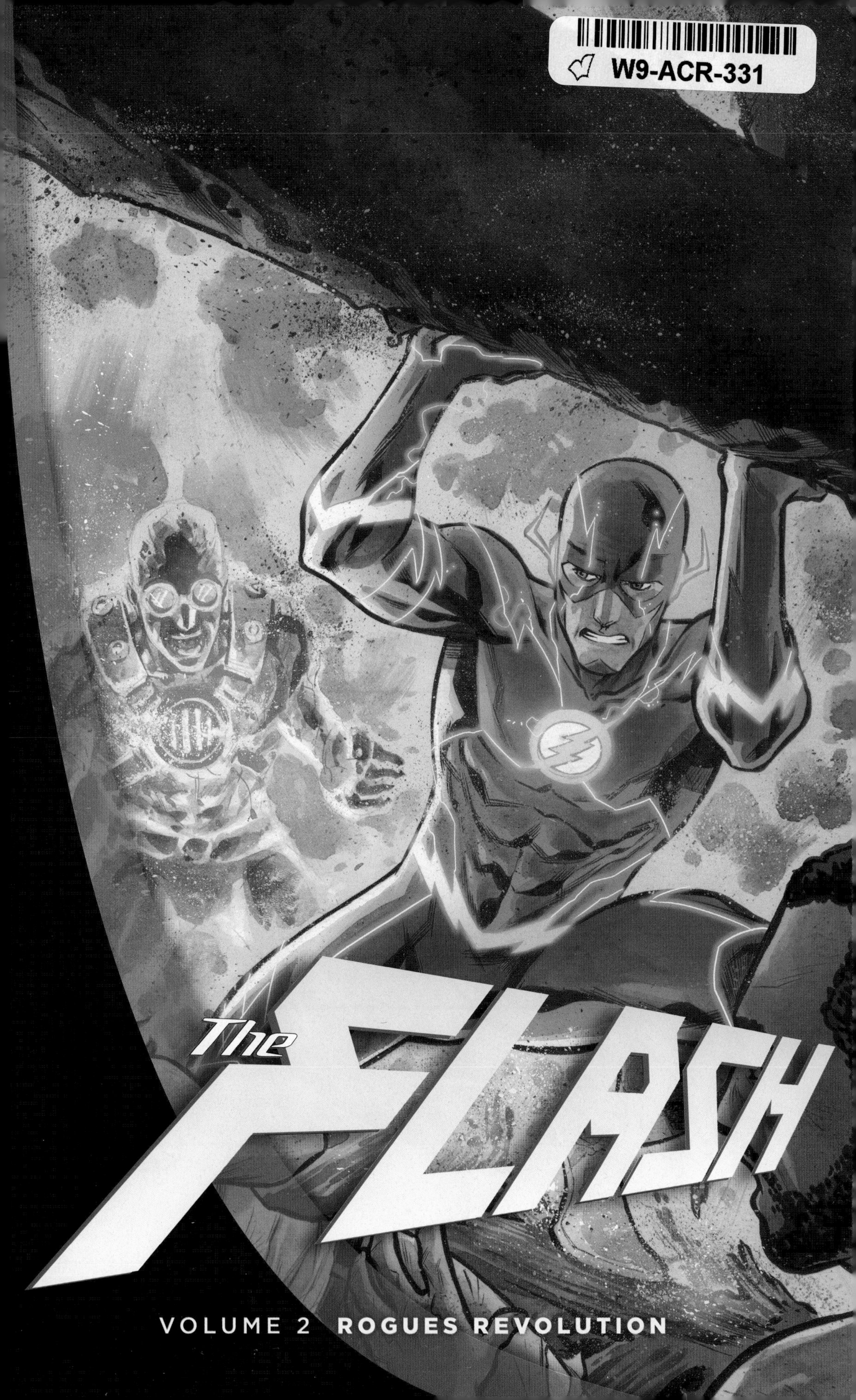
The FLASH
VOLUME 2 ROGUES REVOLUTION

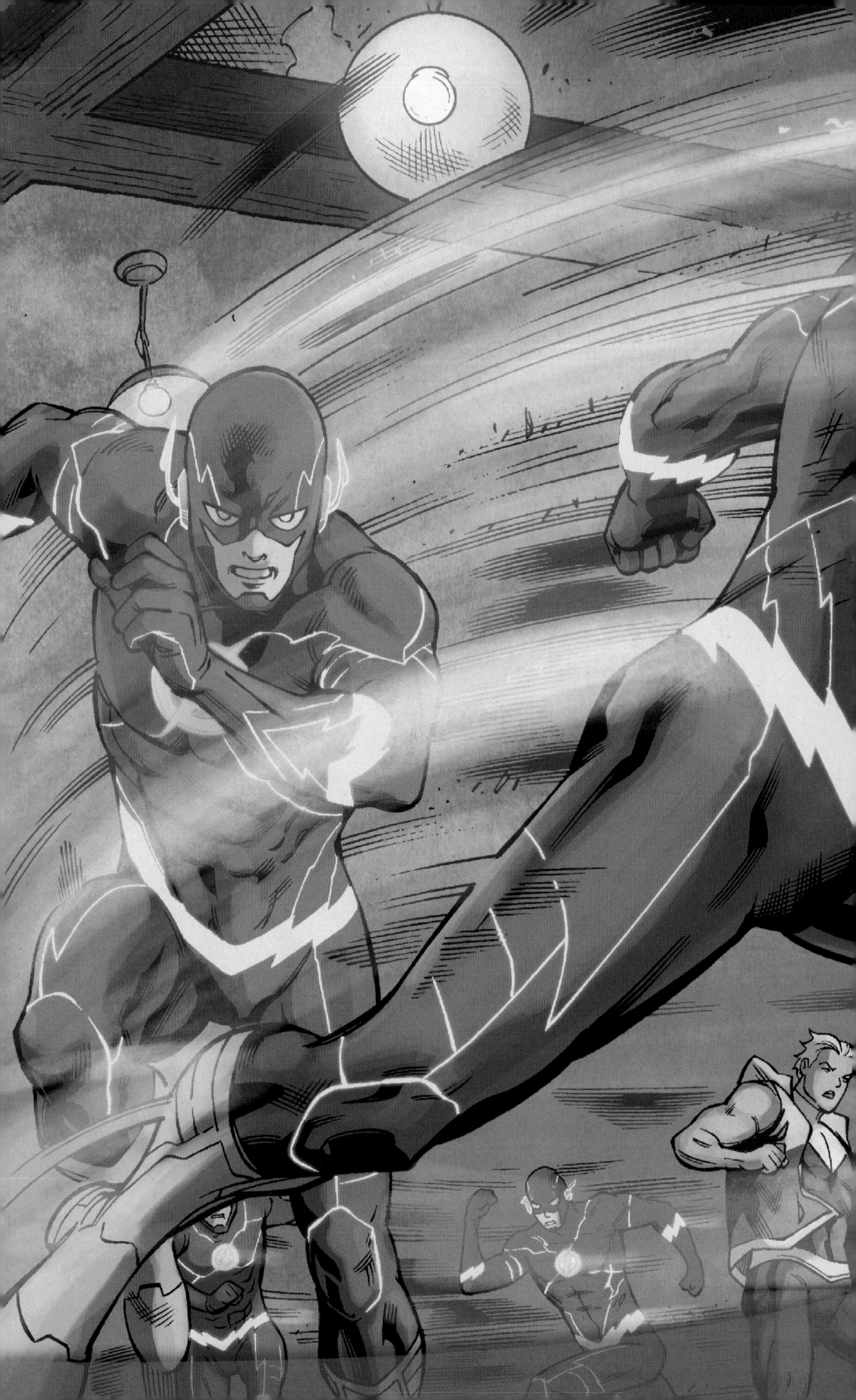

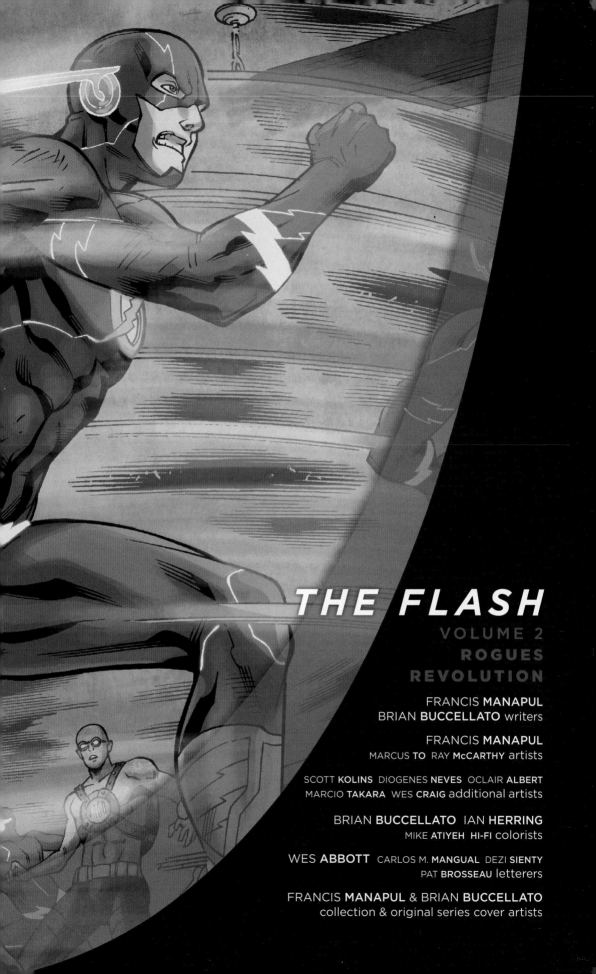

THE FLASH

VOLUME 2
ROGUES
REVOLUTION

FRANCIS **MANAPUL**
BRIAN **BUCCELLATO** writers

FRANCIS **MANAPUL**
MARCUS **TO** RAY **McCARTHY** artists

SCOTT **KOLINS** DIOGENES **NEVES** OCLAIR **ALBERT**
MARCIO **TAKARA** WES **CRAIG** additional artists

BRIAN **BUCCELLATO** IAN **HERRING**
MIKE **ATIYEH** HI-FI colorists

WES **ABBOTT** CARLOS M. **MANGUAL** DEZI **SIENTY**
PAT **BROSSEAU** letterers

FRANCIS **MANAPUL** & BRIAN **BUCCELLATO**
collection & original series cover artists

MATT IDELSON BRIAN CUNNINGHAM Editors – Original Series CHRIS CONROY Associate Editor – Original Series
DARREN SHAN Assistant Editor – Original Series PETER HAMBOUSSI Editor ROBIN WILDMAN Assistant Editor
ROBBIN BROSTERMAN Design Director – Books ROBBIE BIEDERMAN Publication Design

BOB HARRAS Senior VP – Editor-in-Chief, DC Comics

DIANE NELSON President DAN DIDIO and JIM LEE Co-Publishers
GEOFF JOHNS Chief Creative Officer
AMIT DESAI Senior VP – Marketing & Franchise Management
AMY GENKINS Senior VP – Business & Legal Affairs NAIRI GARDINER Senior VP – Finance
JEFF BOISON VP – Publishing Planning MARK CHIARELLO VP – Art Direction & Design
JOHN CUNNINGHAM VP – Marketing TERRI CUNNINGHAM VP – Editorial Administration
LARRY GANEM VP – Talent Relations & Services ALISON GILL Senior VP – Manufacturing & Operations
HANK KANALZ Senior VP – Vertigo & Integrated Publishing JAY KOGAN VP – Business & Legal Affairs, Publishing
JACK MAHAN VP – Business Affairs, Talent NICK NAPOLITANO VP – Manufacturing Administration
SUE POHJA VP – Book Sales FRED RUIZ VP – Manufacturing Operations
COURTNEY SIMMONS Senior VP – Publicity BOB WAYNE Senior VP – Sales

THE FLASH VOLUME 2: ROGUES REVOLUTION

DC Comics, 1700 Broadway, New York, NY 10019
A Warner Bros. Entertainment Company.
Printed by RR Donnelley, Salem, VA, USA. 11/26/14. Third Printing.

HC ISBN: 978-1-4012-4031-8
SC ISBN: 978-1-4012-4273-2

Library of Congress Cataloging-in-Publication Data

Manapul, Francis.
The Flash. Volume 2, Rogues Revolution / Francis Manapul, Brian Buccellato.
pages cm
"Originally published in single magazine form in The Flash 9-12, 0, The Flash Annual 1."
ISBN 978-1-4012-4273-2
1. Graphic novels. I. Buccellato, Brian. II. Title. III. Title: Rogues Revolution.
PN6728.F53M37 2013
741.5'973—dc23
                                            2013010703

SUSTAINABLE
FORESTRY
INITIATIVE

Certified Chain of Custody
20% Certified Forest Content,
80% Certified Sourcing
www.sfiprogram.org
SFI-01042
APPLIES TO TEXT STOCK ONLY

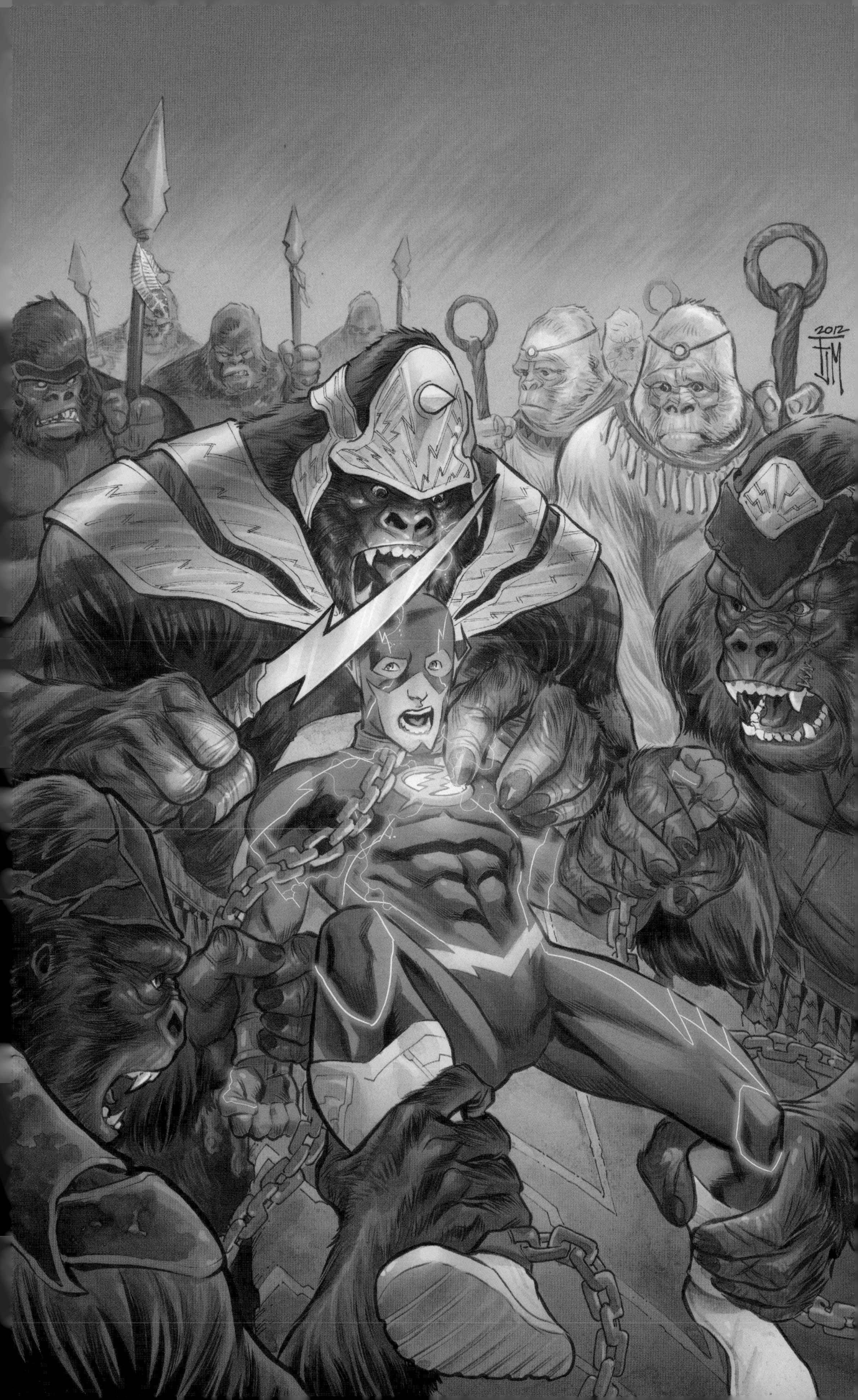

FRANCIS MANAPUL & BRIAN BUCCELLATO writers FRANCIS MANAPUL artist

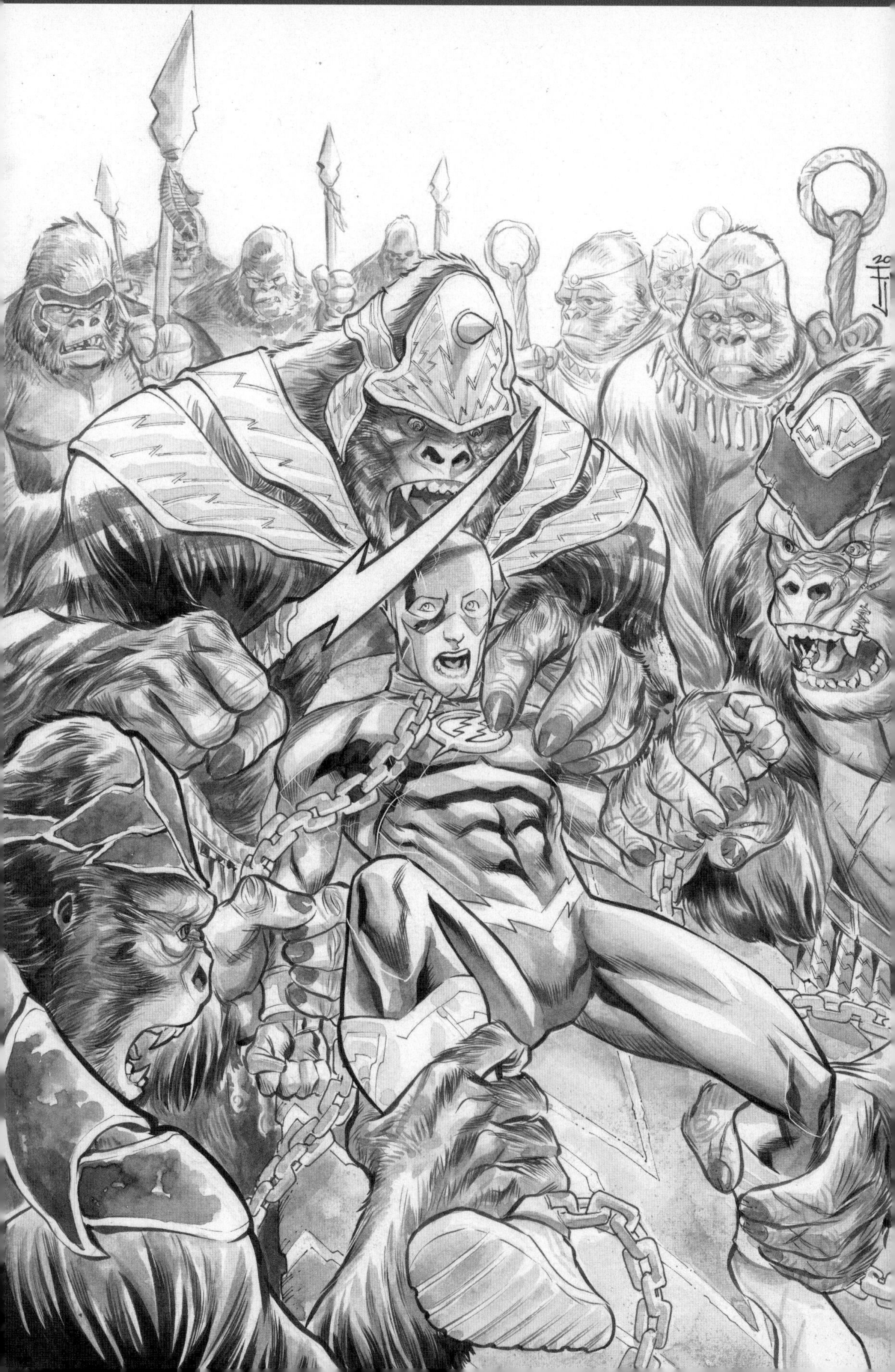

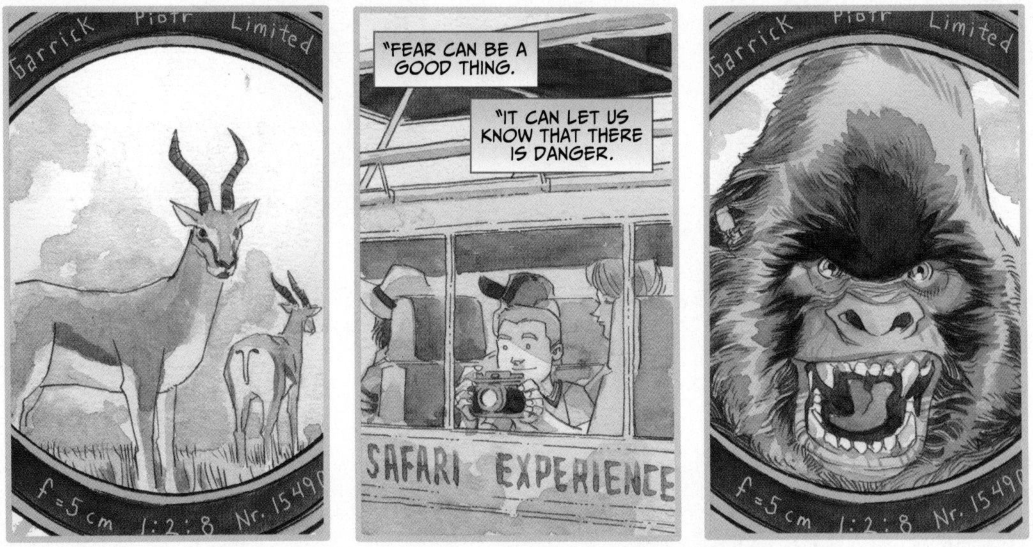
"FEAR CAN BE A GOOD THING.
"IT CAN LET US KNOW THAT THERE IS DANGER.
SAFARI EXPERIENCE

DC COMICS

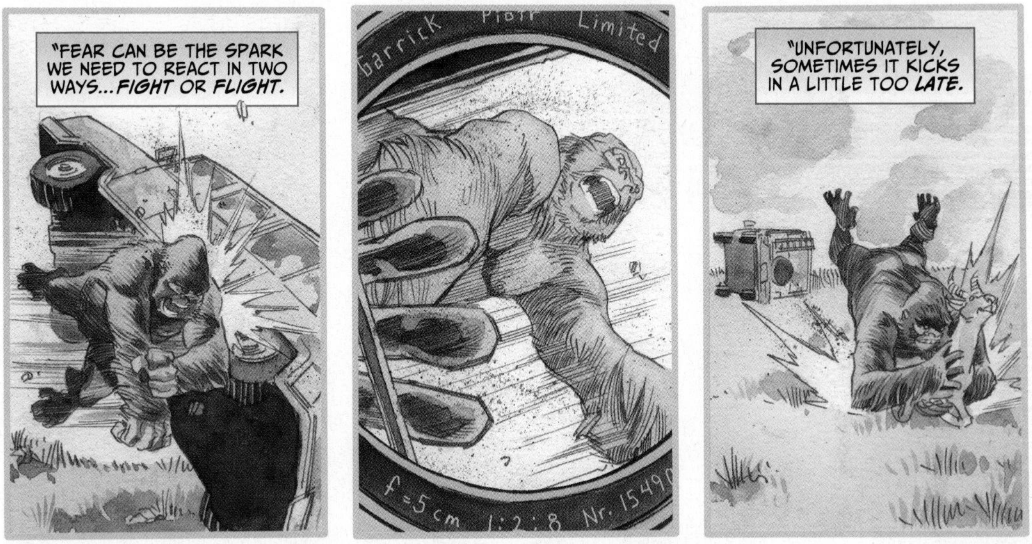
"FEAR CAN BE THE SPARK WE NEED TO REACT IN TWO WAYS...*FIGHT* OR *FLIGHT*.
"UNFORTUNATELY, SOMETIMES IT KICKS IN A LITTLE TOO *LATE*.

PROUDLY PRESENTS

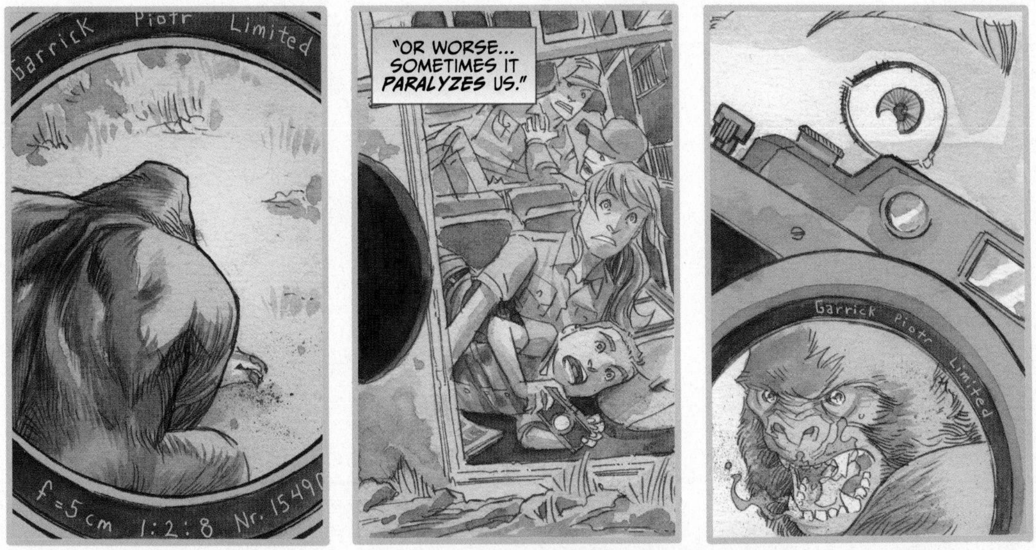
"OR WORSE... SOMETIMES IT *PARALYZES* US."

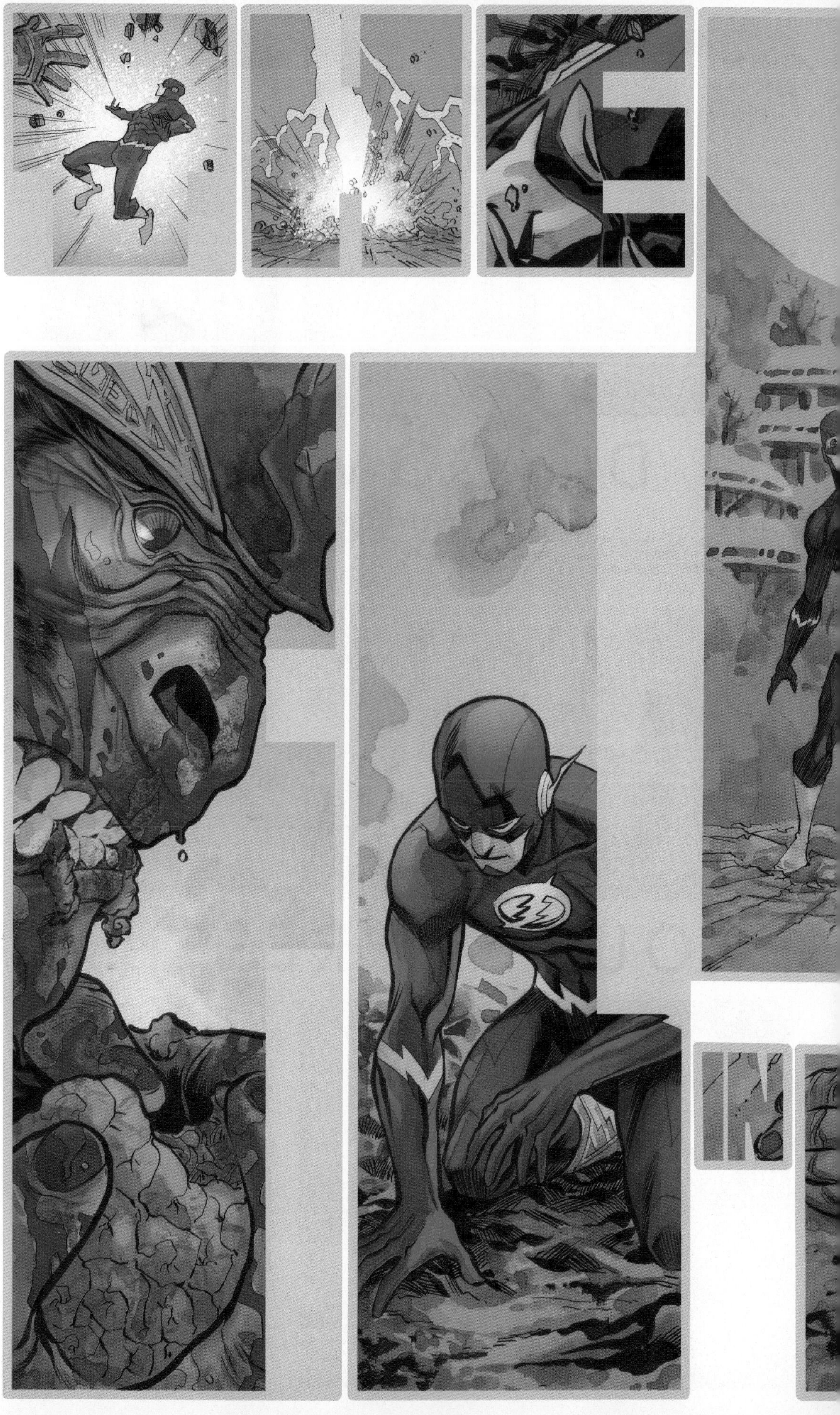
IN

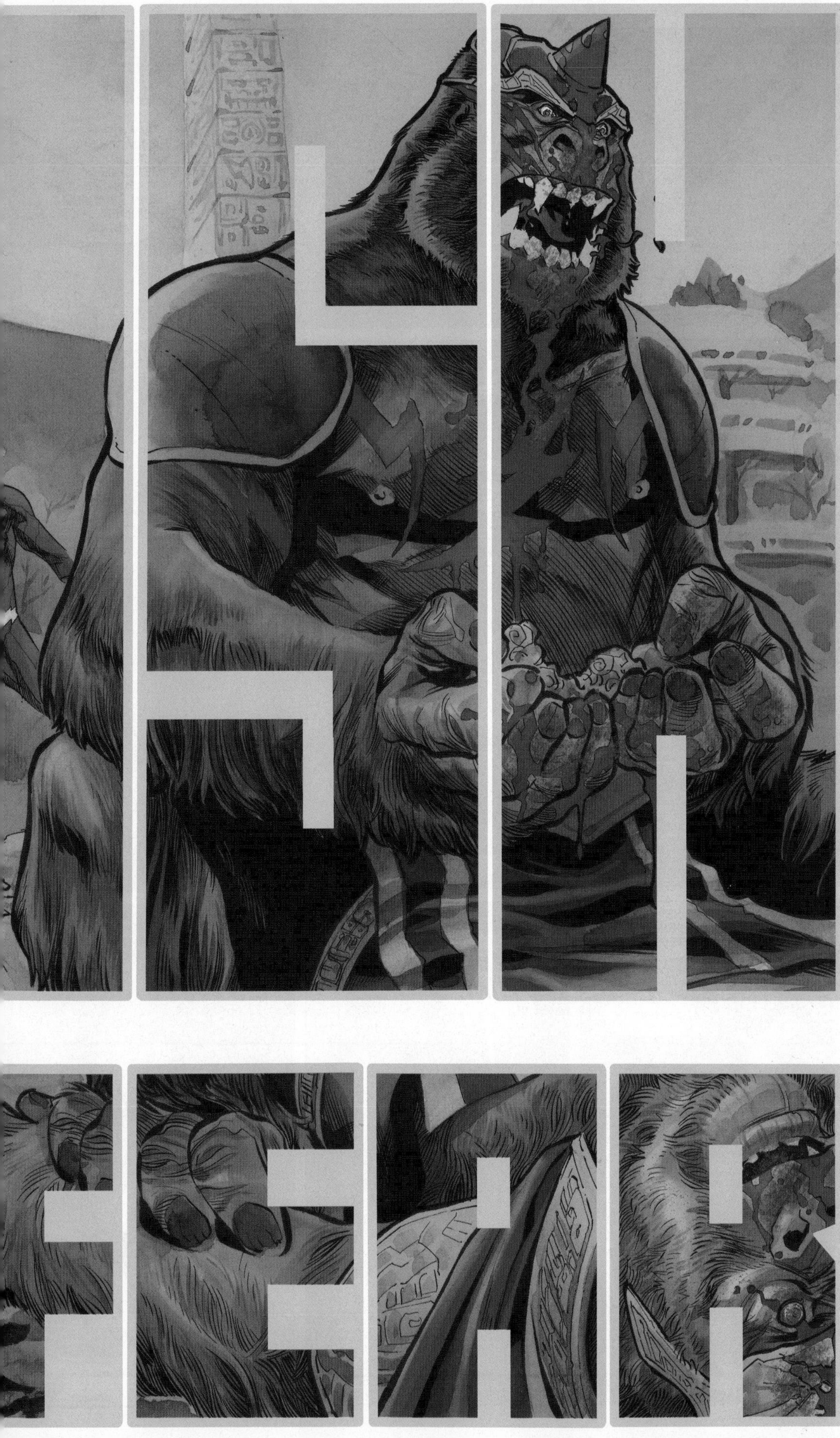

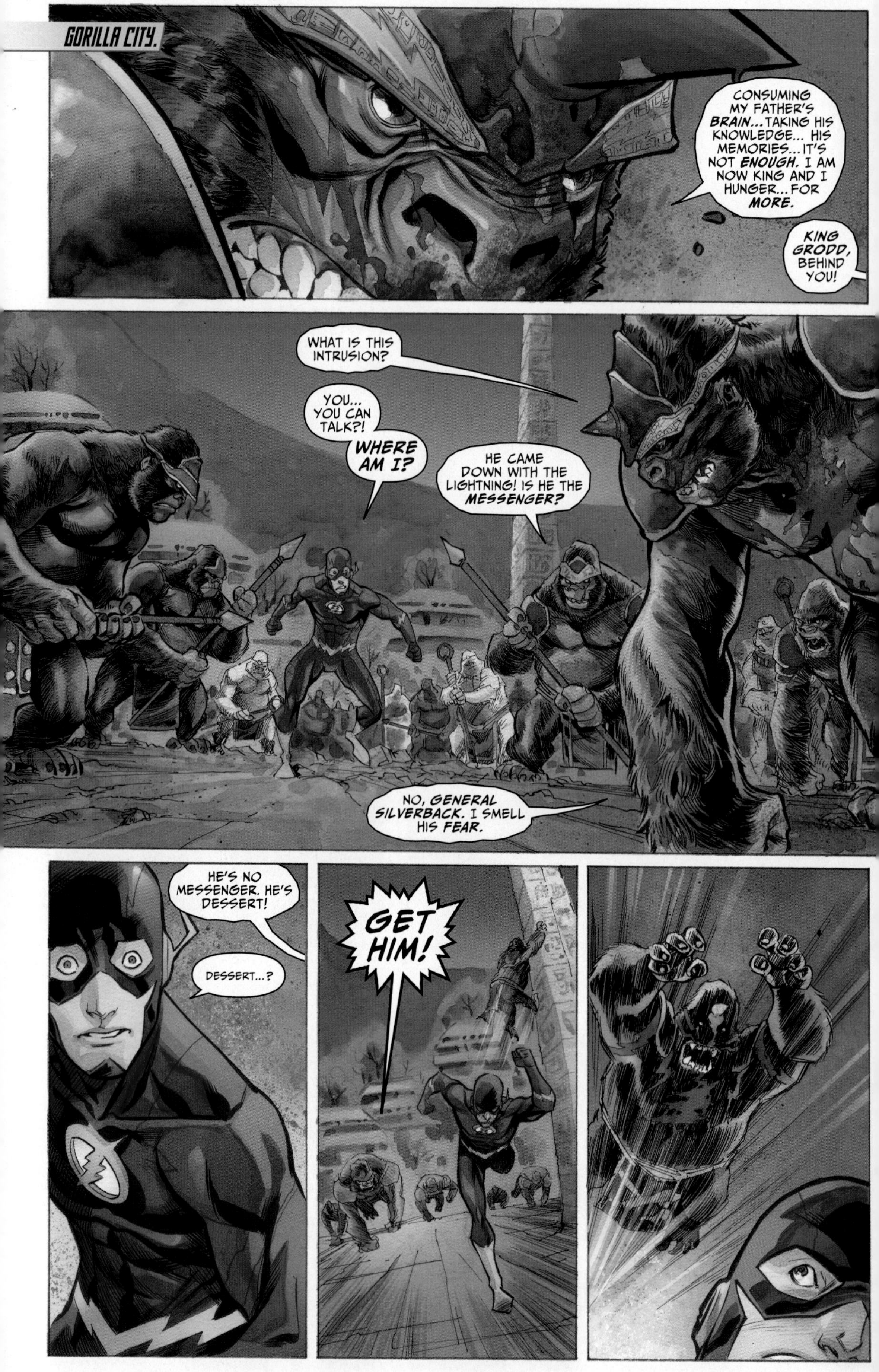
GORILLA CITY.
CONSUMING MY FATHER'S BRAIN... TAKING HIS KNOWLEDGE... HIS MEMORIES... IT'S NOT ENOUGH. I AM NOW KING AND I HUNGER... FOR MORE.
KING GRODD, BEHIND YOU!
WHAT IS THIS INTRUSION?
YOU... YOU CAN TALK?! WHERE AM I?
HE CAME DOWN WITH THE LIGHTNING! IS HE THE MESSENGER?
NO, GENERAL SILVERBACK. I SMELL HIS FEAR.
HE'S NO MESSENGER. HE'S DESSERT!
DESSERT...?
GET HIM!

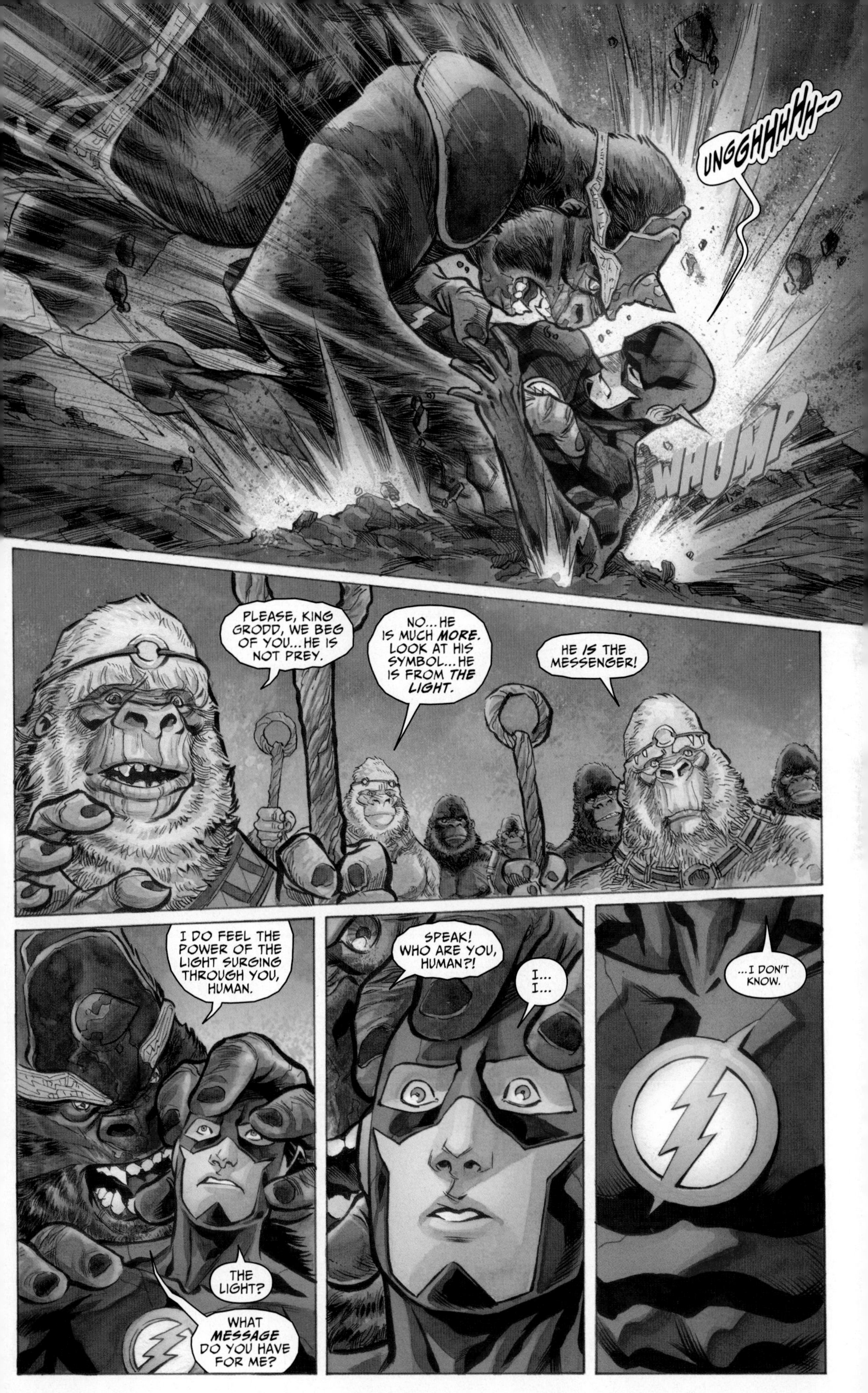
UNGGHHHHH--
WHUMP
PLEASE, KING GRODD, WE BEG OF YOU...HE IS NOT PREY.
NO...HE IS MUCH MORE. LOOK AT HIS SYMBOL...HE IS FROM THE LIGHT.
HE IS THE MESSENGER!
I DO FEEL THE POWER OF THE LIGHT SURGING THROUGH YOU, HUMAN.
THE LIGHT?
WHAT MESSAGE DO YOU HAVE FOR ME?
SPEAK! WHO ARE YOU, HUMAN?!
I... I...
...I DON'T KNOW.

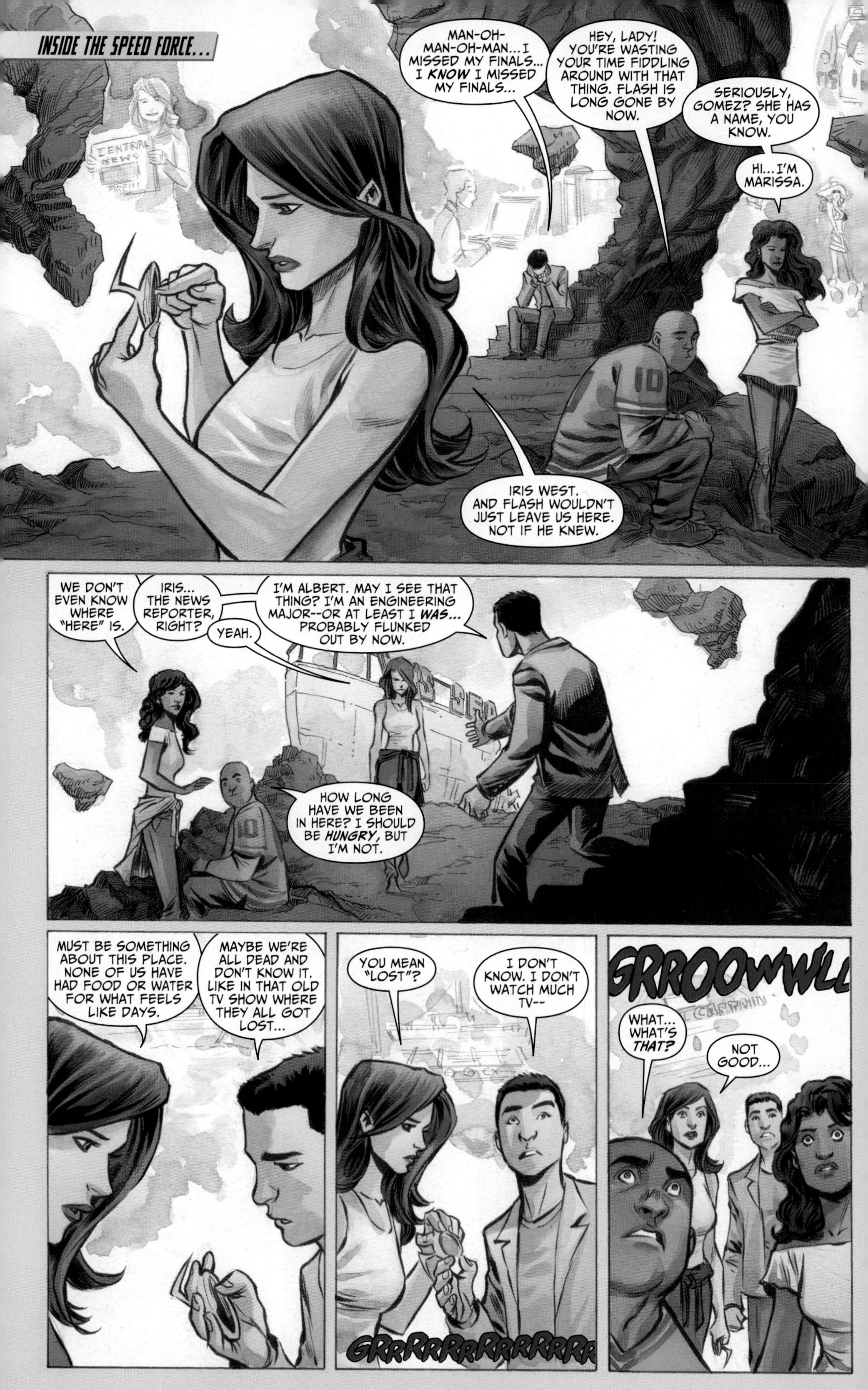
INSIDE THE SPEED FORCE...
MAN-OH-MAN-OH-MAN... I MISSED MY FINALS... I KNOW I MISSED MY FINALS...
HEY, LADY! YOU'RE WASTING YOUR TIME FIDDLING AROUND WITH THAT THING. FLASH IS LONG GONE BY NOW.
SERIOUSLY, GOMEZ? SHE HAS A NAME, YOU KNOW.
HI... I'M MARISSA.
IRIS WEST. AND FLASH WOULDN'T JUST LEAVE US HERE. NOT IF HE KNEW.
CENTRAL NEWS
WE DON'T EVEN KNOW WHERE "HERE" IS.
IRIS... THE NEWS REPORTER, RIGHT?
YEAH.
I'M ALBERT. MAY I SEE THAT THING? I'M AN ENGINEERING MAJOR--OR AT LEAST I WAS... PROBABLY FLUNKED OUT BY NOW.
HOW LONG HAVE WE BEEN IN HERE? I SHOULD BE HUNGRY, BUT I'M NOT.
MUST BE SOMETHING ABOUT THIS PLACE. NONE OF US HAVE HAD FOOD OR WATER FOR WHAT FEELS LIKE DAYS.
MAYBE WE'RE ALL DEAD AND DON'T KNOW IT. LIKE IN THAT OLD TV SHOW WHERE THEY ALL GOT LOST...
YOU MEAN "LOST"?
I DON'T KNOW. I DON'T WATCH MUCH TV--
GRRRRRRRRRRRRRRR
GRROOWWLL
WHAT... WHAT'S THAT?
NOT GOOD...

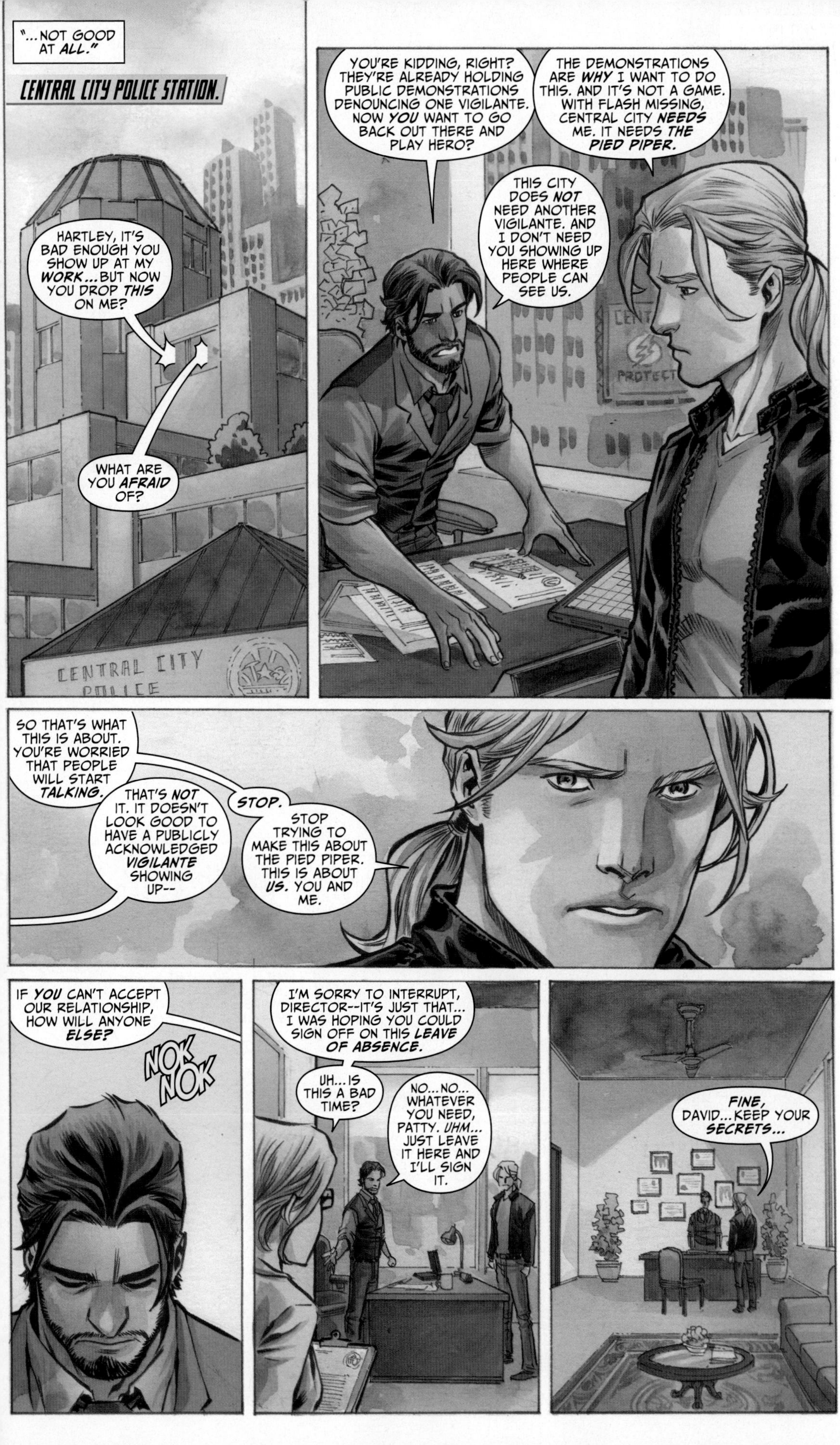

"...NOT GOOD AT ALL."
CENTRAL CITY POLICE STATION.
HARTLEY, IT'S BAD ENOUGH YOU SHOW UP AT MY WORK... BUT NOW YOU DROP THIS ON ME?
WHAT ARE YOU AFRAID OF?
CENTRAL CITY POLICE
YOU'RE KIDDING, RIGHT? THEY'RE ALREADY HOLDING PUBLIC DEMONSTRATIONS DENOUNCING ONE VIGILANTE. NOW YOU WANT TO GO BACK OUT THERE AND PLAY HERO?
THE DEMONSTRATIONS ARE WHY I WANT TO DO THIS. AND IT'S NOT A GAME. WITH FLASH MISSING, CENTRAL CITY NEEDS ME. IT NEEDS THE PIED PIPER.
THIS CITY DOES NOT NEED ANOTHER VIGILANTE. AND I DON'T NEED YOU SHOWING UP HERE WHERE PEOPLE CAN SEE US.
SO THAT'S WHAT THIS IS ABOUT. YOU'RE WORRIED THAT PEOPLE WILL START TALKING.
THAT'S NOT IT. IT DOESN'T LOOK GOOD TO HAVE A PUBLICLY ACKNOWLEDGED VIGILANTE SHOWING UP--
STOP.
STOP TRYING TO MAKE THIS ABOUT THE PIED PIPER. THIS IS ABOUT US. YOU AND ME.
IF YOU CAN'T ACCEPT OUR RELATIONSHIP, HOW WILL ANYONE ELSE?
NOK NOK
I'M SORRY TO INTERRUPT, DIRECTOR--IT'S JUST THAT... I WAS HOPING YOU COULD SIGN OFF ON THIS LEAVE OF ABSENCE.
UH... IS THIS A BAD TIME?
NO... NO... WHATEVER YOU NEED, PATTY. UHM... JUST LEAVE IT HERE AND I'LL SIGN IT.
FINE, DAVID... KEEP YOUR SECRETS...

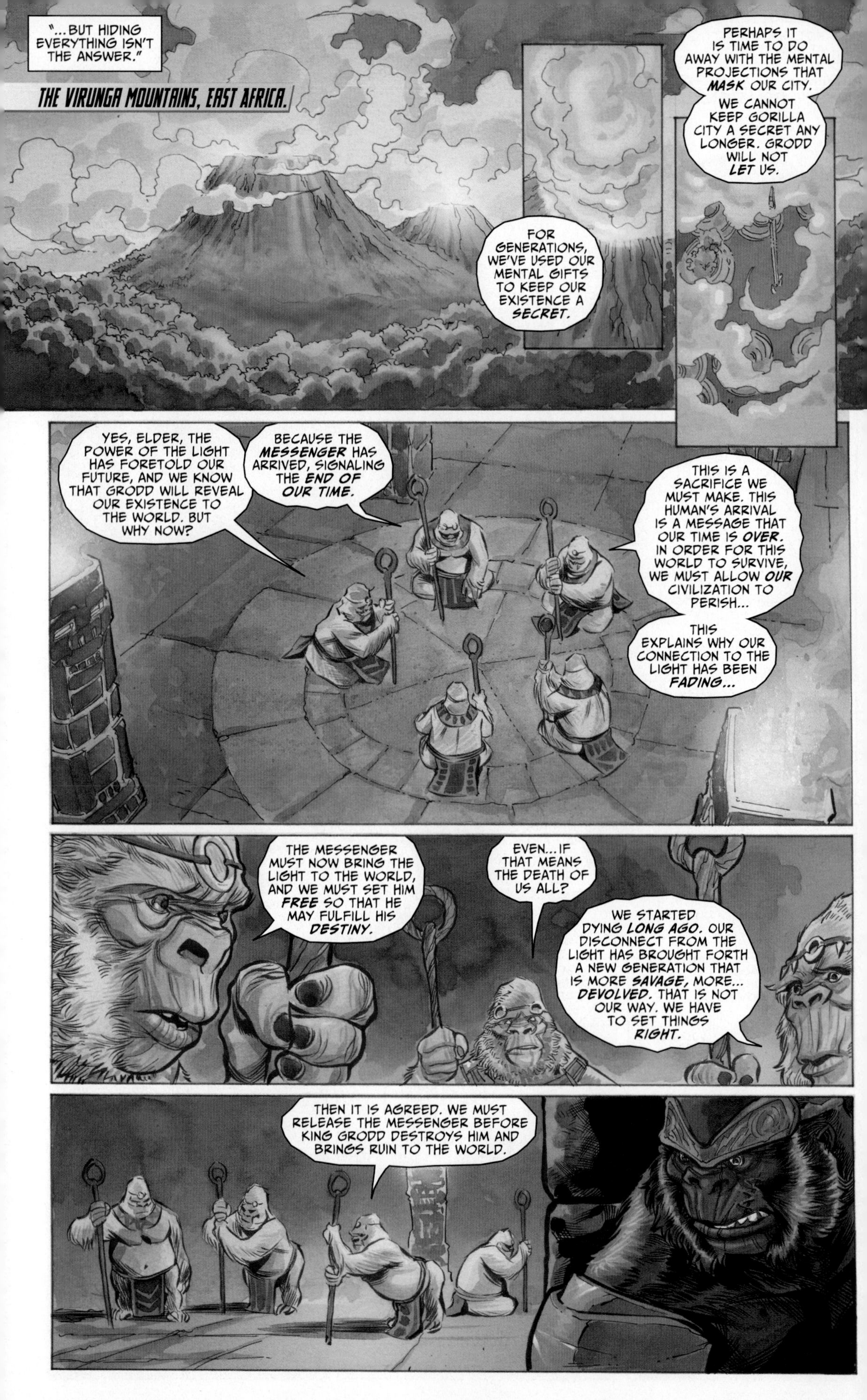
"...BUT HIDING EVERYTHING ISN'T THE ANSWER."
THE VIRUNGA MOUNTAINS, EAST AFRICA.
FOR GENERATIONS, WE'VE USED OUR MENTAL GIFTS TO KEEP OUR EXISTENCE A SECRET.
PERHAPS IT IS TIME TO DO AWAY WITH THE MENTAL PROJECTIONS THAT MASK OUR CITY.
WE CANNOT KEEP GORILLA CITY A SECRET ANY LONGER. GRODD WILL NOT LET US.
YES, ELDER, THE POWER OF THE LIGHT HAS FORETOLD OUR FUTURE, AND WE KNOW THAT GRODD WILL REVEAL OUR EXISTENCE TO THE WORLD. BUT WHY NOW?
BECAUSE THE MESSENGER HAS ARRIVED, SIGNALING THE END OF OUR TIME.
THIS IS A SACRIFICE WE MUST MAKE. THIS HUMAN'S ARRIVAL IS A MESSAGE THAT OUR TIME IS OVER. IN ORDER FOR THIS WORLD TO SURVIVE, WE MUST ALLOW OUR CIVILIZATION TO PERISH...
THIS EXPLAINS WHY OUR CONNECTION TO THE LIGHT HAS BEEN FADING...
THE MESSENGER MUST NOW BRING THE LIGHT TO THE WORLD, AND WE MUST SET HIM FREE SO THAT HE MAY FULFILL HIS DESTINY.
EVEN... IF THAT MEANS THE DEATH OF US ALL?
WE STARTED DYING LONG AGO. OUR DISCONNECT FROM THE LIGHT HAS BROUGHT FORTH A NEW GENERATION THAT IS MORE SAVAGE, MORE... DEVOLVED. THAT IS NOT OUR WAY. WE HAVE TO SET THINGS RIGHT.
THEN IT IS AGREED. WE MUST RELEASE THE MESSENGER BEFORE KING GRODD DESTROYS HIM AND BRINGS RUIN TO THE WORLD.

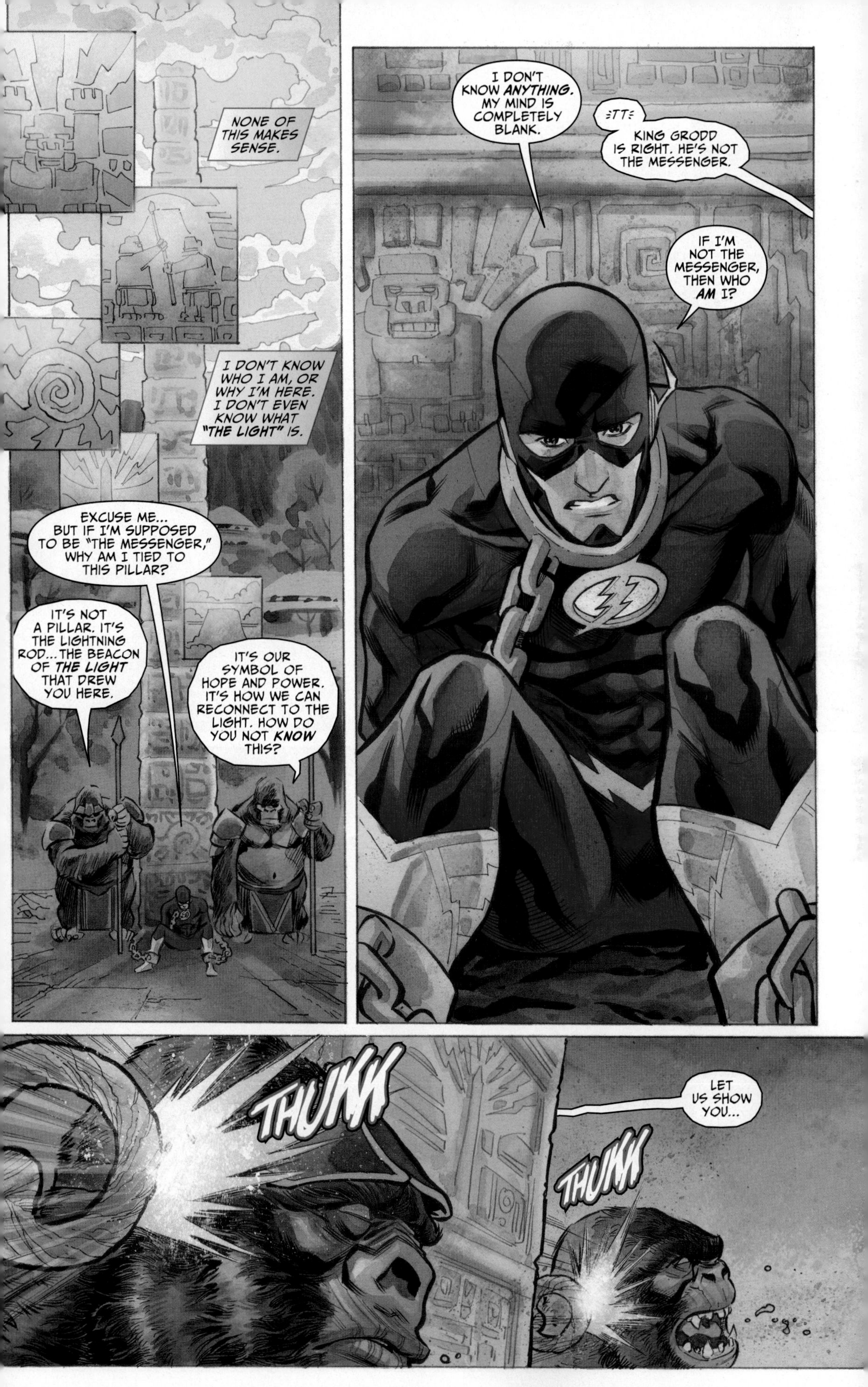
NONE OF THIS MAKES SENSE.
I DON'T KNOW WHO I AM, OR WHY I'M HERE. I DON'T EVEN KNOW WHAT "THE LIGHT" IS.
EXCUSE ME... BUT IF I'M SUPPOSED TO BE "THE MESSENGER," WHY AM I TIED TO THIS PILLAR?
IT'S NOT A PILLAR. IT'S THE LIGHTNING ROD... THE BEACON OF THE LIGHT THAT DREW YOU HERE.
IT'S OUR SYMBOL OF HOPE AND POWER. IT'S HOW WE CAN RECONNECT TO THE LIGHT. HOW DO YOU NOT KNOW THIS?
I DON'T KNOW ANYTHING. MY MIND IS COMPLETELY BLANK.
TT
KING GRODD IS RIGHT. HE'S NOT THE MESSENGER.
IF I'M NOT THE MESSENGER, THEN WHO AM I?
THUKK
LET US SHOW YOU...
THUKK

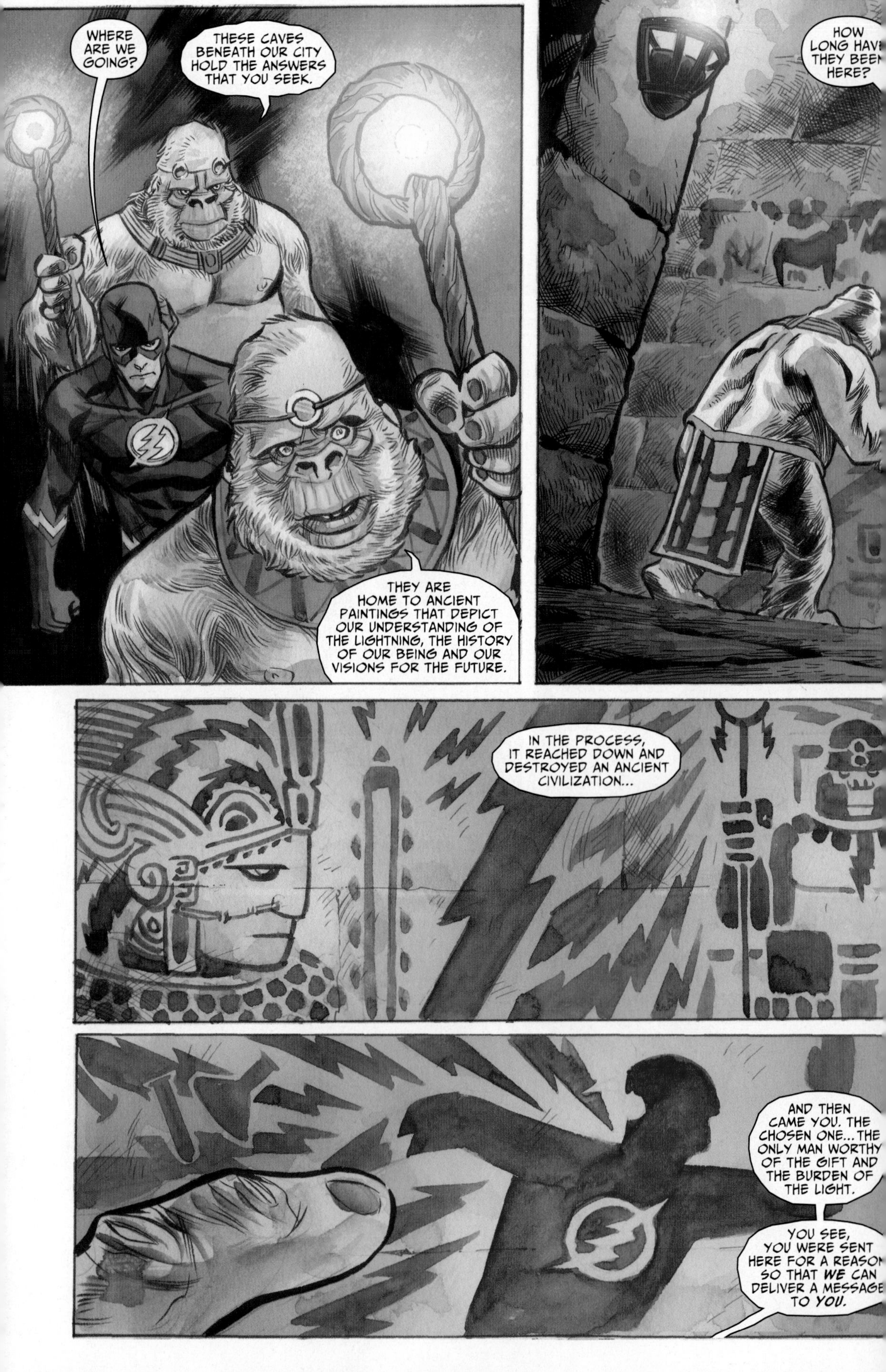

WHERE ARE WE GOING?
THESE CAVES BENEATH OUR CITY HOLD THE ANSWERS THAT YOU SEEK.
THEY ARE HOME TO ANCIENT PAINTINGS THAT DEPICT OUR UNDERSTANDING OF THE LIGHTNING, THE HISTORY OF OUR BEING AND OUR VISIONS FOR THE FUTURE.
HOW LONG HAVE THEY BEEN HERE?
IN THE PROCESS, IT REACHED DOWN AND DESTROYED AN ANCIENT CIVILIZATION...
AND THEN CAME YOU. THE CHOSEN ONE... THE ONLY MAN WORTHY OF THE GIFT AND THE BURDEN OF THE LIGHT.
YOU SEE, YOU WERE SENT HERE FOR A REASON SO THAT *WE* CAN DELIVER A MESSAGE TO *YOU*.

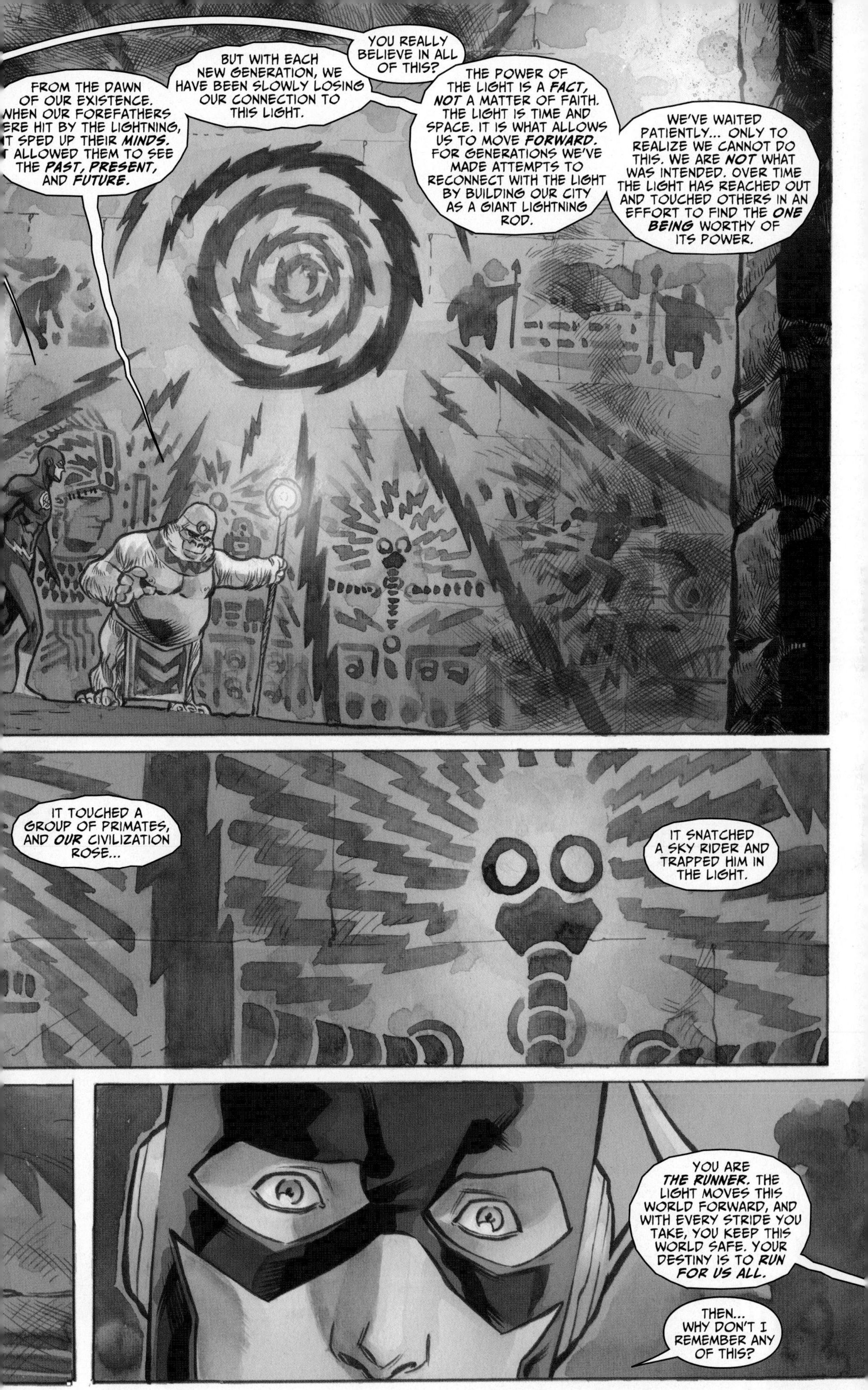

FROM THE DAWN OF OUR EXISTENCE. WHEN OUR FOREFATHERS ERE HIT BY THE LIGHTNING, T SPED UP THEIR MINDS. T ALLOWED THEM TO SEE THE PAST, PRESENT, AND FUTURE.
BUT WITH EACH NEW GENERATION, WE HAVE BEEN SLOWLY LOSING OUR CONNECTION TO THIS LIGHT.
YOU REALLY BELIEVE IN ALL OF THIS?
THE POWER OF THE LIGHT IS A FACT, NOT A MATTER OF FAITH. THE LIGHT IS TIME AND SPACE. IT IS WHAT ALLOWS US TO MOVE FORWARD. FOR GENERATIONS WE'VE MADE ATTEMPTS TO RECONNECT WITH THE LIGHT BY BUILDING OUR CITY AS A GIANT LIGHTNING ROD.
WE'VE WAITED PATIENTLY... ONLY TO REALIZE WE CANNOT DO THIS. WE ARE NOT WHAT WAS INTENDED. OVER TIME THE LIGHT HAS REACHED OUT AND TOUCHED OTHERS IN AN EFFORT TO FIND THE ONE BEING WORTHY OF ITS POWER.
IT TOUCHED A GROUP OF PRIMATES, AND OUR CIVILIZATION ROSE...
IT SNATCHED A SKY RIDER AND TRAPPED HIM IN THE LIGHT.
YOU ARE THE RUNNER. THE LIGHT MOVES THIS WORLD FORWARD, AND WITH EVERY STRIDE YOU TAKE, YOU KEEP THIS WORLD SAFE. YOUR DESTINY IS TO RUN FOR US ALL.
THEN... WHY DON'T I REMEMBER ANY OF THIS?

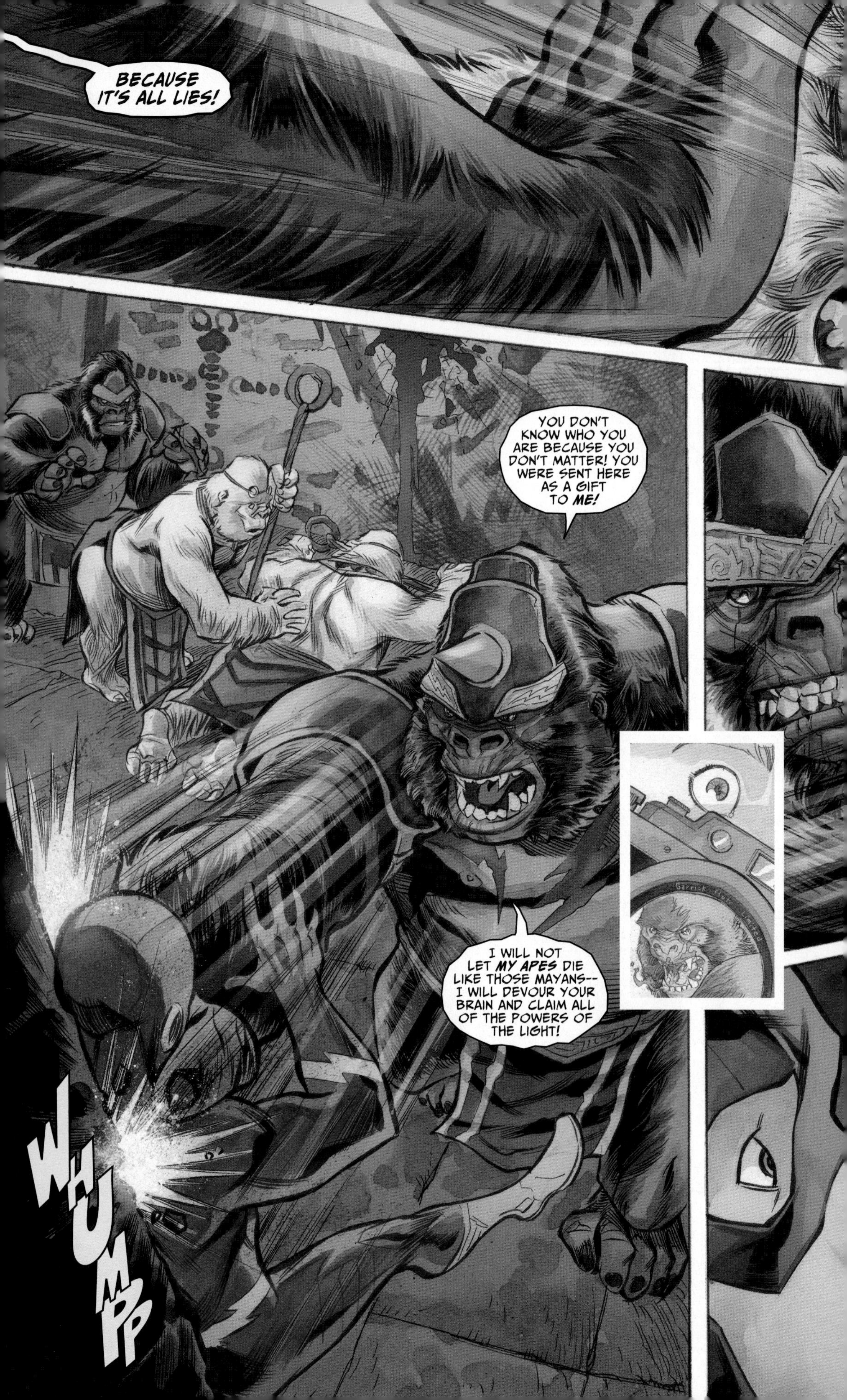

BECAUSE IT'S ALL LIES!
YOU DON'T KNOW WHO YOU ARE BECAUSE YOU DON'T MATTER! YOU WERE SENT HERE AS A GIFT TO ME!
I WILL NOT LET MY APES DIE LIKE THOSE MAYANS-- I WILL DEVOUR YOUR BRAIN AND CLAIM ALL OF THE POWERS OF THE LIGHT!
WHUMPP

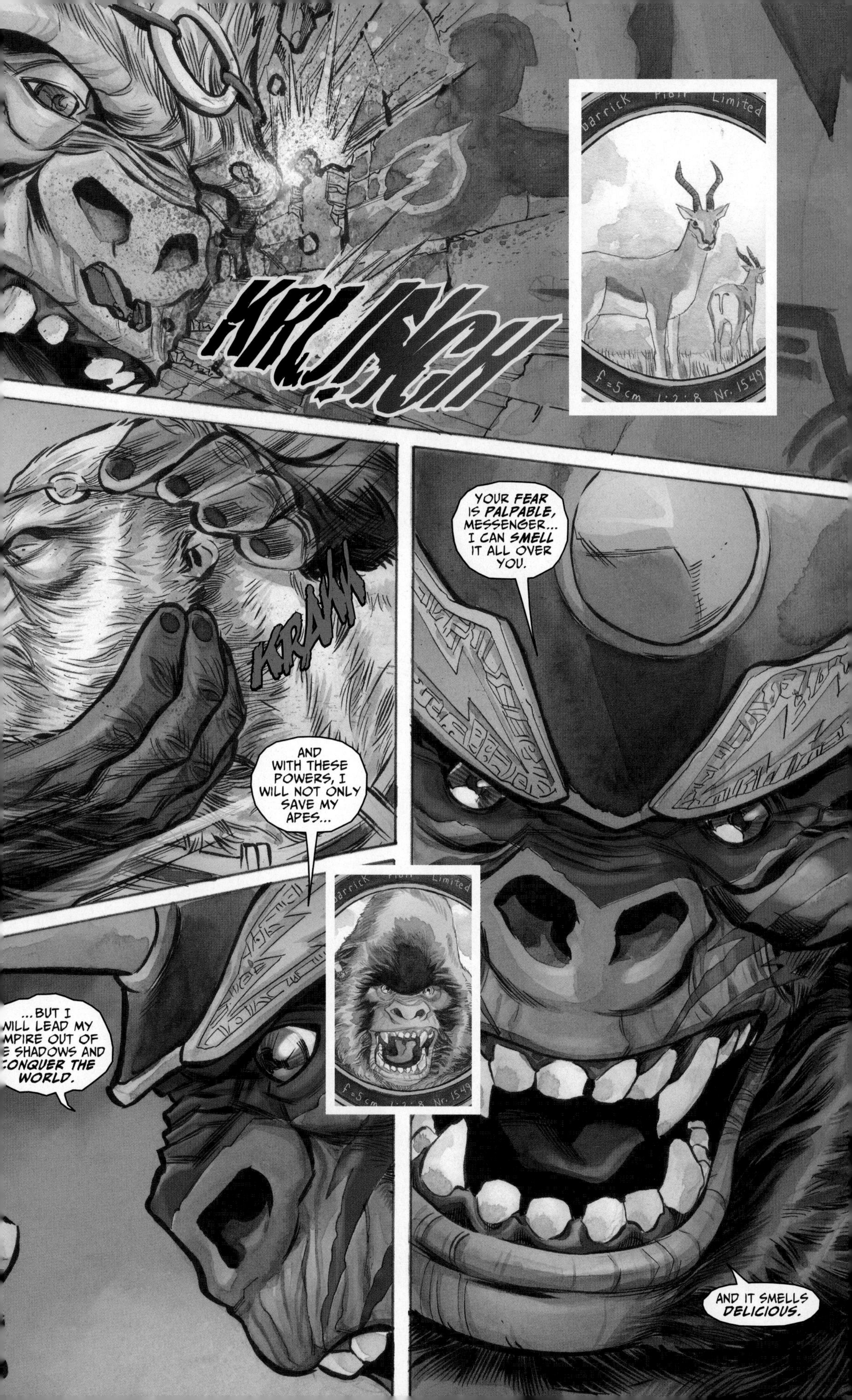
KRUNCH
KRAKK
YOUR FEAR IS PALPABLE, MESSENGER... I CAN SMELL IT ALL OVER YOU.
AND WITH THESE POWERS, I WILL NOT ONLY SAVE MY APES...
...BUT I WILL LEAD MY MPIRE OUT OF E SHADOWS AND CONQUER THE WORLD.
AND IT SMELLS DELICIOUS.

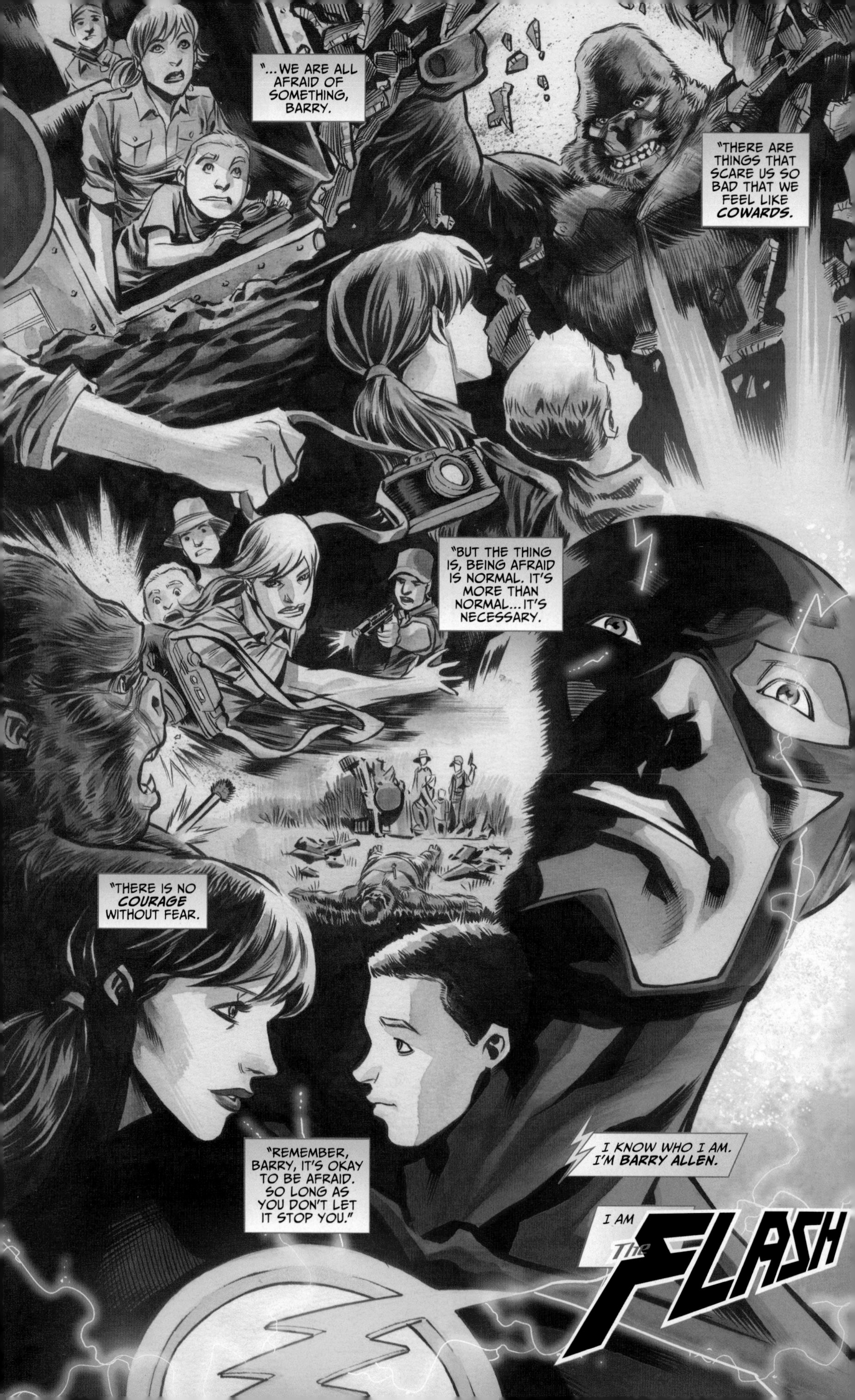
"...WE ARE ALL AFRAID OF SOMETHING, BARRY.
"THERE ARE THINGS THAT SCARE US SO BAD THAT WE FEEL LIKE COWARDS.
"BUT THE THING IS, BEING AFRAID IS NORMAL. IT'S MORE THAN NORMAL...IT'S NECESSARY.
"THERE IS NO COURAGE WITHOUT FEAR.
"REMEMBER, BARRY, IT'S OKAY TO BE AFRAID. SO LONG AS YOU DON'T LET IT STOP YOU."
I KNOW WHO I AM. I'M BARRY ALLEN.
I AM
The FLASH

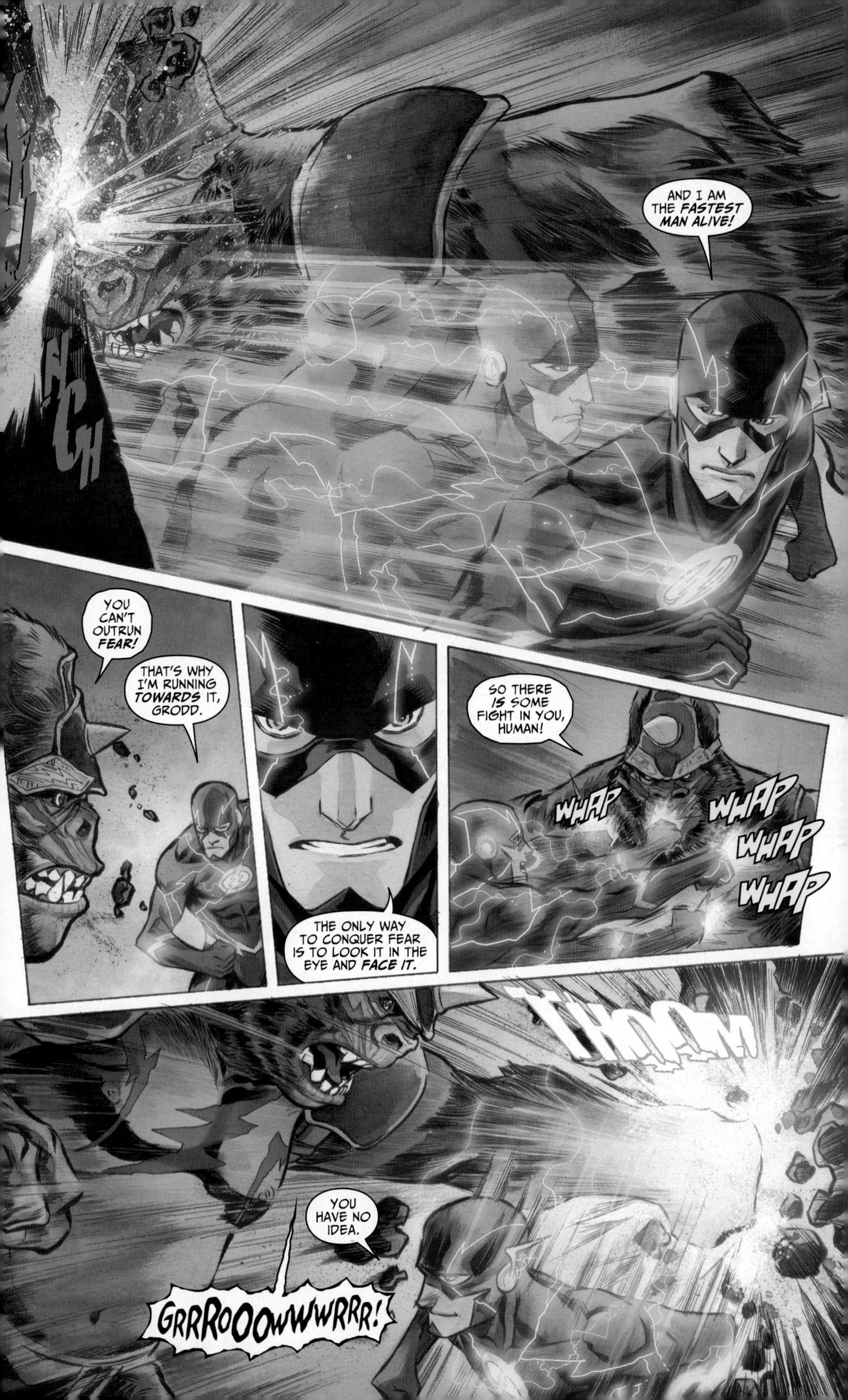

AND I AM THE *FASTEST MAN ALIVE!*
YOU CAN'T OUTRUN *FEAR!*
THAT'S WHY I'M RUNNING *TOWARDS* IT, GRODD.
THE ONLY WAY TO CONQUER FEAR IS TO LOOK IT IN THE EYE AND *FACE IT.*
SO THERE *IS* SOME FIGHT IN YOU, HUMAN!
WHAP
WHAP
WHAP
WHAP
THOOM
YOU HAVE NO IDEA.
GRRROOOWWWRRR!

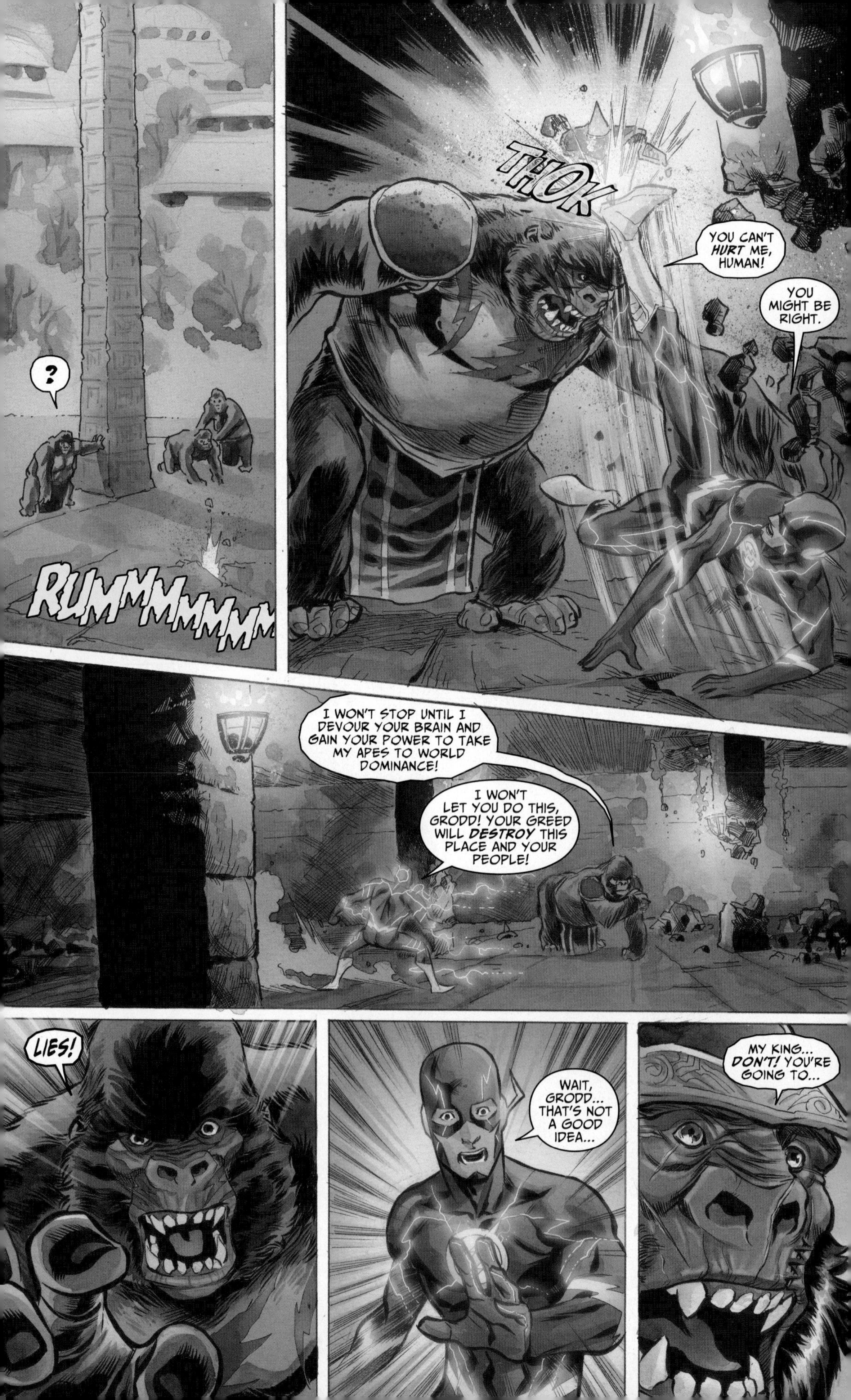
?
RUMMMMMMMM
THOK
YOU CAN'T *HURT* ME, HUMAN!
YOU MIGHT BE RIGHT.
I WON'T STOP UNTIL I DEVOUR YOUR BRAIN AND GAIN YOUR POWER TO TAKE MY APES TO WORLD DOMINANCE!
I WON'T LET YOU DO THIS, GRODD! YOUR GREED WILL *DESTROY* THIS PLACE AND YOUR PEOPLE!
LIES!
WAIT, GRODD... THAT'S NOT A GOOD IDEA...
MY KING... *DON'T!* YOU'RE GOING TO...

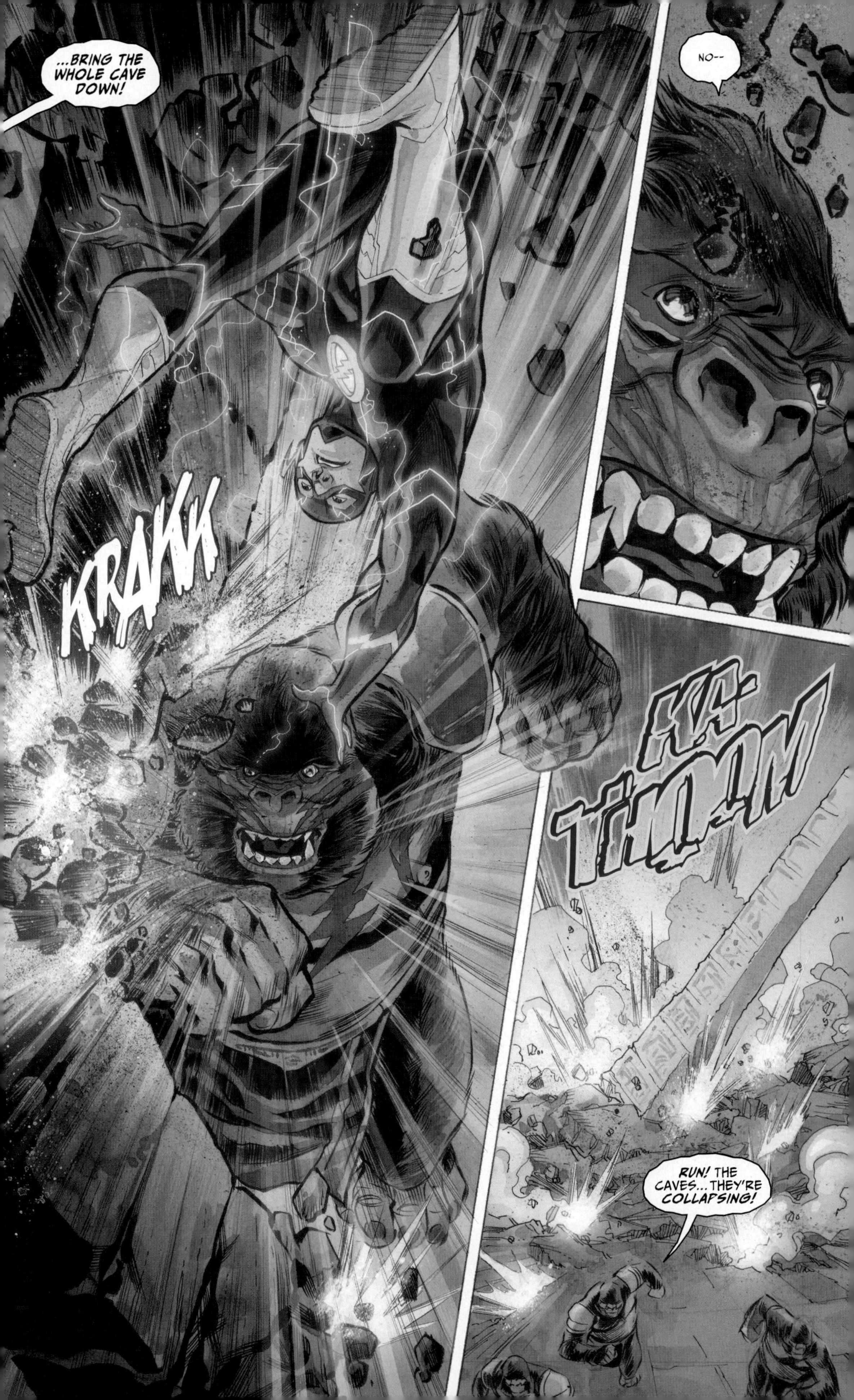
...BRING THE WHOLE CAVE DOWN!
KRAKK
NO--
KA-THOOM
RUN! THE CAVES... THEY'RE COLLAPSING!

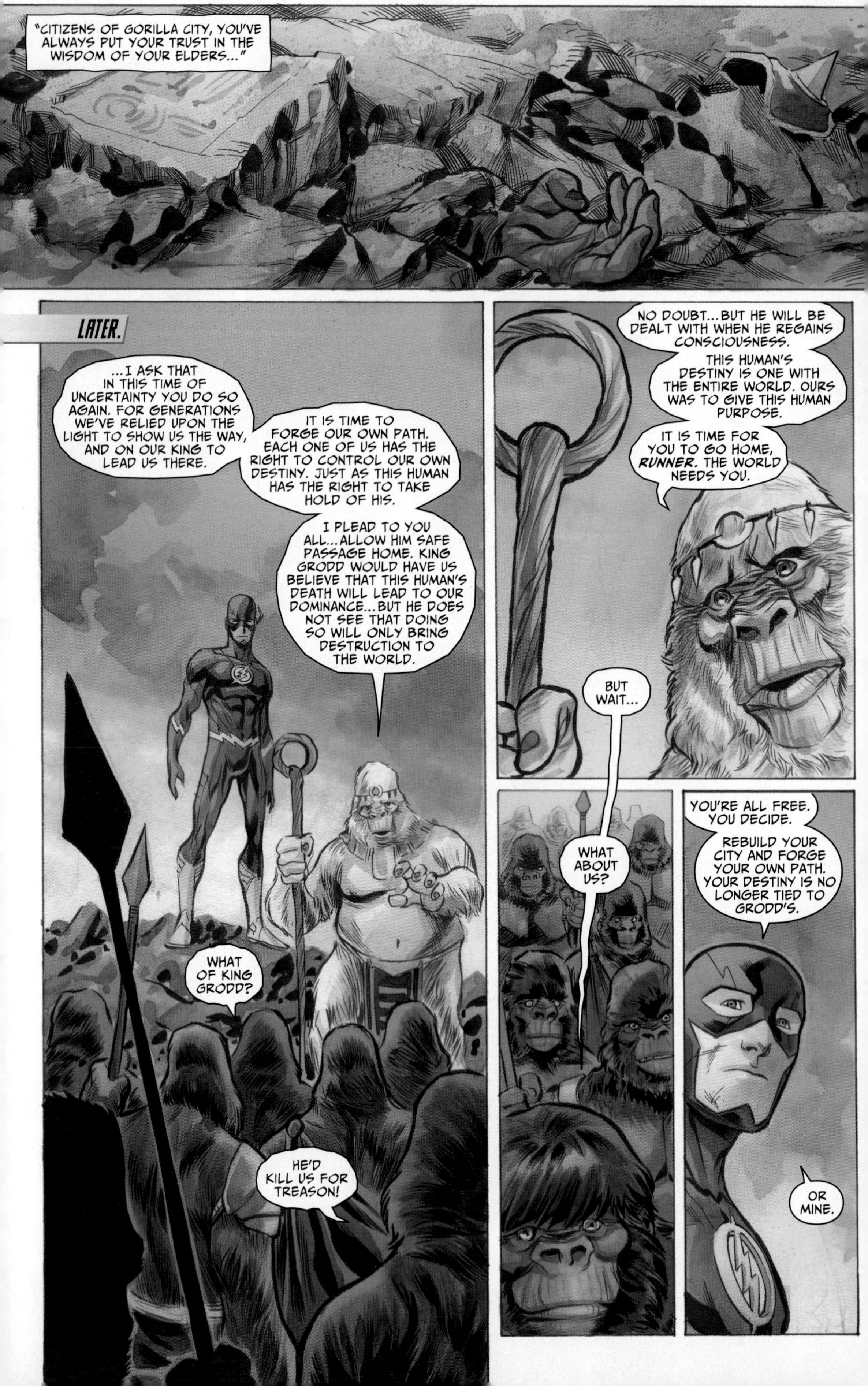
"CITIZENS OF GORILLA CITY, YOU'VE ALWAYS PUT YOUR TRUST IN THE WISDOM OF YOUR ELDERS..."
LATER.
...I ASK THAT IN THIS TIME OF UNCERTAINTY YOU DO SO AGAIN. FOR GENERATIONS WE'VE RELIED UPON THE LIGHT TO SHOW US THE WAY, AND ON OUR KING TO LEAD US THERE.
IT IS TIME TO FORGE OUR OWN PATH. EACH ONE OF US HAS THE RIGHT TO CONTROL OUR OWN DESTINY. JUST AS THIS HUMAN HAS THE RIGHT TO TAKE HOLD OF HIS.
I PLEAD TO YOU ALL...ALLOW HIM SAFE PASSAGE HOME. KING GRODD WOULD HAVE US BELIEVE THAT THIS HUMAN'S DEATH WILL LEAD TO OUR DOMINANCE...BUT HE DOES NOT SEE THAT DOING SO WILL ONLY BRING DESTRUCTION TO THE WORLD.
WHAT OF KING GRODD?
HE'D KILL US FOR TREASON!
NO DOUBT...BUT HE WILL BE DEALT WITH WHEN HE REGAINS CONSCIOUSNESS.
THIS HUMAN'S DESTINY IS ONE WITH THE ENTIRE WORLD. OURS WAS TO GIVE THIS HUMAN PURPOSE.
IT IS TIME FOR YOU TO GO HOME, RUNNER. THE WORLD NEEDS YOU.
BUT WAIT...
WHAT ABOUT US?
YOU'RE ALL FREE. YOU DECIDE.
REBUILD YOUR CITY AND FORGE YOUR OWN PATH. YOUR DESTINY IS NO LONGER TIED TO GRODD'S.
OR MINE.

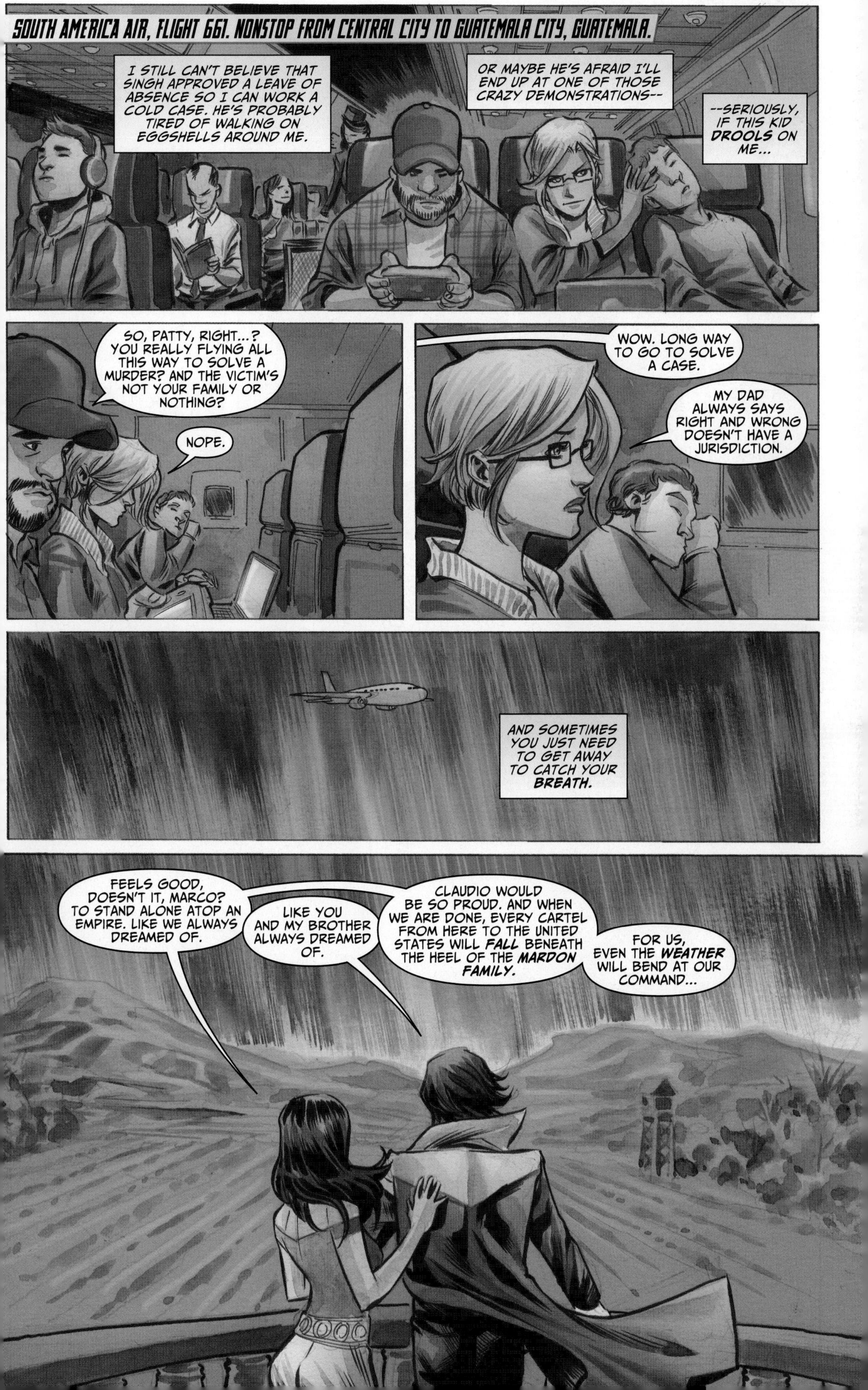
SOUTH AMERICA AIR, FLIGHT 661. NONSTOP FROM CENTRAL CITY TO GUATEMALA CITY, GUATEMALA.
I STILL CAN'T BELIEVE THAT SINGH APPROVED A LEAVE OF ABSENCE SO I CAN WORK A COLD CASE. HE'S PROBABLY TIRED OF WALKING ON EGGSHELLS AROUND ME.
OR MAYBE HE'S AFRAID I'LL END UP AT ONE OF THOSE CRAZY DEMONSTRATIONS--
--SERIOUSLY, IF THIS KID DROOLS ON ME...
SO, PATTY, RIGHT...? YOU REALLY FLYING ALL THIS WAY TO SOLVE A MURDER? AND THE VICTIM'S NOT YOUR FAMILY OR NOTHING?
NOPE.
WOW. LONG WAY TO GO TO SOLVE A CASE.
MY DAD ALWAYS SAYS RIGHT AND WRONG DOESN'T HAVE A JURISDICTION.
AND SOMETIMES YOU JUST NEED TO GET AWAY TO CATCH YOUR BREATH.
FEELS GOOD, DOESN'T IT, MARCO? TO STAND ALONE ATOP AN EMPIRE. LIKE WE ALWAYS DREAMED OF.
LIKE YOU AND MY BROTHER ALWAYS DREAMED OF.
CLAUDIO WOULD BE SO PROUD. AND WHEN WE ARE DONE, EVERY CARTEL FROM HERE TO THE UNITED STATES WILL FALL BENEATH THE HEEL OF THE MARDON FAMILY.
FOR US, EVEN THE WEATHER WILL BEND AT OUR COMMAND...

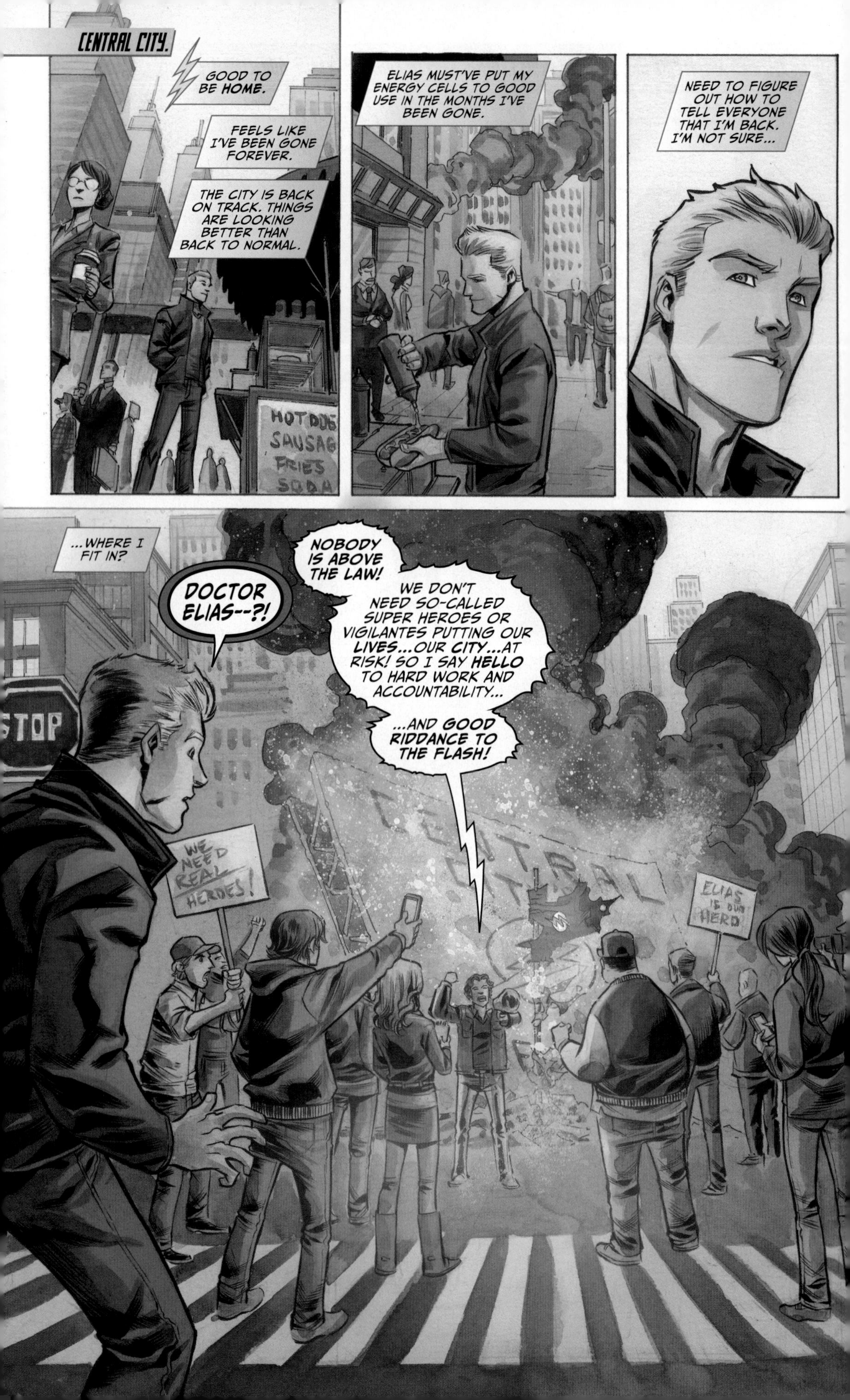
CENTRAL CITY.
GOOD TO BE HOME.
FEELS LIKE I'VE BEEN GONE FOREVER.
THE CITY IS BACK ON TRACK. THINGS ARE LOOKING BETTER THAN BACK TO NORMAL.
FRIES
SODA
ELIAS MUST'VE PUT MY ENERGY CELLS TO GOOD USE IN THE MONTHS I'VE BEEN GONE.
NEED TO FIGURE OUT HOW TO TELL EVERYONE THAT I'M BACK. I'M NOT SURE...
...WHERE I FIT IN?
DOCTOR ELIAS--?!
NOBODY IS ABOVE THE LAW!
WE DON'T NEED SO-CALLED SUPER HEROES OR VIGILANTES PUTTING OUR LIVES...OUR CITY...AT RISK! SO I SAY HELLO TO HARD WORK AND ACCOUNTABILITY...
...AND GOOD RIDDANCE TO THE FLASH!
STOP
WE NEED REAL HEROES!
ELIAS IS OUR HERO

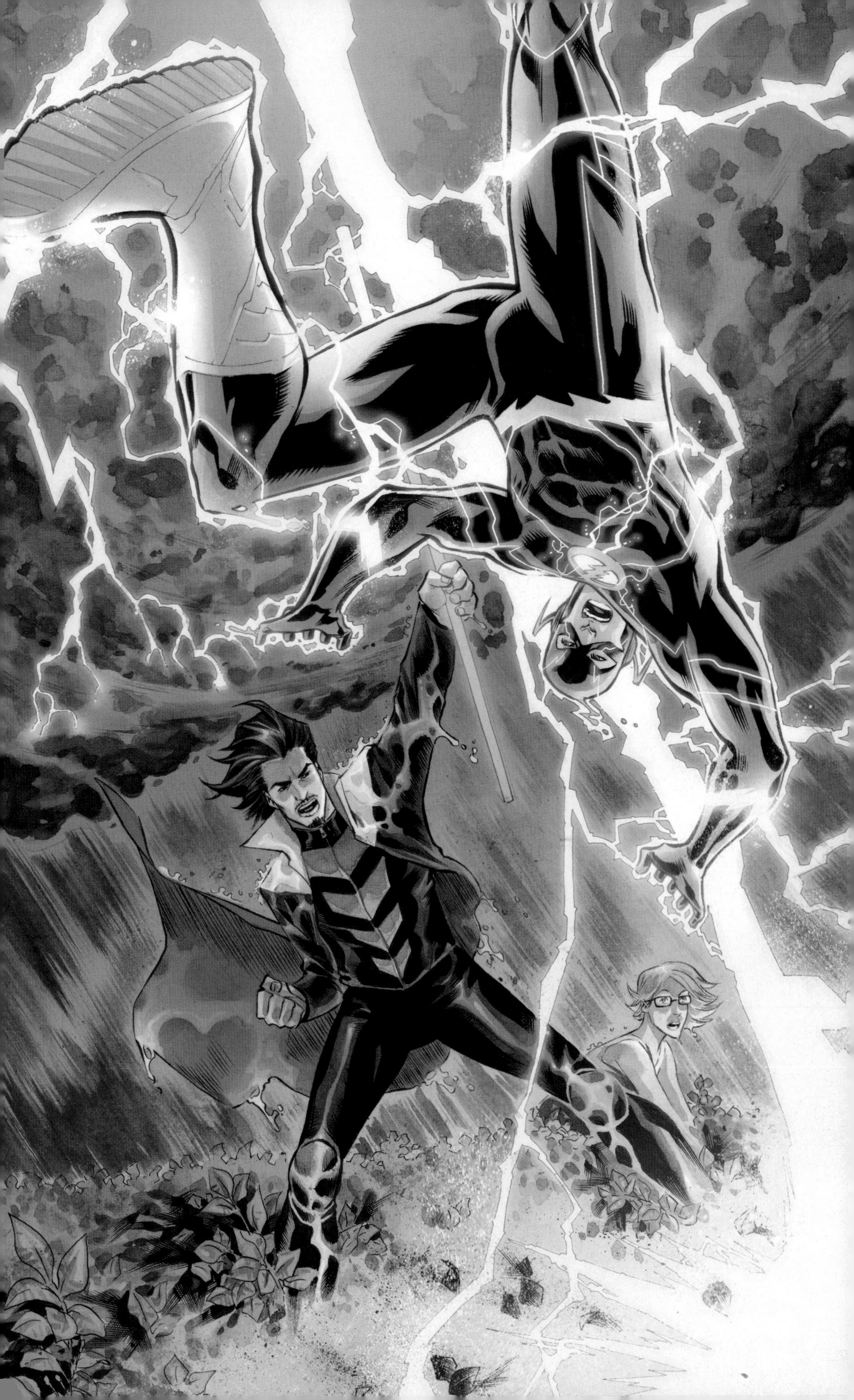

FRANCIS MANAPUL & BRIAN BUCCELLATO writers MARCUS TO penciller RAY McCARTHY inker

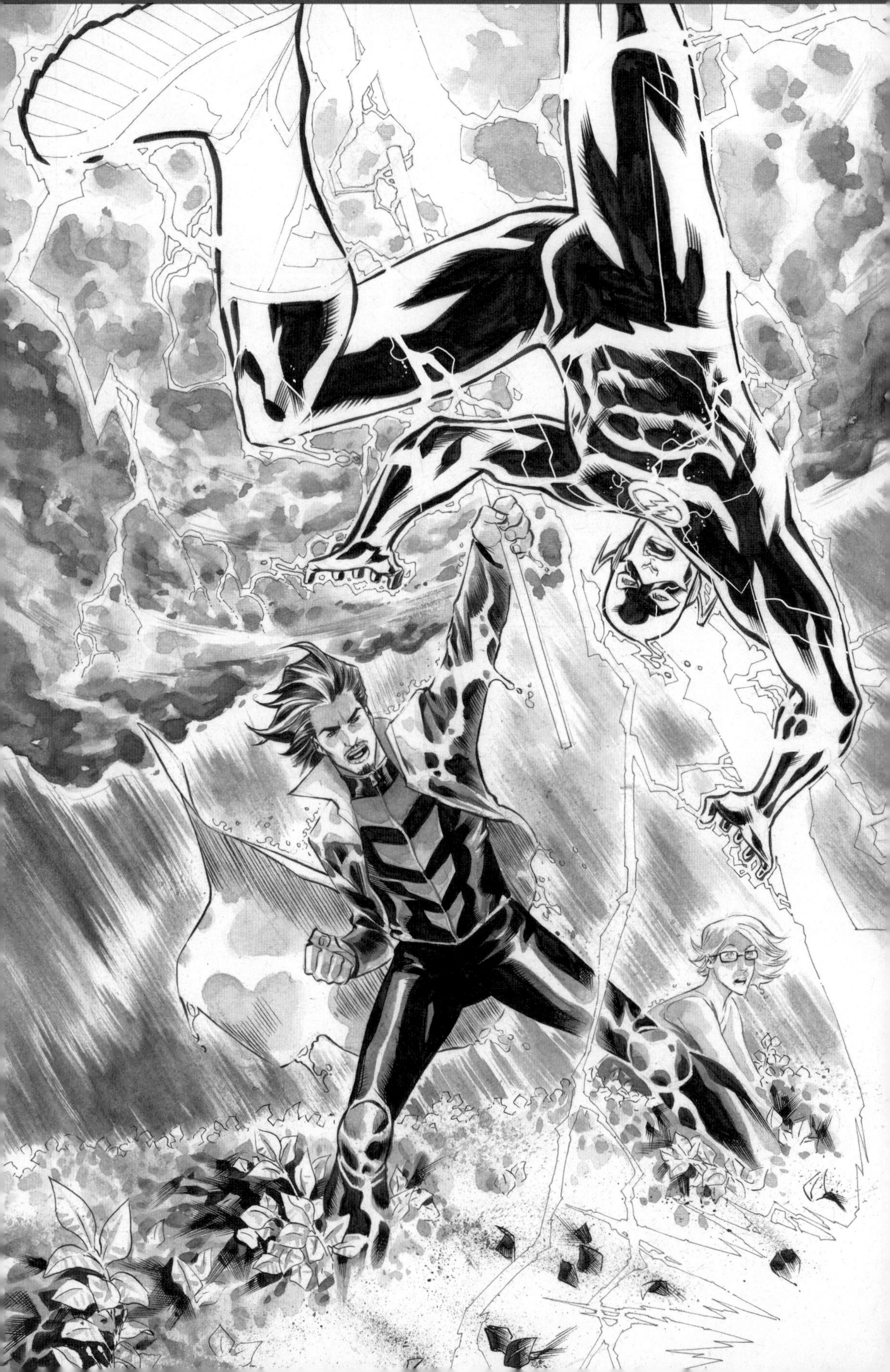

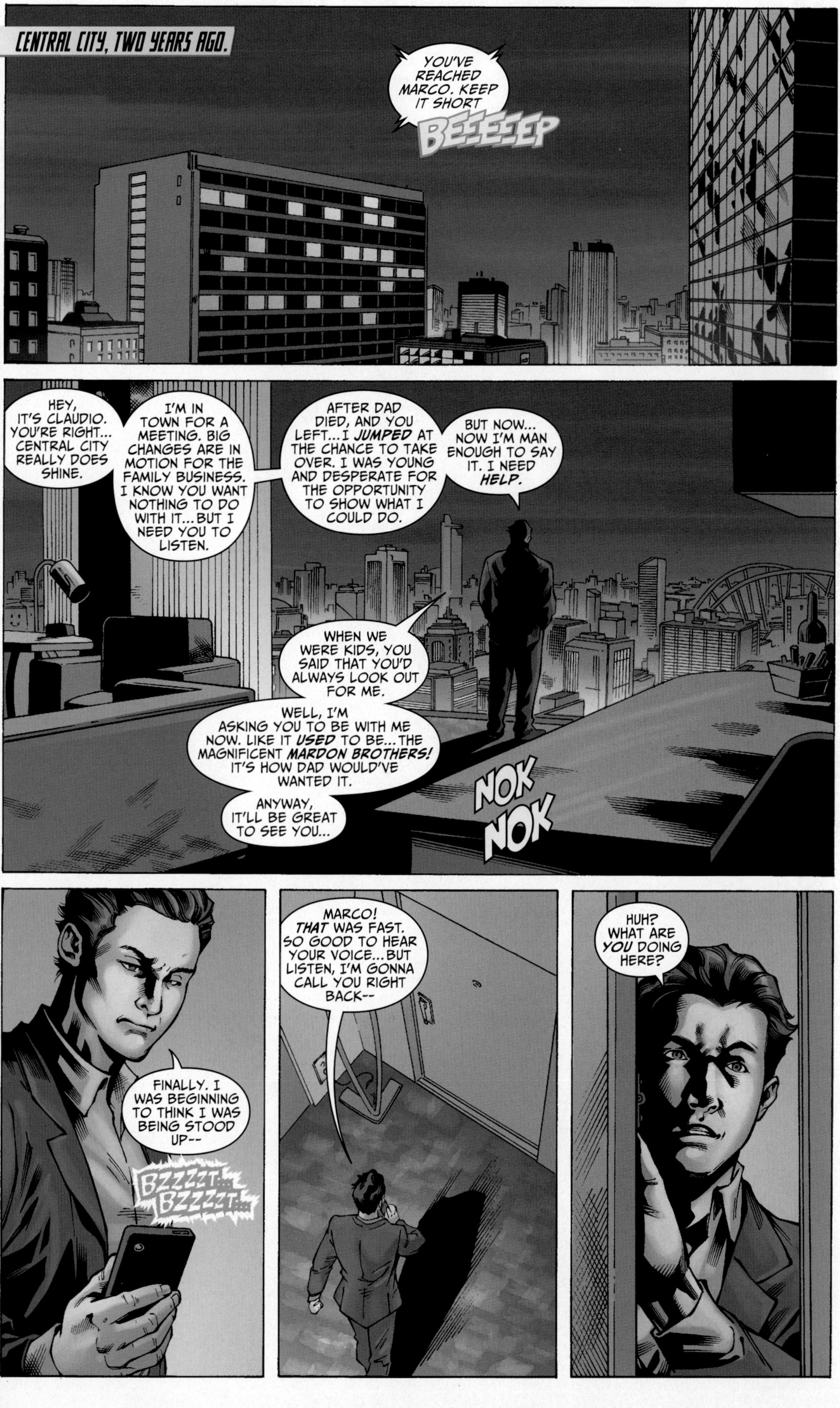
CENTRAL CITY, TWO YEARS AGO.
YOU'VE REACHED MARCO. KEEP IT SHORT
BEEEEEP
HEY, IT'S CLAUDIO. YOU'RE RIGHT... CENTRAL CITY REALLY DOES SHINE.
I'M IN TOWN FOR A MEETING. BIG CHANGES ARE IN MOTION FOR THE FAMILY BUSINESS. I KNOW YOU WANT NOTHING TO DO WITH IT...BUT I NEED YOU TO LISTEN.
AFTER DAD DIED, AND YOU LEFT...I JUMPED AT THE CHANCE TO TAKE OVER. I WAS YOUNG AND DESPERATE FOR THE OPPORTUNITY TO SHOW WHAT I COULD DO.
BUT NOW... NOW I'M MAN ENOUGH TO SAY IT. I NEED HELP.
WHEN WE WERE KIDS, YOU SAID THAT YOU'D ALWAYS LOOK OUT FOR ME.
WELL, I'M ASKING YOU TO BE WITH ME NOW. LIKE IT USED TO BE...THE MAGNIFICENT MARDON BROTHERS! IT'S HOW DAD WOULD'VE WANTED IT.
ANYWAY, IT'LL BE GREAT TO SEE YOU...
NOK NOK
FINALLY. I WAS BEGINNING TO THINK I WAS BEING STOOD UP--
BZZZZT... BZZZZT...
MARCO! THAT WAS FAST. SO GOOD TO HEAR YOUR VOICE...BUT LISTEN, I'M GONNA CALL YOU RIGHT BACK--
HUH? WHAT ARE YOU DOING HERE?

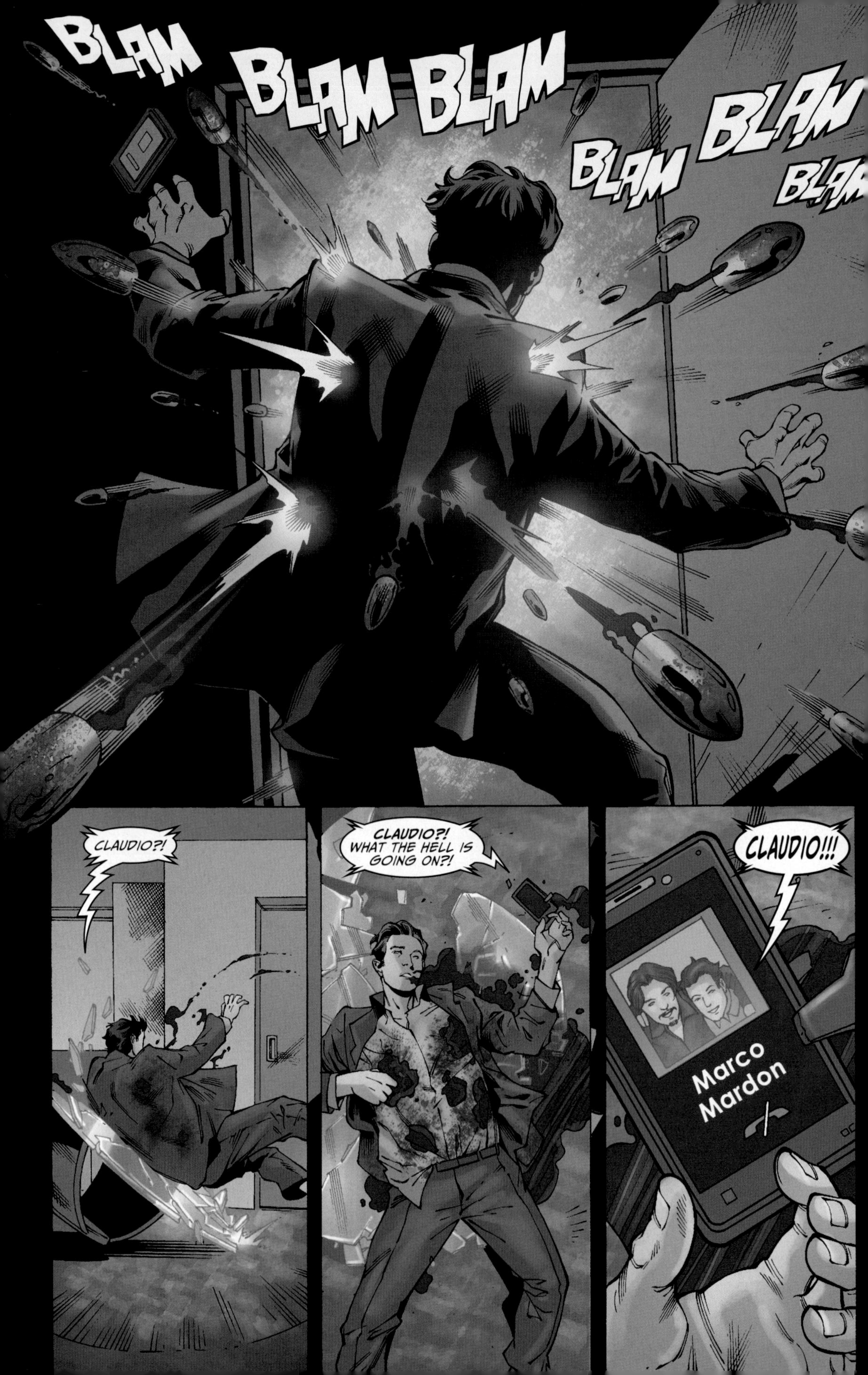
BLAM
BLAM BLAM
BLAM
BLAM
BLAM
BLAM
CLAUDIO?!
CLAUDIO?! WHAT THE HELL IS GOING ON?!
CLAUDIO!!!
Marco Mardon

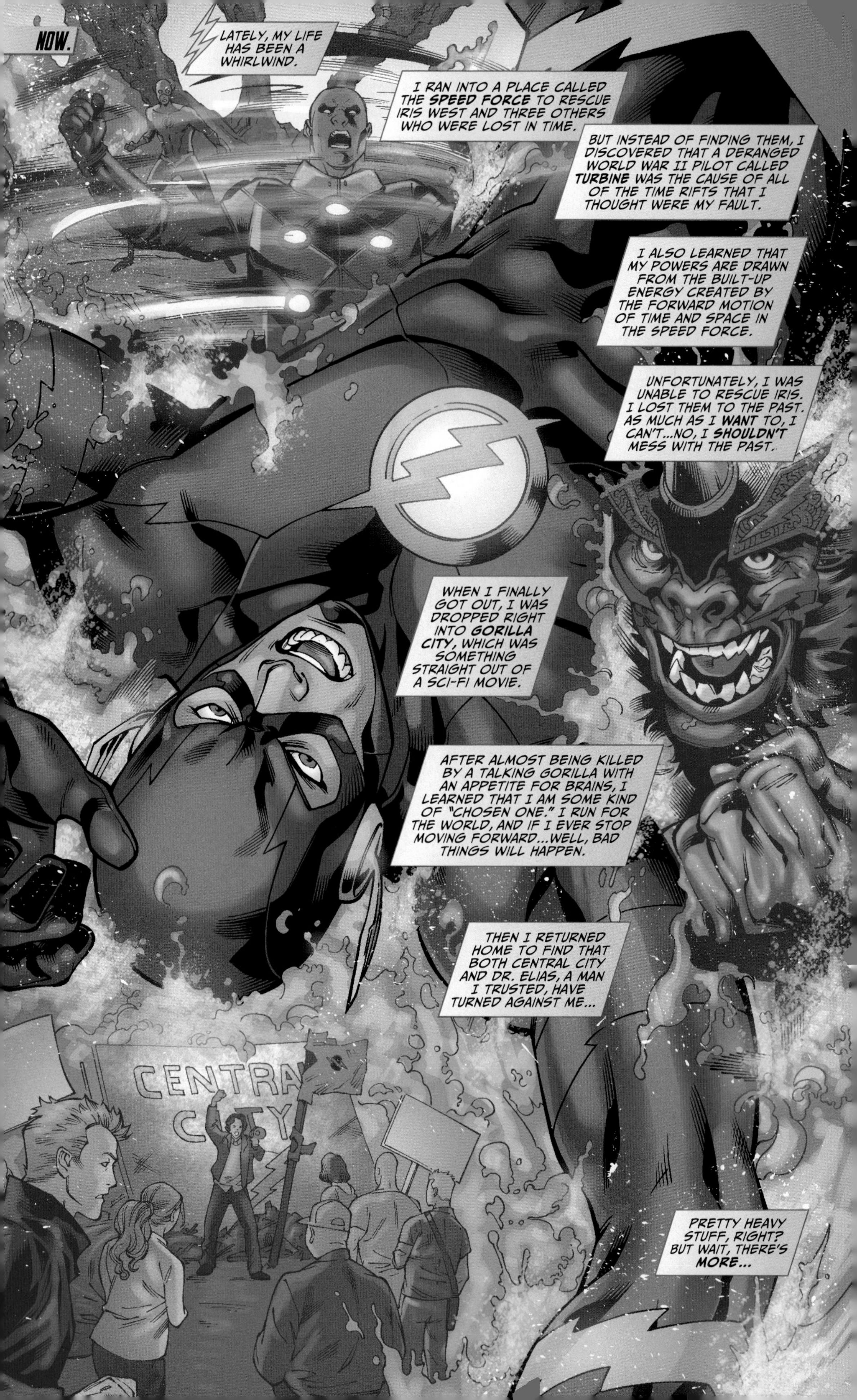
NOW.
LATELY, MY LIFE HAS BEEN A WHIRLWIND.
I RAN INTO A PLACE CALLED THE SPEED FORCE TO RESCUE IRIS WEST AND THREE OTHERS WHO WERE LOST IN TIME.
BUT INSTEAD OF FINDING THEM, I DISCOVERED THAT A DERANGED WORLD WAR II PILOT CALLED TURBINE WAS THE CAUSE OF ALL OF THE TIME RIFTS THAT I THOUGHT WERE MY FAULT.
I ALSO LEARNED THAT MY POWERS ARE DRAWN FROM THE BUILT-UP ENERGY CREATED BY THE FORWARD MOTION OF TIME AND SPACE IN THE SPEED FORCE.
UNFORTUNATELY, I WAS UNABLE TO RESCUE IRIS. I LOST THEM TO THE PAST. AS MUCH AS I WANT TO, I CAN'T...NO, I SHOULDN'T MESS WITH THE PAST.
WHEN I FINALLY GOT OUT, I WAS DROPPED RIGHT INTO GORILLA CITY, WHICH WAS SOMETHING STRAIGHT OUT OF A SCI-FI MOVIE.
AFTER ALMOST BEING KILLED BY A TALKING GORILLA WITH AN APPETITE FOR BRAINS, I LEARNED THAT I AM SOME KIND OF "CHOSEN ONE." I RUN FOR THE WORLD, AND IF I EVER STOP MOVING FORWARD...WELL, BAD THINGS WILL HAPPEN.
THEN I RETURNED HOME TO FIND THAT BOTH CENTRAL CITY AND DR. ELIAS, A MAN I TRUSTED, HAVE TURNED AGAINST ME...
PRETTY HEAVY STUFF, RIGHT? BUT WAIT, THERE'S MORE...

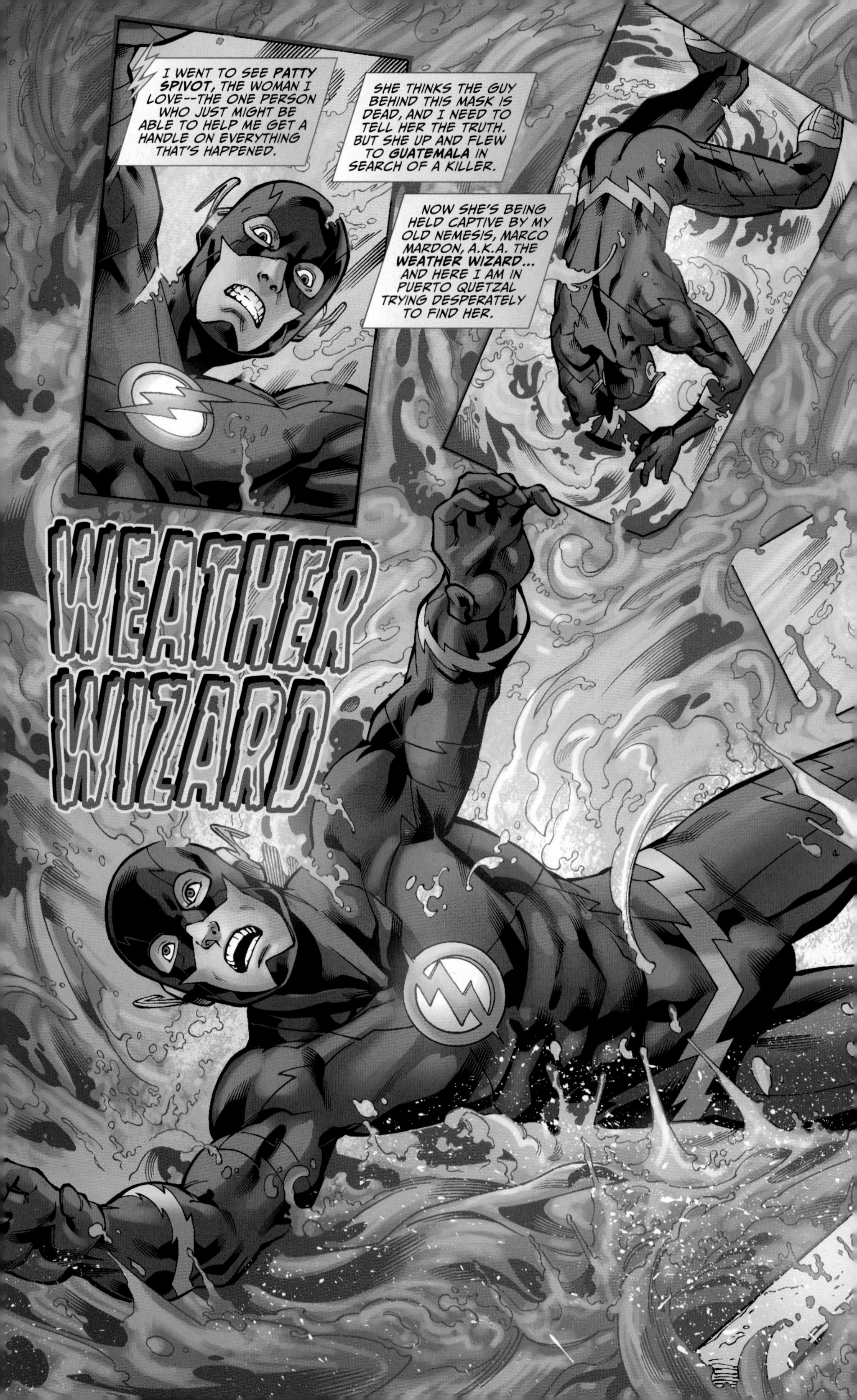

I WENT TO SEE PATTY SPIVOT, THE WOMAN I LOVE--THE ONE PERSON WHO JUST MIGHT BE ABLE TO HELP ME GET A HANDLE ON EVERYTHING THAT'S HAPPENED.
SHE THINKS THE GUY BEHIND THIS MASK IS DEAD, AND I NEED TO TELL HER THE TRUTH. BUT SHE UP AND FLEW TO GUATEMALA IN SEARCH OF A KILLER.
NOW SHE'S BEING HELD CAPTIVE BY MY OLD NEMESIS, MARCO MARDON, A.K.A. THE WEATHER WIZARD... AND HERE I AM IN PUERTO QUETZAL TRYING DESPERATELY TO FIND HER.
WEATHER WIZARD

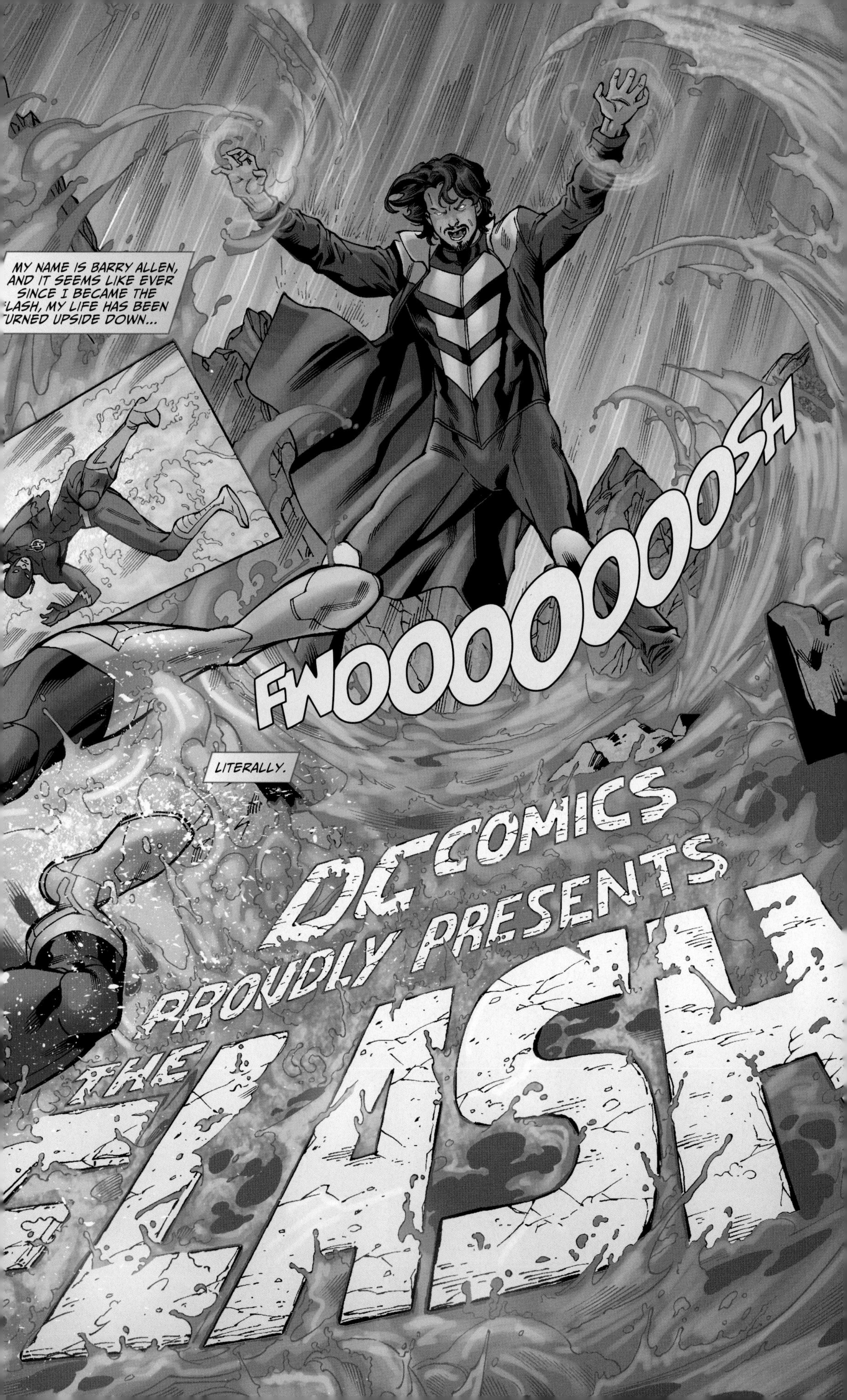
MY NAME IS BARRY ALLEN, AND IT SEEMS LIKE EVER SINCE I BECAME THE FLASH, MY LIFE HAS BEEN TURNED UPSIDE DOWN...
FWOOOOOOOOOSH
LITERALLY.
DC COMICS PROUDLY PRESENTS
THE FLASH

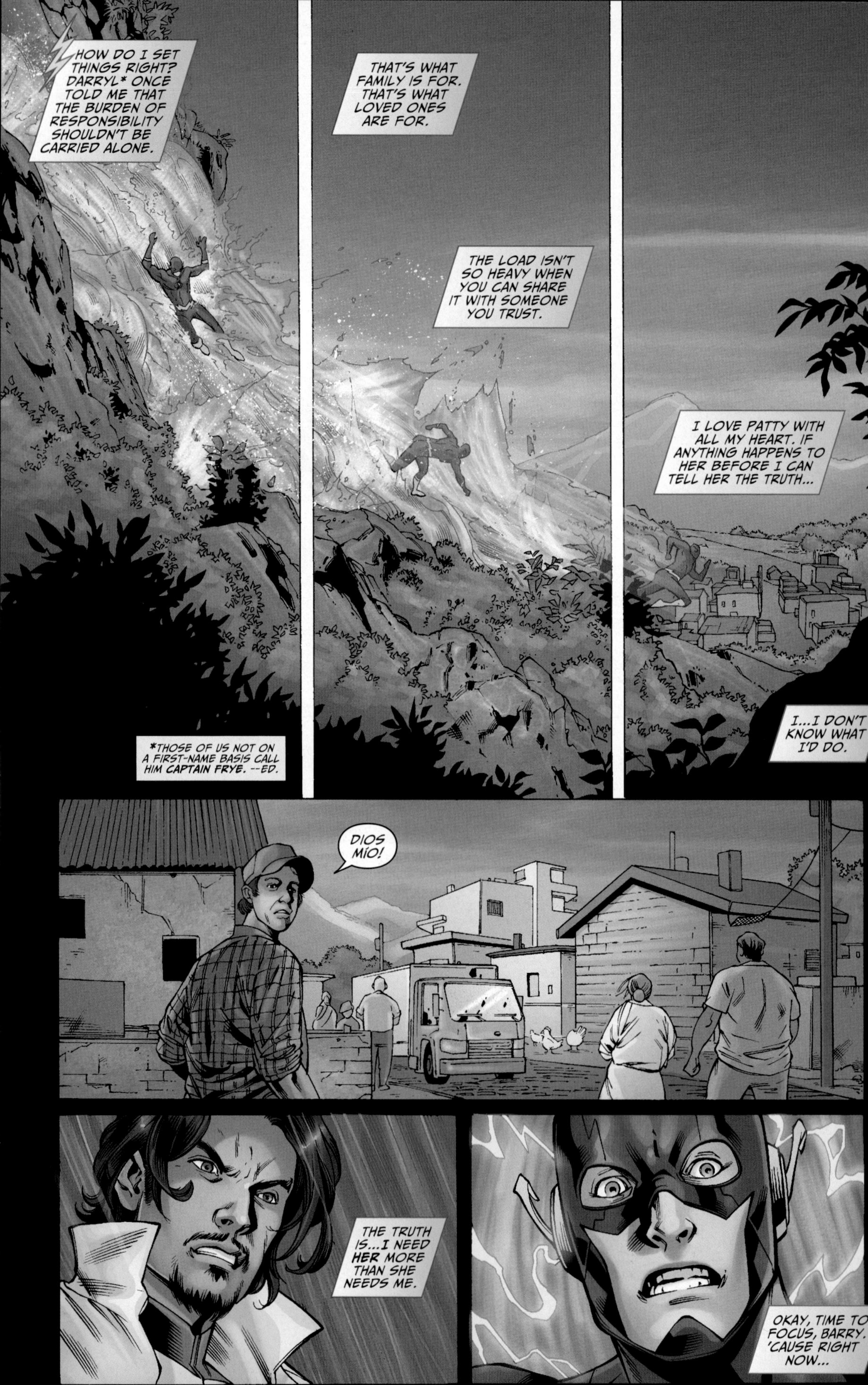
HOW DO I SET THINGS RIGHT? DARRYL* ONCE TOLD ME THAT THE BURDEN OF RESPONSIBILITY SHOULDN'T BE CARRIED ALONE.
*THOSE OF US NOT ON A FIRST-NAME BASIS CALL HIM CAPTAIN FRYE. --ED.
THAT'S WHAT FAMILY IS FOR. THAT'S WHAT LOVED ONES ARE FOR.
THE LOAD ISN'T SO HEAVY WHEN YOU CAN SHARE IT WITH SOMEONE YOU TRUST.
I LOVE PATTY WITH ALL MY HEART. IF ANYTHING HAPPENS TO HER BEFORE I CAN TELL HER THE TRUTH...
I...I DON'T KNOW WHAT I'D DO.
DIOS MÍO!
THE TRUTH IS...I NEED HER MORE THAN SHE NEEDS ME.
OKAY, TIME TO FOCUS, BARRY. 'CAUSE RIGHT NOW...

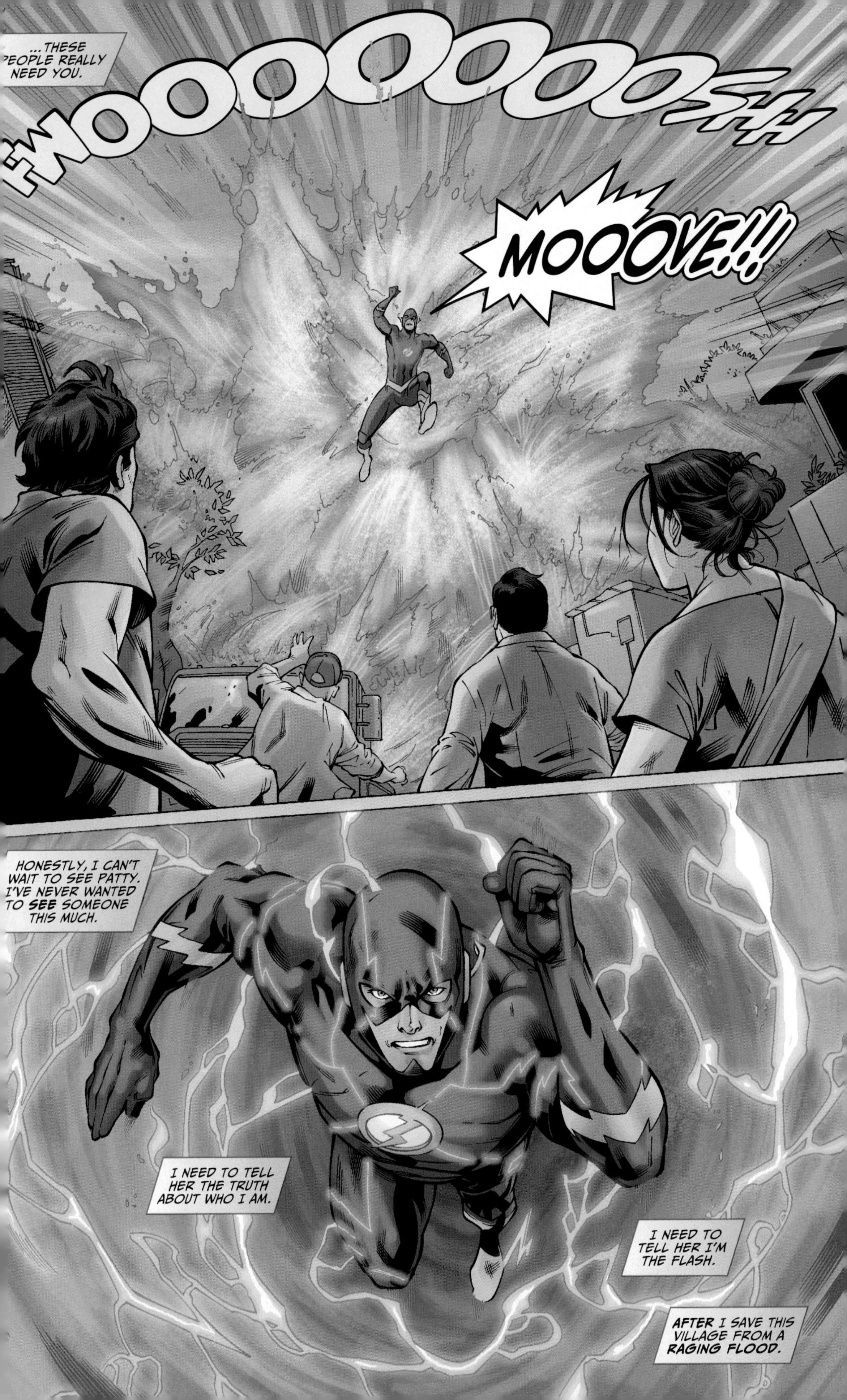
...THESE PEOPLE REALLY NEED YOU.
FWOOOOOOOOSH
MOOOVE!!
HONESTLY, I CAN'T WAIT TO SEE PATTY. I'VE NEVER WANTED TO SEE SOMEONE THIS MUCH.
I NEED TO TELL HER THE TRUTH ABOUT WHO I AM.
I NEED TO TELL HER I'M THE FLASH.
AFTER I SAVE THIS VILLAGE FROM A RAGING FLOOD.

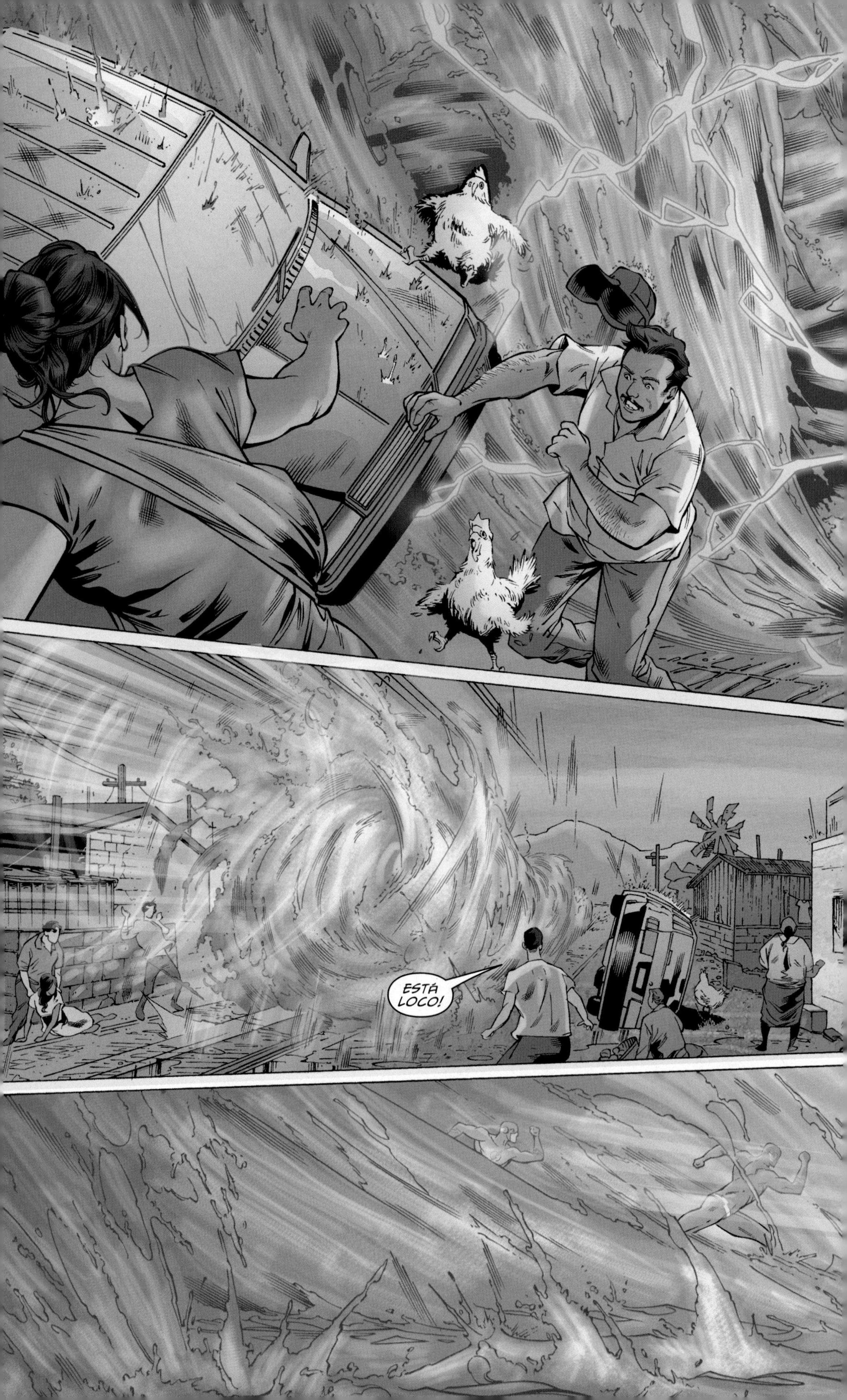
ESTÁ LOCO!

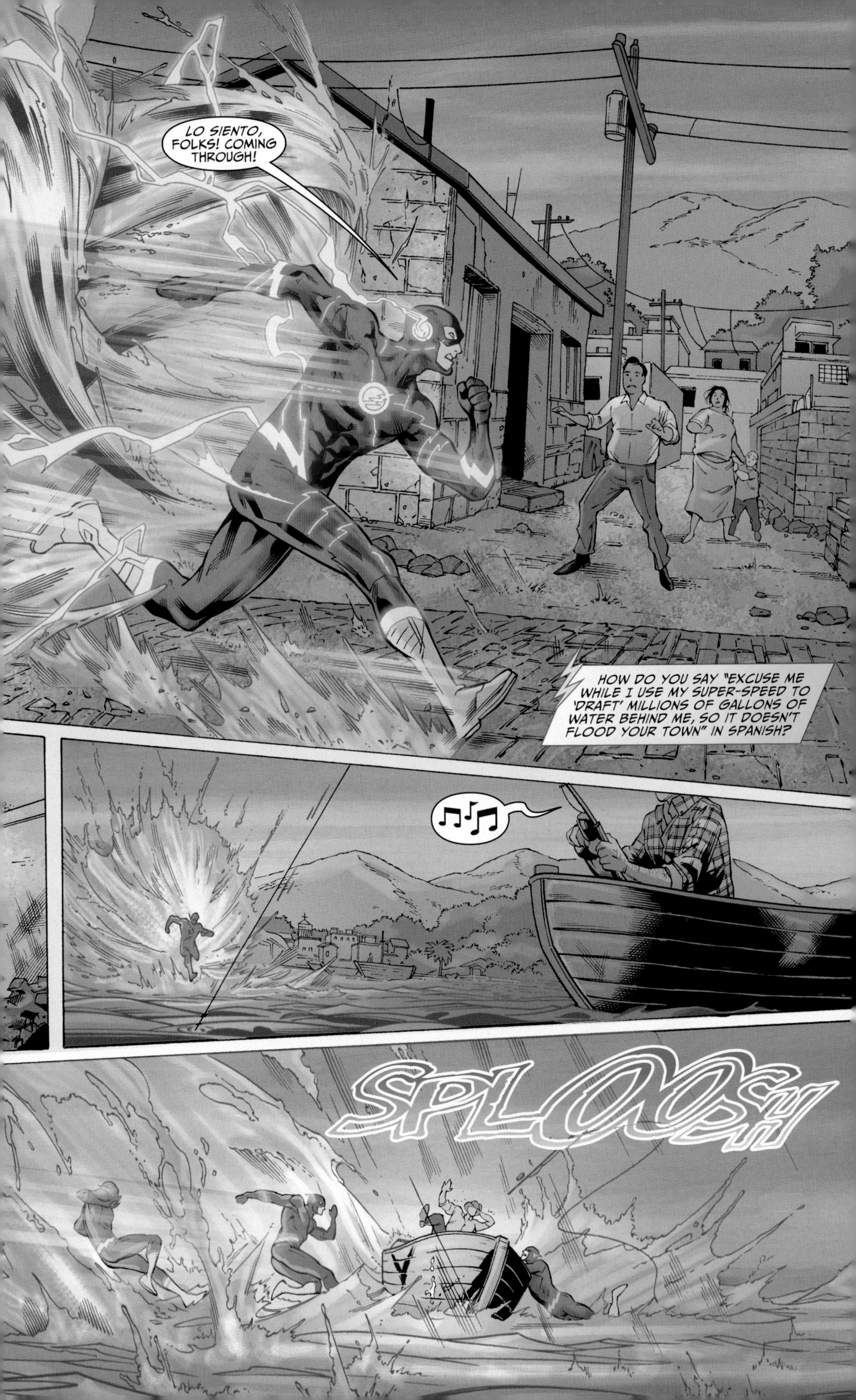
LO SIENTO, FOLKS! COMING THROUGH!
HOW DO YOU SAY "EXCUSE ME WHILE I USE MY SUPER-SPEED TO 'DRAFT' MILLIONS OF GALLONS OF WATER BEHIND ME, SO IT DOESN'T FLOOD YOUR TOWN" IN SPANISH?
♫♪♫
SPLOOSH

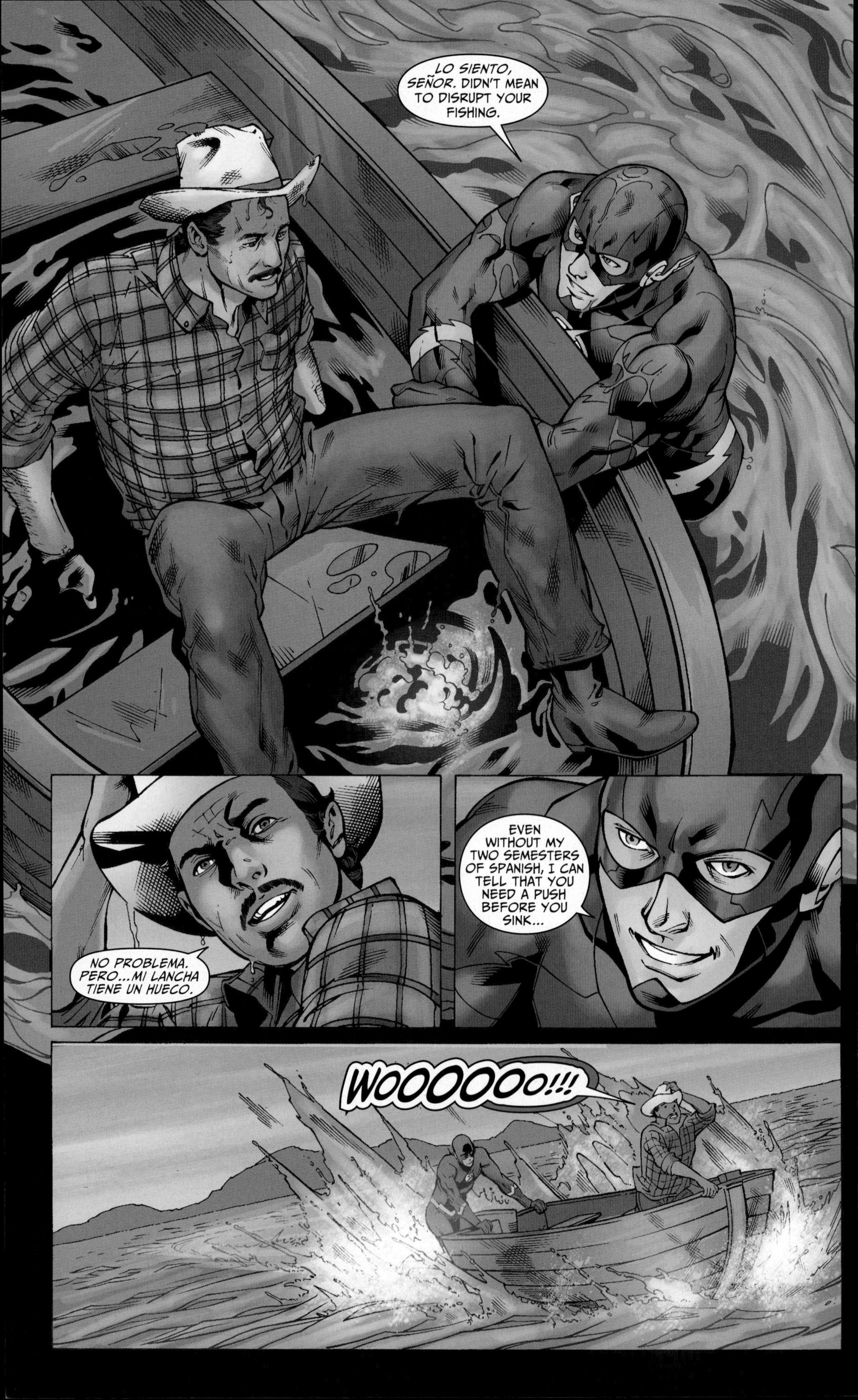
LO SIENTO, SEÑOR. DIDN'T MEAN TO DISRUPT YOUR FISHING.
NO PROBLEMA. PERO...MI LANCHA TIENE UN HUECO.
EVEN WITHOUT MY TWO SEMESTERS OF SPANISH, I CAN TELL THAT YOU NEED A PUSH BEFORE YOU SINK...
WOOOOOOo!!!

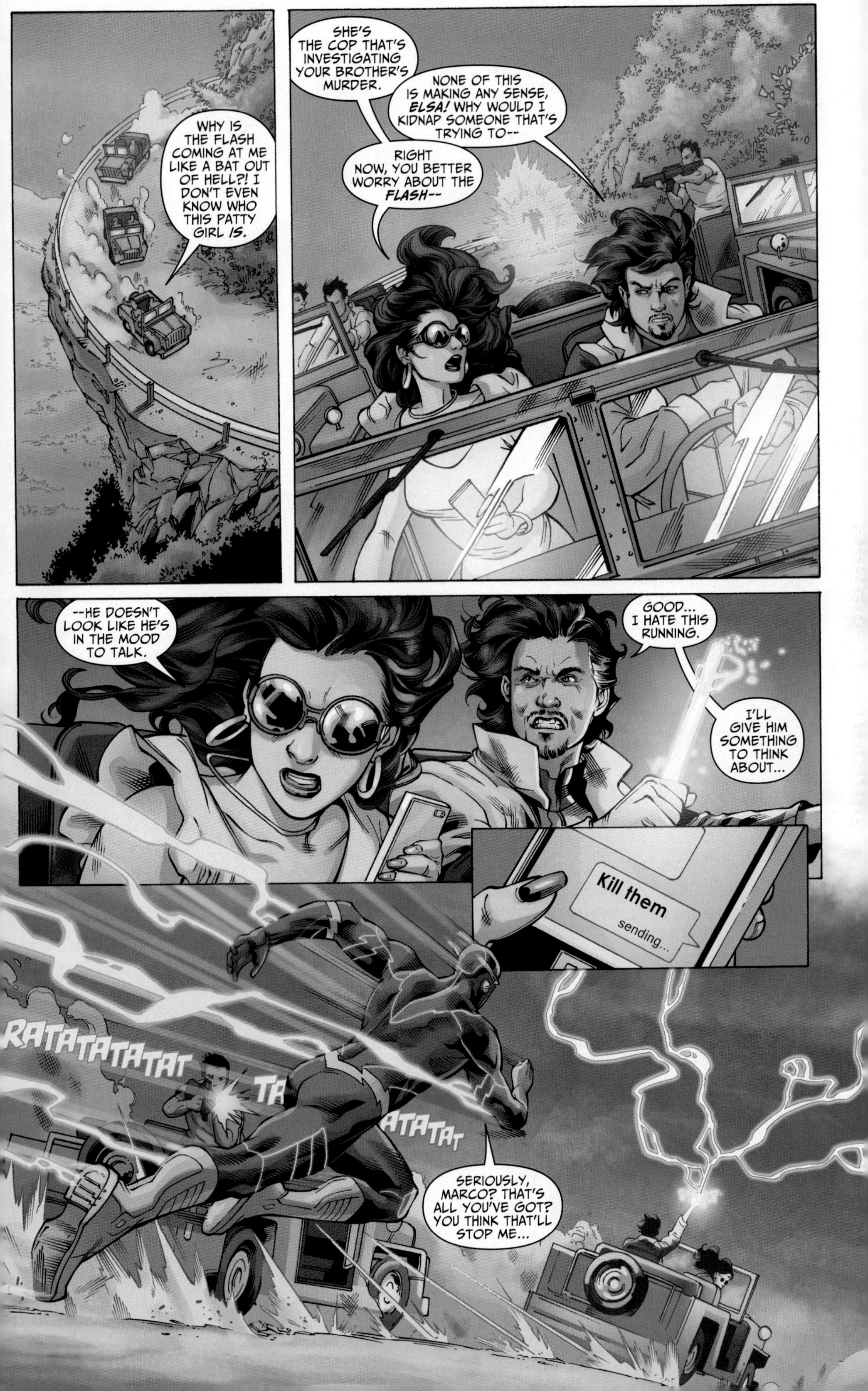
WHY IS THE FLASH COMING AT ME LIKE A BAT OUT OF HELL?! I DON'T EVEN KNOW WHO THIS PATTY GIRL IS.
SHE'S THE COP THAT'S INVESTIGATING YOUR BROTHER'S MURDER.
NONE OF THIS IS MAKING ANY SENSE, ELSA! WHY WOULD I KIDNAP SOMEONE THAT'S TRYING TO--
RIGHT NOW, YOU BETTER WORRY ABOUT THE FLASH--
--HE DOESN'T LOOK LIKE HE'S IN THE MOOD TO TALK.
GOOD... I HATE THIS RUNNING.
I'LL GIVE HIM SOMETHING TO THINK ABOUT...
Kill them
sending...
RATATATATAT
TA
ATATAT
SERIOUSLY, MARCO? THAT'S ALL YOU'VE GOT? YOU THINK THAT'LL STOP ME...

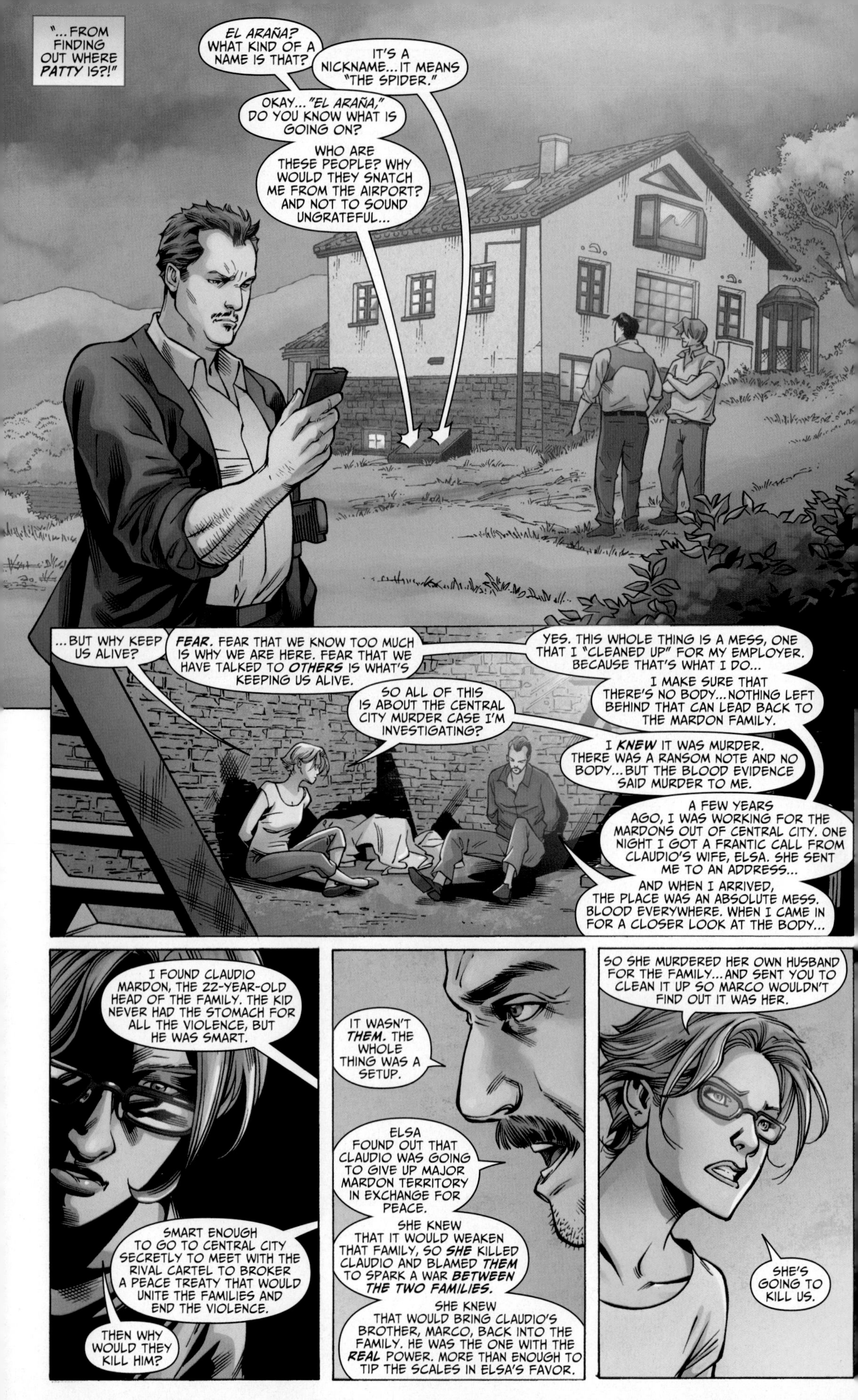

"...FROM FINDING OUT WHERE *PATTY* IS?!"
EL ARAÑA? WHAT KIND OF A NAME IS THAT?
IT'S A NICKNAME... IT MEANS "THE SPIDER."
OKAY... *"EL ARAÑA,"* DO YOU KNOW WHAT IS GOING ON?
WHO ARE THESE PEOPLE? WHY WOULD THEY SNATCH ME FROM THE AIRPORT? AND NOT TO SOUND UNGRATEFUL...
...BUT WHY KEEP US ALIVE?
FEAR. FEAR THAT WE KNOW TOO MUCH IS WHY WE ARE HERE. FEAR THAT WE HAVE TALKED TO ***OTHERS*** IS WHAT'S KEEPING US ALIVE.
SO ALL OF THIS IS ABOUT THE CENTRAL CITY MURDER CASE I'M INVESTIGATING?
YES. THIS WHOLE THING IS A MESS, ONE THAT I "CLEANED UP" FOR MY EMPLOYER. BECAUSE THAT'S WHAT I DO...
I MAKE SURE THAT THERE'S NO BODY...NOTHING LEFT BEHIND THAT CAN LEAD BACK TO THE MARDON FAMILY.
I ***KNEW*** IT WAS MURDER. THERE WAS A RANSOM NOTE AND NO BODY...BUT THE BLOOD EVIDENCE SAID MURDER TO ME.
A FEW YEARS AGO, I WAS WORKING FOR THE MARDONS OUT OF CENTRAL CITY. ONE NIGHT I GOT A FRANTIC CALL FROM CLAUDIO'S WIFE, ELSA. SHE SENT ME TO AN ADDRESS...
AND WHEN I ARRIVED, THE PLACE WAS AN ABSOLUTE MESS. BLOOD EVERYWHERE. WHEN I CAME IN FOR A CLOSER LOOK AT THE BODY...
I FOUND CLAUDIO MARDON, THE 22-YEAR-OLD HEAD OF THE FAMILY. THE KID NEVER HAD THE STOMACH FOR ALL THE VIOLENCE, BUT HE WAS SMART.
SMART ENOUGH TO GO TO CENTRAL CITY SECRETLY TO MEET WITH THE RIVAL CARTEL TO BROKER A PEACE TREATY THAT WOULD UNITE THE FAMILIES AND END THE VIOLENCE.
THEN WHY WOULD THEY KILL HIM?
IT WASN'T ***THEM.*** THE WHOLE THING WAS A SETUP.
ELSA FOUND OUT THAT CLAUDIO WAS GOING TO GIVE UP MAJOR MARDON TERRITORY IN EXCHANGE FOR PEACE.
SHE KNEW THAT IT WOULD WEAKEN THAT FAMILY, SO ***SHE*** KILLED CLAUDIO AND BLAMED ***THEM*** TO SPARK A WAR ***BETWEEN THE TWO FAMILIES.***
SHE KNEW THAT WOULD BRING CLAUDIO'S BROTHER, MARCO, BACK INTO THE FAMILY. HE WAS THE ONE WITH THE ***REAL*** POWER. MORE THAN ENOUGH TO TIP THE SCALES IN ELSA'S FAVOR.
SO SHE MURDERED HER OWN HUSBAND FOR THE FAMILY...AND SENT YOU TO CLEAN IT UP SO MARCO WOULDN'T FIND OUT IT WAS HER.
SHE'S GOING TO KILL US.

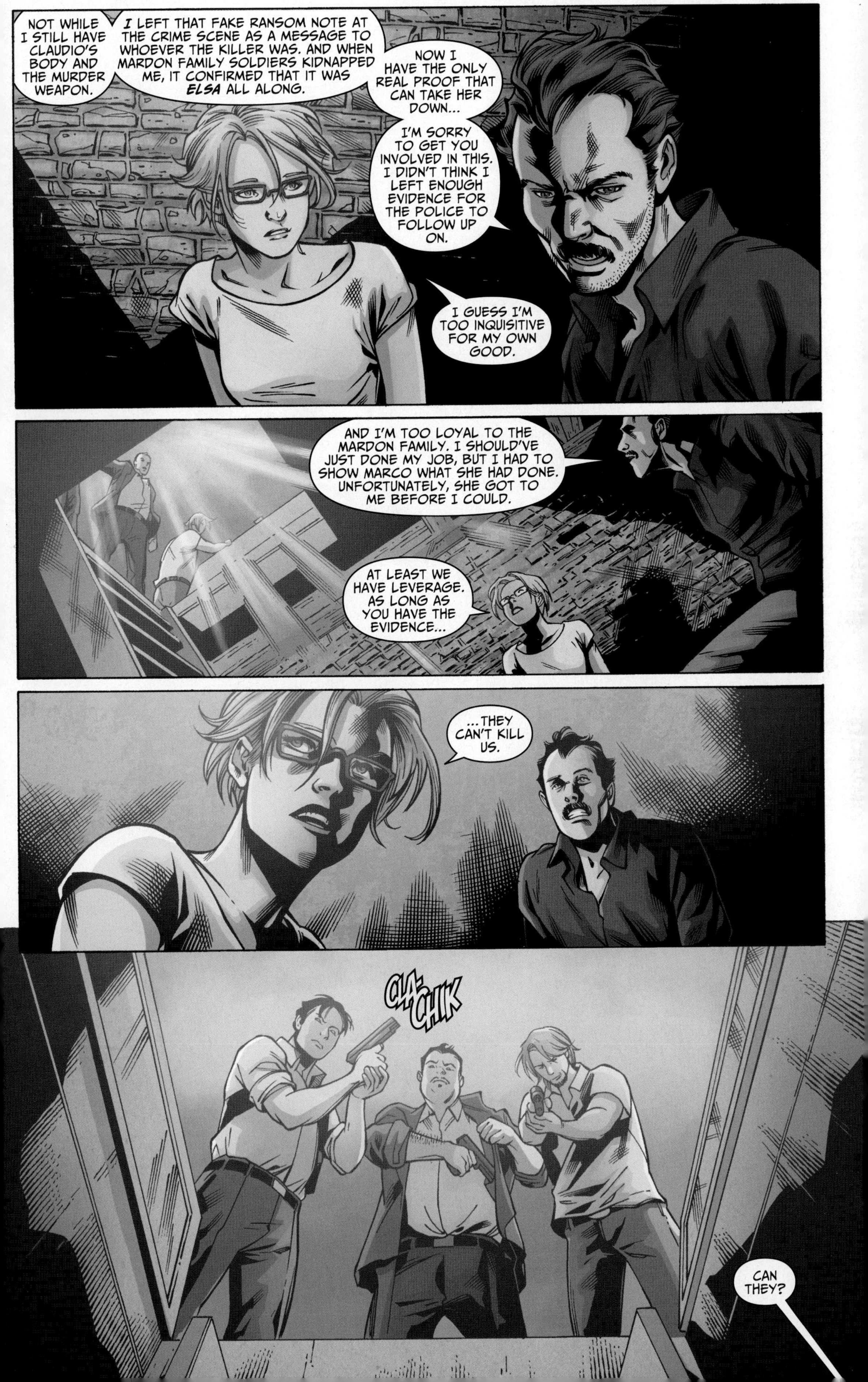
NOT WHILE I STILL HAVE CLAUDIO'S BODY AND THE MURDER WEAPON.
I LEFT THAT FAKE RANSOM NOTE AT THE CRIME SCENE AS A MESSAGE TO WHOEVER THE KILLER WAS. AND WHEN MARDON FAMILY SOLDIERS KIDNAPPED ME, IT CONFIRMED THAT IT WAS ELSA ALL ALONG.
NOW I HAVE THE ONLY REAL PROOF THAT CAN TAKE HER DOWN...
I'M SORRY TO GET YOU INVOLVED IN THIS. I DIDN'T THINK I LEFT ENOUGH EVIDENCE FOR THE POLICE TO FOLLOW UP ON.
I GUESS I'M TOO INQUISITIVE FOR MY OWN GOOD.
AND I'M TOO LOYAL TO THE MARDON FAMILY. I SHOULD'VE JUST DONE MY JOB, BUT I HAD TO SHOW MARCO WHAT SHE HAD DONE. UNFORTUNATELY, SHE GOT TO ME BEFORE I COULD.
AT LEAST WE HAVE LEVERAGE. AS LONG AS YOU HAVE THE EVIDENCE...
...THEY CAN'T KILL US.
CLA-CHIK
CAN THEY?

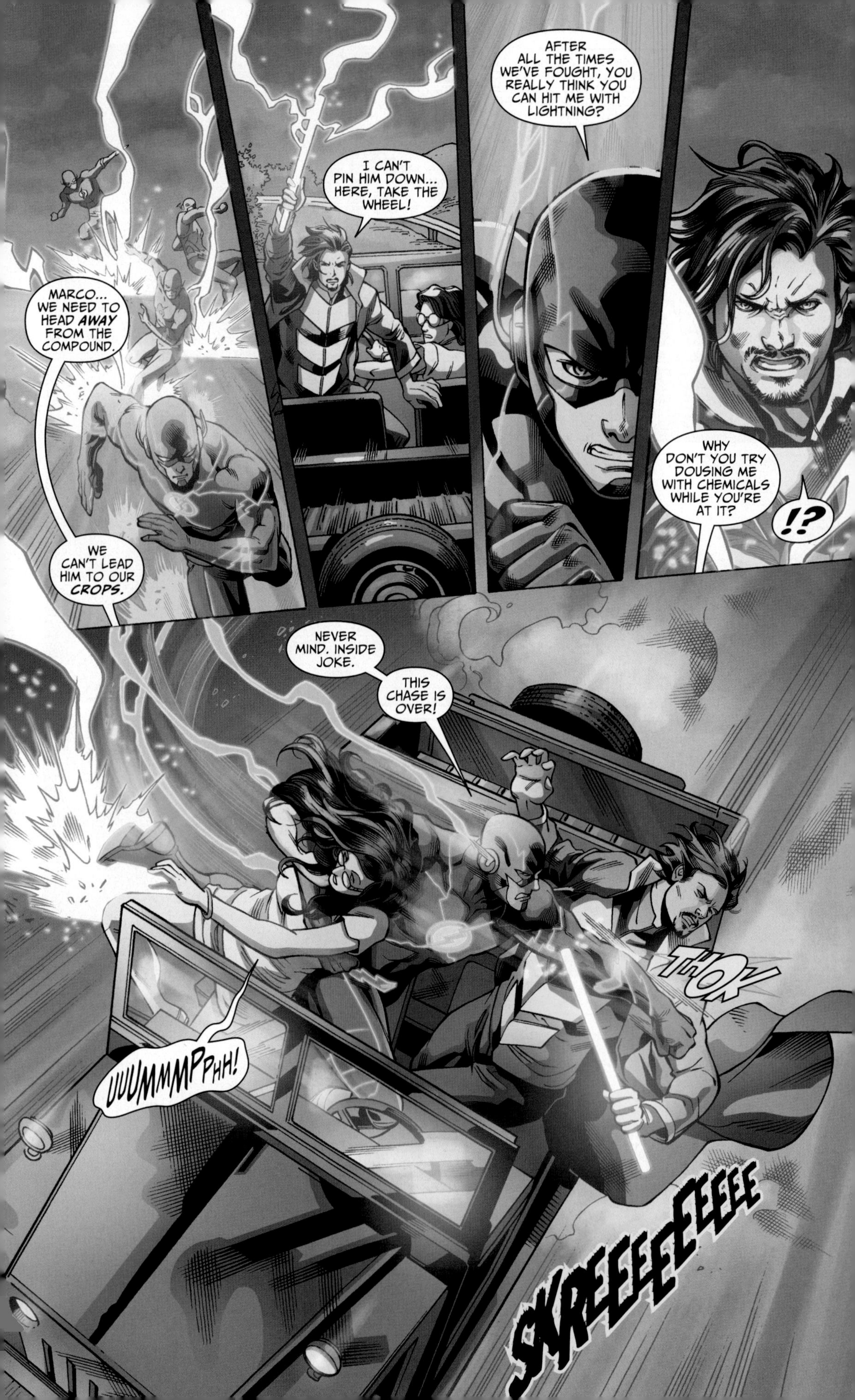
MARCO... WE NEED TO HEAD AWAY FROM THE COMPOUND.
WE CAN'T LEAD HIM TO OUR CROPS.
I CAN'T PIN HIM DOWN... HERE, TAKE THE WHEEL!
AFTER ALL THE TIMES WE'VE FOUGHT, YOU REALLY THINK YOU CAN HIT ME WITH LIGHTNING?
WHY DON'T YOU TRY DOUSING ME WITH CHEMICALS WHILE YOU'RE AT IT?
!?
NEVER MIND. INSIDE JOKE.
THIS CHASE IS OVER!
THOK
UUUMMMPHH!
SKREEEEEEEEEE

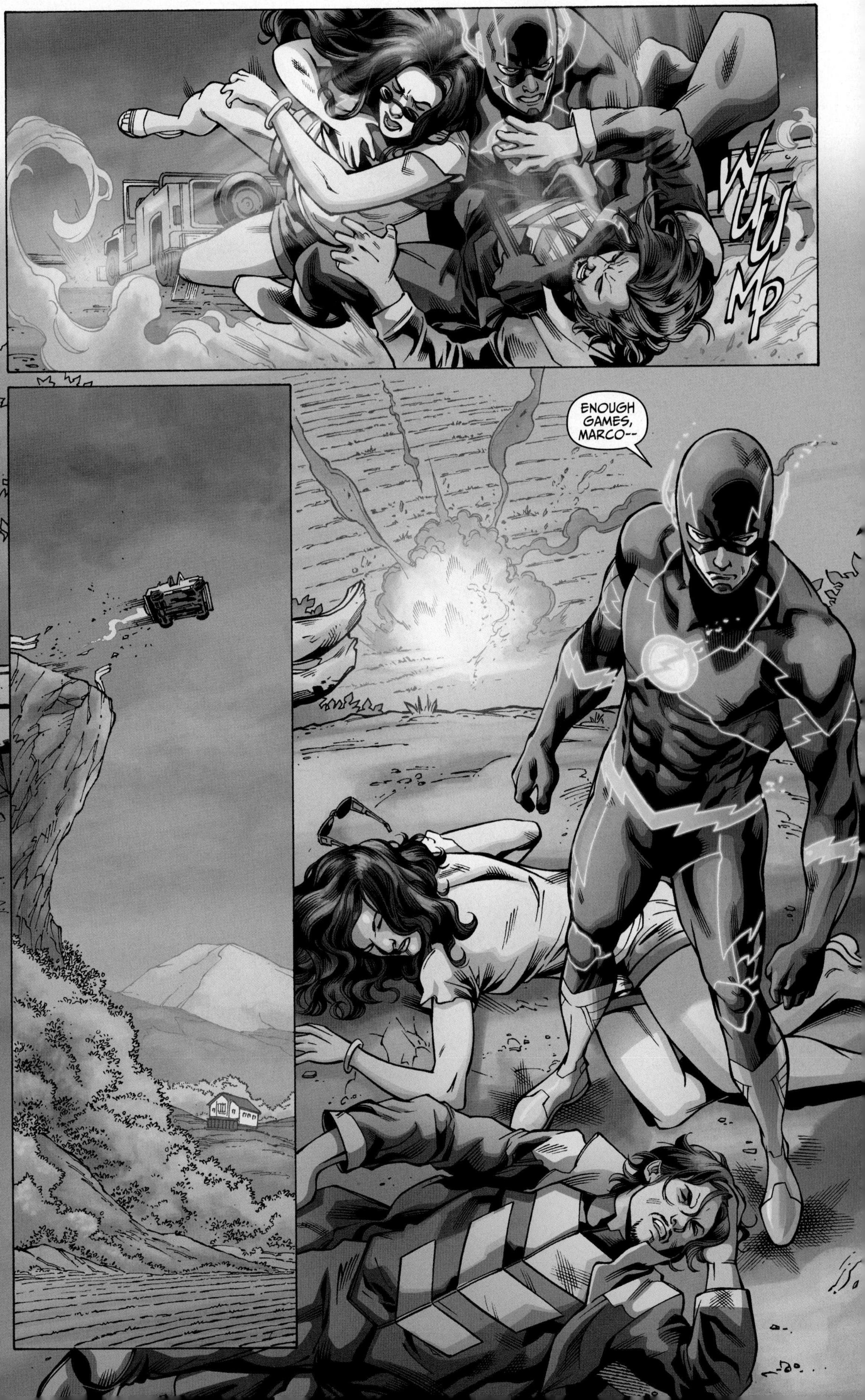
WUUMP
ENOUGH GAMES, MARCO--

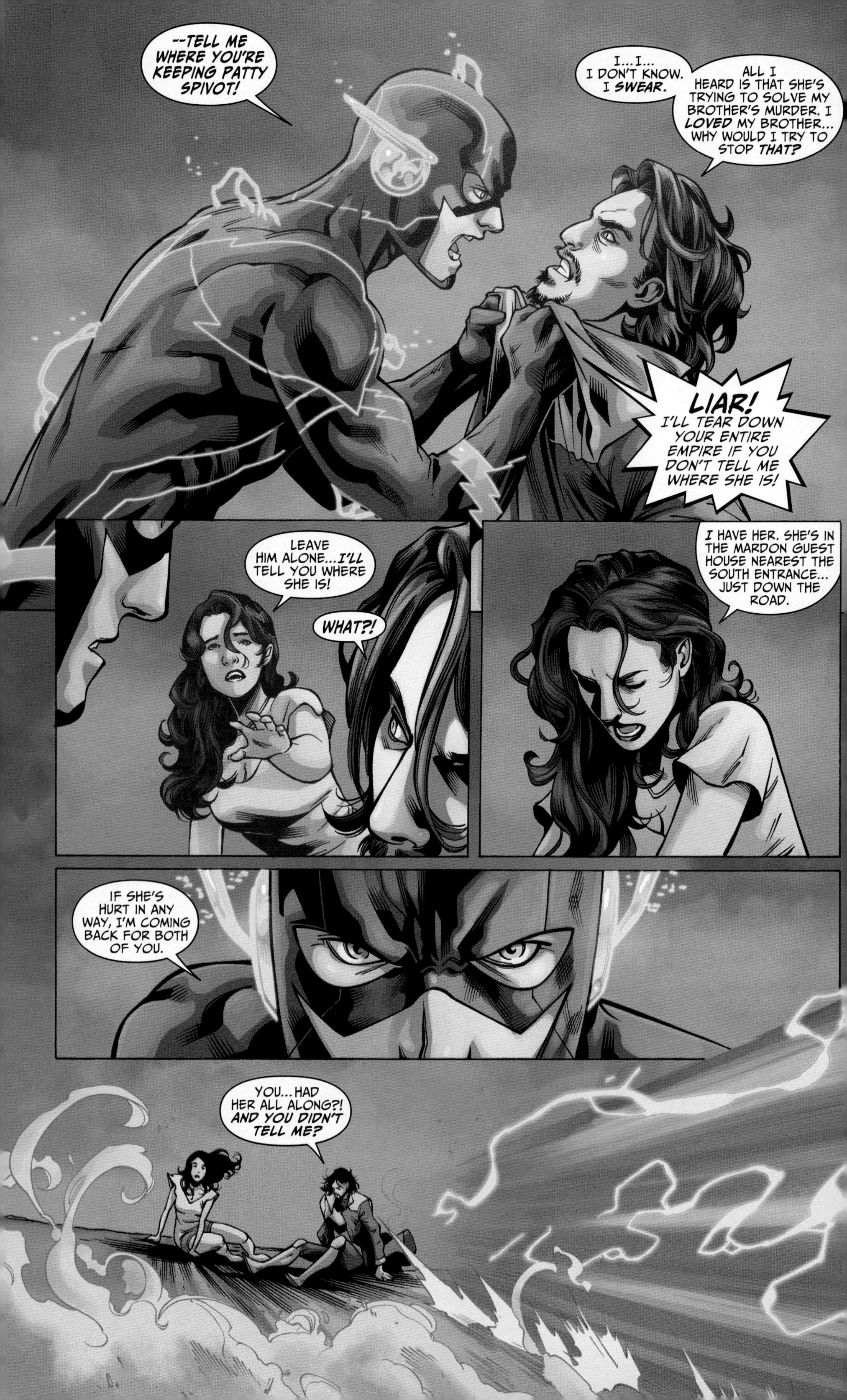
--TELL ME WHERE YOU'RE KEEPING PATTY SPIVOT!
I...I... I DON'T KNOW. I SWEAR.
ALL I HEARD IS THAT SHE'S TRYING TO SOLVE MY BROTHER'S MURDER. I LOVED MY BROTHER... WHY WOULD I TRY TO STOP THAT?
LIAR! I'LL TEAR DOWN YOUR ENTIRE EMPIRE IF YOU DON'T TELL ME WHERE SHE IS!
LEAVE HIM ALONE...I'LL TELL YOU WHERE SHE IS!
WHAT?!
I HAVE HER. SHE'S IN THE MARDON GUEST HOUSE NEAREST THE SOUTH ENTRANCE... JUST DOWN THE ROAD.
IF SHE'S HURT IN ANY WAY, I'M COMING BACK FOR BOTH OF YOU.
YOU...HAD HER ALL ALONG?! AND YOU DIDN'T TELL ME?

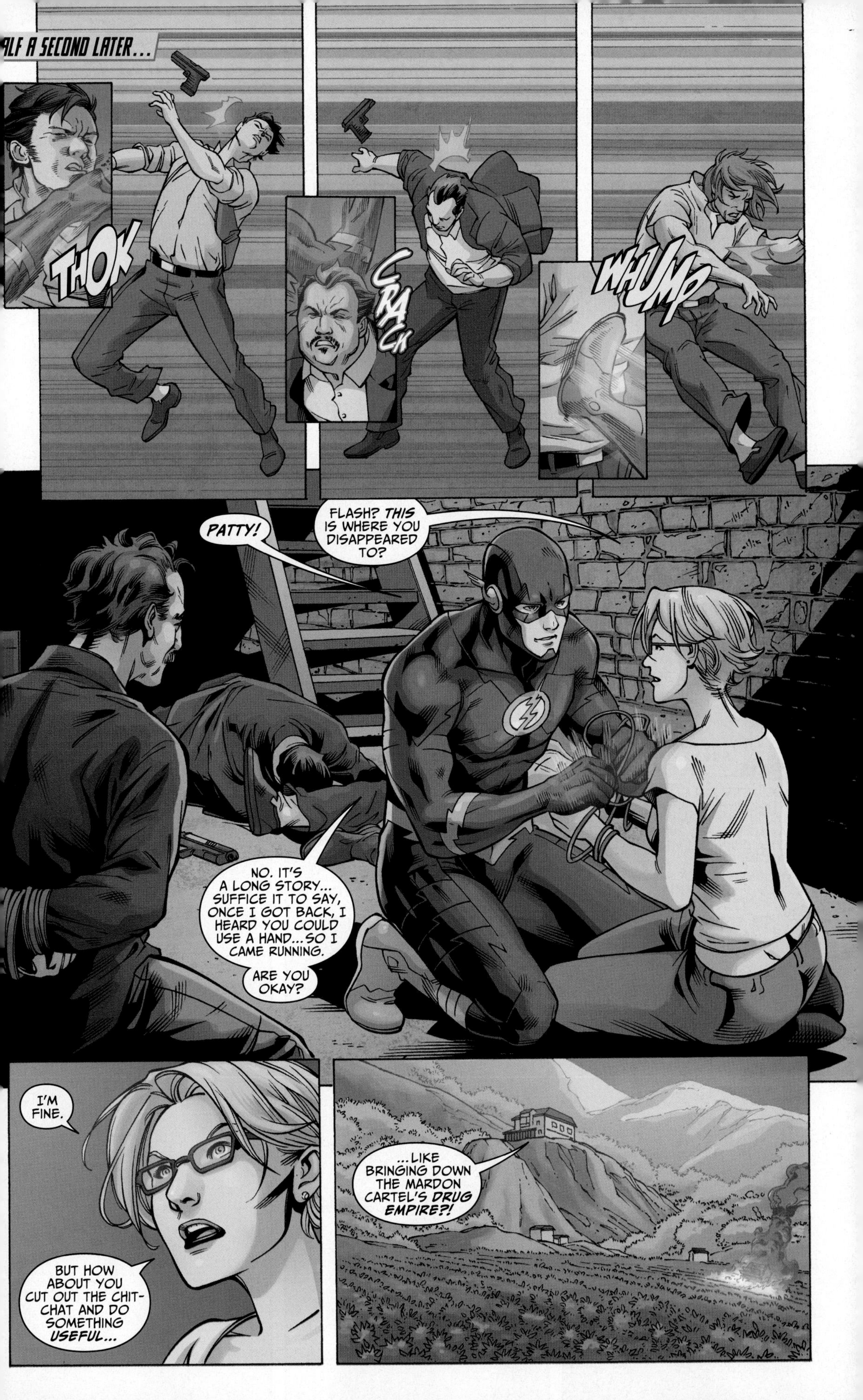

ALF A SECOND LATER...
THOK
CRACK
WHUMP
PATTY!
FLASH? THIS IS WHERE YOU DISAPPEARED TO?
NO. IT'S A LONG STORY... SUFFICE IT TO SAY, ONCE I GOT BACK, I HEARD YOU COULD USE A HAND...SO I CAME RUNNING.
ARE YOU OKAY?
I'M FINE.
BUT HOW ABOUT YOU CUT OUT THE CHIT-CHAT AND DO SOMETHING USEFUL...
...LIKE BRINGING DOWN THE MARDON CARTEL'S DRUG EMPIRE?!

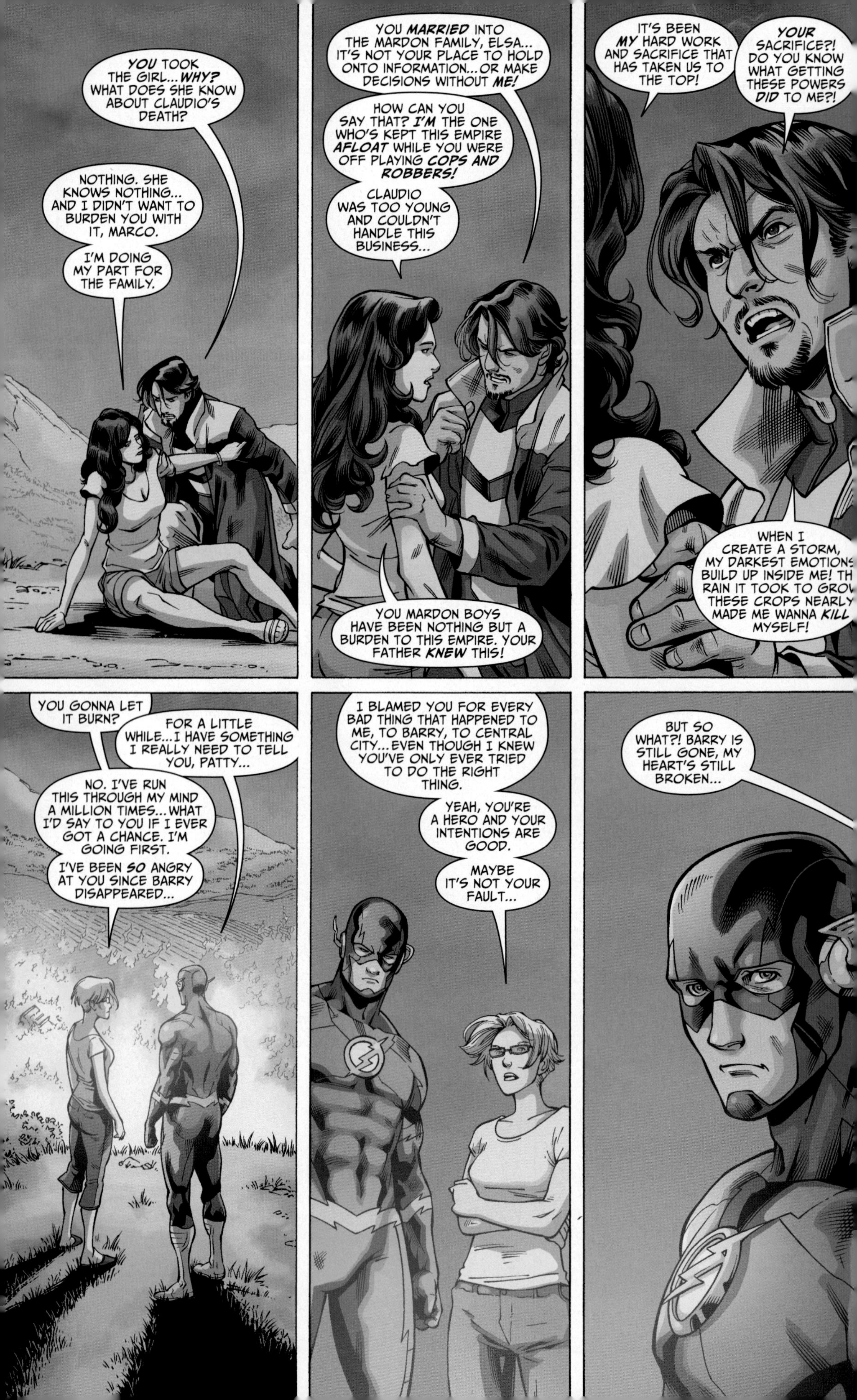
YOU TOOK THE GIRL... WHY? WHAT DOES SHE KNOW ABOUT CLAUDIO'S DEATH?
NOTHING. SHE KNOWS NOTHING... AND I DIDN'T WANT TO BURDEN YOU WITH IT, MARCO.
I'M DOING MY PART FOR THE FAMILY.
YOU MARRIED INTO THE MARDON FAMILY, ELSA... IT'S NOT YOUR PLACE TO HOLD ONTO INFORMATION...OR MAKE DECISIONS WITHOUT ME!
HOW CAN YOU SAY THAT? I'M THE ONE WHO'S KEPT THIS EMPIRE AFLOAT WHILE YOU WERE OFF PLAYING COPS AND ROBBERS!
CLAUDIO WAS TOO YOUNG AND COULDN'T HANDLE THIS BUSINESS...
YOU MARDON BOYS HAVE BEEN NOTHING BUT A BURDEN TO THIS EMPIRE. YOUR FATHER KNEW THIS!
IT'S BEEN MY HARD WORK AND SACRIFICE THAT HAS TAKEN US TO THE TOP!
YOUR SACRIFICE?! DO YOU KNOW WHAT GETTING THESE POWERS DID TO ME?!
WHEN I CREATE A STORM, MY DARKEST EMOTIONS BUILD UP INSIDE ME! TH RAIN IT TOOK TO GROW THESE CROPS NEARLY MADE ME WANNA KILL MYSELF!
YOU GONNA LET IT BURN?
FOR A LITTLE WHILE...I HAVE SOMETHING I REALLY NEED TO TELL YOU, PATTY...
NO. I'VE RUN THIS THROUGH MY MIND A MILLION TIMES...WHAT I'D SAY TO YOU IF I EVER GOT A CHANCE. I'M GOING FIRST.
I'VE BEEN SO ANGRY AT YOU SINCE BARRY DISAPPEARED...
I BLAMED YOU FOR EVERY BAD THING THAT HAPPENED TO ME, TO BARRY, TO CENTRAL CITY...EVEN THOUGH I KNEW YOU'VE ONLY EVER TRIED TO DO THE RIGHT THING.
YEAH, YOU'RE A HERO AND YOUR INTENTIONS ARE GOOD.
MAYBE IT'S NOT YOUR FAULT...
BUT SO WHAT?! BARRY IS STILL GONE, MY HEART'S STILL BROKEN...

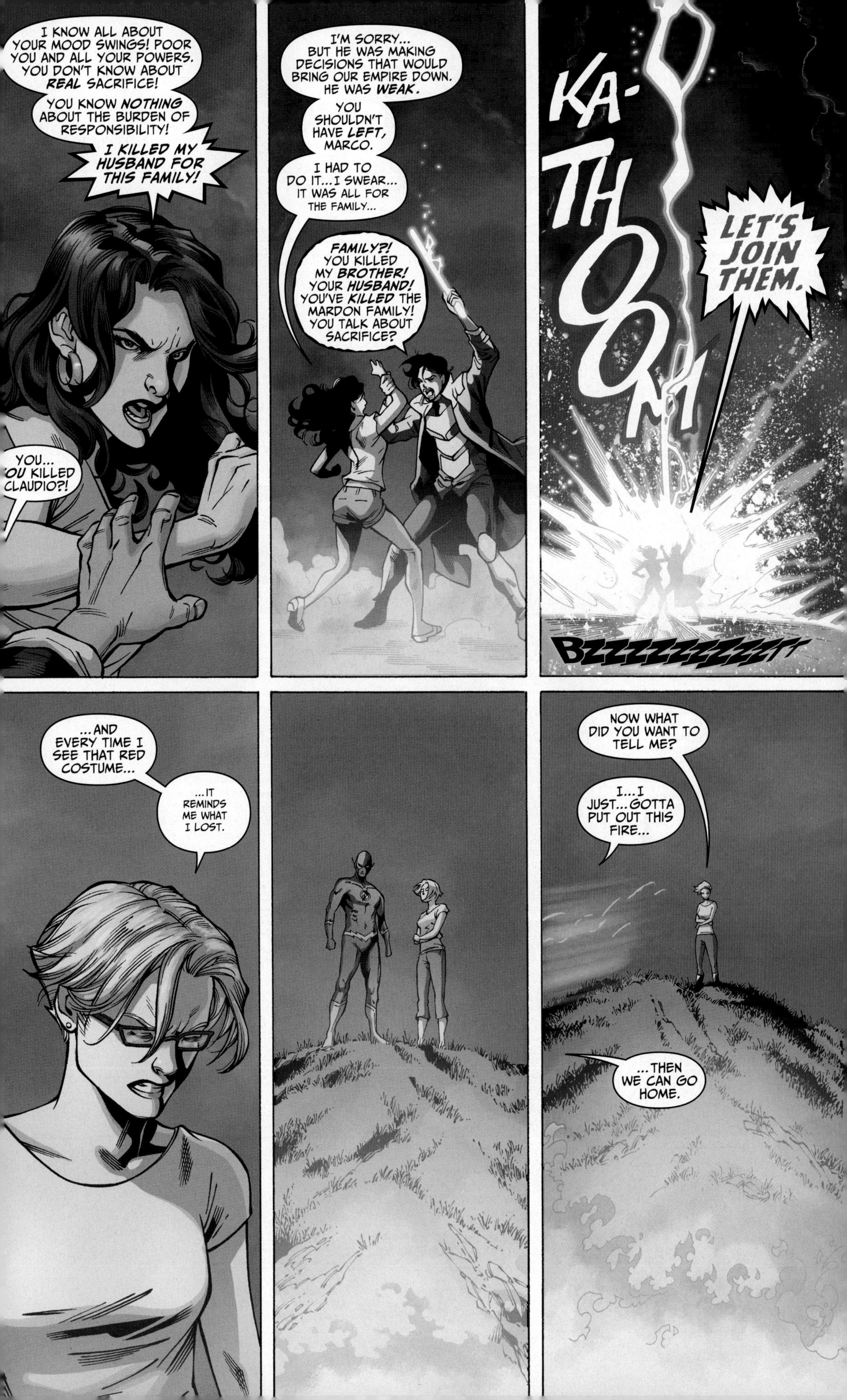
I KNOW ALL ABOUT YOUR MOOD SWINGS! POOR YOU AND ALL YOUR POWERS. YOU DON'T KNOW ABOUT REAL SACRIFICE!
YOU KNOW NOTHING ABOUT THE BURDEN OF RESPONSIBILITY!
I KILLED MY HUSBAND FOR THIS FAMILY!
YOU... OU KILLED CLAUDIO?!
I'M SORRY... BUT HE WAS MAKING DECISIONS THAT WOULD BRING OUR EMPIRE DOWN. HE WAS WEAK.
YOU SHOULDN'T HAVE LEFT, MARCO.
I HAD TO DO IT... I SWEAR... IT WAS ALL FOR THE FAMILY...
FAMILY?! YOU KILLED MY BROTHER! YOUR HUSBAND! YOU'VE KILLED THE MARDON FAMILY! YOU TALK ABOUT SACRIFICE?
KA-THOOM!
LET'S JOIN THEM.
BZZZZZZZZZZZT
...AND EVERY TIME I SEE THAT RED COSTUME...
...IT REMINDS ME WHAT I LOST.
NOW WHAT DID YOU WANT TO TELL ME?
I...I JUST...GOTTA PUT OUT THIS FIRE...
...THEN WE CAN GO HOME.

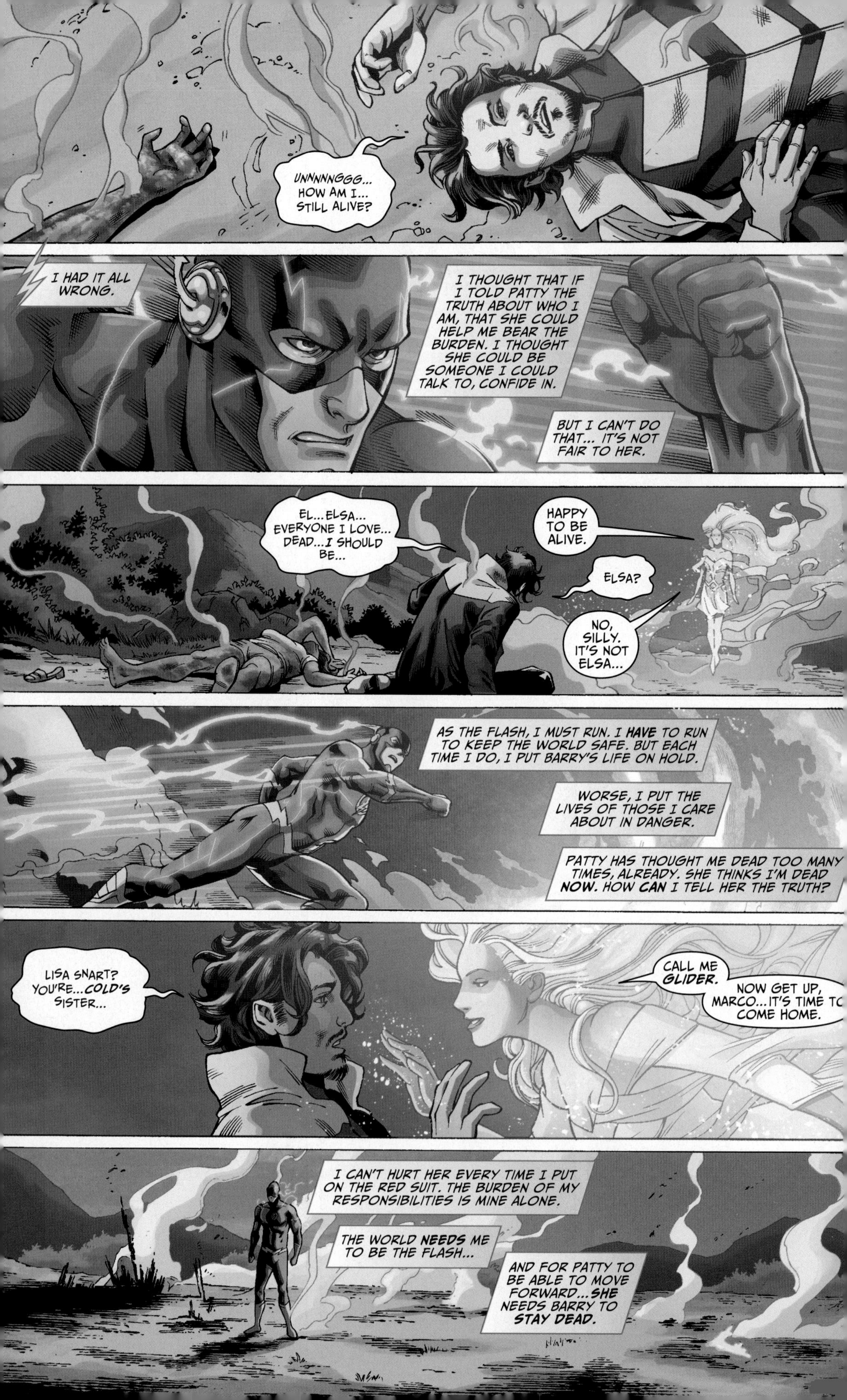
UNNNNGGG... HOW AM I... STILL ALIVE?
I HAD IT ALL WRONG.
I THOUGHT THAT IF I TOLD PATTY THE TRUTH ABOUT WHO I AM, THAT SHE COULD HELP ME BEAR THE BURDEN. I THOUGHT SHE COULD BE SOMEONE I COULD TALK TO, CONFIDE IN.
BUT I CAN'T DO THAT... IT'S NOT FAIR TO HER.
EL...ELSA... EVERYONE I LOVE... DEAD...I SHOULD BE...
HAPPY TO BE ALIVE.
ELSA?
NO, SILLY. IT'S NOT ELSA...
AS THE FLASH, I MUST RUN. I HAVE TO RUN TO KEEP THE WORLD SAFE. BUT EACH TIME I DO, I PUT BARRY'S LIFE ON HOLD.
WORSE, I PUT THE LIVES OF THOSE I CARE ABOUT IN DANGER.
PATTY HAS THOUGHT ME DEAD TOO MANY TIMES, ALREADY. SHE THINKS I'M DEAD NOW. HOW CAN I TELL HER THE TRUTH?
LISA SNART? YOU'RE...COLD'S SISTER...
CALL ME GLIDER.
NOW GET UP, MARCO...IT'S TIME TO COME HOME.
I CAN'T HURT HER EVERY TIME I PUT ON THE RED SUIT. THE BURDEN OF MY RESPONSIBILITIES IS MINE ALONE.
THE WORLD NEEDS ME TO BE THE FLASH...
AND FOR PATTY TO BE ABLE TO MOVE FORWARD...SHE NEEDS BARRY TO STAY DEAD.

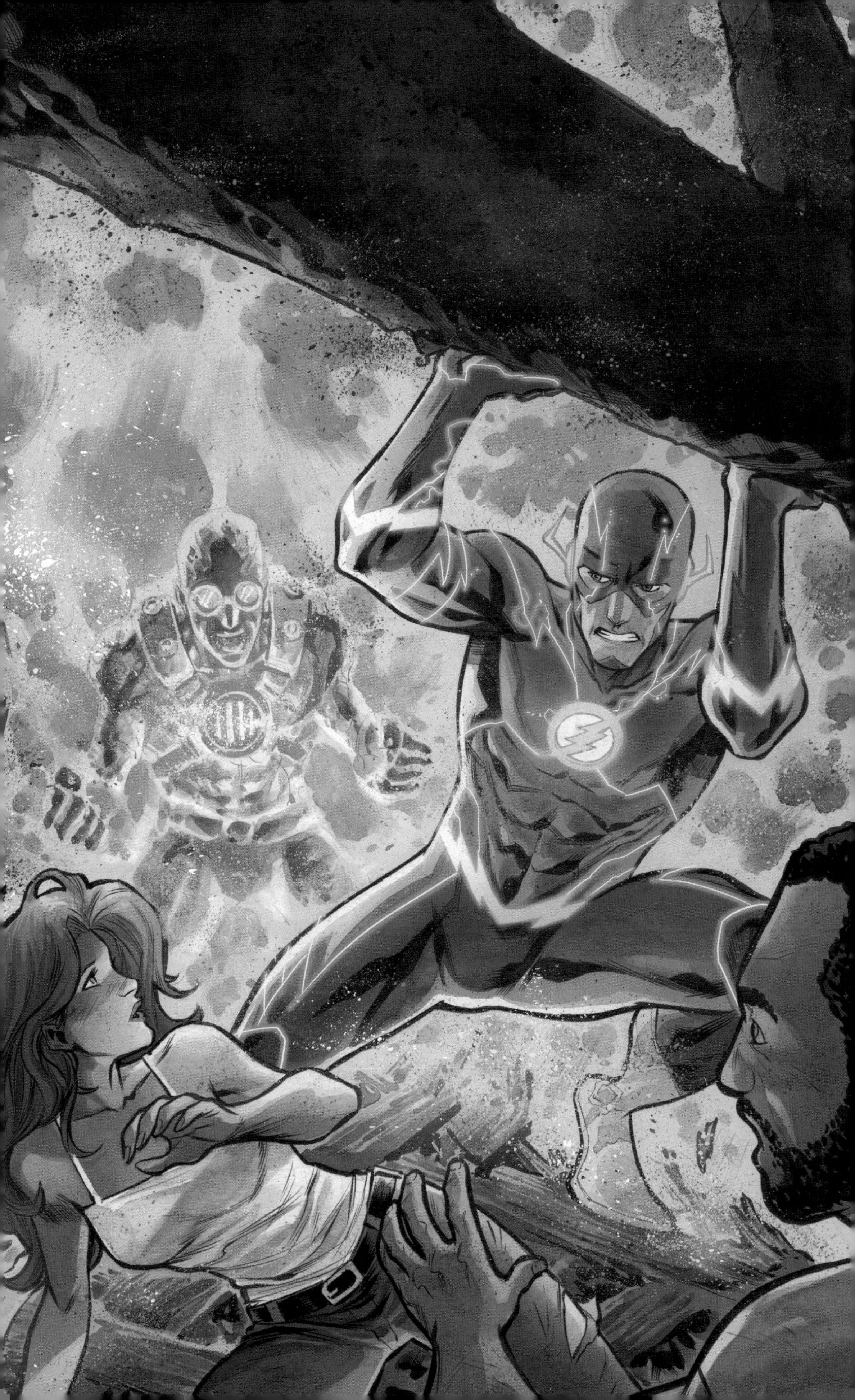

FRANCIS MANAPUL & BRIAN BUCCELLATO writers MARCUS TO penciller RAY McCARTHY inker

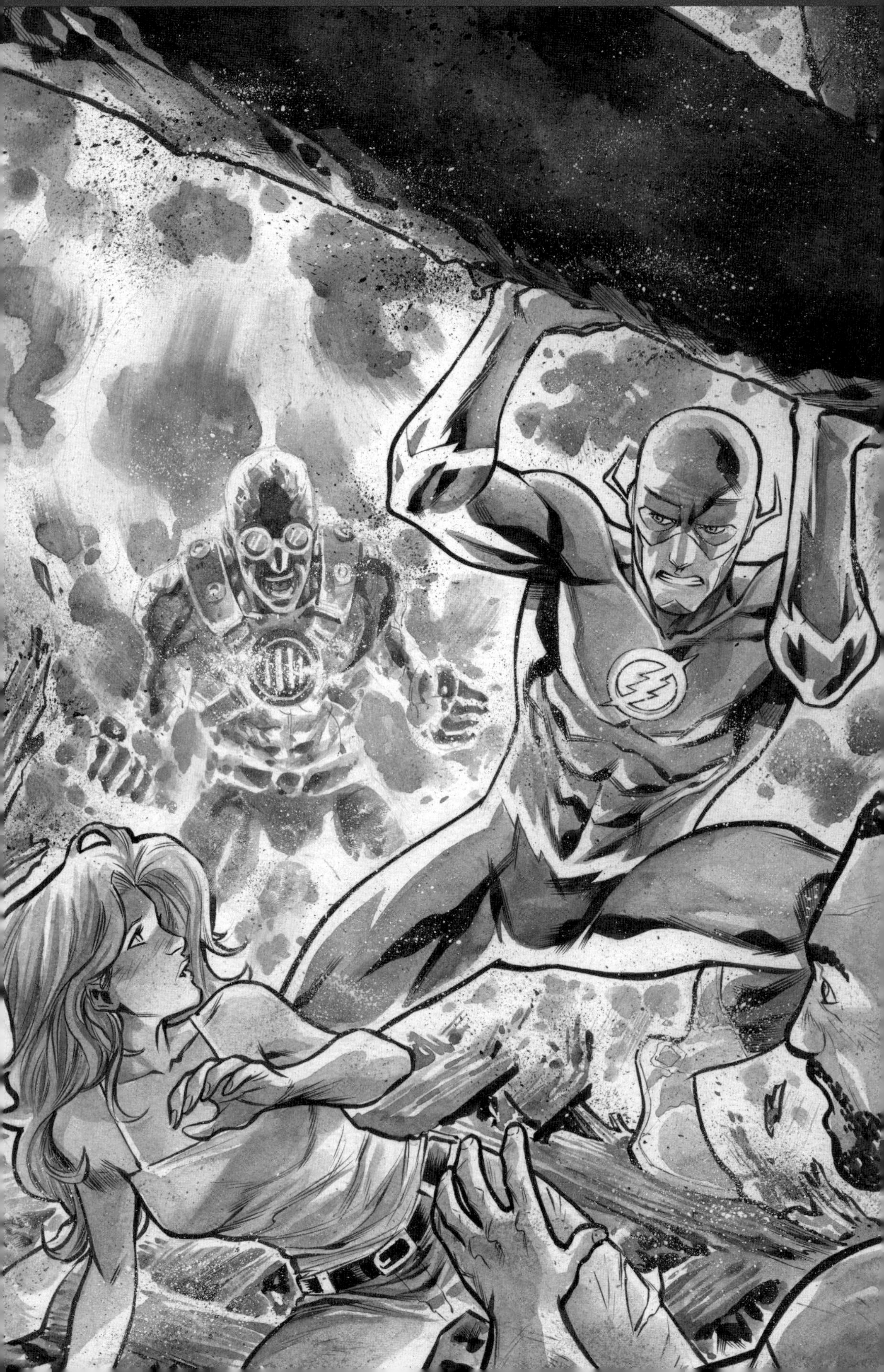

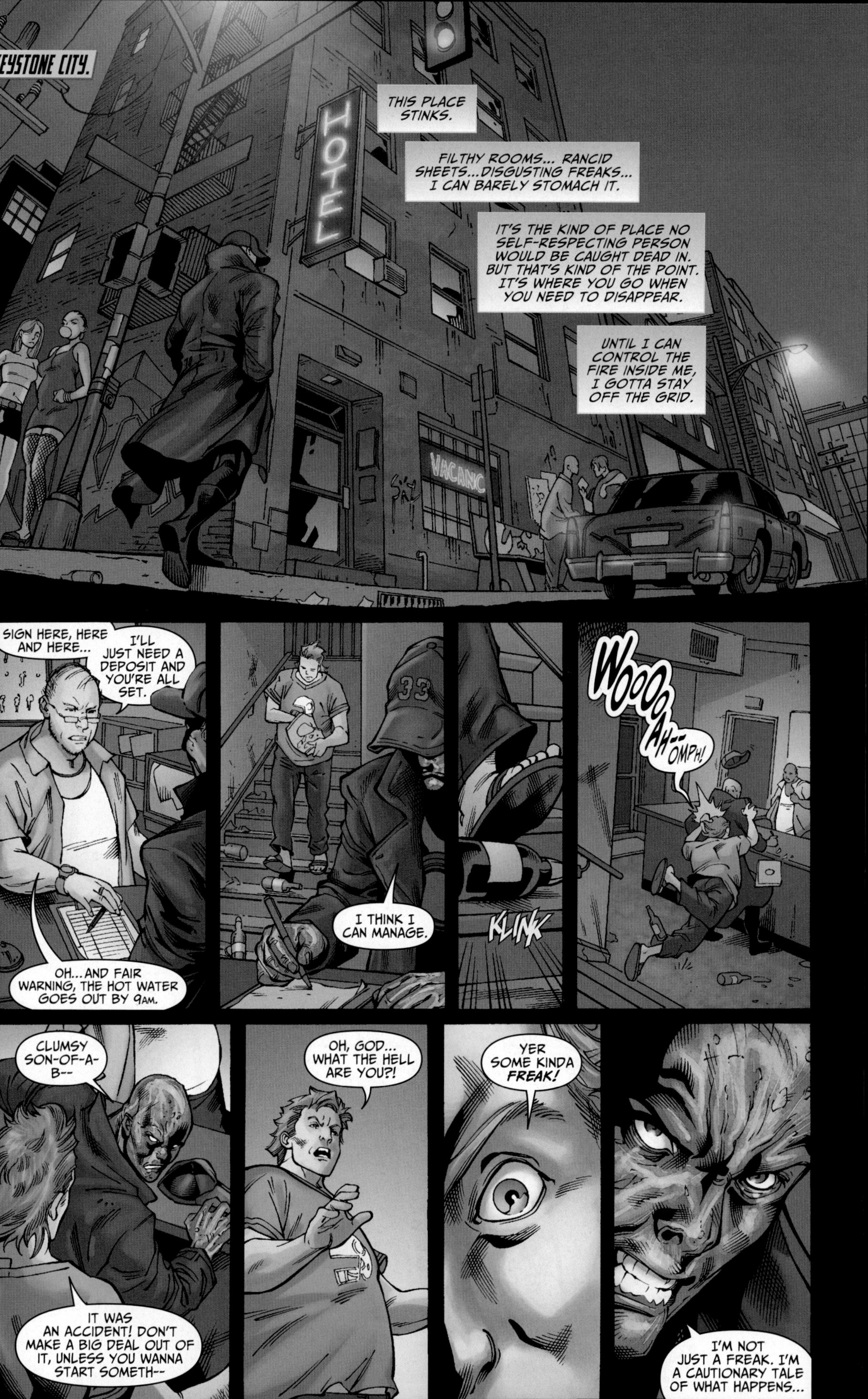

KEYSTONE CITY.
THIS PLACE STINKS.
FILTHY ROOMS... RANCID SHEETS...DISGUSTING FREAKS... I CAN BARELY STOMACH IT.
IT'S THE KIND OF PLACE NO SELF-RESPECTING PERSON WOULD BE CAUGHT DEAD IN. BUT THAT'S KIND OF THE POINT. IT'S WHERE YOU GO WHEN YOU NEED TO DISAPPEAR.
UNTIL I CAN CONTROL THE FIRE INSIDE ME, I GOTTA STAY OFF THE GRID.
HOTEL
VACANC
SIGN HERE, HERE AND HERE...
I'LL JUST NEED A DEPOSIT AND YOU'RE ALL SET.
OH...AND FAIR WARNING, THE HOT WATER GOES OUT BY 9AM.
I THINK I CAN MANAGE.
KLINK
WOOOOAH--OMPH!
CLUMSY SON-OF-A-B--
IT WAS AN ACCIDENT! DON'T MAKE A BIG DEAL OUT OF IT, UNLESS YOU WANNA START SOMETH--
OH, GOD... WHAT THE HELL ARE YOU?!
YER SOME KINDA FREAK!
I'M NOT JUST A FREAK. I'M A CAUTIONARY TALE OF WHAT HAPPENS...

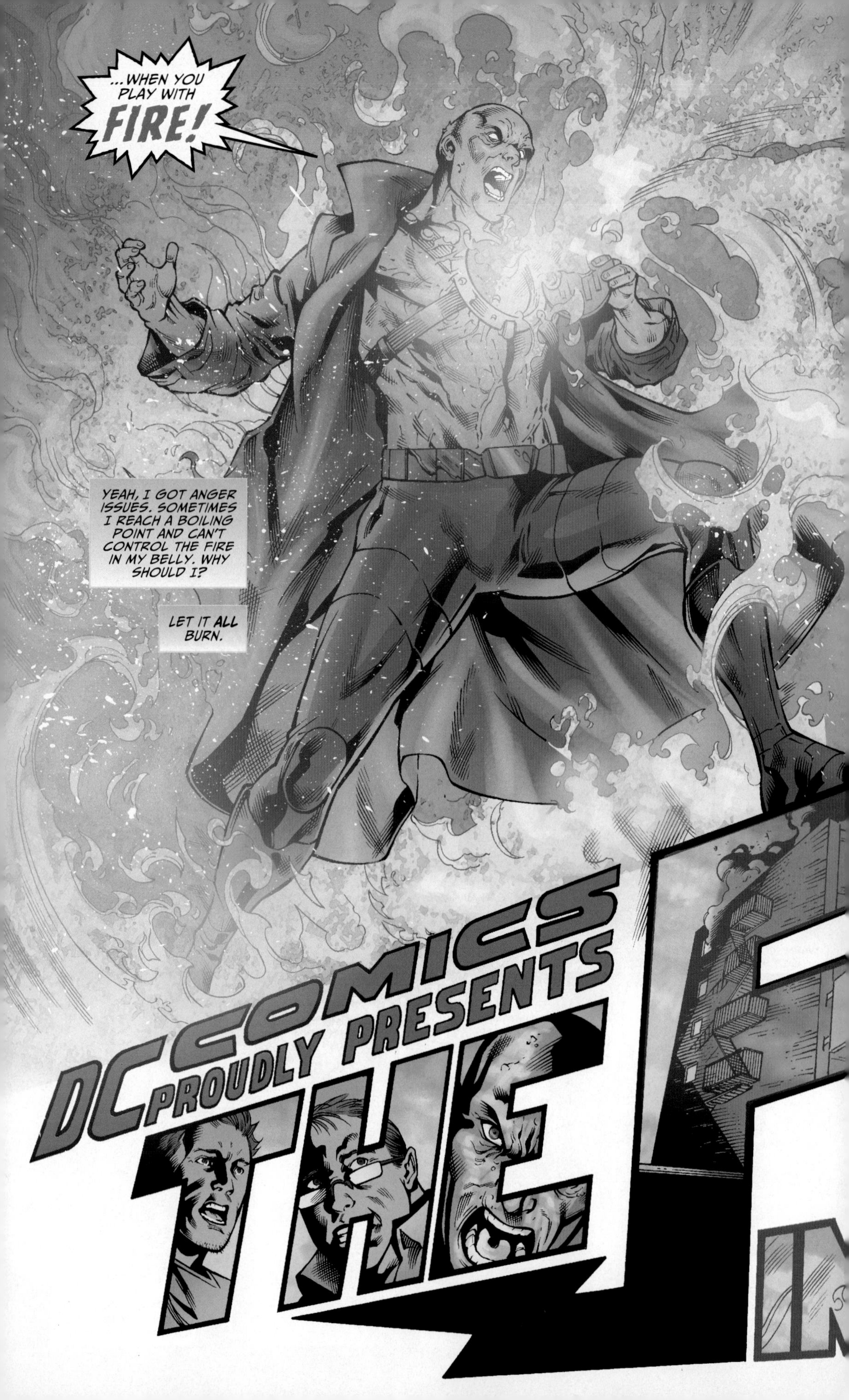
...WHEN YOU PLAY WITH FIRE!
YEAH, I GOT ANGER ISSUES. SOMETIMES I REACH A BOILING POINT AND CAN'T CONTROL THE FIRE IN MY BELLY. WHY SHOULD I?
LET IT ALL BURN.
DC COMICS PROUDLY PRESENTS
THE

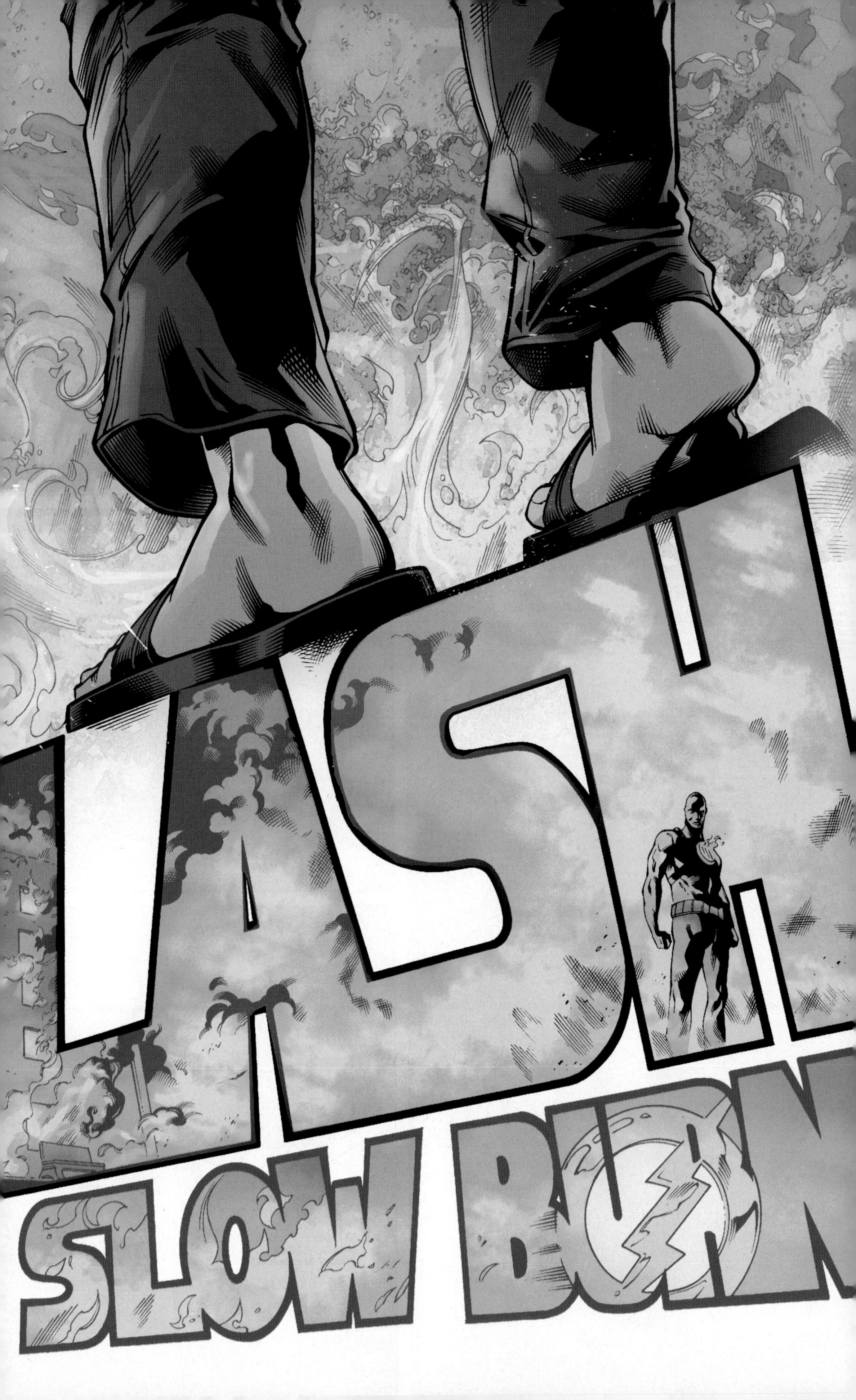
SLOW BURN

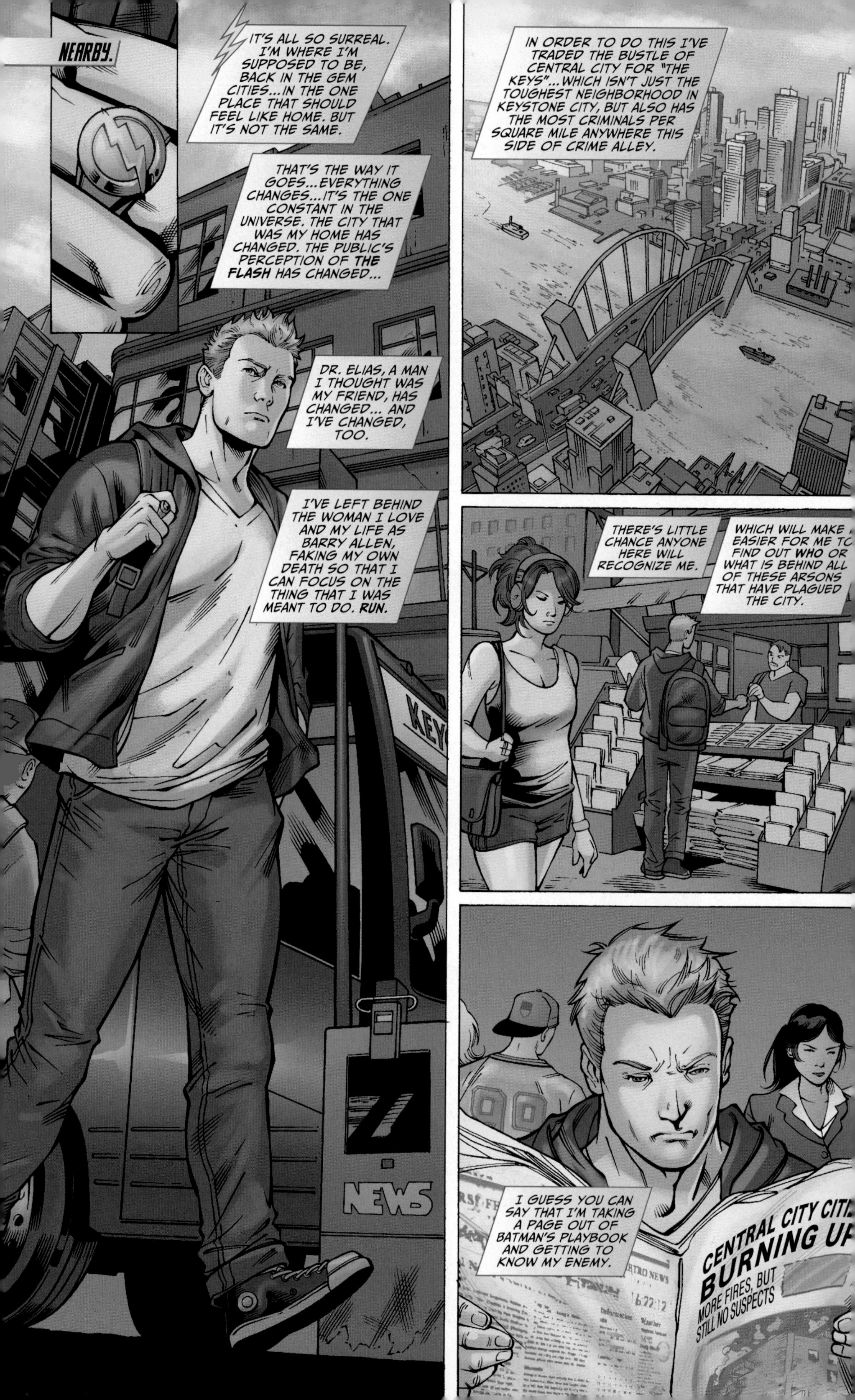
NEARBY.
IT'S ALL SO SURREAL. I'M WHERE I'M SUPPOSED TO BE, BACK IN THE GEM CITIES... IN THE ONE PLACE THAT SHOULD FEEL LIKE HOME. BUT IT'S NOT THE SAME.
THAT'S THE WAY IT GOES... EVERYTHING CHANGES... IT'S THE ONE CONSTANT IN THE UNIVERSE. THE CITY THAT WAS MY HOME HAS CHANGED. THE PUBLIC'S PERCEPTION OF THE FLASH HAS CHANGED...
DR. ELIAS, A MAN I THOUGHT WAS MY FRIEND, HAS CHANGED... AND I'VE CHANGED, TOO.
I'VE LEFT BEHIND THE WOMAN I LOVE AND MY LIFE AS BARRY ALLEN, FAKING MY OWN DEATH SO THAT I CAN FOCUS ON THE THING THAT I WAS MEANT TO DO. RUN.
NEWS
IN ORDER TO DO THIS I'VE TRADED THE BUSTLE OF CENTRAL CITY FOR "THE KEYS"... WHICH ISN'T JUST THE TOUGHEST NEIGHBORHOOD IN KEYSTONE CITY, BUT ALSO HAS THE MOST CRIMINALS PER SQUARE MILE ANYWHERE THIS SIDE OF CRIME ALLEY.
THERE'S LITTLE CHANCE ANYONE HERE WILL RECOGNIZE ME.
WHICH WILL MAKE EASIER FOR ME TO FIND OUT WHO OR WHAT IS BEHIND ALL OF THESE ARSONS THAT HAVE PLAGUED THE CITY.
I GUESS YOU CAN SAY THAT I'M TAKING A PAGE OUT OF BATMAN'S PLAYBOOK AND GETTING TO KNOW MY ENEMY.
CENTRAL CITY CITI
BURNING UP
MORE FIRES, BUT STILL NO SUSPECTS

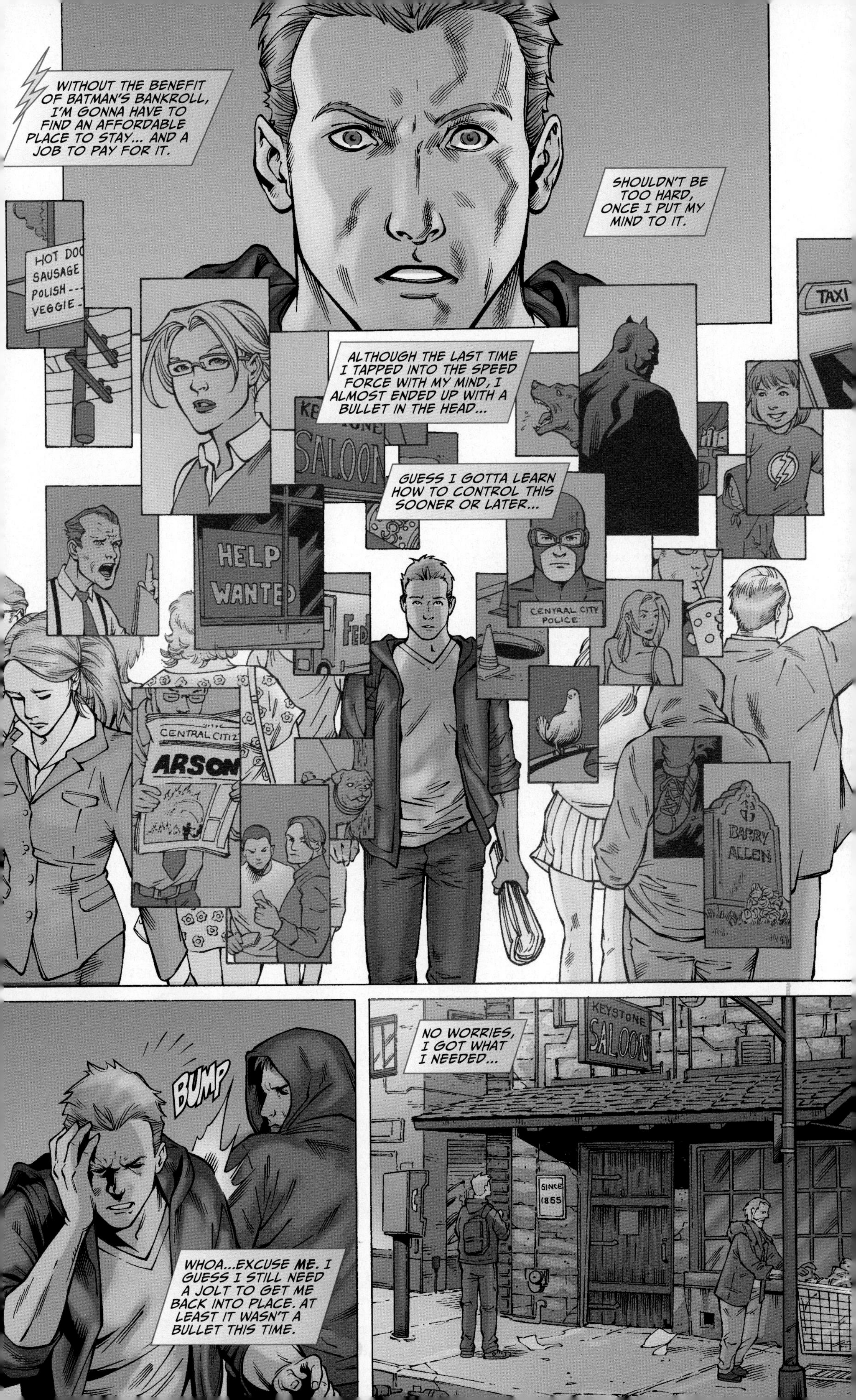
WITHOUT THE BENEFIT OF BATMAN'S BANKROLL, I'M GONNA HAVE TO FIND AN AFFORDABLE PLACE TO STAY... AND A JOB TO PAY FOR IT.
SHOULDN'T BE TOO HARD, ONCE I PUT MY MIND TO IT.
HOT DOG
SAUSAGE
POLISH
VEGGIE
TAXI
ALTHOUGH THE LAST TIME I TAPPED INTO THE SPEED FORCE WITH MY MIND, I ALMOST ENDED UP WITH A BULLET IN THE HEAD...
SALOON
GUESS I GOTTA LEARN HOW TO CONTROL THIS SOONER OR LATER...
HELP WANTED
CENTRAL CITY POLICE
ARSON
BARRY ALLEN
BUMP
WHOA...EXCUSE ME. I GUESS I STILL NEED A JOLT TO GET ME BACK INTO PLACE. AT LEAST IT WASN'T A BULLET THIS TIME.
NO WORRIES, I GOT WHAT I NEEDED...
KEYSTONE SALOON
SINCE 1855

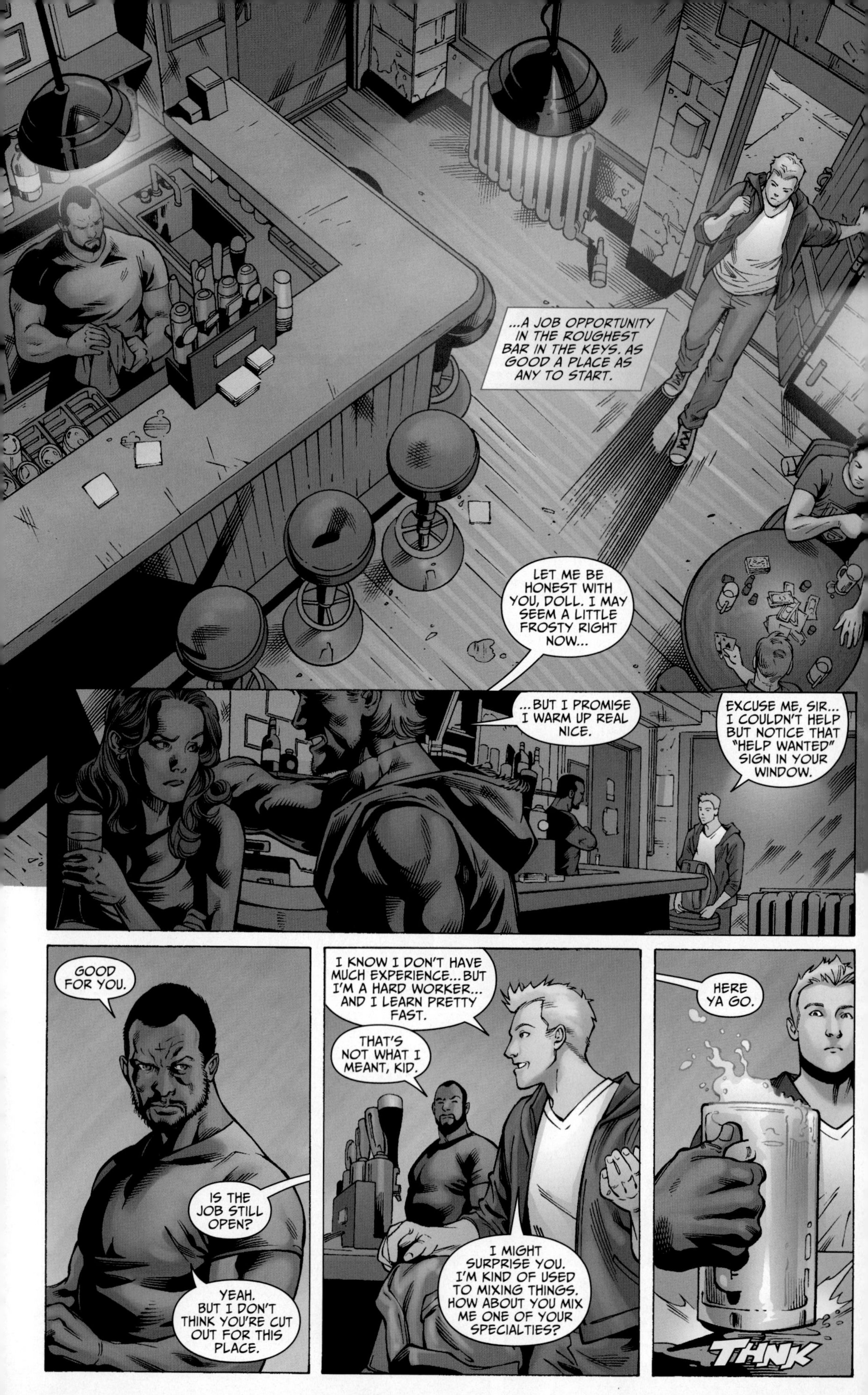
...A JOB OPPORTUNITY IN THE ROUGHEST BAR IN THE KEYS. AS GOOD A PLACE AS ANY TO START.
LET ME BE HONEST WITH YOU, DOLL. I MAY SEEM A LITTLE FROSTY RIGHT NOW...
...BUT I PROMISE I WARM UP REAL NICE.
EXCUSE ME, SIR... I COULDN'T HELP BUT NOTICE THAT "HELP WANTED" SIGN IN YOUR WINDOW.
GOOD FOR YOU.
IS THE JOB STILL OPEN?
YEAH. BUT I DON'T THINK YOU'RE CUT OUT FOR THIS PLACE.
I KNOW I DON'T HAVE MUCH EXPERIENCE... BUT I'M A HARD WORKER... AND I LEARN PRETTY FAST.
THAT'S NOT WHAT I MEANT, KID.
I MIGHT SURPRISE YOU. I'M KIND OF USED TO MIXING THINGS. HOW ABOUT YOU MIX ME ONE OF YOUR SPECIALTIES?
HERE YA GO.
THNK

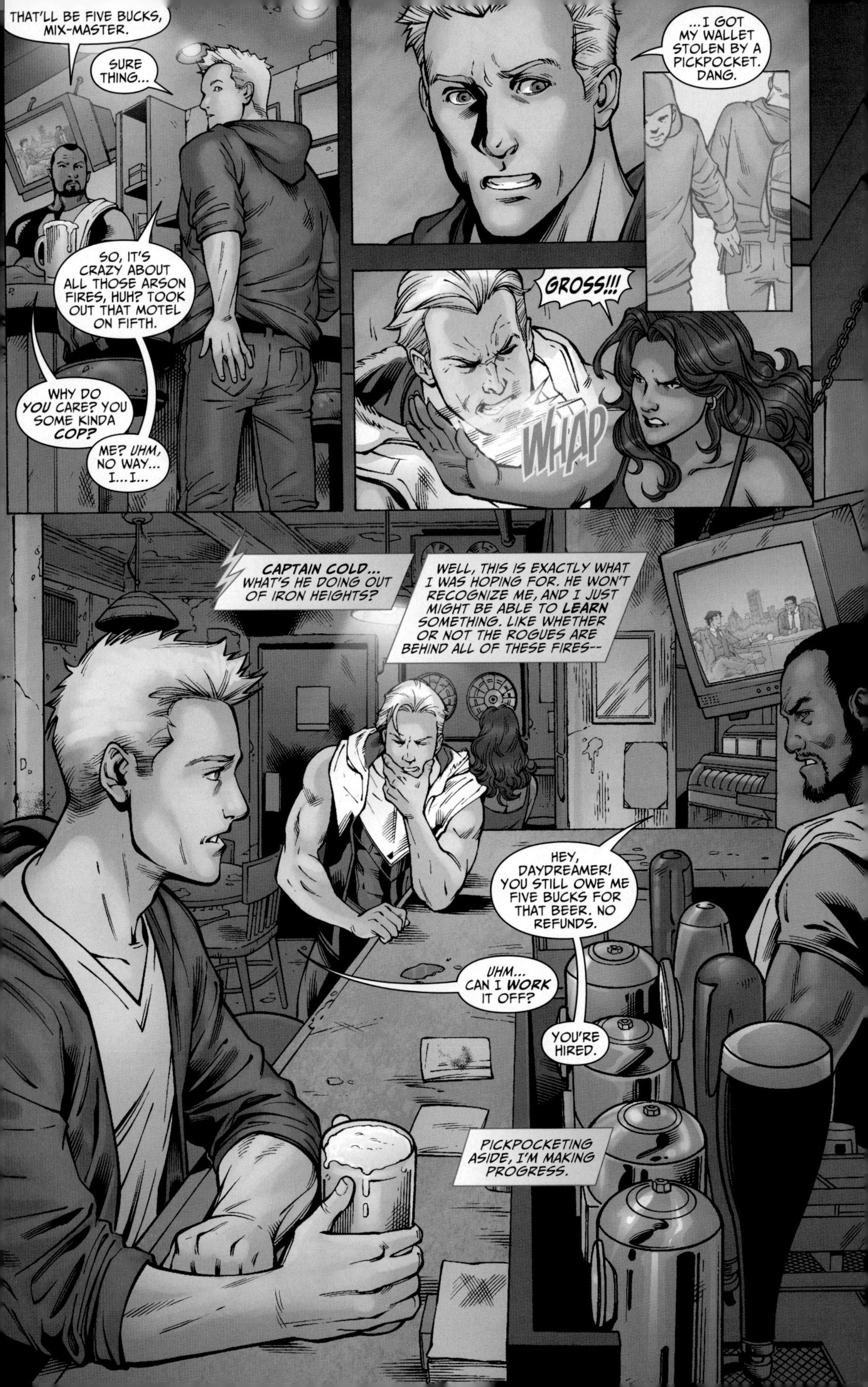
THAT'LL BE FIVE BUCKS, MIX-MASTER.
SURE THING...
SO, IT'S CRAZY ABOUT ALL THOSE ARSON FIRES, HUH? TOOK OUT THAT MOTEL ON FIFTH.
WHY DO YOU CARE? YOU SOME KINDA COP?
ME? UHM, NO WAY... I...I...
...I GOT MY WALLET STOLEN BY A PICKPOCKET. DANG.
GROSS!!!
WHAP
CAPTAIN COLD... WHAT'S HE DOING OUT OF IRON HEIGHTS?
WELL, THIS IS EXACTLY WHAT I WAS HOPING FOR. HE WON'T RECOGNIZE ME, AND I JUST MIGHT BE ABLE TO LEARN SOMETHING. LIKE WHETHER OR NOT THE ROGUES ARE BEHIND ALL OF THESE FIRES--
HEY, DAYDREAMER! YOU STILL OWE ME FIVE BUCKS FOR THAT BEER. NO REFUNDS.
UHM... CAN I WORK IT OFF?
YOU'RE HIRED.
PICKPOCKETING ASIDE, I'M MAKING PROGRESS.

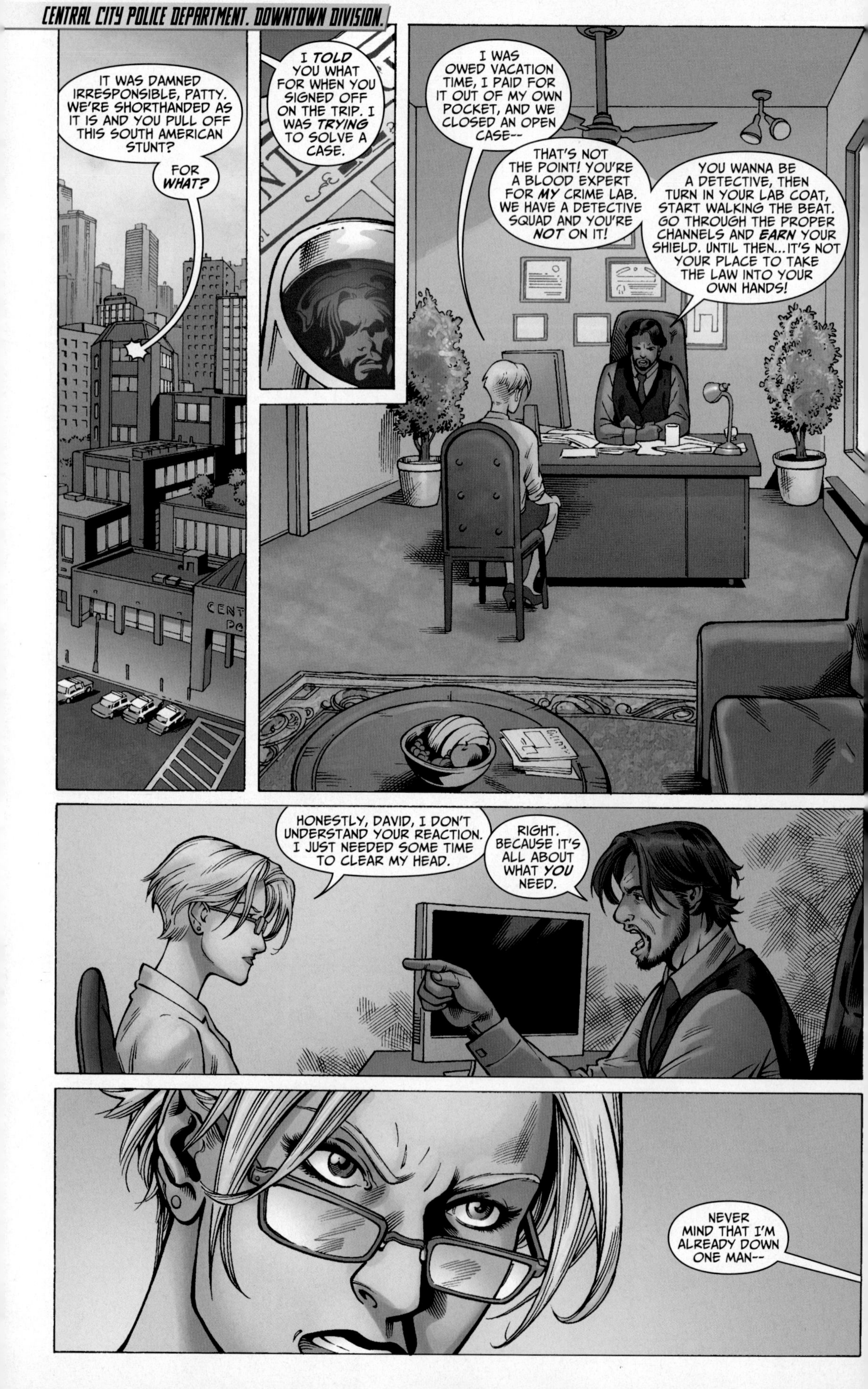
CENTRAL CITY POLICE DEPARTMENT. DOWNTOWN DIVISION.
IT WAS DAMNED IRRESPONSIBLE, PATTY. WE'RE SHORTHANDED AS IT IS AND YOU PULL OFF THIS SOUTH AMERICAN STUNT?
FOR WHAT?
I TOLD YOU WHAT FOR WHEN YOU SIGNED OFF ON THE TRIP. I WAS TRYING TO SOLVE A CASE.
I WAS OWED VACATION TIME, I PAID FOR IT OUT OF MY OWN POCKET, AND WE CLOSED AN OPEN CASE--
THAT'S NOT THE POINT! YOU'RE A BLOOD EXPERT FOR MY CRIME LAB. WE HAVE A DETECTIVE SQUAD AND YOU'RE NOT ON IT!
YOU WANNA BE A DETECTIVE, THEN TURN IN YOUR LAB COAT, START WALKING THE BEAT. GO THROUGH THE PROPER CHANNELS AND EARN YOUR SHIELD. UNTIL THEN... IT'S NOT YOUR PLACE TO TAKE THE LAW INTO YOUR OWN HANDS!
HONESTLY, DAVID, I DON'T UNDERSTAND YOUR REACTION. I JUST NEEDED SOME TIME TO CLEAR MY HEAD.
RIGHT. BECAUSE IT'S ALL ABOUT WHAT YOU NEED.
NEVER MIND THAT I'M ALREADY DOWN ONE MAN--

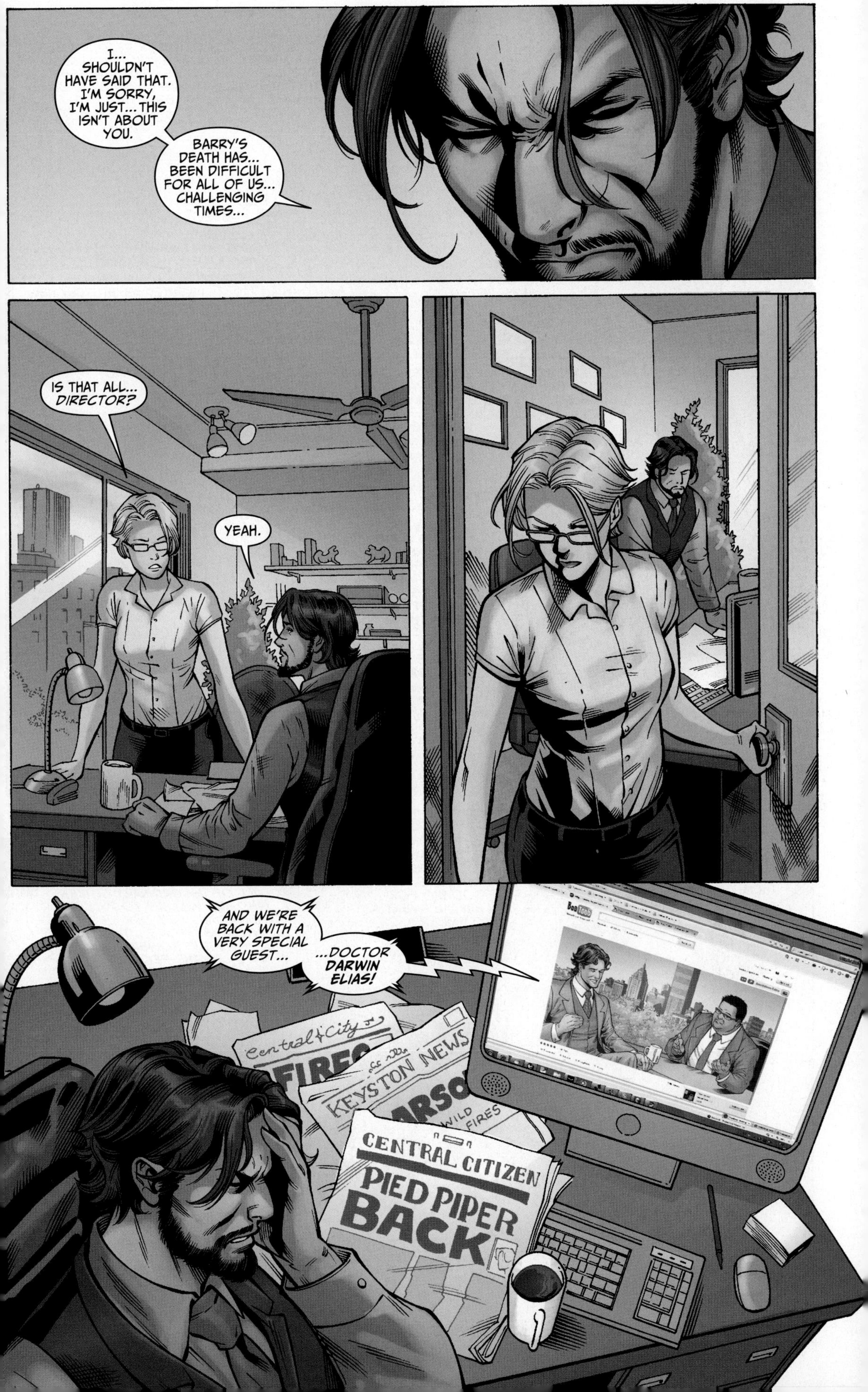
I... SHOULDN'T HAVE SAID THAT. I'M SORRY, I'M JUST...THIS ISN'T ABOUT YOU.
BARRY'S DEATH HAS... BEEN DIFFICULT FOR ALL OF US... CHALLENGING TIMES...
IS THAT ALL... DIRECTOR?
YEAH.
AND WE'RE BACK WITH A VERY SPECIAL GUEST...
...DOCTOR DARWIN ELIAS!
Central City
FIRE
KEYSTON NEWS
ARSO
WILD FIRES
CENTRAL CITIZEN
PIED PIPER BACK

I HESITATE TO CALL YOU THE *"MAN OF THE HOUR"*...BECAUSE *"MAN OF THE YEAR"* SEEMS MORE FITTING, CONSIDERING EVERYTHING THAT HAS GONE ON THE LAST THREE MONTHS.

LET'S FACE IT...YOU'VE CLEANED UP A LOT OF MESSES THIS YEAR. A LOT OF *OTHER* PEOPLE'S MESSES. HECK, AFTER *FLASH* PLUNGED THE GEM CITIES INTO DARKNESS, IT WAS YOU WHO LITERALLY BROUGHT BACK THE LIGHT.

I DON'T DO IT FOR THE ACCOLADES...

COME ON, YOU INVENTED AN ENTIRELY NEW ENERGY SOURCE THAT IS GOING TO KEEP THE LIGHTS ON FOR A HUNDRED YEARS. THAT'S HUGE!

THAT WAS PRETTY GOOD, WASN'T IT?

YOU'VE BEEN ON A TEAR...NOW YOU'VE GOT THIS BRAND-NEW MONORAIL OPENING UP...SERIOUSLY, WHAT'S GOTTEN INTO YOU?

LOOK, WHAT THE CITY NEEDS IS PRACTICAL SOLUTIONS. ENERGY THAT WILL MAKE OUR CITY SELF-SUFFICIENT IS JUST THE START. I'M NOT ONE TO CAST STONES...BUT IT'S NO COINCIDENCE THAT CENTRAL CITY HAS SEEN MORE PROGRESS IN THE MONTHS SINCE FLASH'S TRAGIC DISAPPEARANCE THAN TOOK PLACE IN THE FIVE YEARS HE "WATCHED OVER US."

I'VE DONE MY RESEARCH, HATCH, AND THE DATA ARE CLEAR...ALL *VIGILANTISM* DOES IS BRING OUT THE WORST IN SOCIETY. WE HAVE LAWS. WE HAVE CODES OF CONDUCT...

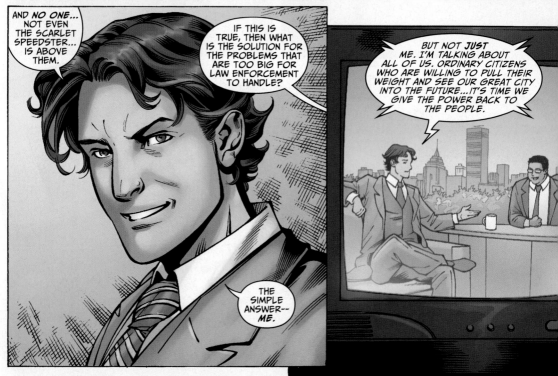

AND *NO ONE*... NOT EVEN THE SCARLET SPEEDSTER... IS ABOVE THEM.

IF THIS IS TRUE, THEN WHAT IS THE SOLUTION FOR THE PROBLEMS THAT ARE TOO BIG FOR LAW ENFORCEMENT TO HANDLE?

BUT NOT *JUST* ME. I'M TALKING ABOUT ALL OF US. ORDINARY CITIZENS WHO ARE WILLING TO PULL THEIR WEIGHT AND SEE OUR GREAT CITY INTO THE FUTURE...IT'S TIME WE GIVE THE POWER BACK TO THE PEOPLE.

THE SIMPLE ANSWER-- *ME.*

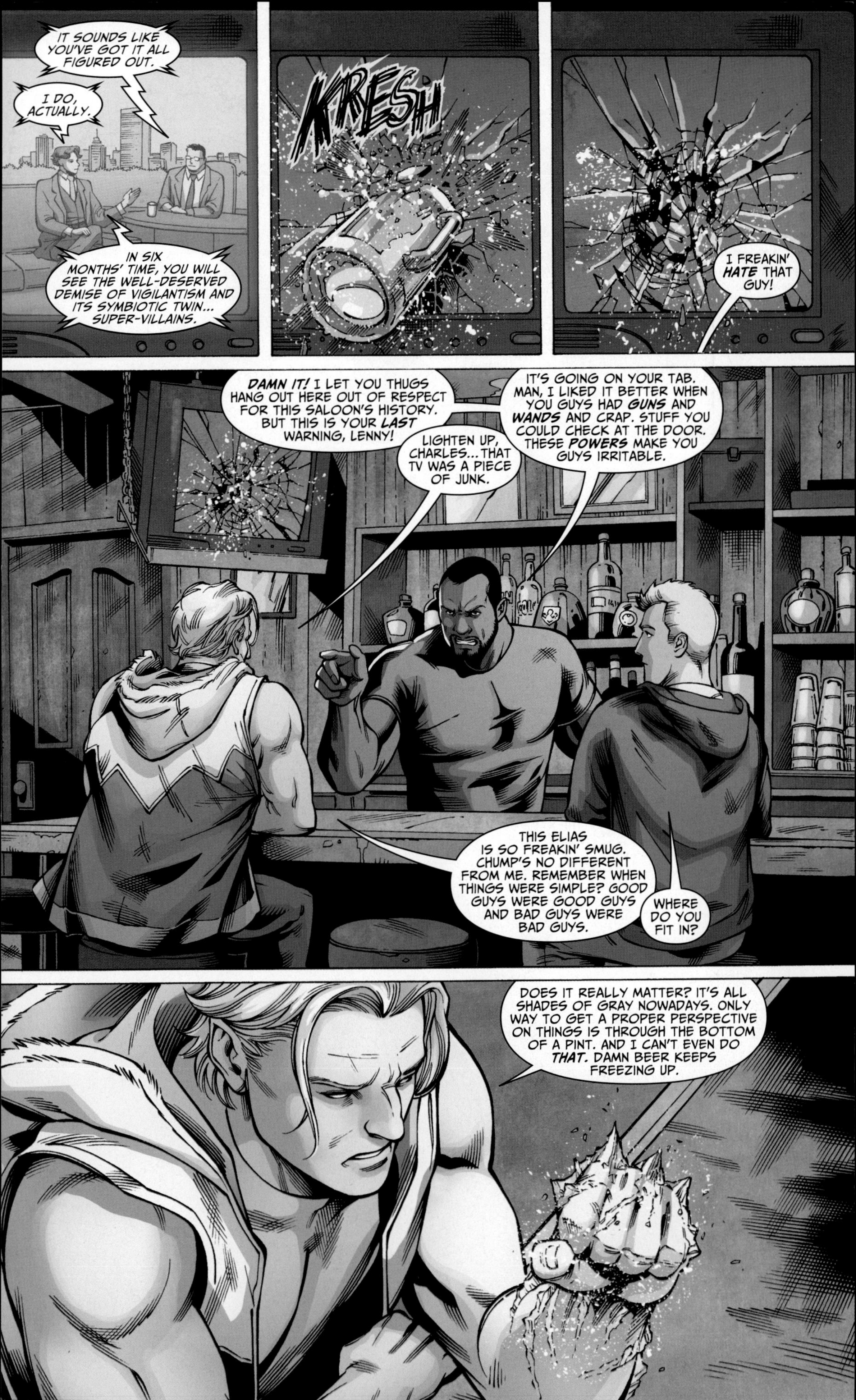
IT SOUNDS LIKE YOU'VE GOT IT ALL FIGURED OUT.
I DO, ACTUALLY.
IN SIX MONTHS' TIME, YOU WILL SEE THE WELL-DESERVED DEMISE OF VIGILANTISM AND ITS SYMBIOTIC TWIN... SUPER-VILLAINS.
KRESH
I FREAKIN' HATE THAT GUY!
DAMN IT! I LET YOU THUGS HANG OUT HERE OUT OF RESPECT FOR THIS SALOON'S HISTORY. BUT THIS IS YOUR LAST WARNING, LENNY!
IT'S GOING ON YOUR TAB. MAN, I LIKED IT BETTER WHEN YOU GUYS HAD GUNS AND WANDS AND CRAP. STUFF YOU COULD CHECK AT THE DOOR. THESE POWERS MAKE YOU GUYS IRRITABLE.
LIGHTEN UP, CHARLES... THAT TV WAS A PIECE OF JUNK.
THIS ELIAS IS SO FREAKIN' SMUG. CHUMP'S NO DIFFERENT FROM ME. REMEMBER WHEN THINGS WERE SIMPLE? GOOD GUYS WERE GOOD GUYS AND BAD GUYS WERE BAD GUYS.
WHERE DO YOU FIT IN?
DOES IT REALLY MATTER? IT'S ALL SHADES OF GRAY NOWADAYS. ONLY WAY TO GET A PROPER PERSPECTIVE ON THINGS IS THROUGH THE BOTTOM OF A PINT. AND I CAN'T EVEN DO THAT. DAMN BEER KEEPS FREEZING UP.

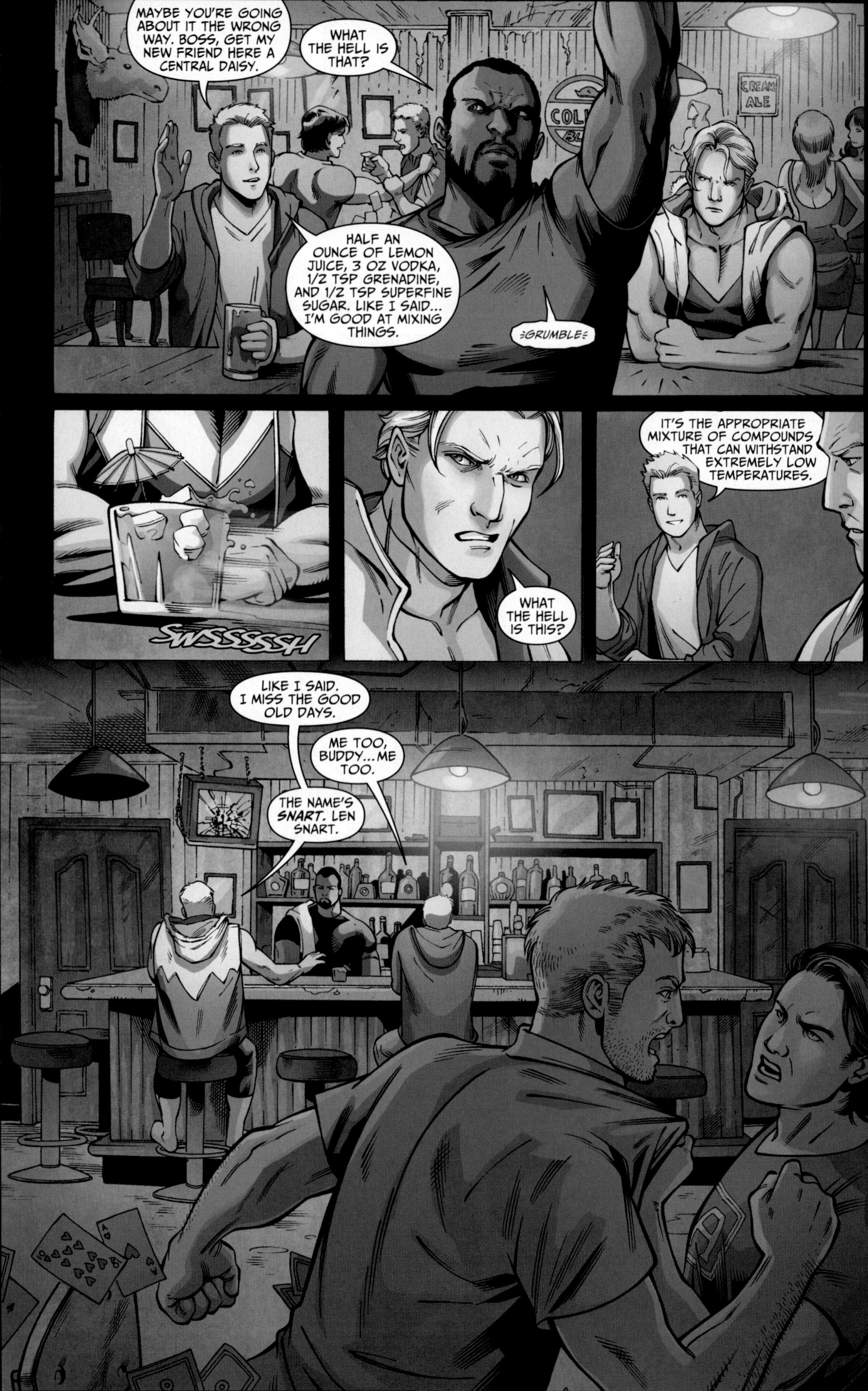
MAYBE YOU'RE GOING ABOUT IT THE WRONG WAY. BOSS, GET MY NEW FRIEND HERE A CENTRAL DAISY.
WHAT THE HELL IS THAT?
HALF AN OUNCE OF LEMON JUICE, 3 OZ VODKA, 1/2 TSP GRENADINE, AND 1/2 TSP SUPERFINE SUGAR. LIKE I SAID... I'M GOOD AT MIXING THINGS.
GRUMBLE
COLD
CREAM ALE
SWSSSSSH
WHAT THE HELL IS THIS?
IT'S THE APPROPRIATE MIXTURE OF COMPOUNDS THAT CAN WITHSTAND EXTREMELY LOW TEMPERATURES.
LIKE I SAID. I MISS THE GOOD OLD DAYS.
ME TOO, BUDDY...ME TOO.
THE NAME'S SNART. LEN SNART.

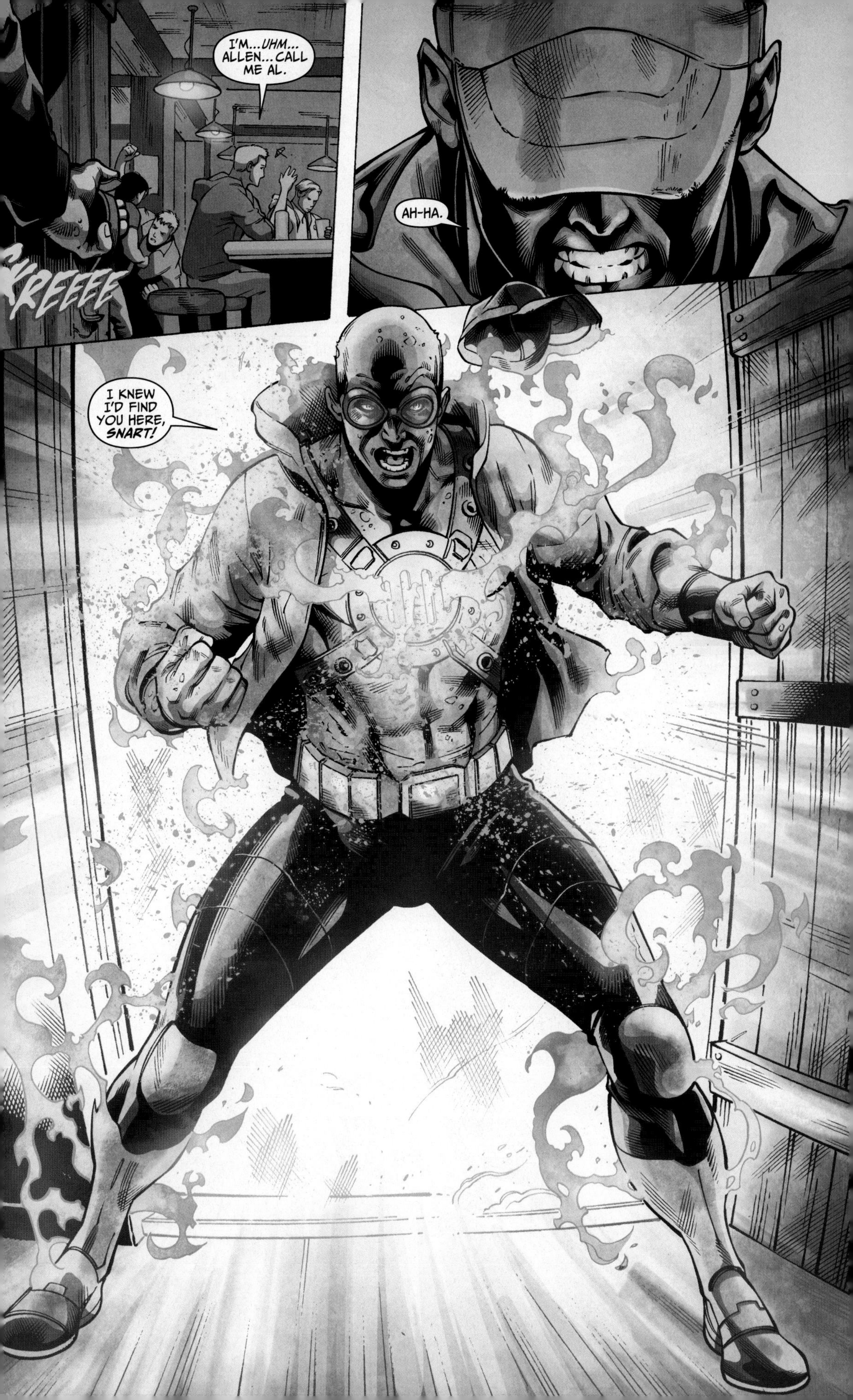
I'M...UHM... ALLEN...CALL ME AL.
SKREEEE
AH-HA.
I KNEW I'D FIND YOU HERE, SNART!

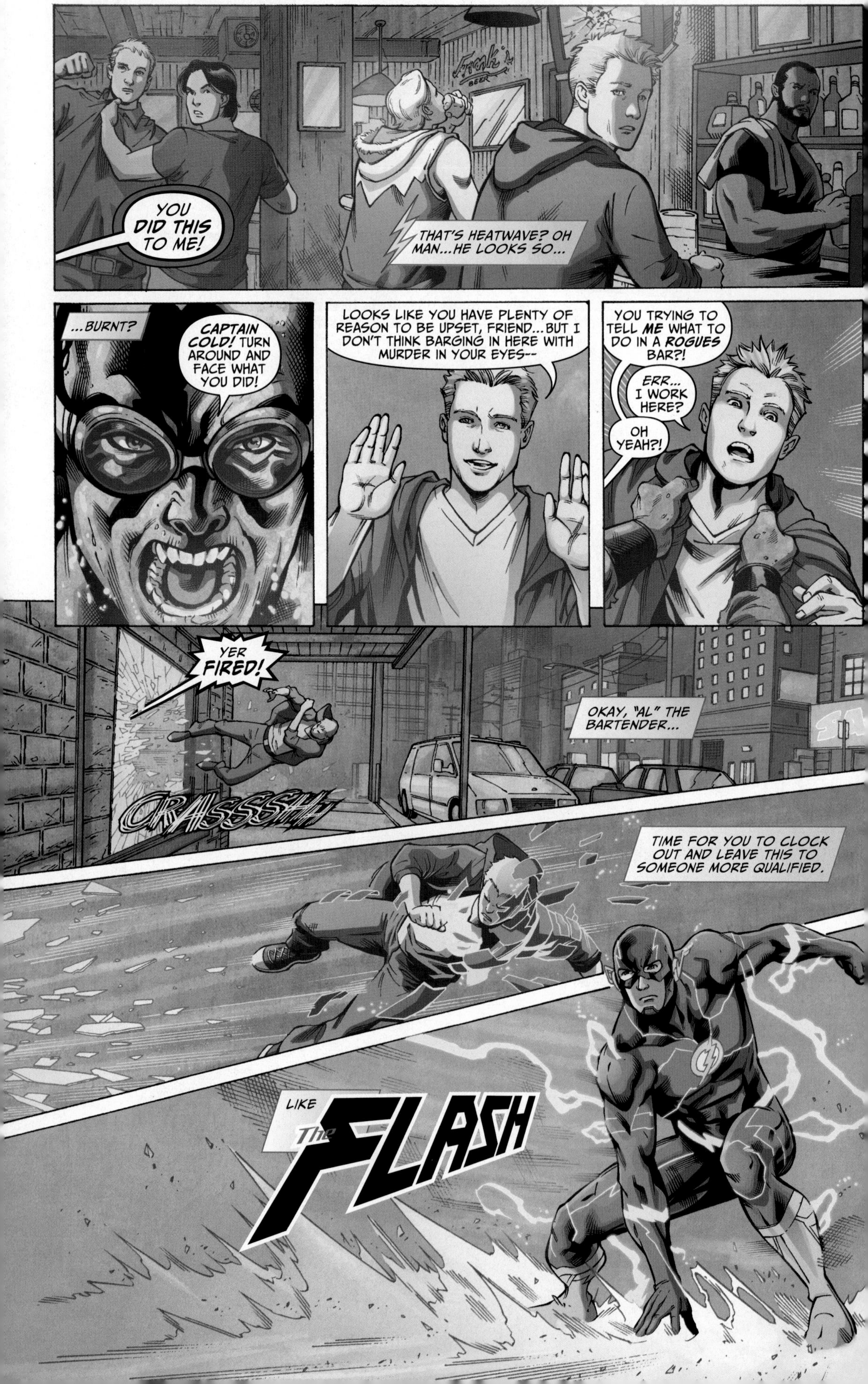

YOU DID THIS TO ME!
THAT'S HEATWAVE? OH MAN...HE LOOKS SO...
...BURNT?
CAPTAIN COLD! TURN AROUND AND FACE WHAT YOU DID!
LOOKS LIKE YOU HAVE PLENTY OF REASON TO BE UPSET, FRIEND...BUT I DON'T THINK BARGING IN HERE WITH MURDER IN YOUR EYES--
YOU TRYING TO TELL ME WHAT TO DO IN A ROGUES BAR?!
ERR... I WORK HERE?
OH YEAH?!
YER FIRED!
CRASSSHH
OKAY, "AL" THE BARTENDER...
TIME FOR YOU TO CLOCK OUT AND LEAVE THIS TO SOMEONE MORE QUALIFIED.
LIKE
The FLASH

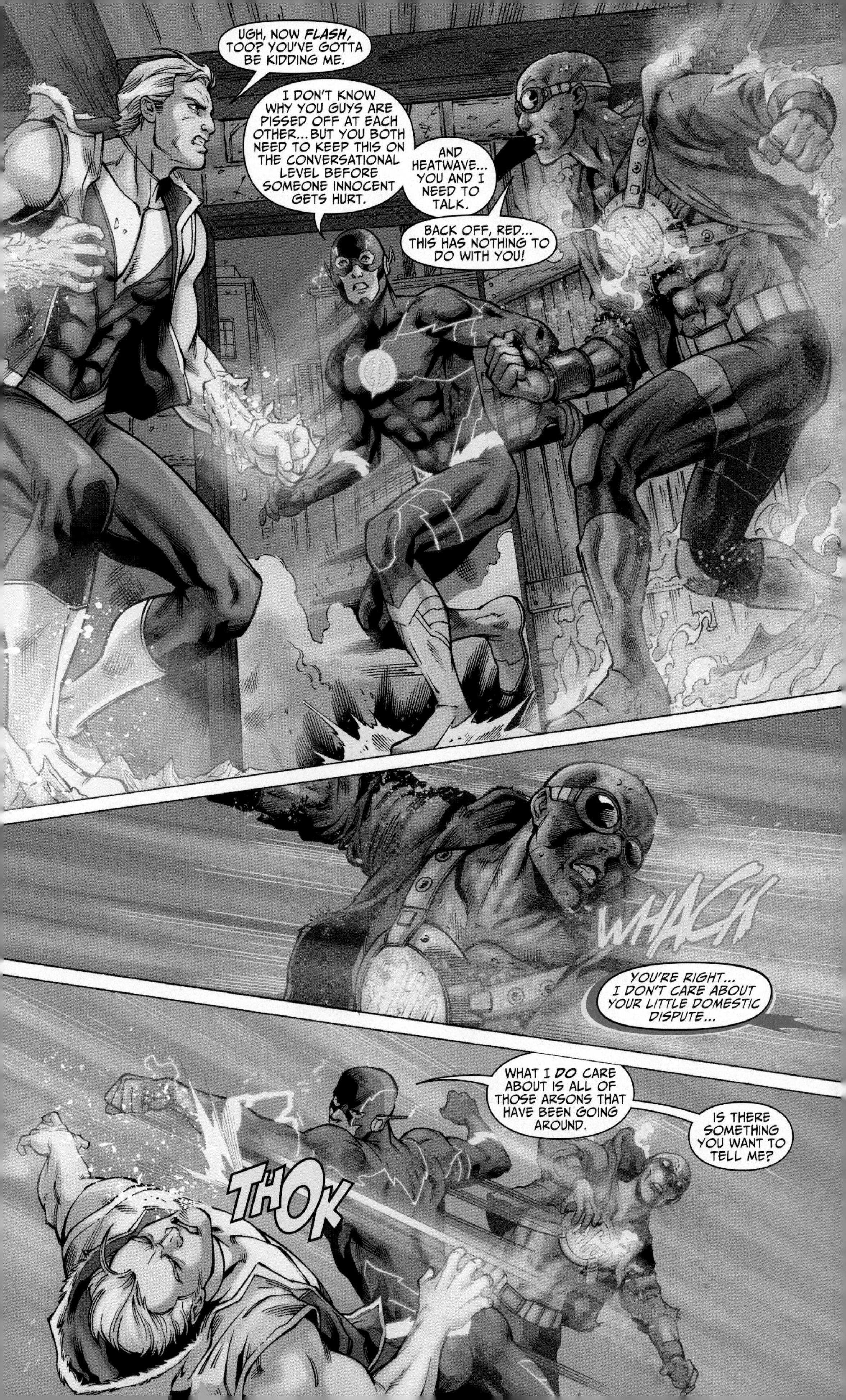

UGH, NOW FLASH, TOO? YOU'VE GOTTA BE KIDDING ME.
I DON'T KNOW WHY YOU GUYS ARE PISSED OFF AT EACH OTHER... BUT YOU BOTH NEED TO KEEP THIS ON THE CONVERSATIONAL LEVEL BEFORE SOMEONE INNOCENT GETS HURT.
AND HEATWAVE... YOU AND I NEED TO TALK.
BACK OFF, RED... THIS HAS NOTHING TO DO WITH YOU!
WHACK
YOU'RE RIGHT... I DON'T CARE ABOUT YOUR LITTLE DOMESTIC DISPUTE...
WHAT I DO CARE ABOUT IS ALL OF THOSE ARSONS THAT HAVE BEEN GOING AROUND.
IS THERE SOMETHING YOU WANT TO TELL ME?
THOK

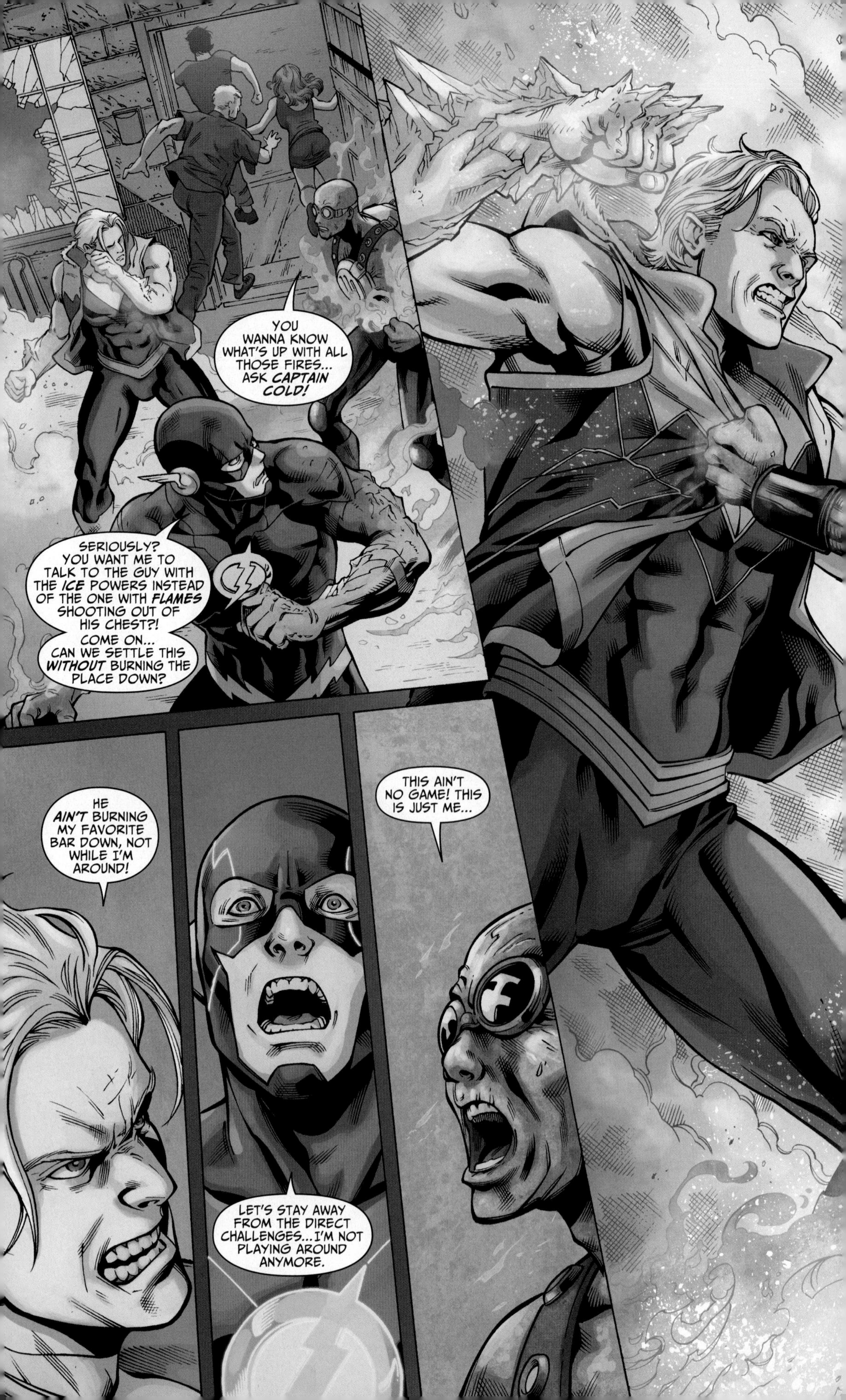
YOU WANNA KNOW WHAT'S UP WITH ALL THOSE FIRES... ASK CAPTAIN COLD!
SERIOUSLY? YOU WANT ME TO TALK TO THE GUY WITH THE ICE POWERS INSTEAD OF THE ONE WITH FLAMES SHOOTING OUT OF HIS CHEST?!
COME ON... CAN WE SETTLE THIS WITHOUT BURNING THE PLACE DOWN?
HE AIN'T BURNING MY FAVORITE BAR DOWN, NOT WHILE I'M AROUND!
LET'S STAY AWAY FROM THE DIRECT CHALLENGES...I'M NOT PLAYING AROUND ANYMORE.
THIS AIN'T NO GAME! THIS IS JUST ME...

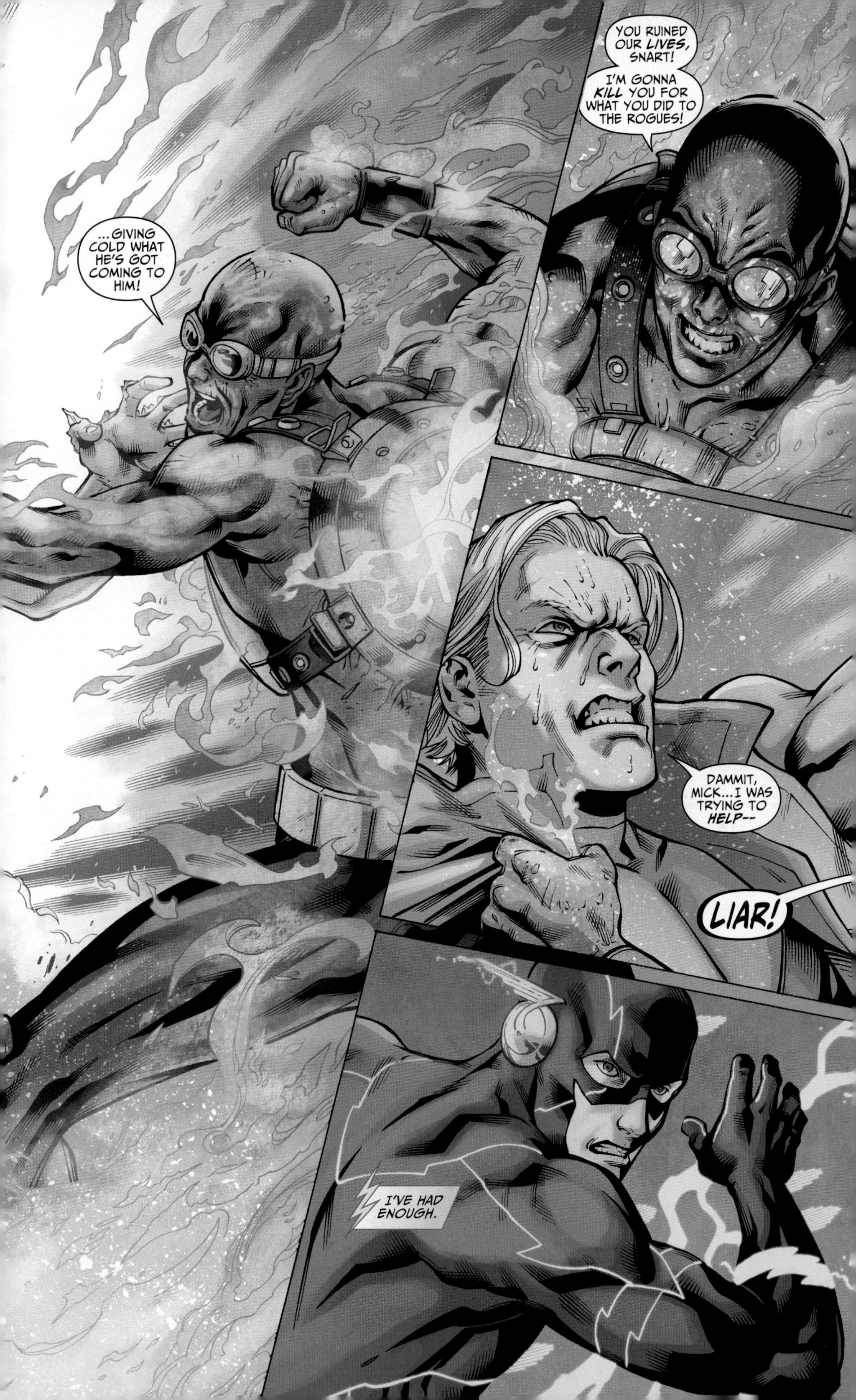
...GIVING COLD WHAT HE'S GOT COMING TO HIM!
YOU RUINED OUR LIVES, SNART!
I'M GONNA KILL YOU FOR WHAT YOU DID TO THE ROGUES!
DAMMIT, MICK...I WAS TRYING TO HELP--
LIAR!
I'VE HAD ENOUGH.

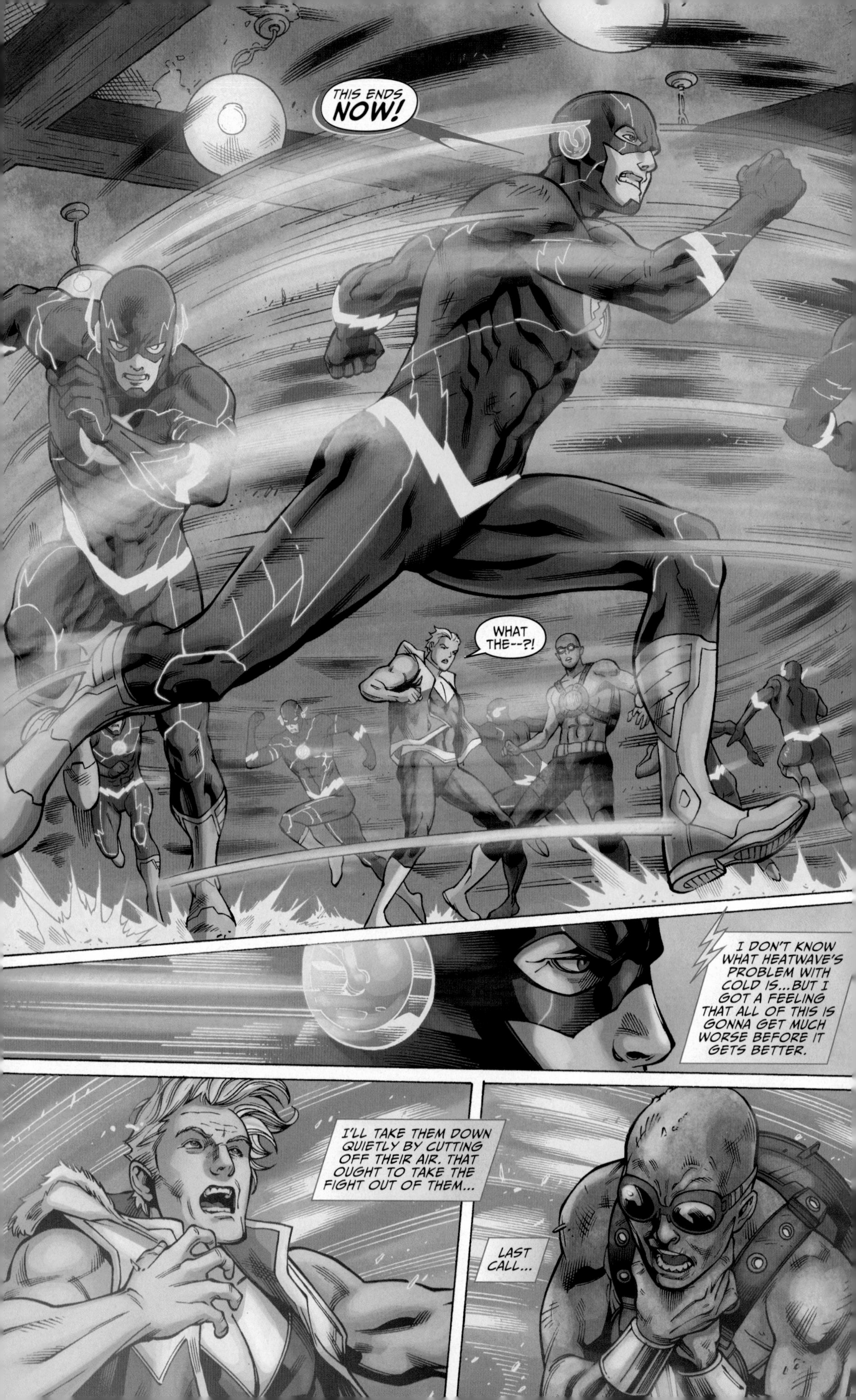

THIS ENDS NOW!
WHAT THE--?!
I DON'T KNOW WHAT HEATWAVE'S PROBLEM WITH COLD IS...BUT I GOT A FEELING THAT ALL OF THIS IS GONNA GET MUCH WORSE BEFORE IT GETS BETTER.
I'LL TAKE THEM DOWN QUIETLY BY CUTTING OFF THEIR AIR. THAT OUGHT TO TAKE THE FIGHT OUT OF THEM...
LAST CALL...

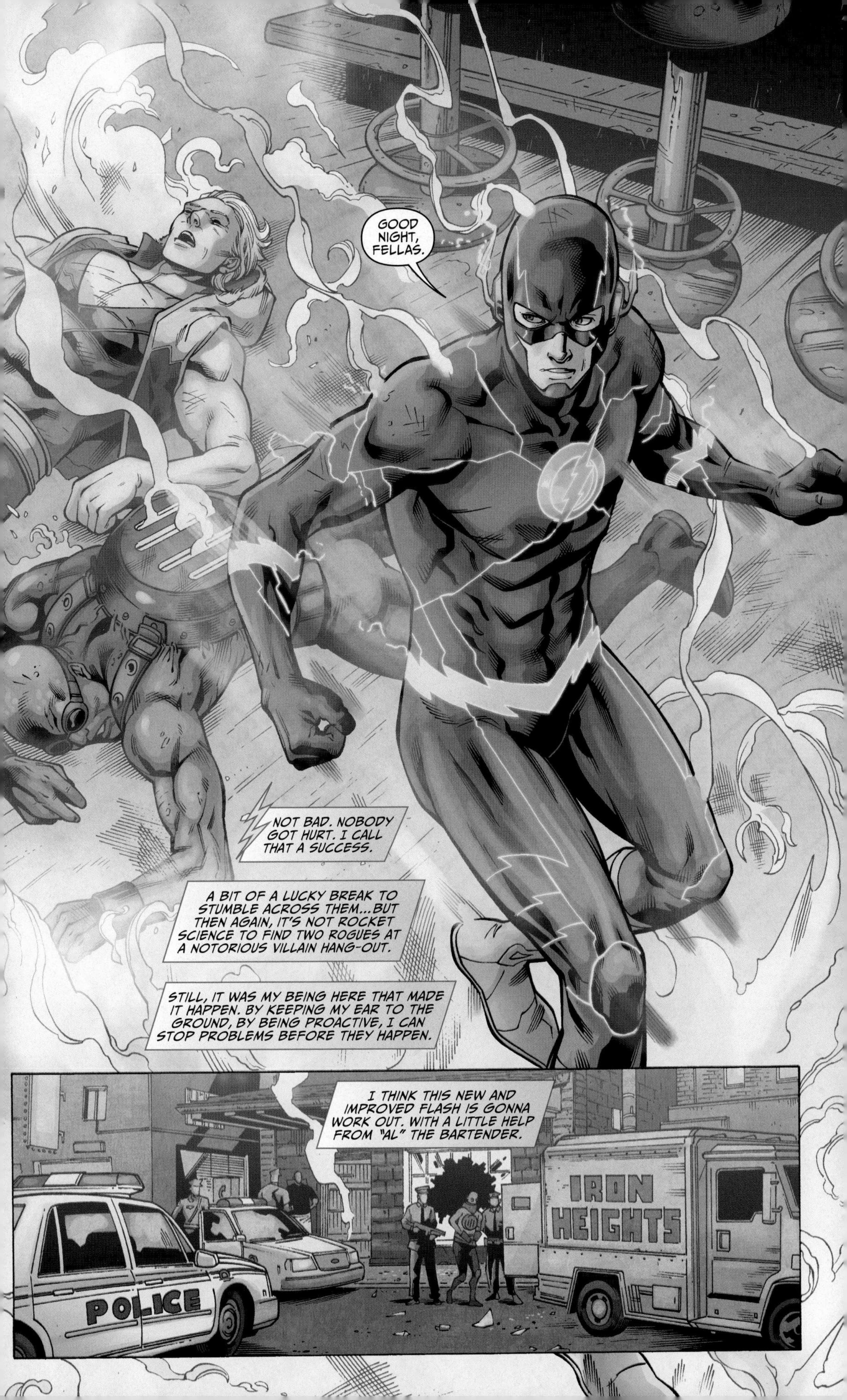
GOOD NIGHT, FELLAS.
NOT BAD. NOBODY GOT HURT. I CALL THAT A SUCCESS.
A BIT OF A LUCKY BREAK TO STUMBLE ACROSS THEM...BUT THEN AGAIN, IT'S NOT ROCKET SCIENCE TO FIND TWO ROGUES AT A NOTORIOUS VILLAIN HANG-OUT.
STILL, IT WAS MY BEING HERE THAT MADE IT HAPPEN. BY KEEPING MY EAR TO THE GROUND, BY BEING PROACTIVE, I CAN STOP PROBLEMS BEFORE THEY HAPPEN.
I THINK THIS NEW AND IMPROVED FLASH IS GONNA WORK OUT. WITH A LITTLE HELP FROM "AL" THE BARTENDER.
IRON HEIGHTS
POLICE

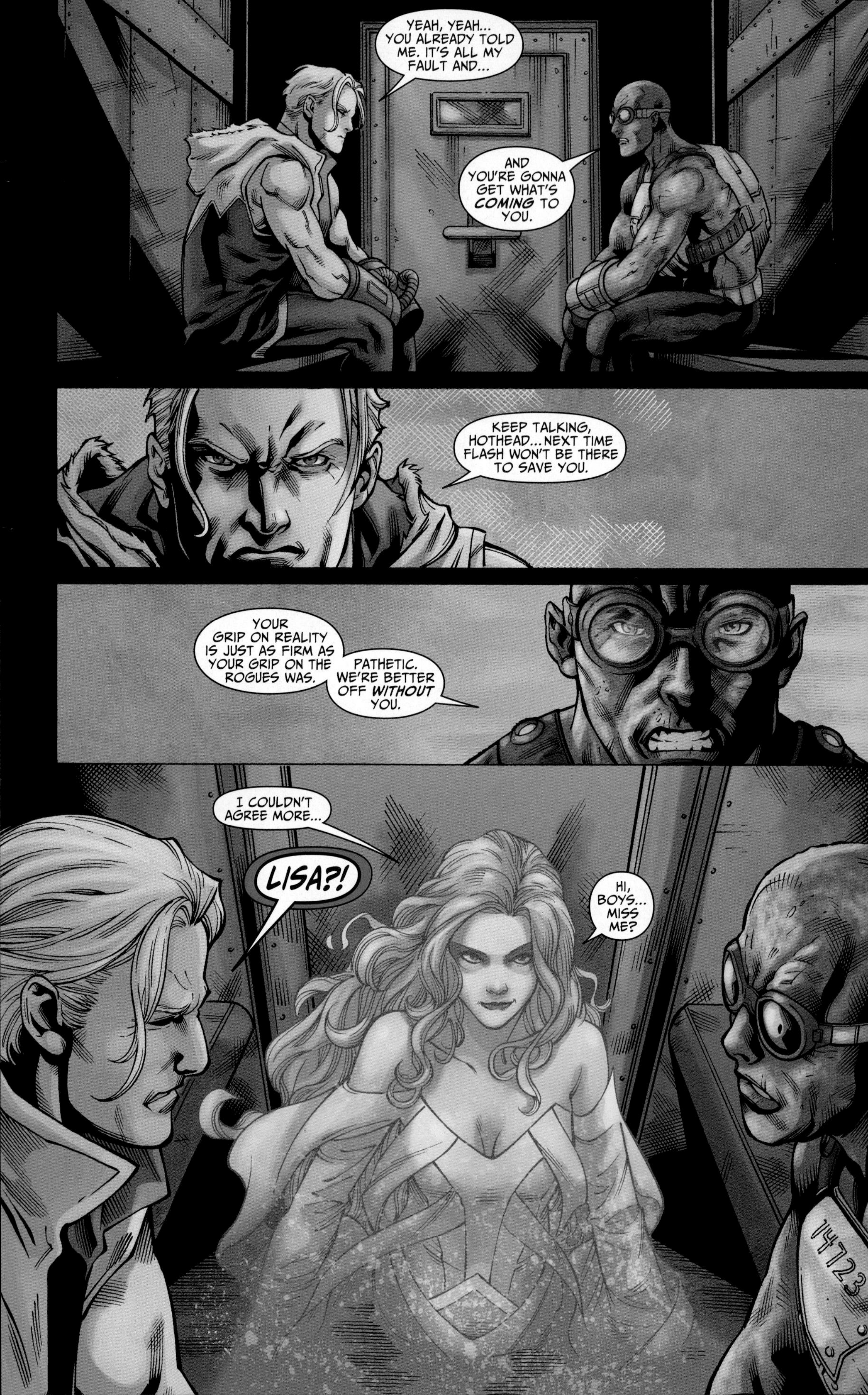
YEAH, YEAH... YOU ALREADY TOLD ME. IT'S ALL MY FAULT AND...
AND YOU'RE GONNA GET WHAT'S COMING TO YOU.
KEEP TALKING, HOTHEAD...NEXT TIME FLASH WON'T BE THERE TO SAVE YOU.
YOUR GRIP ON REALITY IS JUST AS FIRM AS YOUR GRIP ON THE ROGUES WAS.
PATHETIC. WE'RE BETTER OFF WITHOUT YOU.
I COULDN'T AGREE MORE...
LISA?!
HI, BOYS... MISS ME?
14723

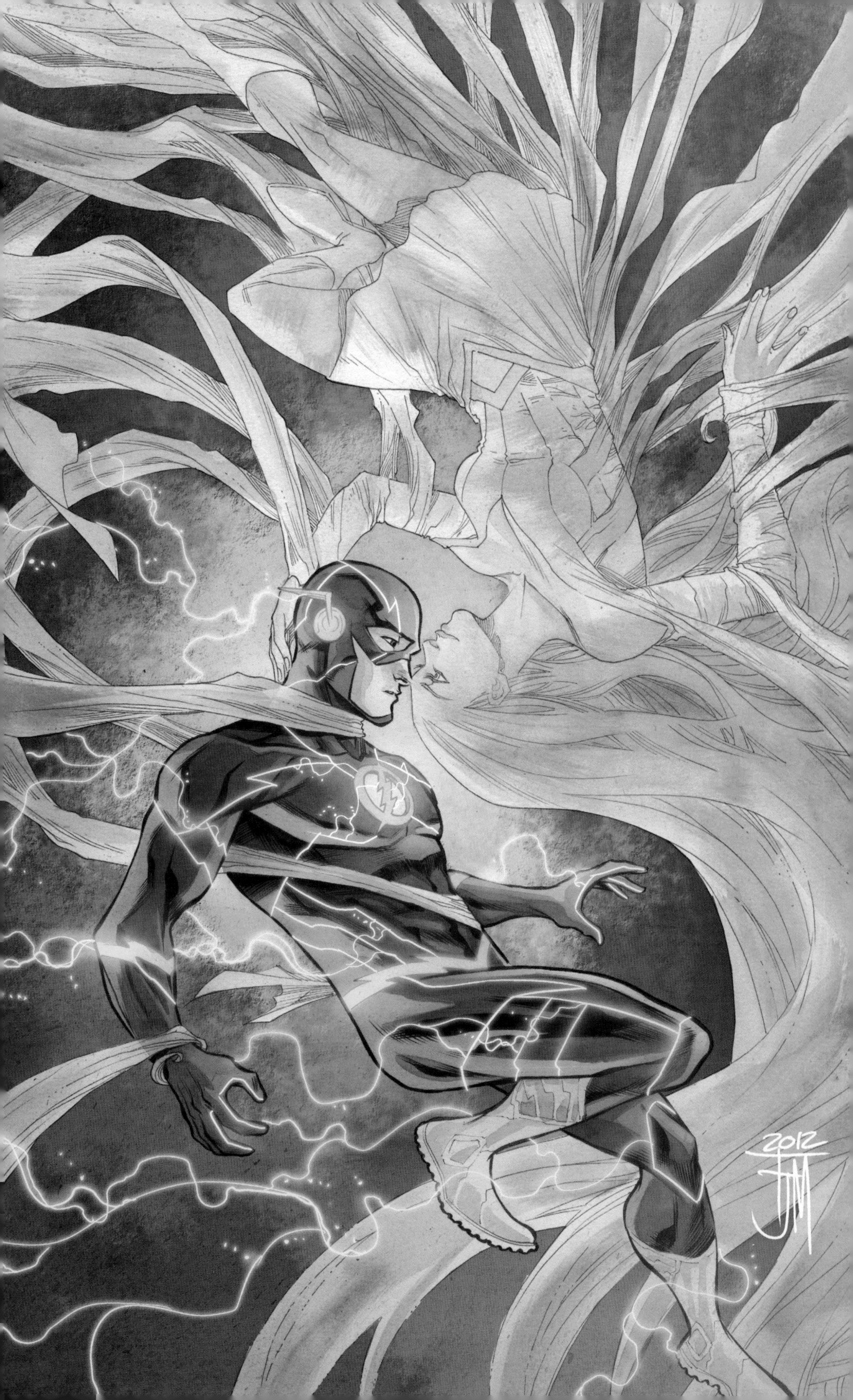

FRANCIS MANAPUL & BRIAN BUCCELLATO writers FRANCIS MANAPUL artist

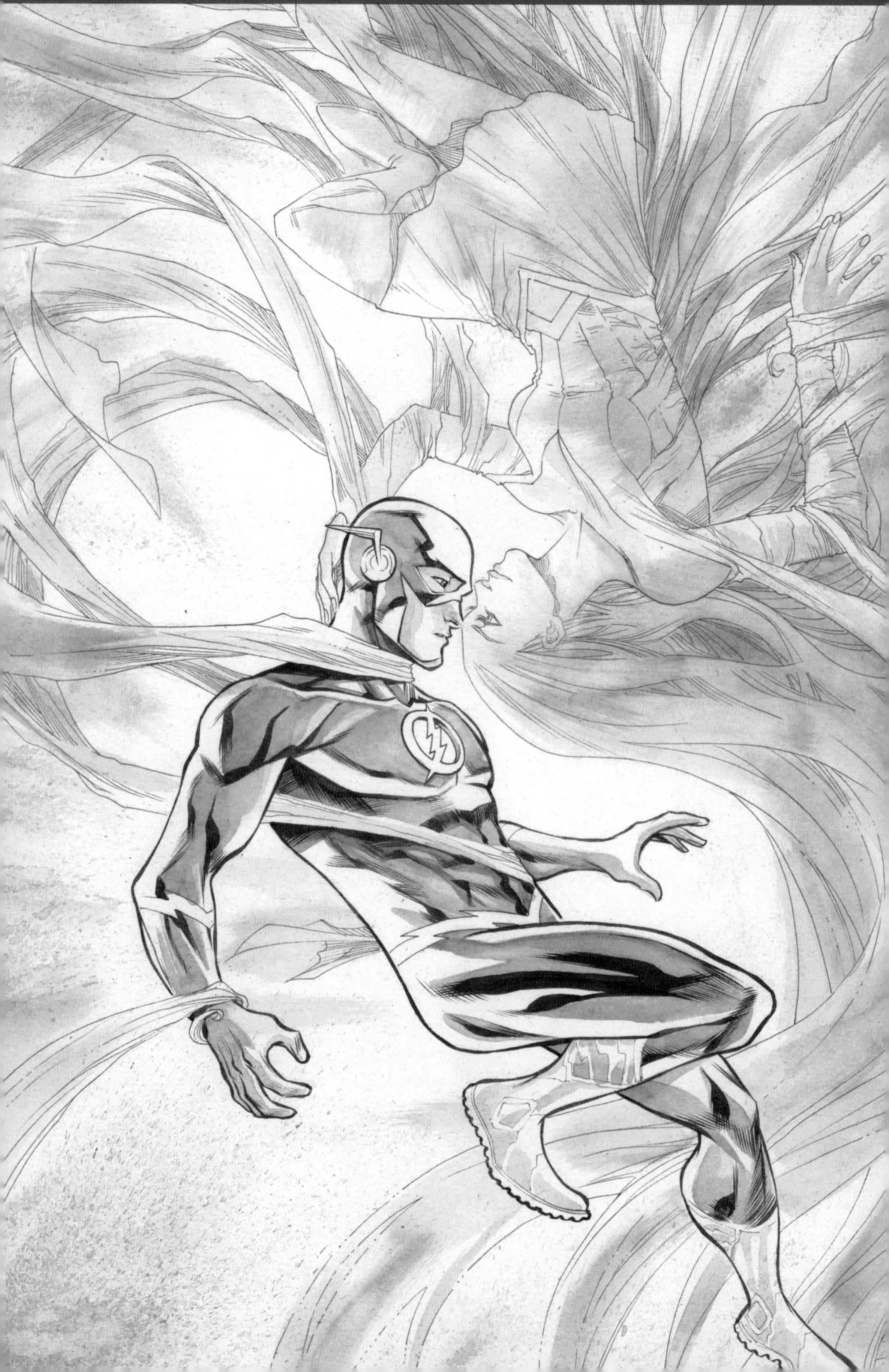

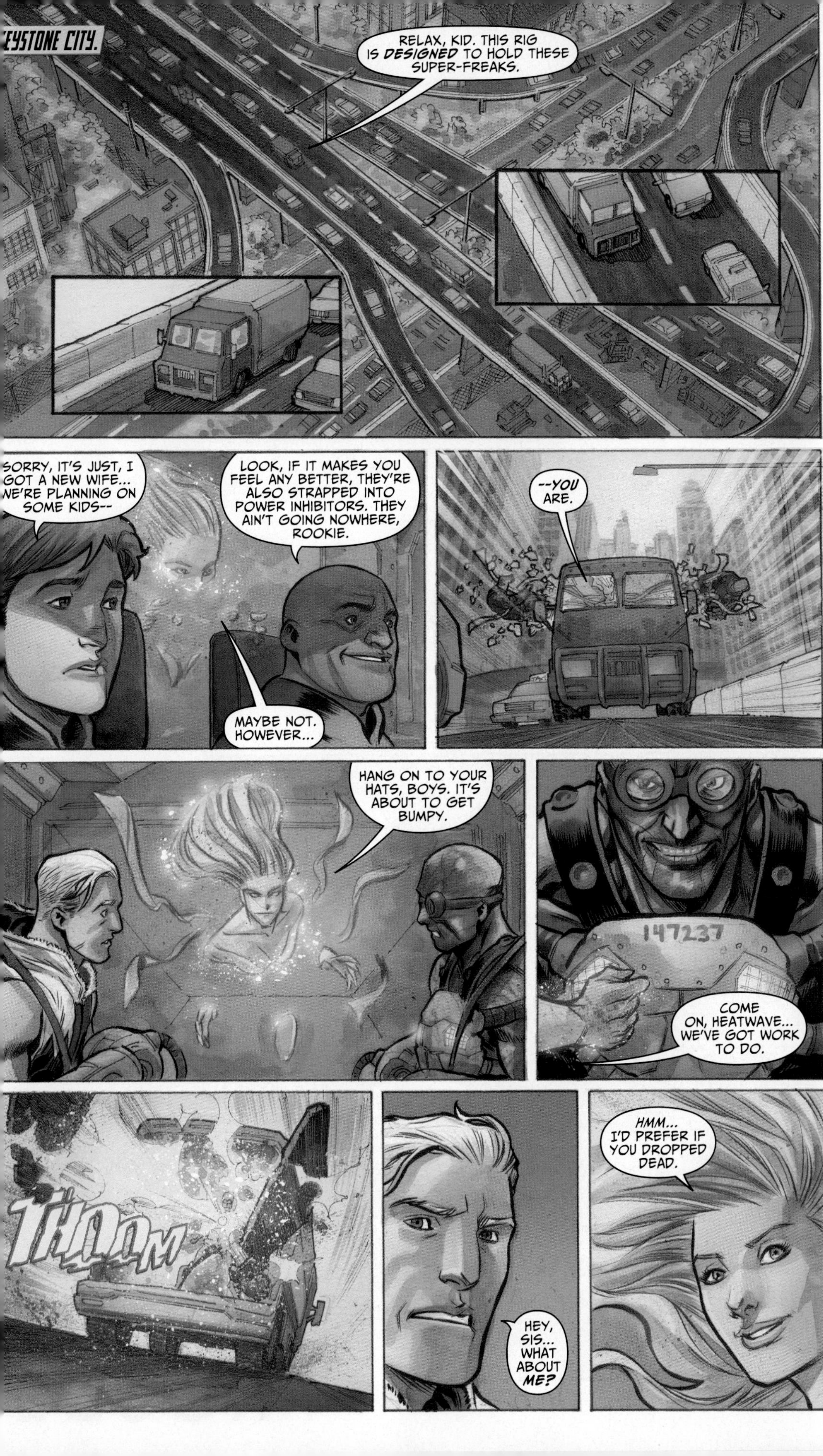
EYSTONE CITY.
RELAX, KID. THIS RIG IS DESIGNED TO HOLD THESE SUPER-FREAKS.
SORRY, IT'S JUST, I GOT A NEW WIFE... WE'RE PLANNING ON SOME KIDS--
LOOK, IF IT MAKES YOU FEEL ANY BETTER, THEY'RE ALSO STRAPPED INTO POWER INHIBITORS. THEY AIN'T GOING NOWHERE, ROOKIE.
MAYBE NOT. HOWEVER...
--YOU ARE.
HANG ON TO YOUR HATS, BOYS. IT'S ABOUT TO GET BUMPY.
147237
COME ON, HEATWAVE... WE'VE GOT WORK TO DO.
THOOM
HEY, SIS... WHAT ABOUT ME?
HMM... I'D PREFER IF YOU DROPPED DEAD.

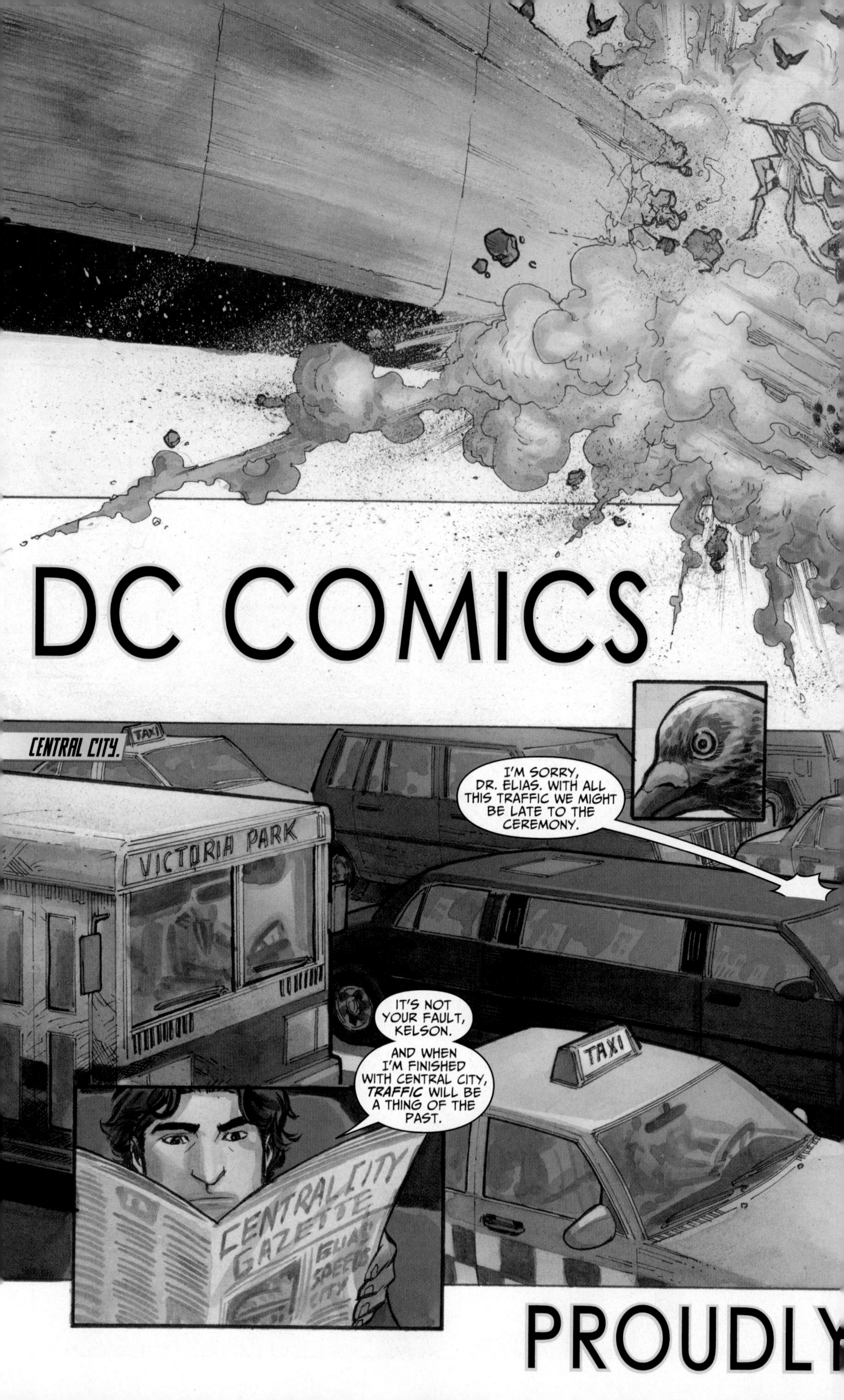
DC COMICS
CENTRAL CITY.
TAXI
I'M SORRY, DR. ELIAS. WITH ALL THIS TRAFFIC WE MIGHT BE LATE TO THE CEREMONY.
VICTORIA PARK
IT'S NOT YOUR FAULT, KELSON.
AND WHEN I'M FINISHED WITH CENTRAL CITY, *TRAFFIC* WILL BE A THING OF THE PAST.
TAXI
CENTRAL CITY GAZETTE
PROUDLY

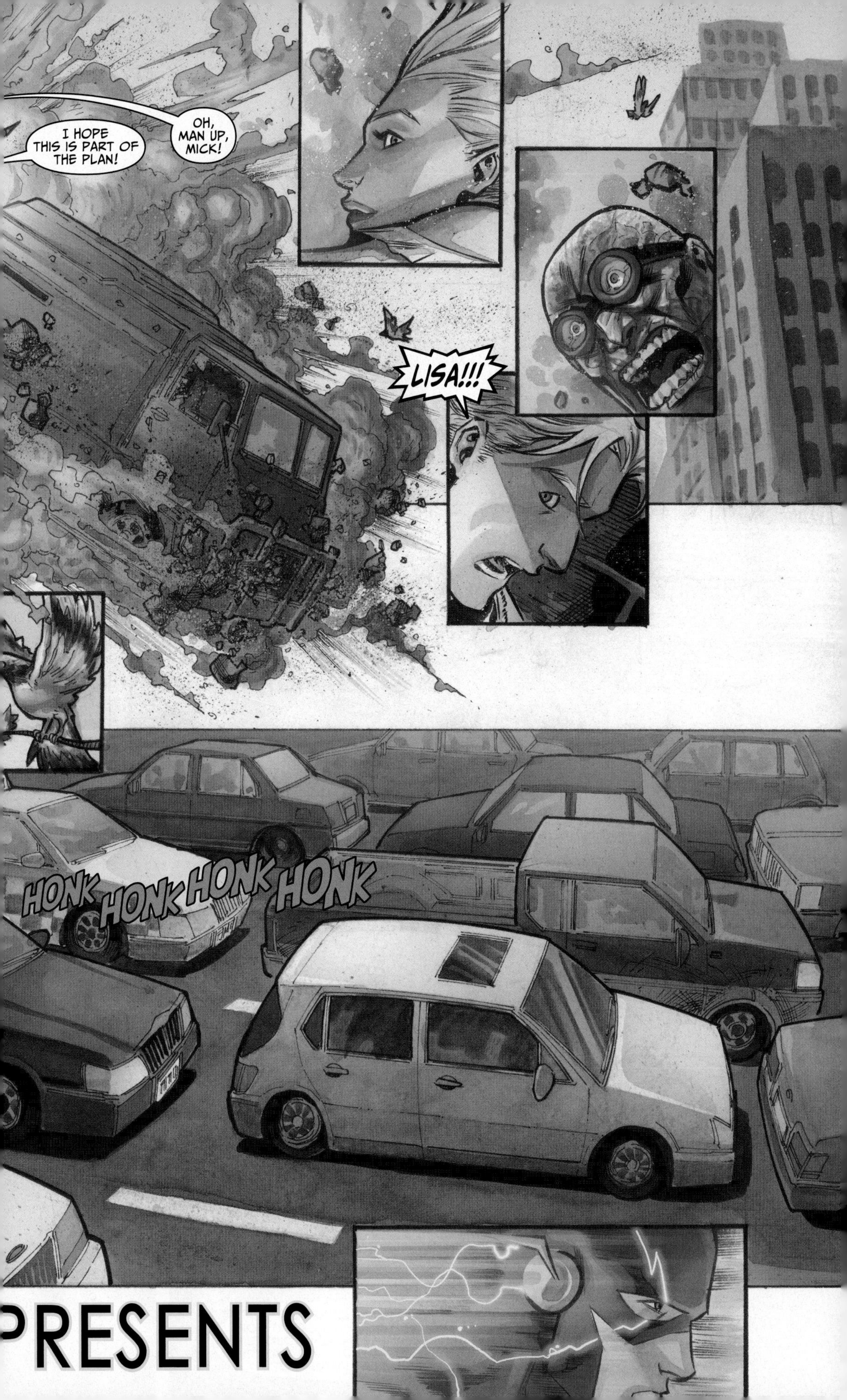

I HOPE THIS IS PART OF THE PLAN!
OH, MAN UP, MICK!
LISA!!!
HONK HONK HONK HONK

PRESENTS

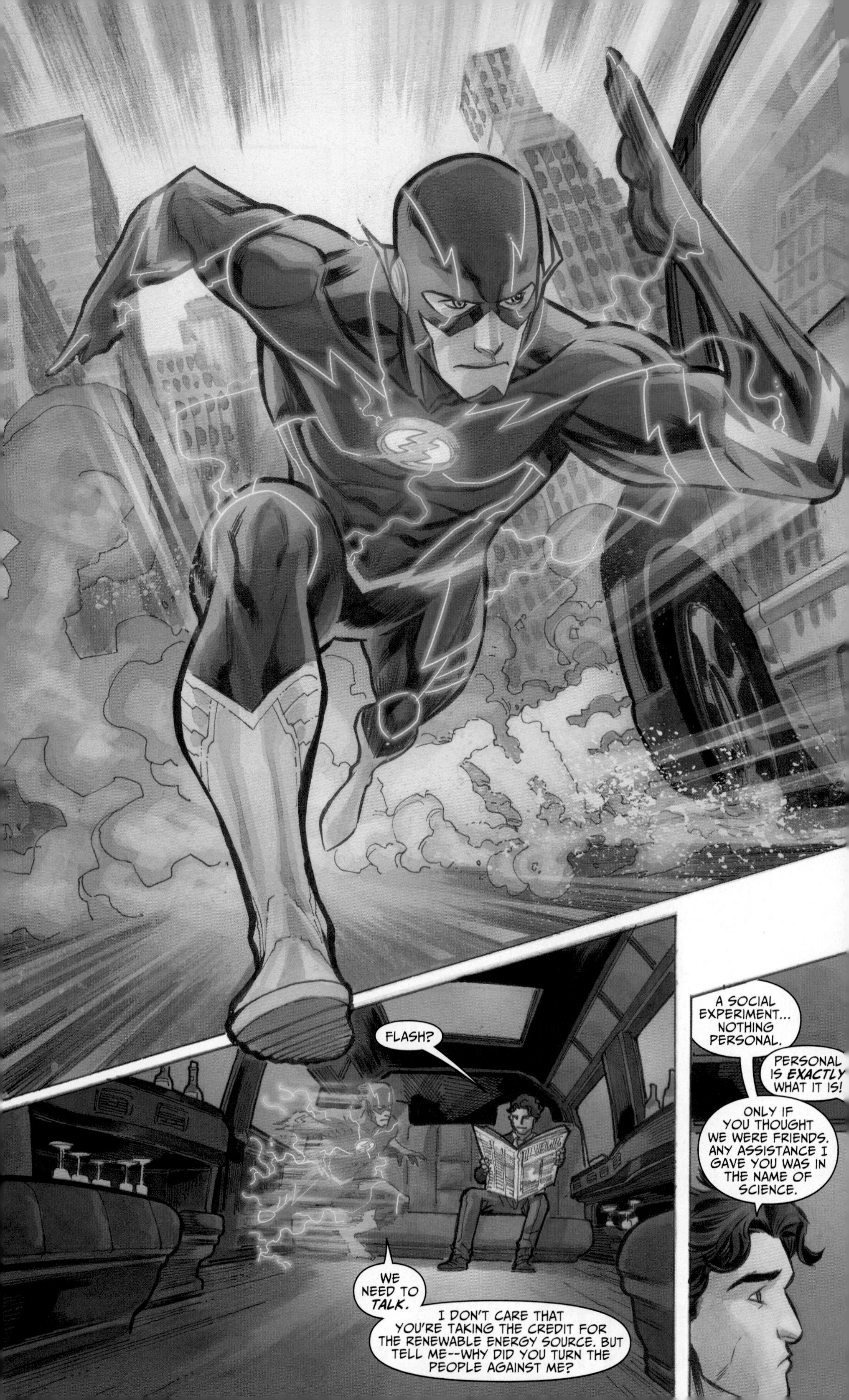
FLASH?
WE NEED TO *TALK.*
I DON'T CARE THAT YOU'RE TAKING THE CREDIT FOR THE RENEWABLE ENERGY SOURCE. BUT TELL ME--WHY DID YOU TURN THE PEOPLE AGAINST ME?
A SOCIAL EXPERIMENT... NOTHING PERSONAL.
PERSONAL IS *EXACTLY* WHAT IT IS!
ONLY IF YOU THOUGHT WE WERE FRIENDS. ANY ASSISTANCE I GAVE YOU WAS IN THE NAME OF SCIENCE.

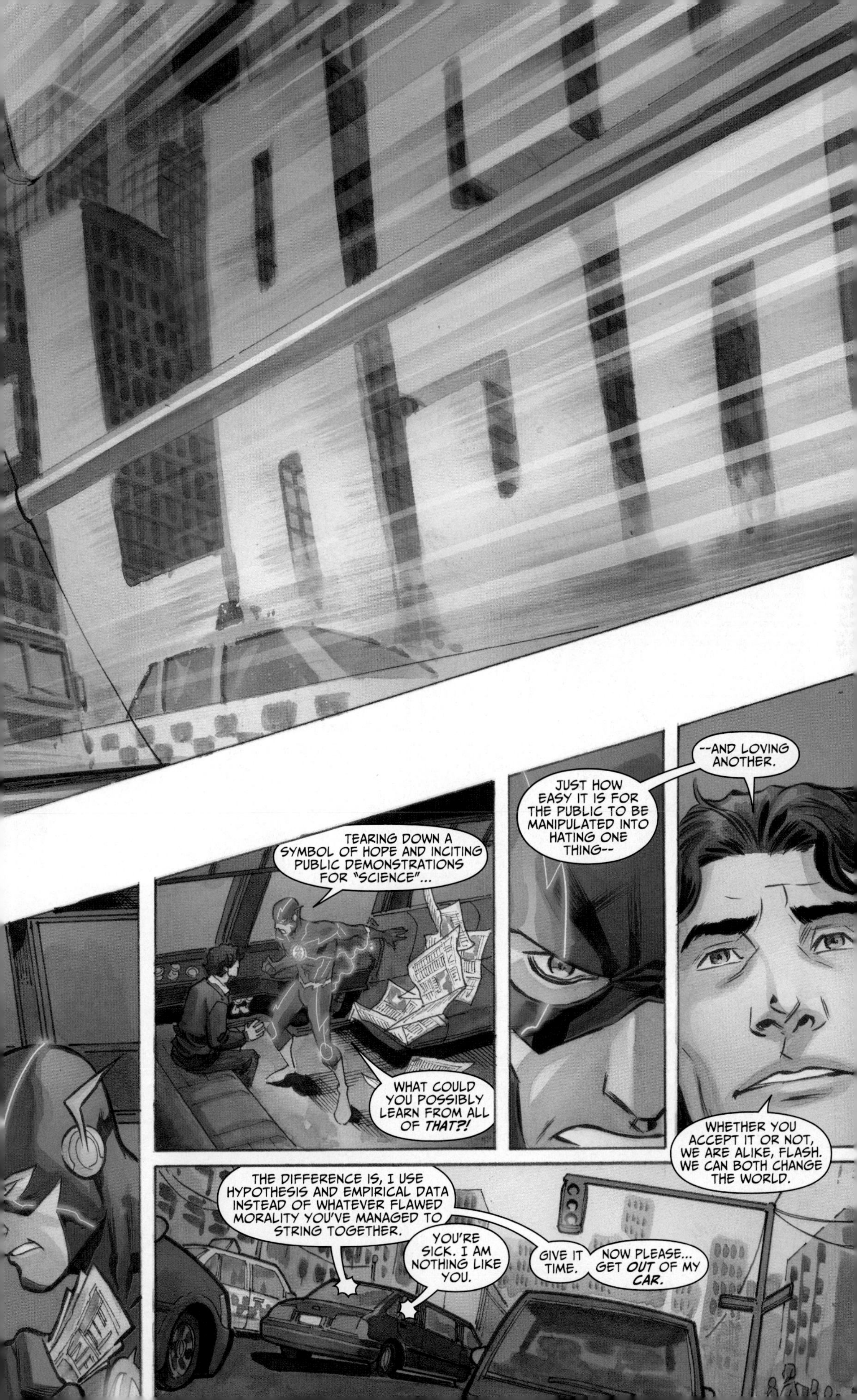
TEARING DOWN A SYMBOL OF HOPE AND INCITING PUBLIC DEMONSTRATIONS FOR "SCIENCE"...
WHAT COULD YOU POSSIBLY LEARN FROM ALL OF *THAT?!*
JUST HOW EASY IT IS FOR THE PUBLIC TO BE MANIPULATED INTO HATING ONE THING--
--AND LOVING ANOTHER.
WHETHER YOU ACCEPT IT OR NOT, WE ARE ALIKE, FLASH. WE CAN BOTH CHANGE THE WORLD.
THE DIFFERENCE IS, I USE HYPOTHESIS AND EMPIRICAL DATA INSTEAD OF WHATEVER FLAWED MORALITY YOU'VE MANAGED TO STRING TOGETHER.
YOU'RE SICK. I AM NOTHING LIKE YOU.
GIVE IT TIME.
NOW PLEASE... GET *OUT* OF MY *CAR.*

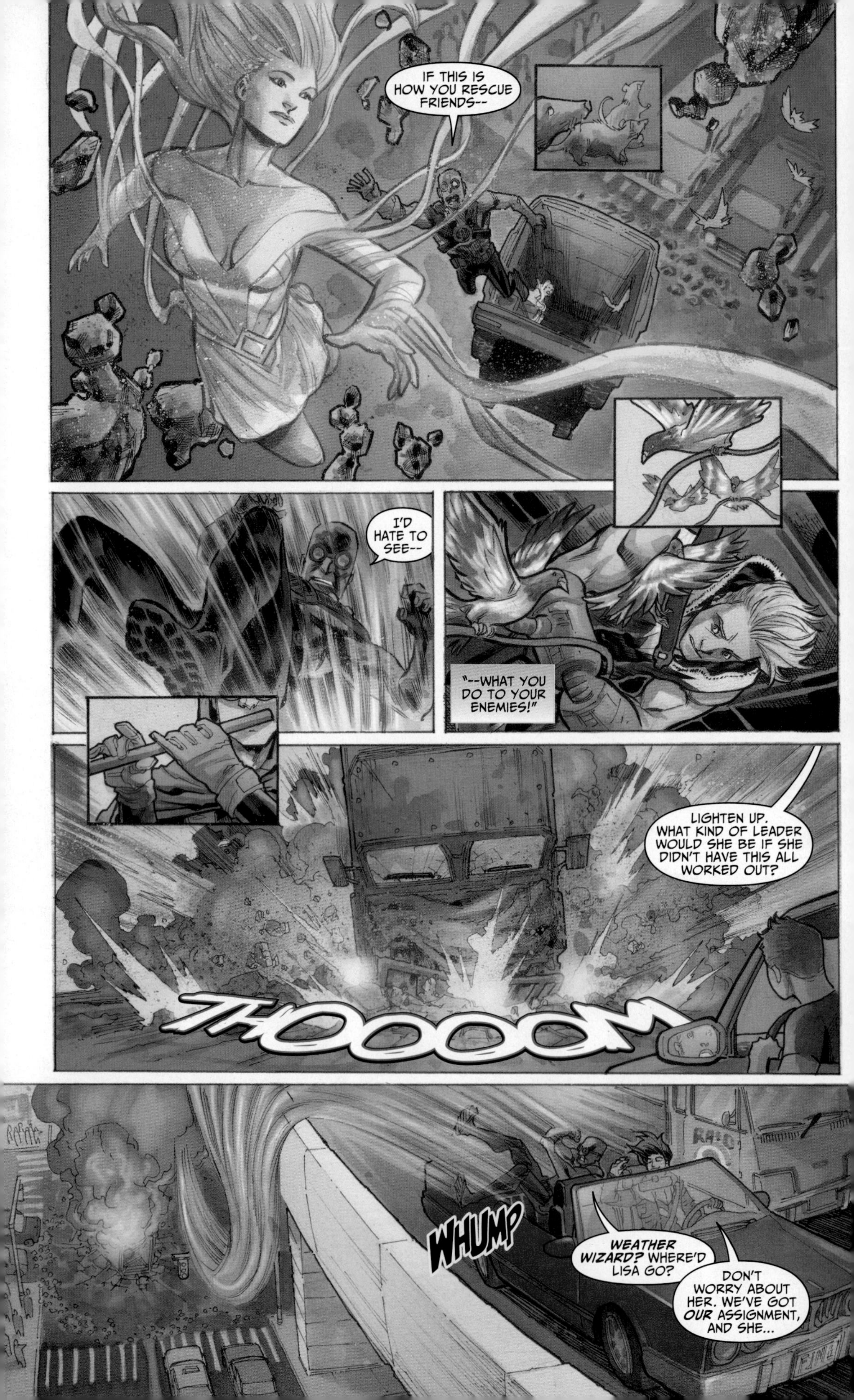
IF THIS IS HOW YOU RESCUE FRIENDS--
I'D HATE TO SEE--
"--WHAT YOU DO TO YOUR ENEMIES!"
LIGHTEN UP. WHAT KIND OF LEADER WOULD SHE BE IF SHE DIDN'T HAVE THIS ALL WORKED OUT?
THOOOOM
WHUMP
WEATHER WIZARD? WHERE'D LISA GO?
DON'T WORRY ABOUT HER. WE'VE GOT OUR ASSIGNMENT, AND SHE...

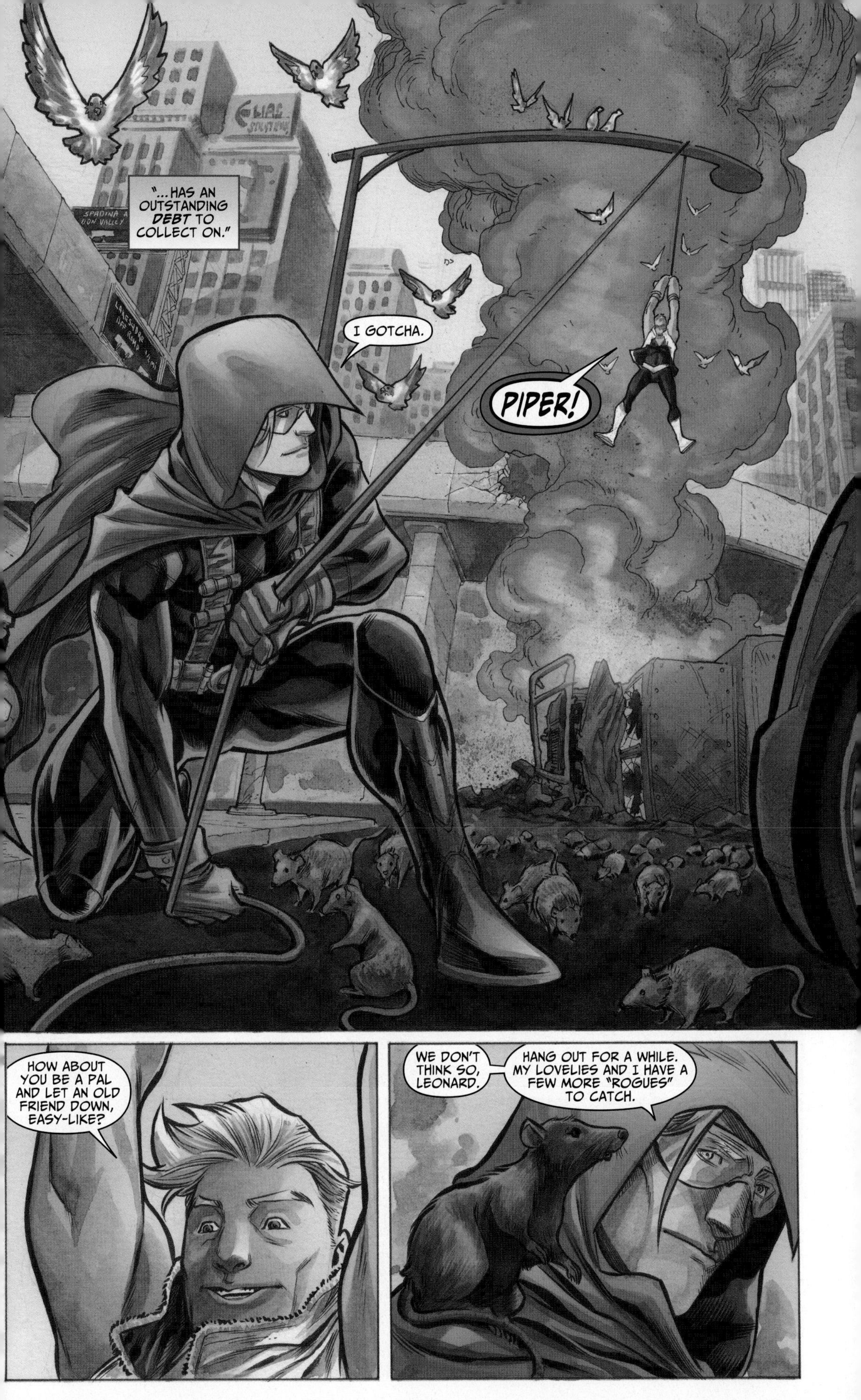
"...HAS AN OUTSTANDING *DEBT* TO COLLECT ON."
I GOTCHA.
PIPER!
HOW ABOUT YOU BE A PAL AND LET AN OLD FRIEND DOWN, EASY-LIKE?
WE DON'T THINK SO, LEONARD.
HANG OUT FOR A WHILE. MY LOVELIES AND I HAVE A FEW MORE "ROGUES" TO CATCH.

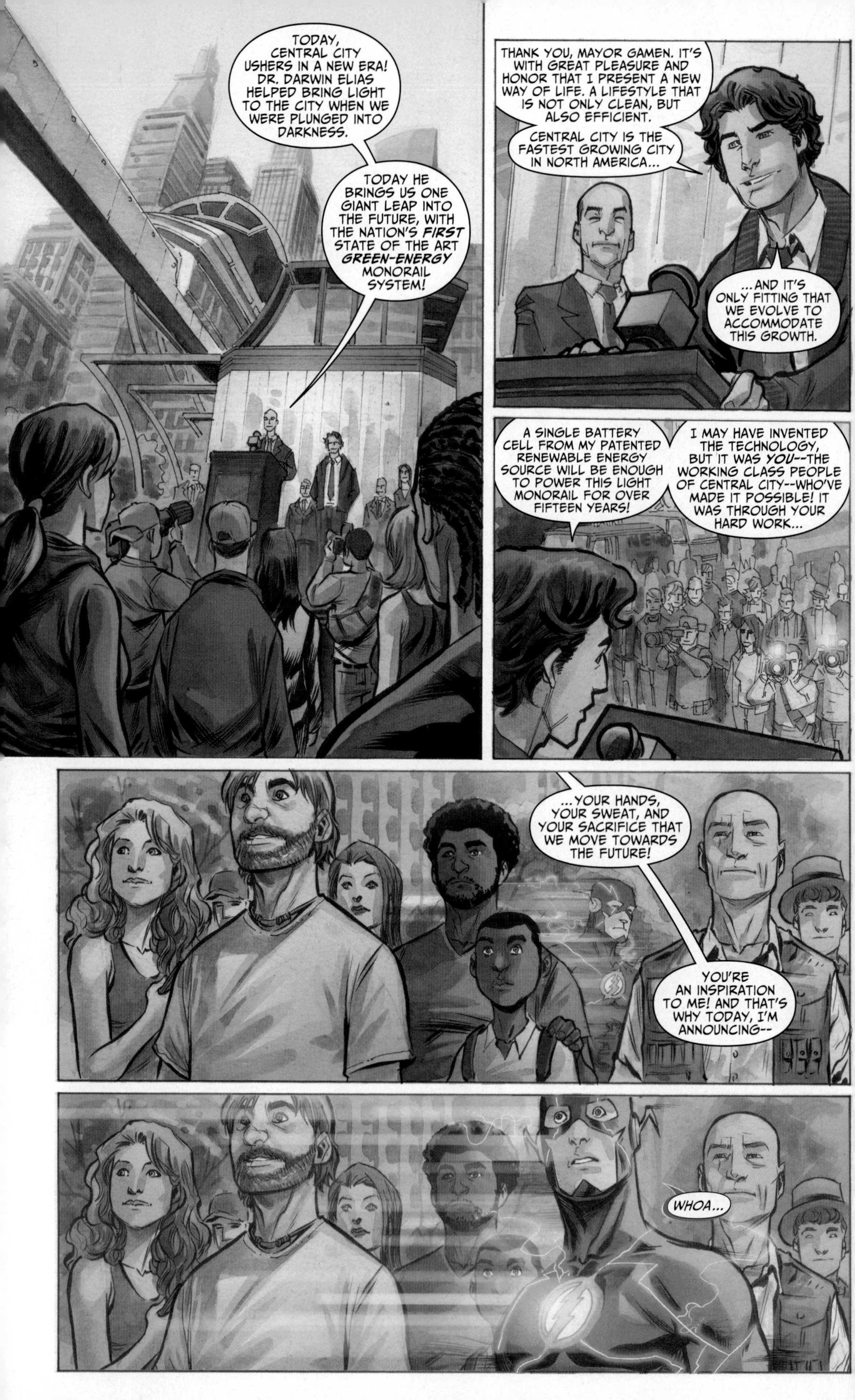
TODAY, CENTRAL CITY USHERS IN A NEW ERA! DR. DARWIN ELIAS HELPED BRING LIGHT TO THE CITY WHEN WE WERE PLUNGED INTO DARKNESS.
TODAY HE BRINGS US ONE GIANT LEAP INTO THE FUTURE, WITH THE NATION'S *FIRST* STATE OF THE ART *GREEN-ENERGY* MONORAIL SYSTEM!
THANK YOU, MAYOR GAMEN. IT'S WITH GREAT PLEASURE AND HONOR THAT I PRESENT A NEW WAY OF LIFE. A LIFESTYLE THAT IS NOT ONLY CLEAN, BUT ALSO EFFICIENT.
CENTRAL CITY IS THE FASTEST GROWING CITY IN NORTH AMERICA...
...AND IT'S ONLY FITTING THAT WE EVOLVE TO ACCOMMODATE THIS GROWTH.
A SINGLE BATTERY CELL FROM MY PATENTED RENEWABLE ENERGY SOURCE WILL BE ENOUGH TO POWER THIS LIGHT MONORAIL FOR OVER FIFTEEN YEARS!
I MAY HAVE INVENTED THE TECHNOLOGY, BUT IT WAS *YOU*--THE WORKING CLASS PEOPLE OF CENTRAL CITY--WHO'VE MADE IT POSSIBLE! IT WAS THROUGH YOUR HARD WORK...
...YOUR HANDS, YOUR SWEAT, AND YOUR SACRIFICE THAT WE MOVE TOWARDS THE FUTURE!
YOU'RE AN INSPIRATION TO ME! AND THAT'S WHY TODAY, I'M ANNOUNCING--
WHOA...

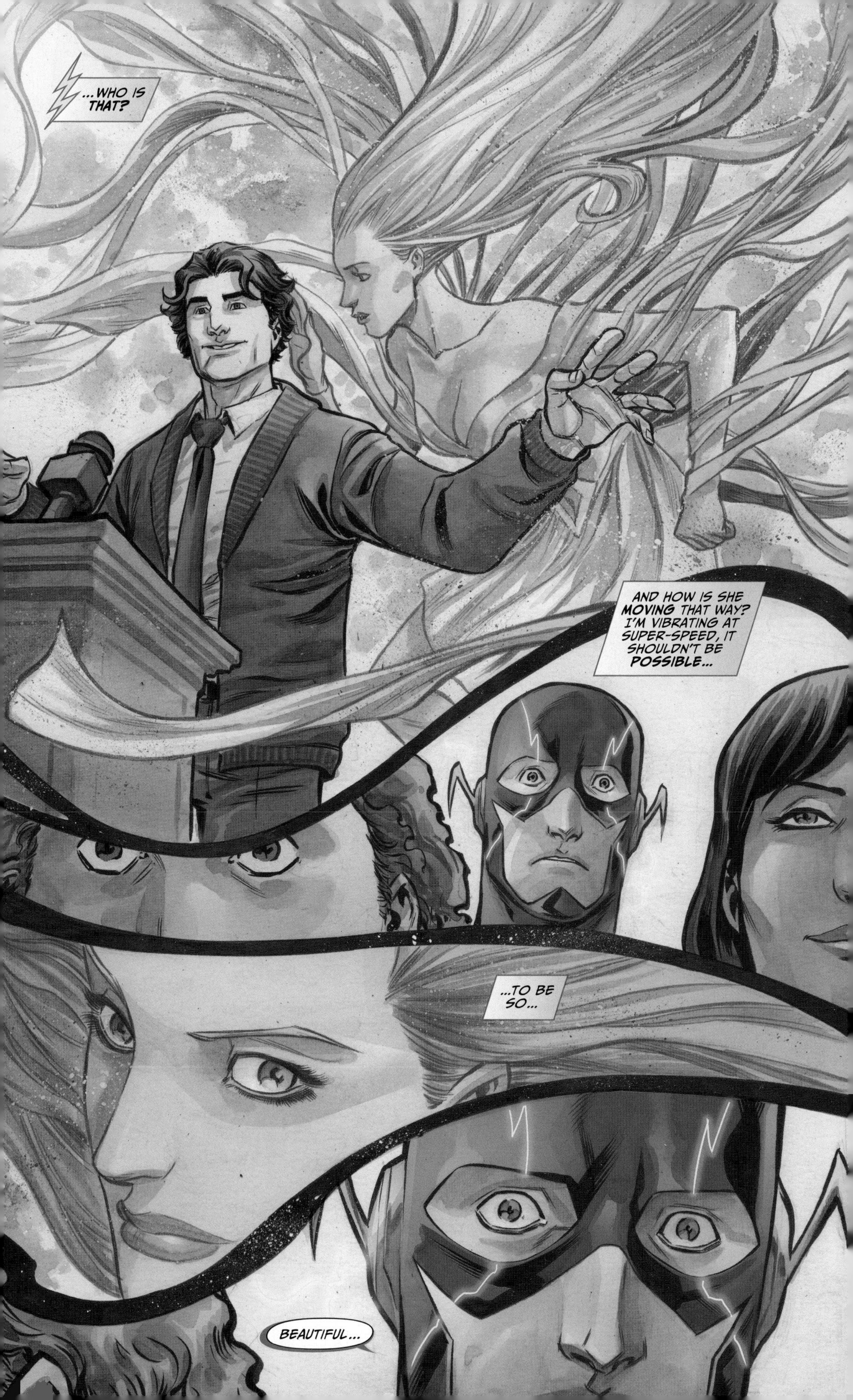
...WHO IS THAT?
AND HOW IS SHE MOVING THAT WAY? I'M VIBRATING AT SUPER-SPEED, IT SHOULDN'T BE POSSIBLE...
...TO BE SO...
BEAUTIFUL...

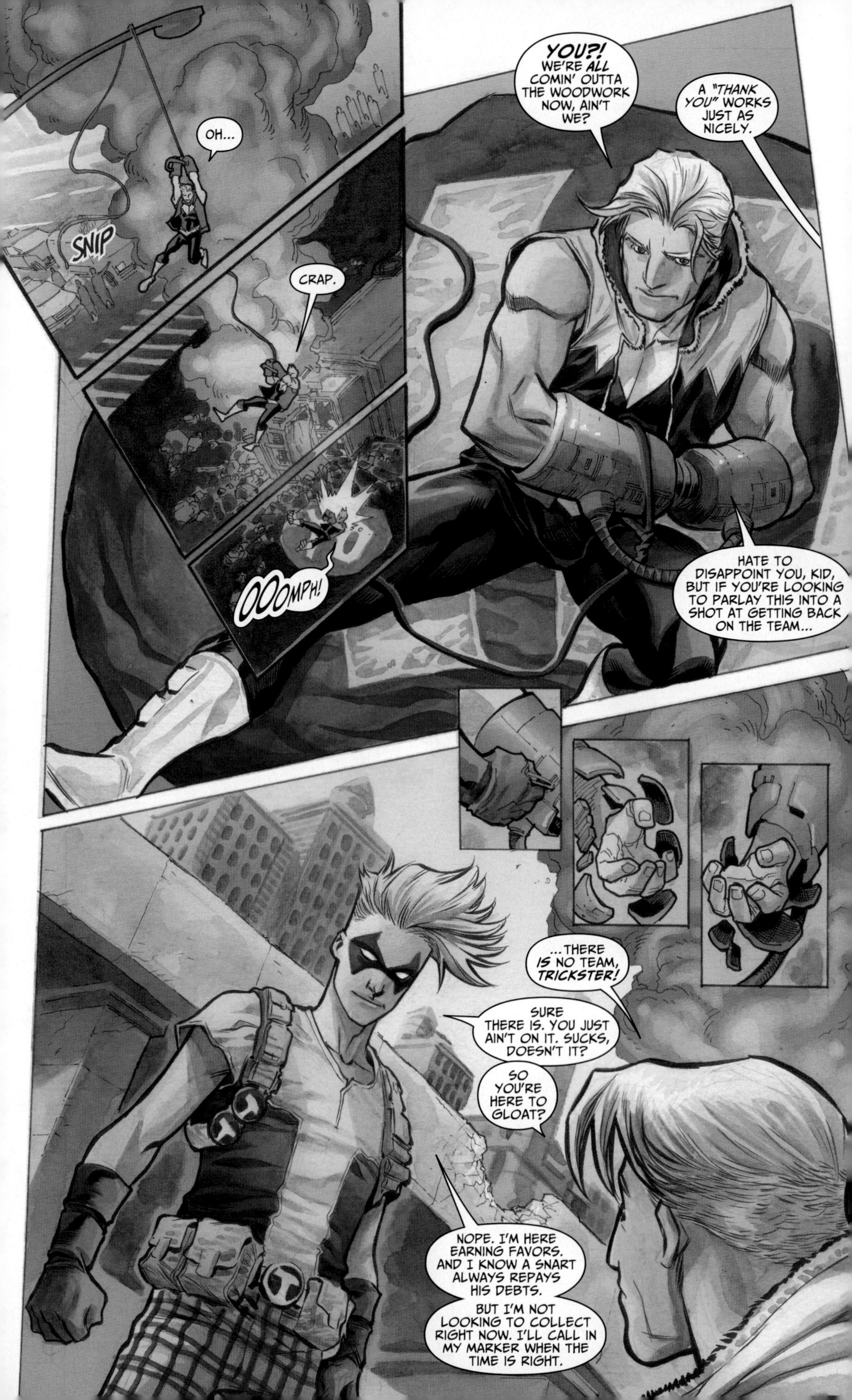
OH...
SNIP
CRAP.
OOOMPH!
YOU?! WE'RE ALL COMIN' OUTTA THE WOODWORK NOW, AIN'T WE?
A "THANK YOU" WORKS JUST AS NICELY.
HATE TO DISAPPOINT YOU, KID, BUT IF YOU'RE LOOKING TO PARLAY THIS INTO A SHOT AT GETTING BACK ON THE TEAM...
...THERE IS NO TEAM, TRICKSTER!
SURE THERE IS. YOU JUST AIN'T ON IT. SUCKS, DOESN'T IT?
SO YOU'RE HERE TO GLOAT?
NOPE. I'M HERE EARNING FAVORS. AND I KNOW A SNART ALWAYS REPAYS HIS DEBTS.
BUT I'M NOT LOOKING TO COLLECT RIGHT NOW. I'LL CALL IN MY MARKER WHEN THE TIME IS RIGHT.

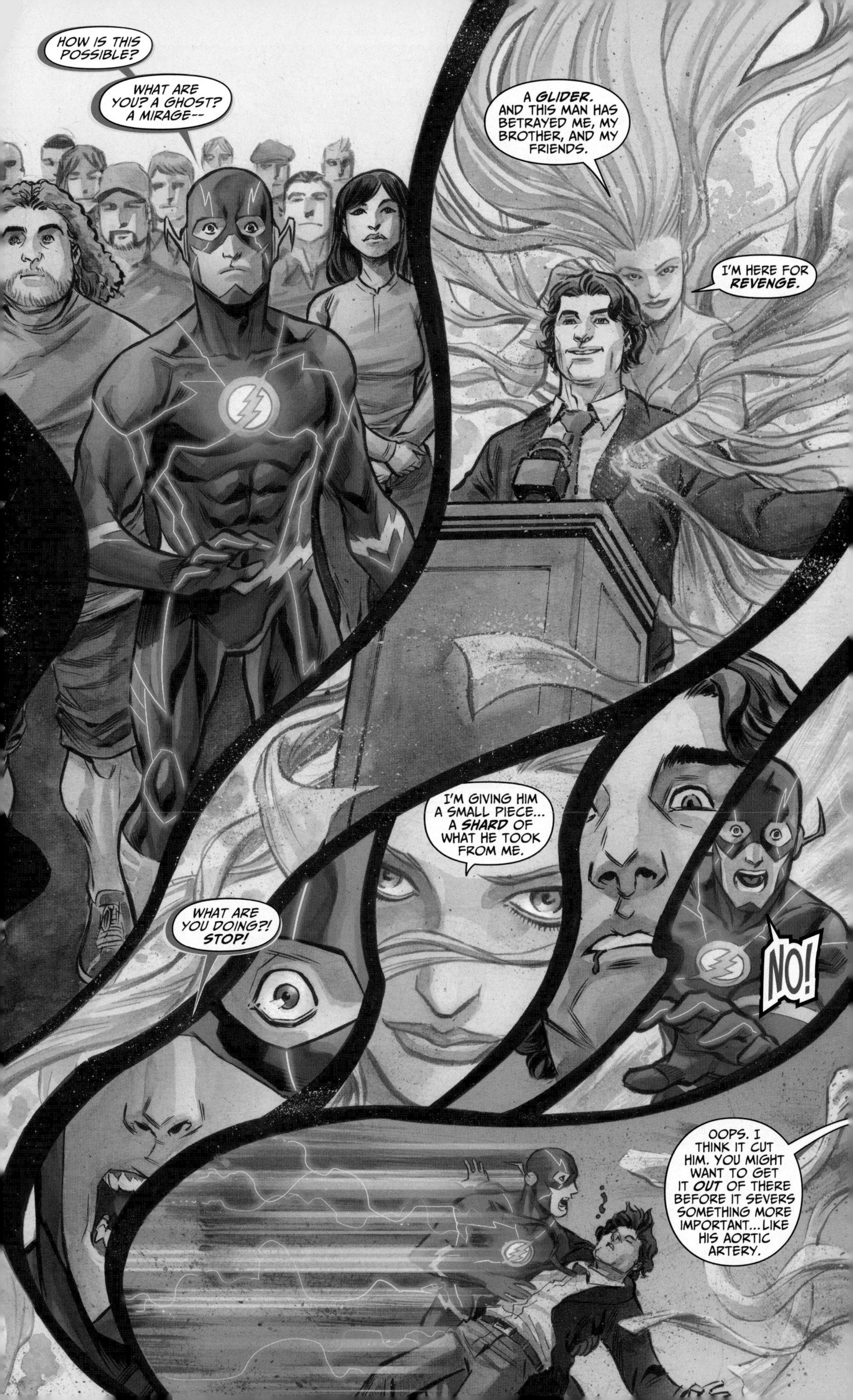
HOW IS THIS POSSIBLE?
WHAT ARE YOU? A GHOST? A MIRAGE--
A GLIDER. AND THIS MAN HAS BETRAYED ME, MY BROTHER, AND MY FRIENDS.
I'M HERE FOR REVENGE.
I'M GIVING HIM A SMALL PIECE... A SHARD OF WHAT HE TOOK FROM ME.
WHAT ARE YOU DOING?! STOP!
NO!
OOPS. I THINK IT CUT HIM. YOU MIGHT WANT TO GET IT OUT OF THERE BEFORE IT SEVERS SOMETHING MORE IMPORTANT... LIKE HIS AORTIC ARTERY.

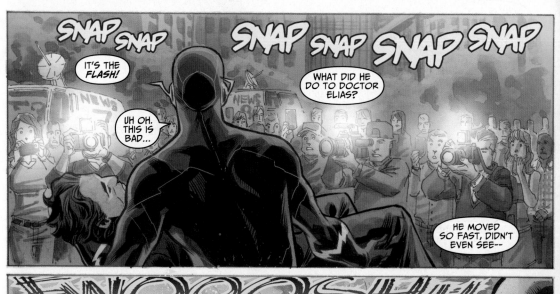

SNAP SNAP SNAP SNAP SNAP SNAP

IT'S THE FLASH!

WHAT DID HE DO TO DOCTOR ELIAS?

UH OH. THIS IS BAD...

HE MOVED SO FAST, DIDN'T EVEN SEE--

FWOOOSHHH

WHAT THE HELL!?!?

--I'LL HAVE TO CALL YOU BACK!

GOOD JOB, MICK...THAT WALL OF FIRE SHOULD KEEP THEM OUTTA THE WAY. YOU KNOW WHAT TO DO NEXT.

YEAH, YEAH. BUT I'M GONNA NEED A LIFT.

...AND IT'S GONNA GET A LOT WORSE IF I CAN'T GET THIS SHARD OUT OF ELIAS.

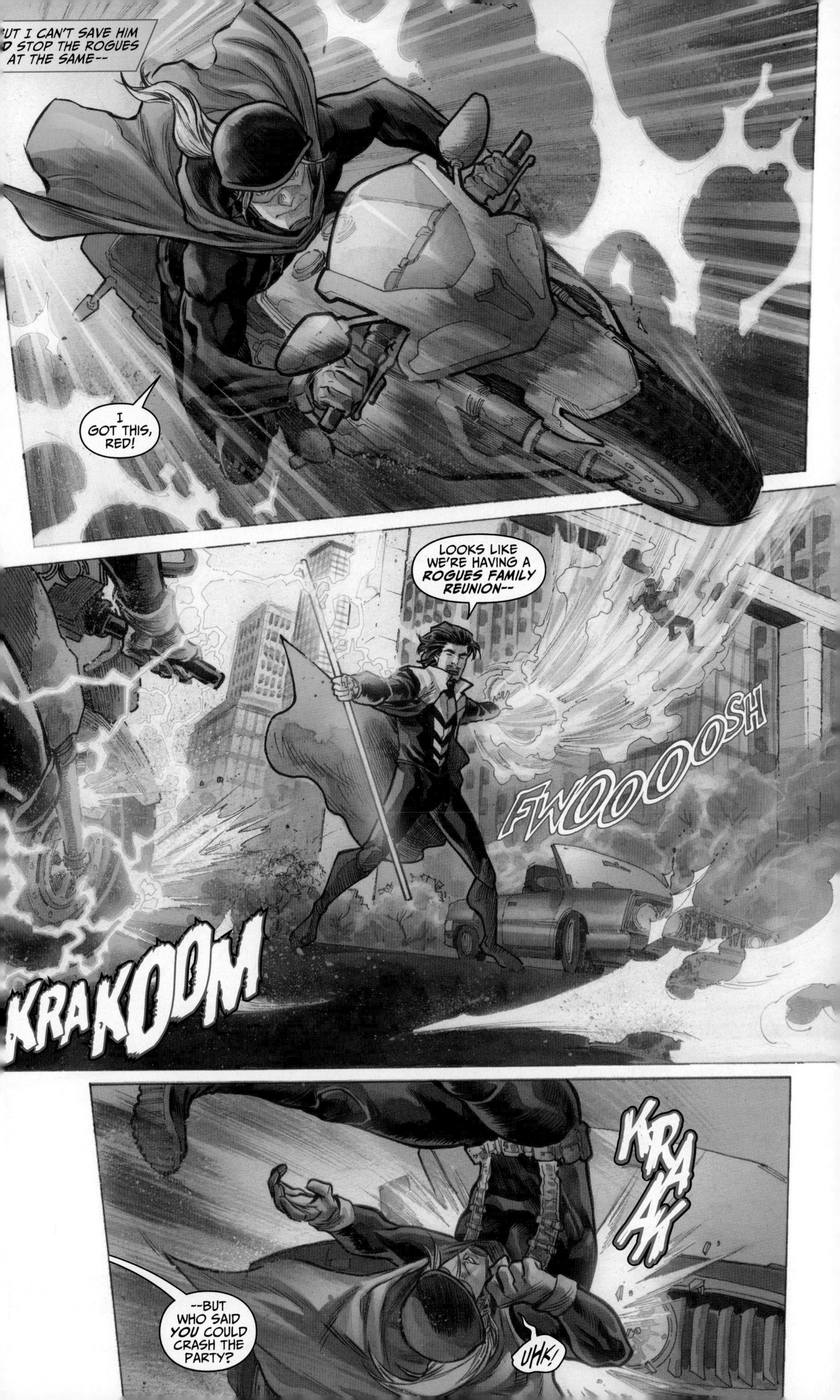

'UT I CAN'T SAVE HIM
D STOP THE ROGUES
AT THE SAME--
I GOT THIS, RED!
LOOKS LIKE WE'RE HAVING A ROGUES FAMILY REUNION--
FWOOOOOSH
KRAKOOM
KRAAK
--BUT WHO SAID YOU COULD CRASH THE PARTY?
UHK!

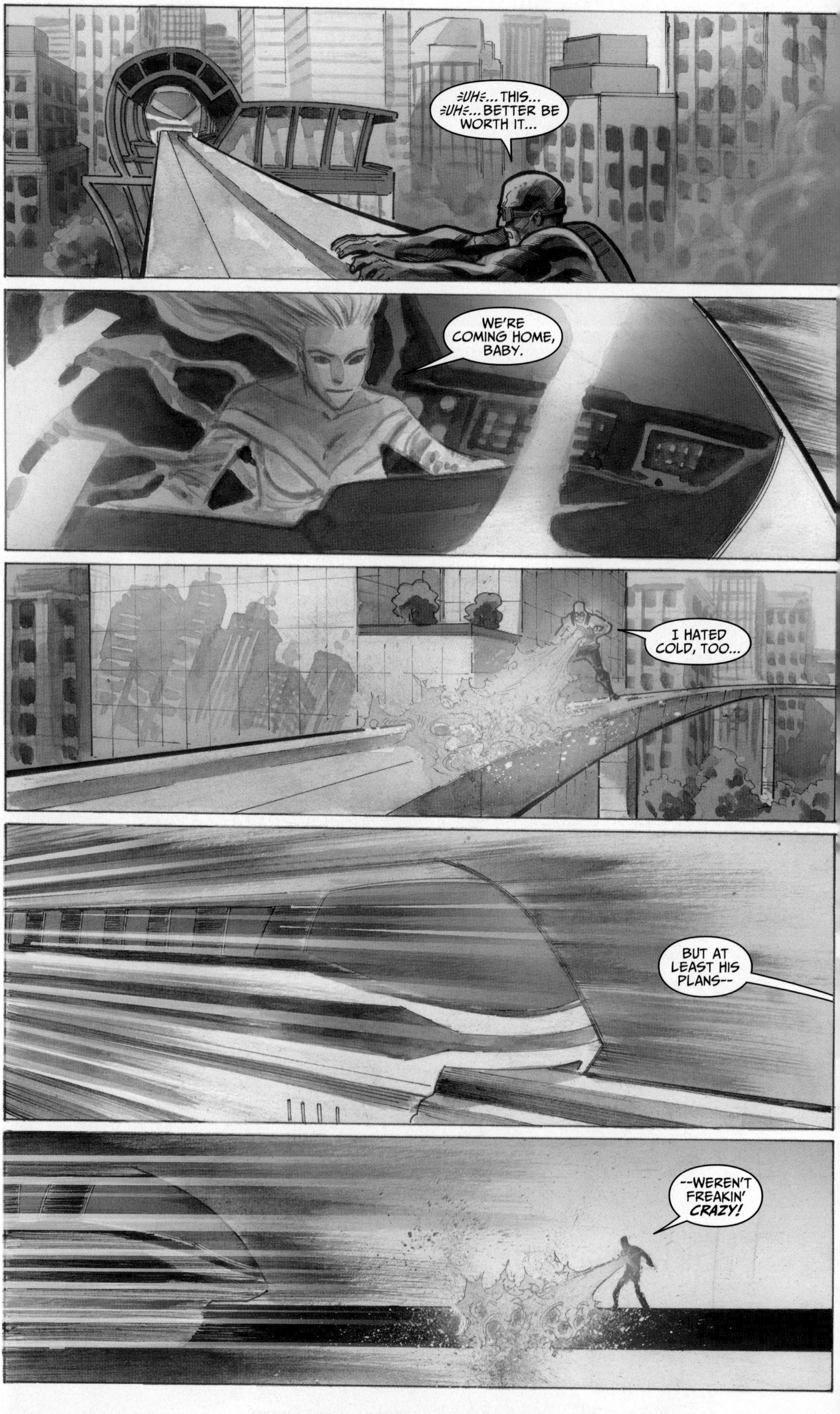
≡UH≡... THIS... ≡UH≡... BETTER BE WORTH IT...
WE'RE COMING HOME, BABY.
I HATED COLD, TOO...
BUT AT LEAST HIS PLANS--
--WEREN'T FREAKIN' *CRAZY!*

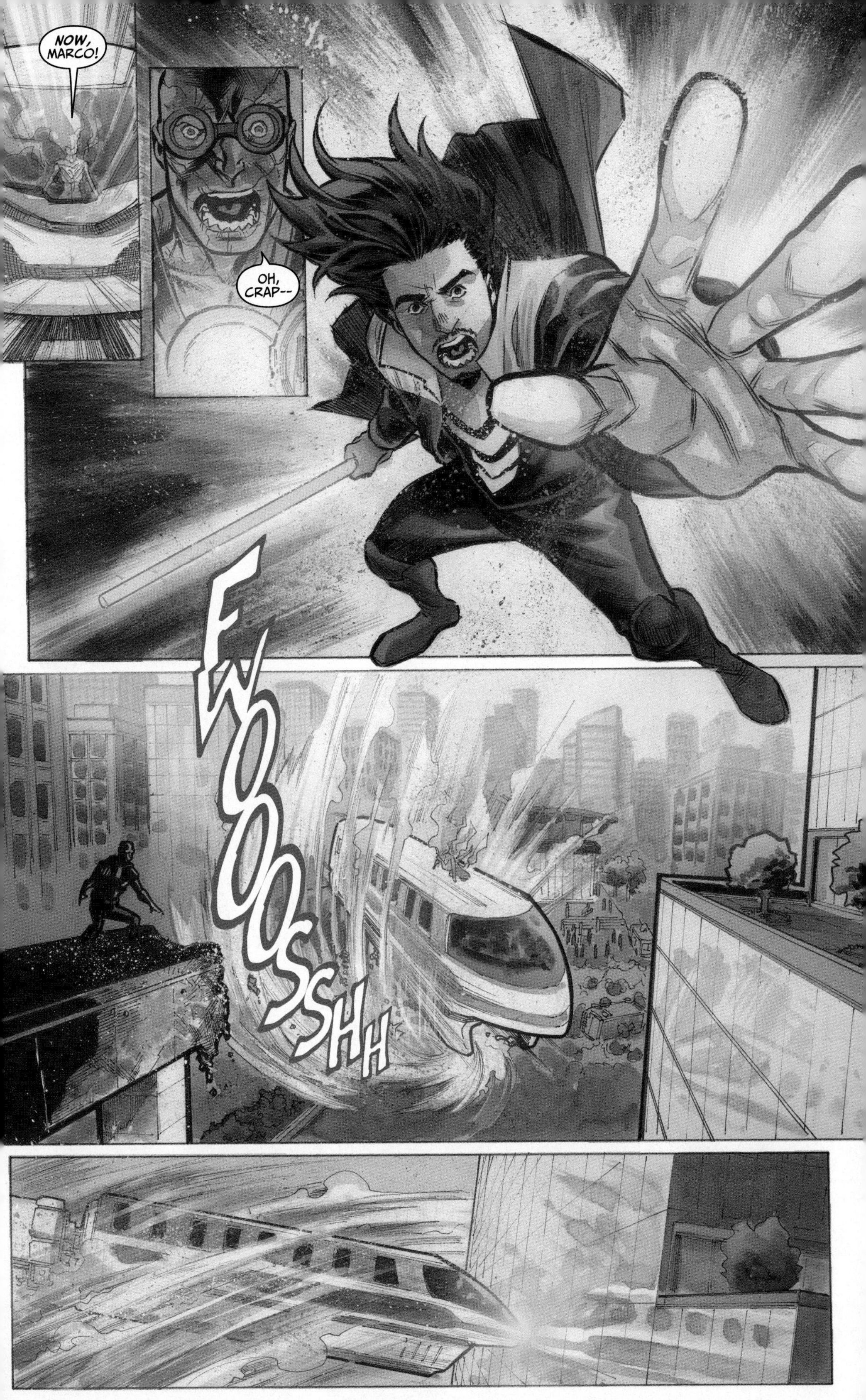
NOW, MARCO!
OH, CRAP--
FWOOOSSHH

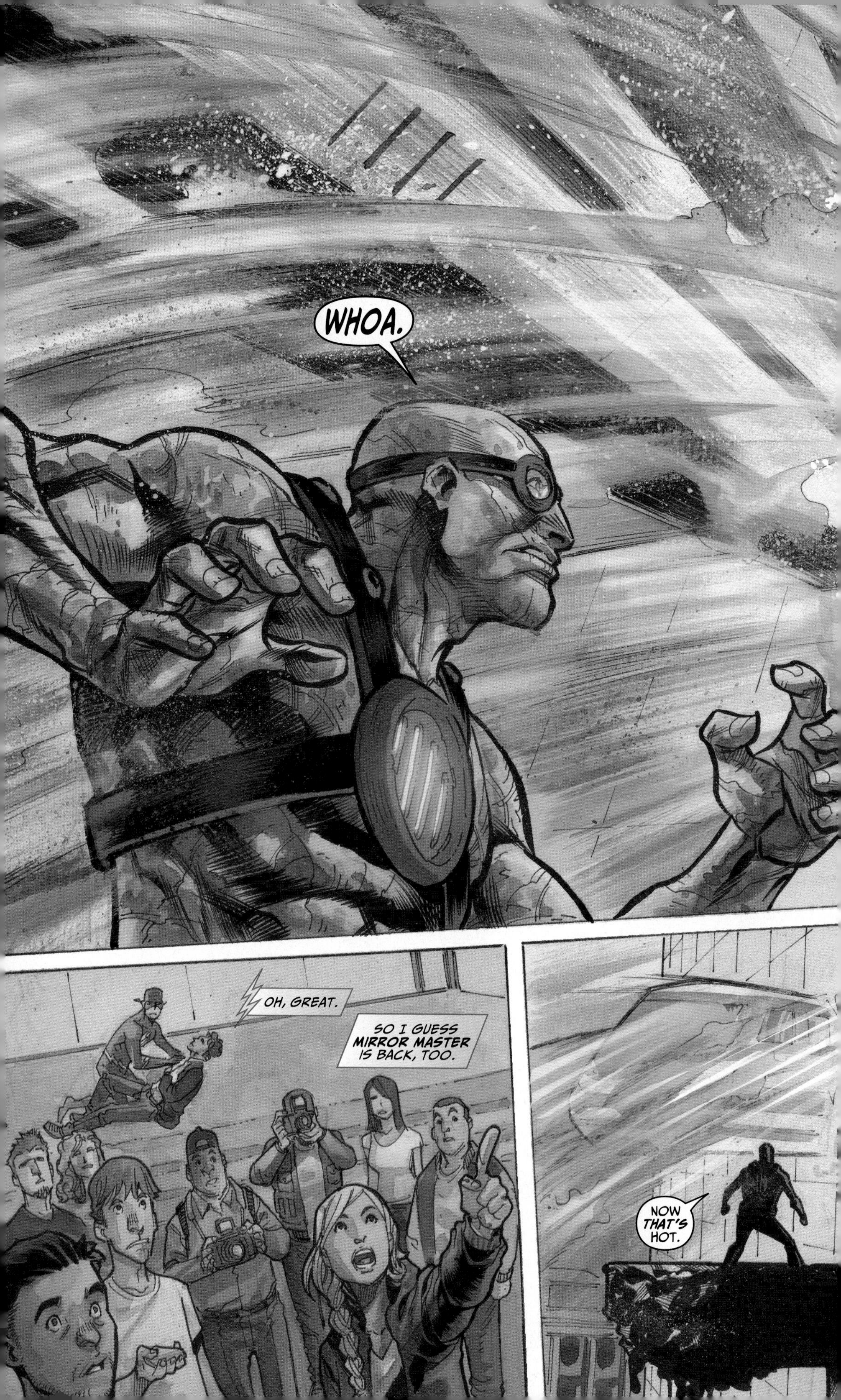
WHOA.
OH, GREAT.
SO I GUESS MIRROR MASTER IS BACK, TOO.
NOW THAT'S HOT.

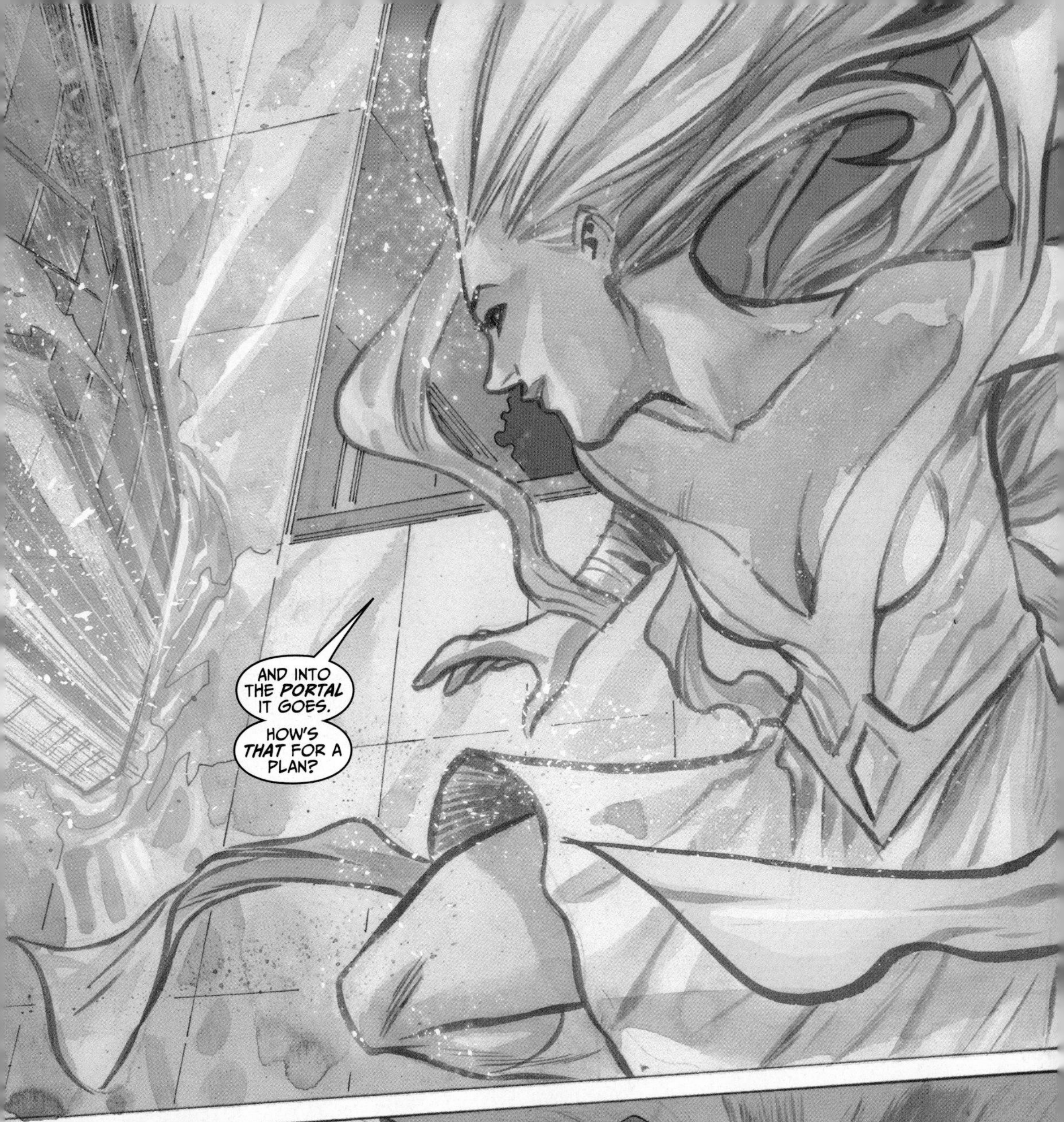
AND INTO THE PORTAL IT GOES.
HOW'S THAT FOR A PLAN?

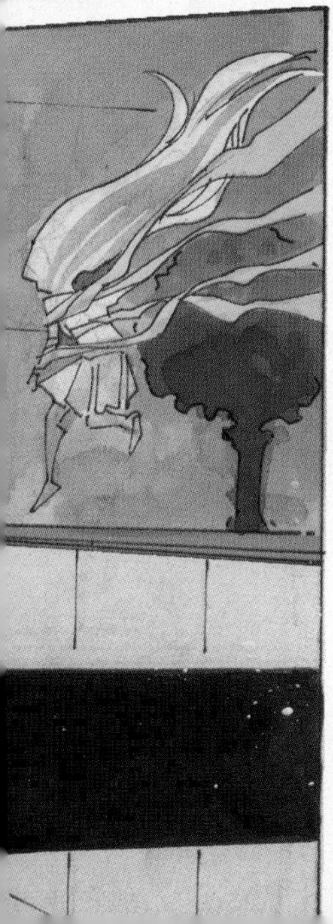

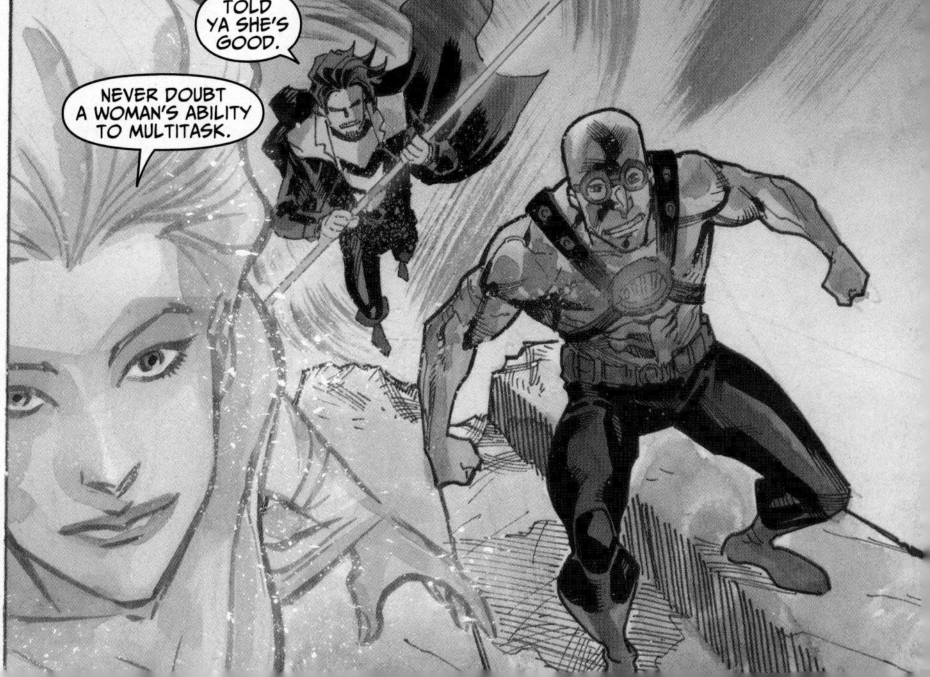
TOLD YA SHE'S GOOD.
NEVER DOUBT A WOMAN'S ABILITY TO MULTITASK.

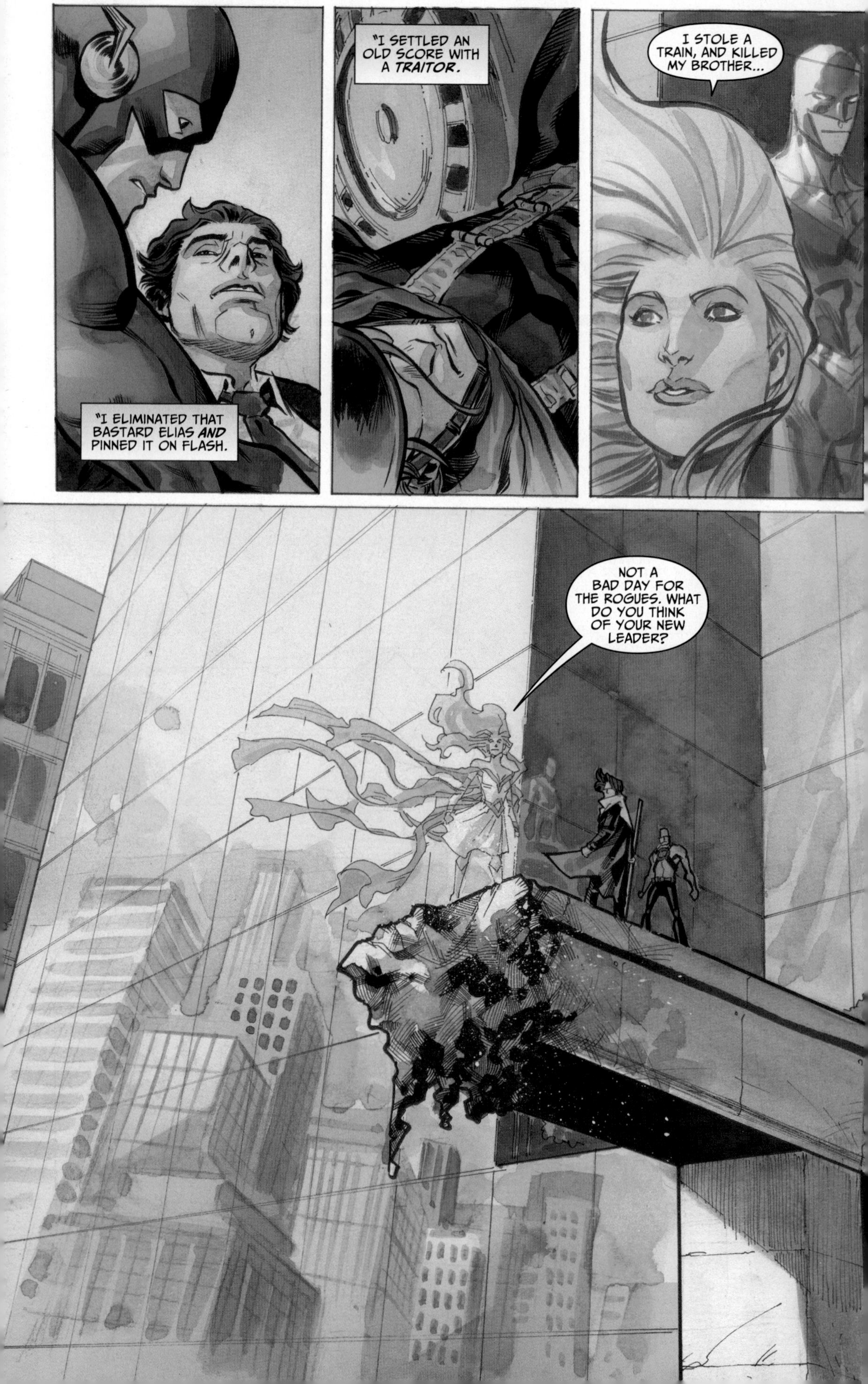
"I ELIMINATED THAT BASTARD ELIAS AND PINNED IT ON FLASH.
"I SETTLED AN OLD SCORE WITH A TRAITOR.
I STOLE A TRAIN, AND KILLED MY BROTHER...
NOT A BAD DAY FOR THE ROGUES. WHAT DO YOU THINK OF YOUR NEW LEADER?

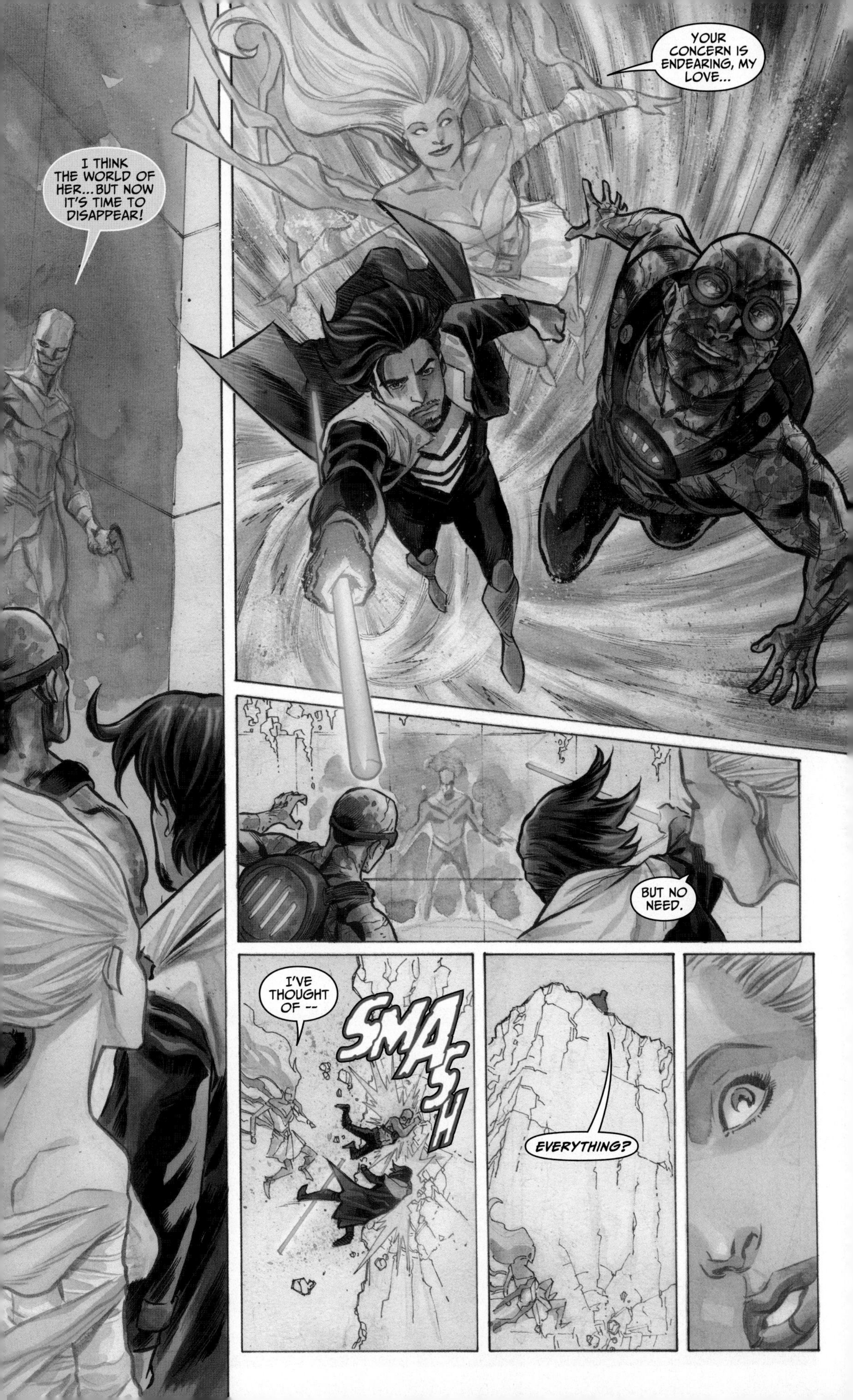
YOUR CONCERN IS ENDEARING, MY LOVE...
I THINK THE WORLD OF HER...BUT NOW IT'S TIME TO DISAPPEAR!
BUT NO NEED.
I'VE THOUGHT OF --
SMASH
EVERYTHING?

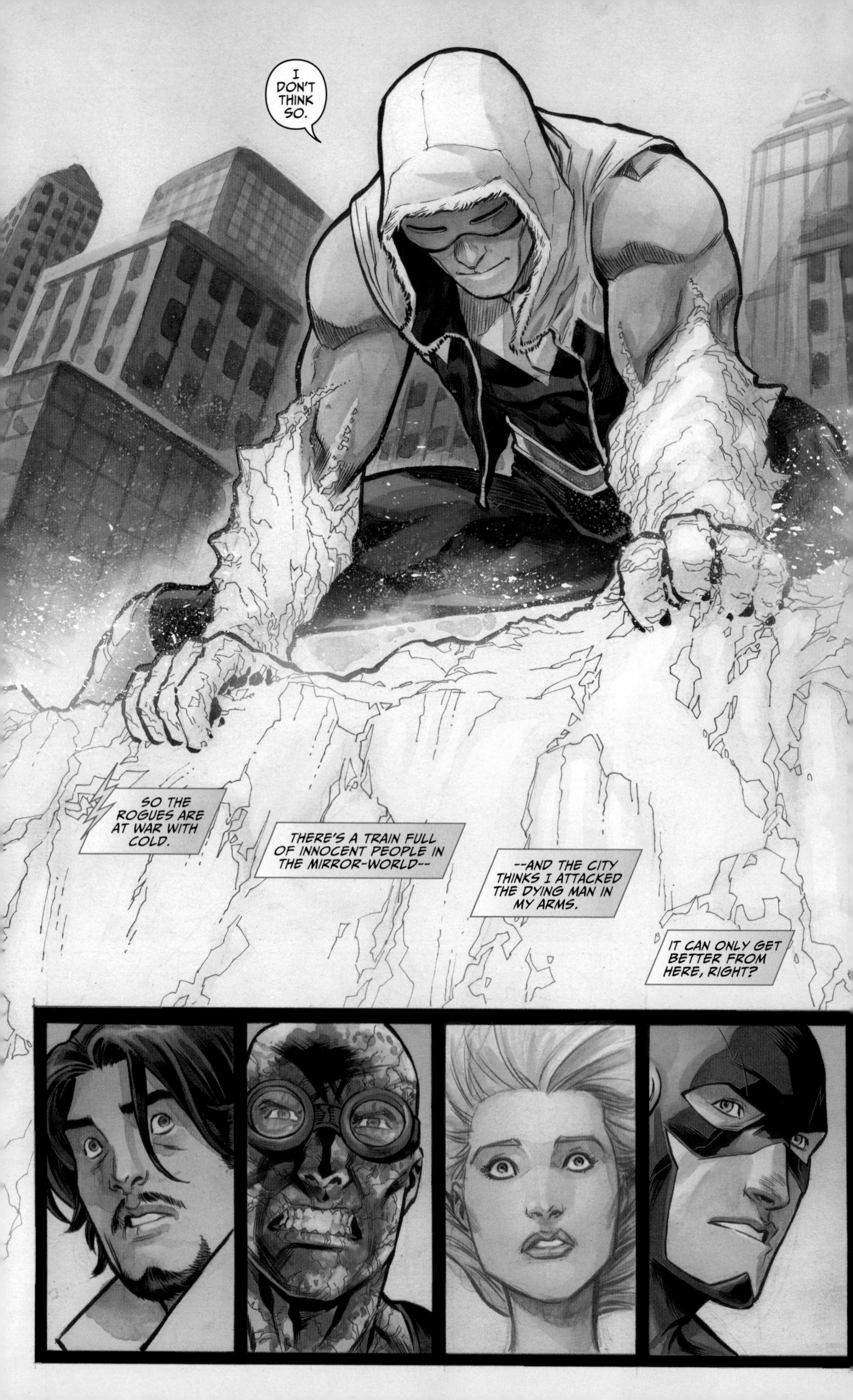
I DON'T THINK SO.
SO THE ROGUES ARE AT WAR WITH COLD.
THERE'S A TRAIN FULL OF INNOCENT PEOPLE IN THE MIRROR-WORLD--
--AND THE CITY THINKS I ATTACKED THE DYING MAN IN MY ARMS.
IT CAN ONLY GET BETTER FROM HERE, RIGHT?

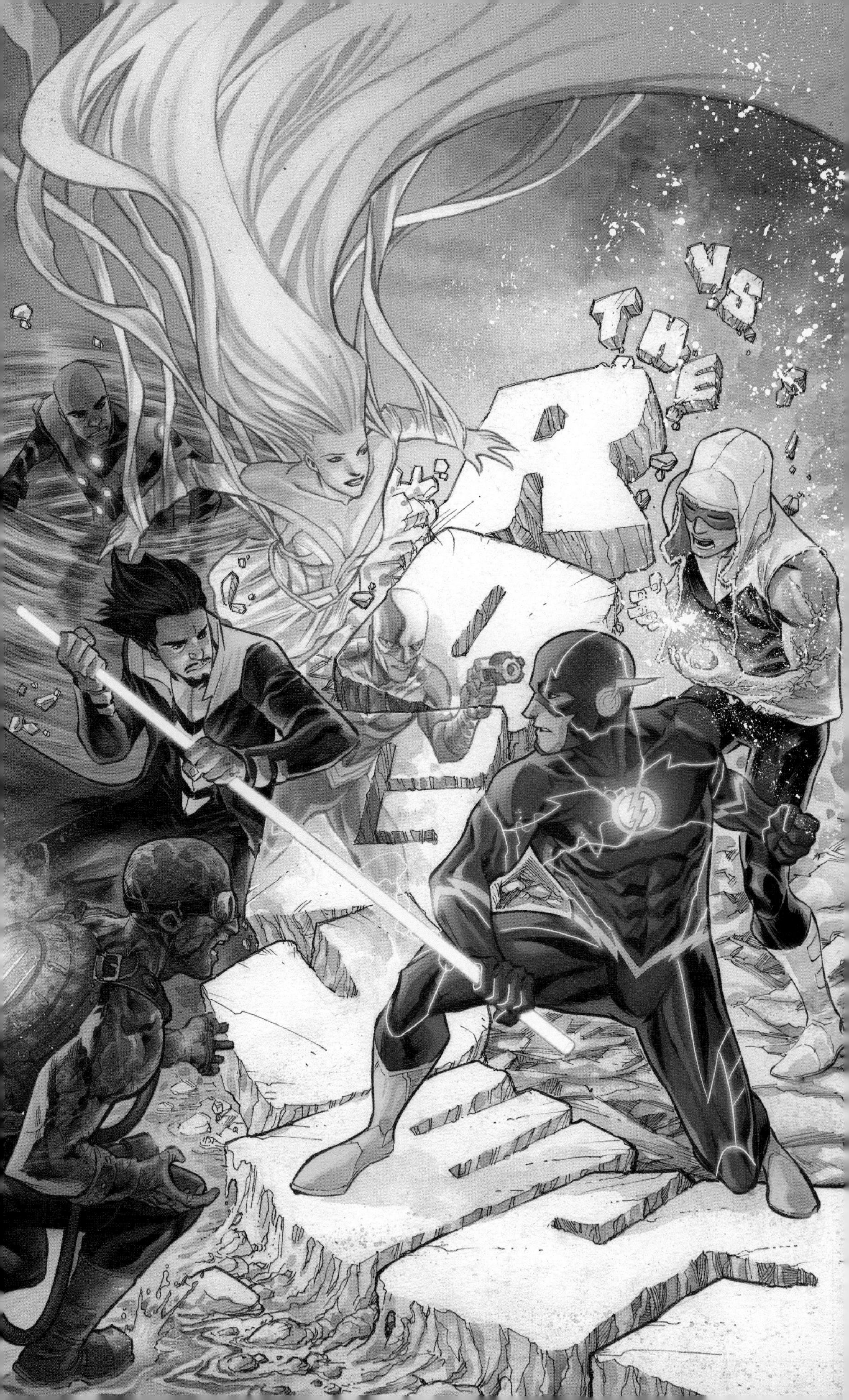
VS
THE

FRANCIS MANAPUL & BRIAN BUCCELLATO writers FRANCIS MANAPUL breakdowns MARCUS TO & RAY McCARTHY artists – chapter one
SCOTT KOLINS artist – chapter two DIOGENES NEVES & OCLAIR ALBERT artists – chapter three
MARCIO TAKARA artist – chapter four WES CRAIG artist – chapter five

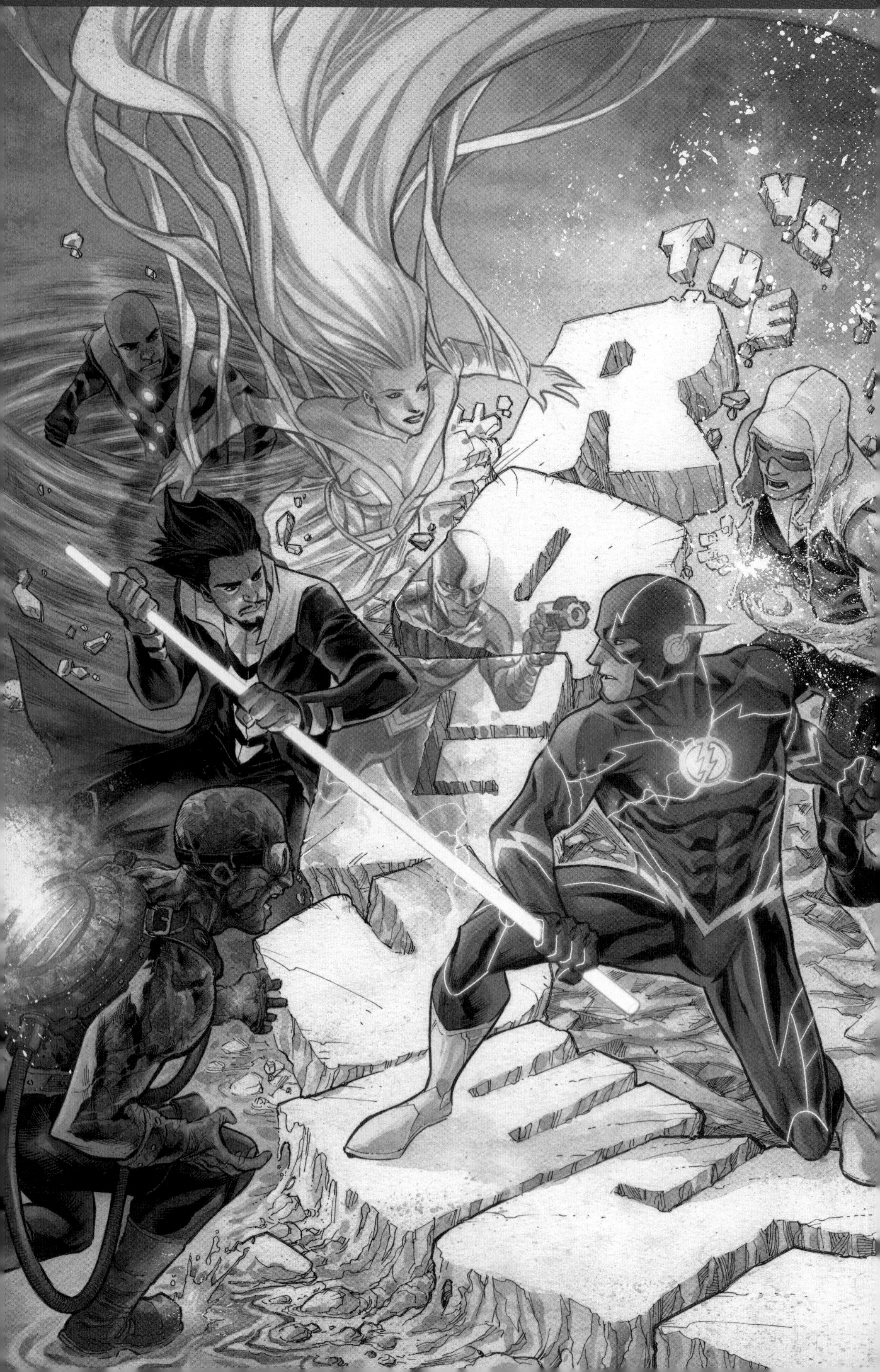
THE
VS

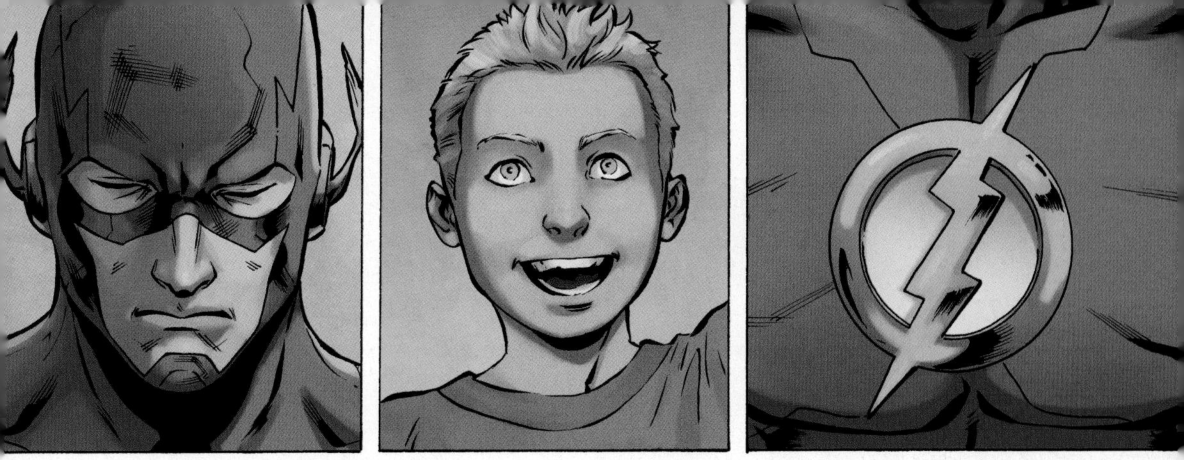

UNITED THEY FALL
CHAPTER 1: THE FLATS

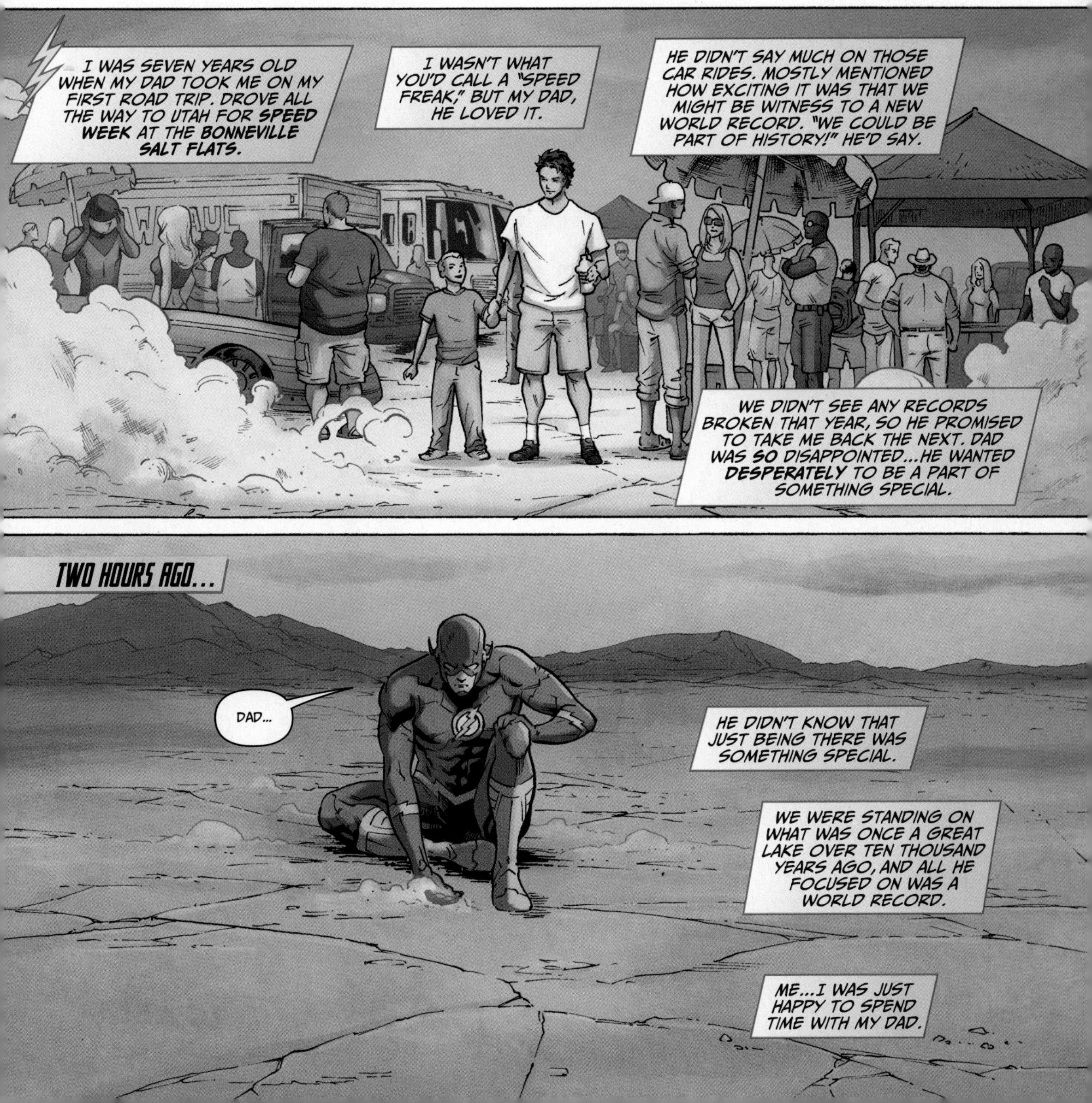
I WAS SEVEN YEARS OLD WHEN MY DAD TOOK ME ON MY FIRST ROAD TRIP. DROVE ALL THE WAY TO UTAH FOR SPEED WEEK AT THE BONNEVILLE SALT FLATS.
I WASN'T WHAT YOU'D CALL A "SPEED FREAK," BUT MY DAD, HE LOVED IT.
HE DIDN'T SAY MUCH ON THOSE CAR RIDES. MOSTLY MENTIONED HOW EXCITING IT WAS THAT WE MIGHT BE WITNESS TO A NEW WORLD RECORD. "WE COULD BE PART OF HISTORY!" HE'D SAY.
WE DIDN'T SEE ANY RECORDS BROKEN THAT YEAR, SO HE PROMISED TO TAKE ME BACK THE NEXT. DAD WAS SO DISAPPOINTED...HE WANTED DESPERATELY TO BE A PART OF SOMETHING SPECIAL.
TWO HOURS AGO...
DAD...
HE DIDN'T KNOW THAT JUST BEING THERE WAS SOMETHING SPECIAL.
WE WERE STANDING ON WHAT WAS ONCE A GREAT LAKE OVER TEN THOUSAND YEARS AGO, AND ALL HE FOCUSED ON WAS A WORLD RECORD.
ME...I WAS JUST HAPPY TO SPEND TIME WITH MY DAD.

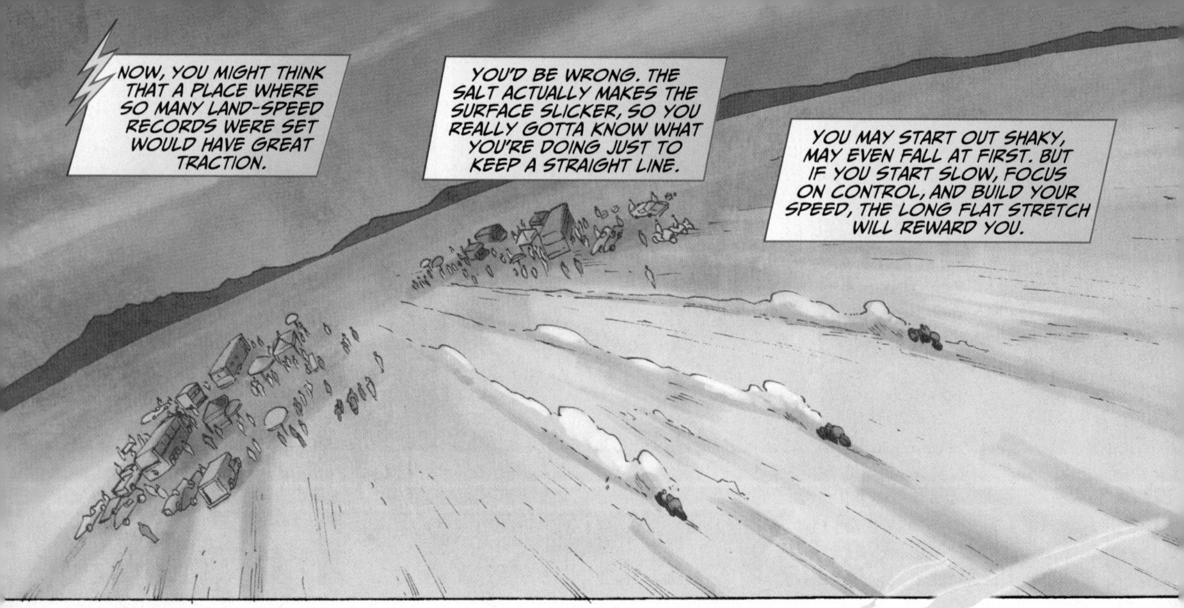
NOW, YOU MIGHT THINK THAT A PLACE WHERE SO MANY LAND-SPEED RECORDS WERE SET WOULD HAVE GREAT TRACTION.
YOU'D BE WRONG. THE SALT ACTUALLY MAKES THE SURFACE SLICKER, SO YOU REALLY GOTTA KNOW WHAT YOU'RE DOING JUST TO KEEP A STRAIGHT LINE.
YOU MAY START OUT SHAKY, MAY EVEN FALL AT FIRST. BUT IF YOU START SLOW, FOCUS ON CONTROL, AND BUILD YOUR SPEED, THE LONG FLAT STRETCH WILL REWARD YOU.

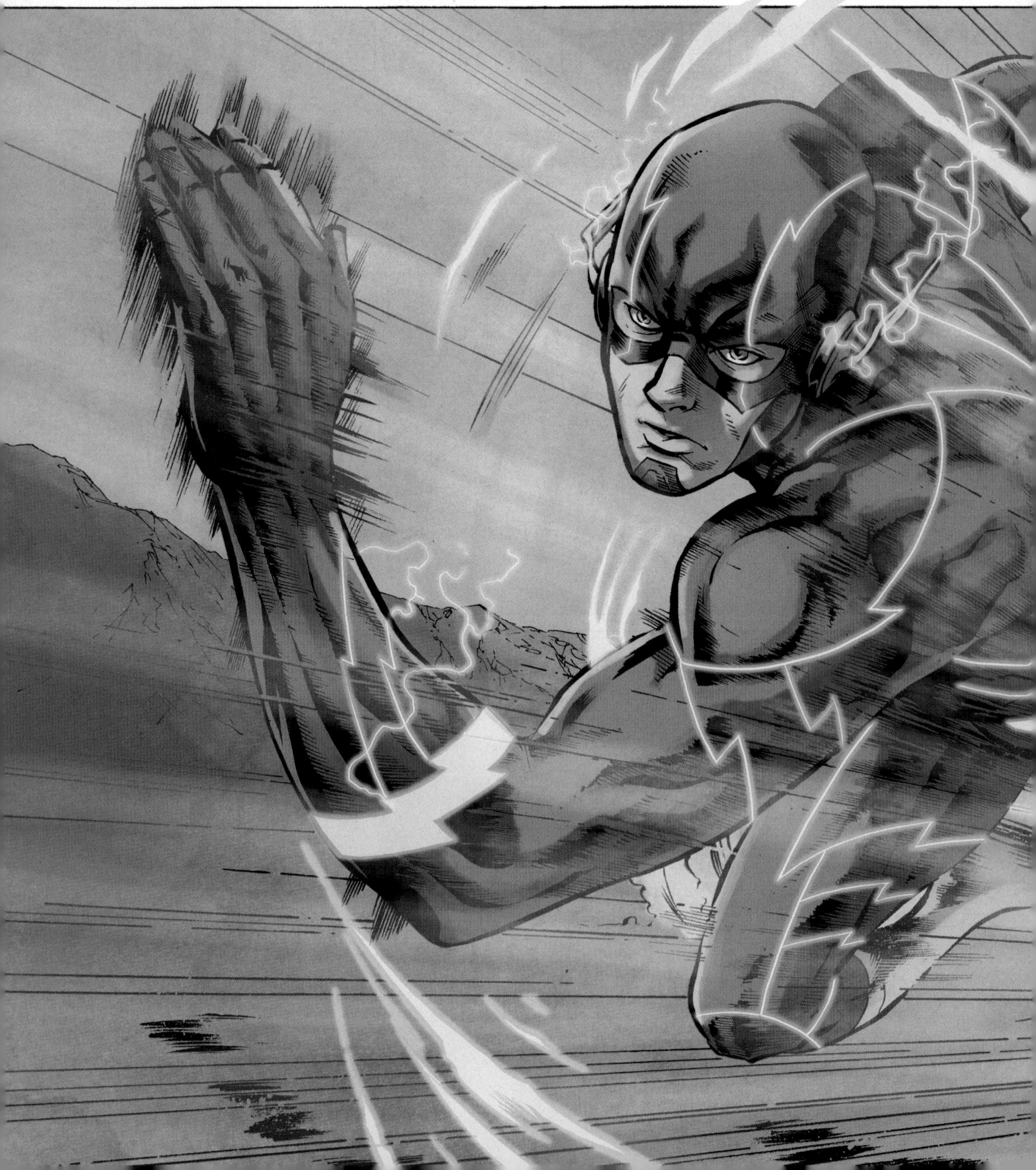

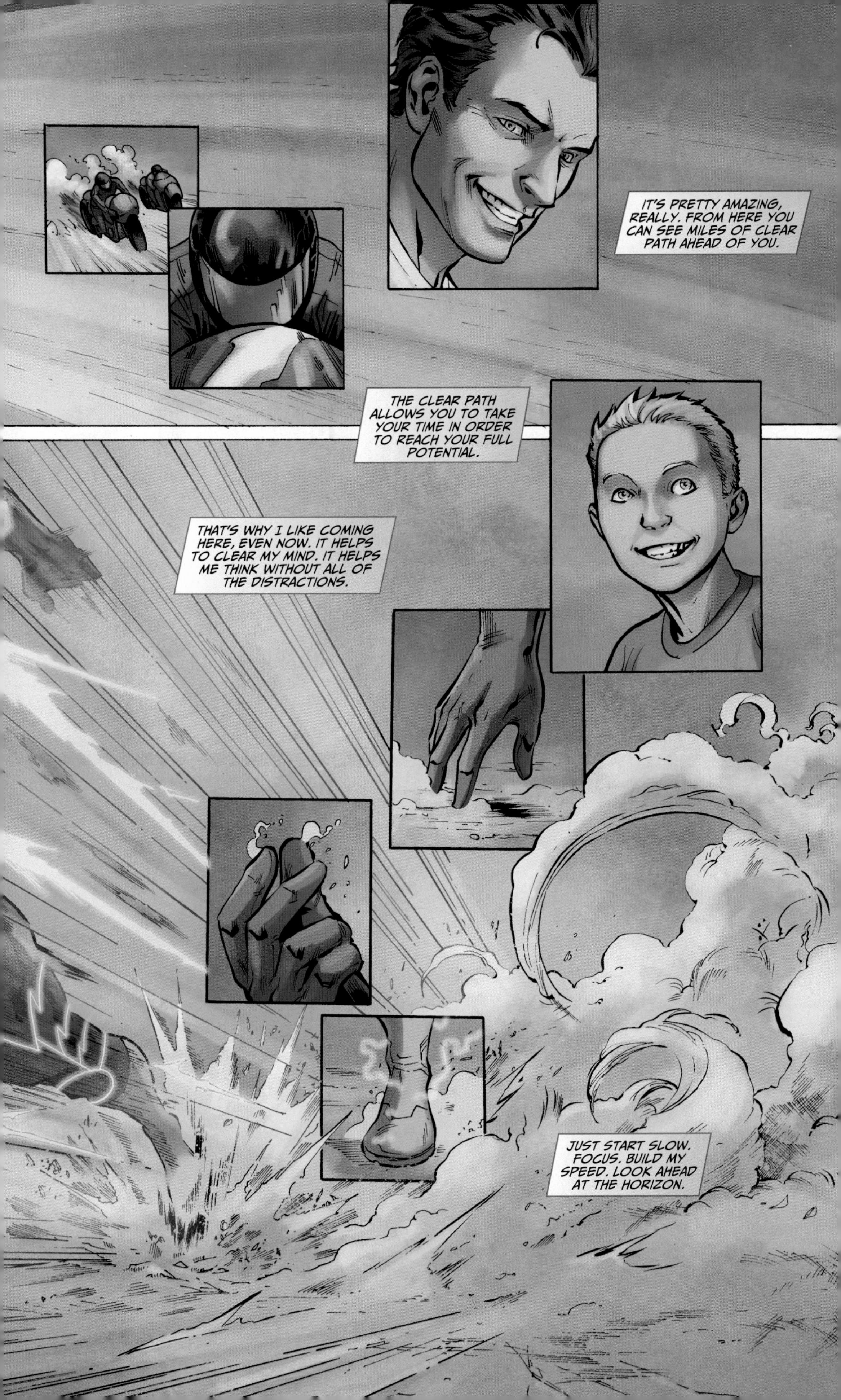
IT'S PRETTY AMAZING, REALLY. FROM HERE YOU CAN SEE MILES OF CLEAR PATH AHEAD OF YOU.
THE CLEAR PATH ALLOWS YOU TO TAKE YOUR TIME IN ORDER TO REACH YOUR FULL POTENTIAL.
THAT'S WHY I LIKE COMING HERE, EVEN NOW. IT HELPS TO CLEAR MY MIND. IT HELPS ME THINK WITHOUT ALL OF THE DISTRACTIONS.
JUST START SLOW. FOCUS. BUILD MY SPEED. LOOK AHEAD AT THE HORIZON.

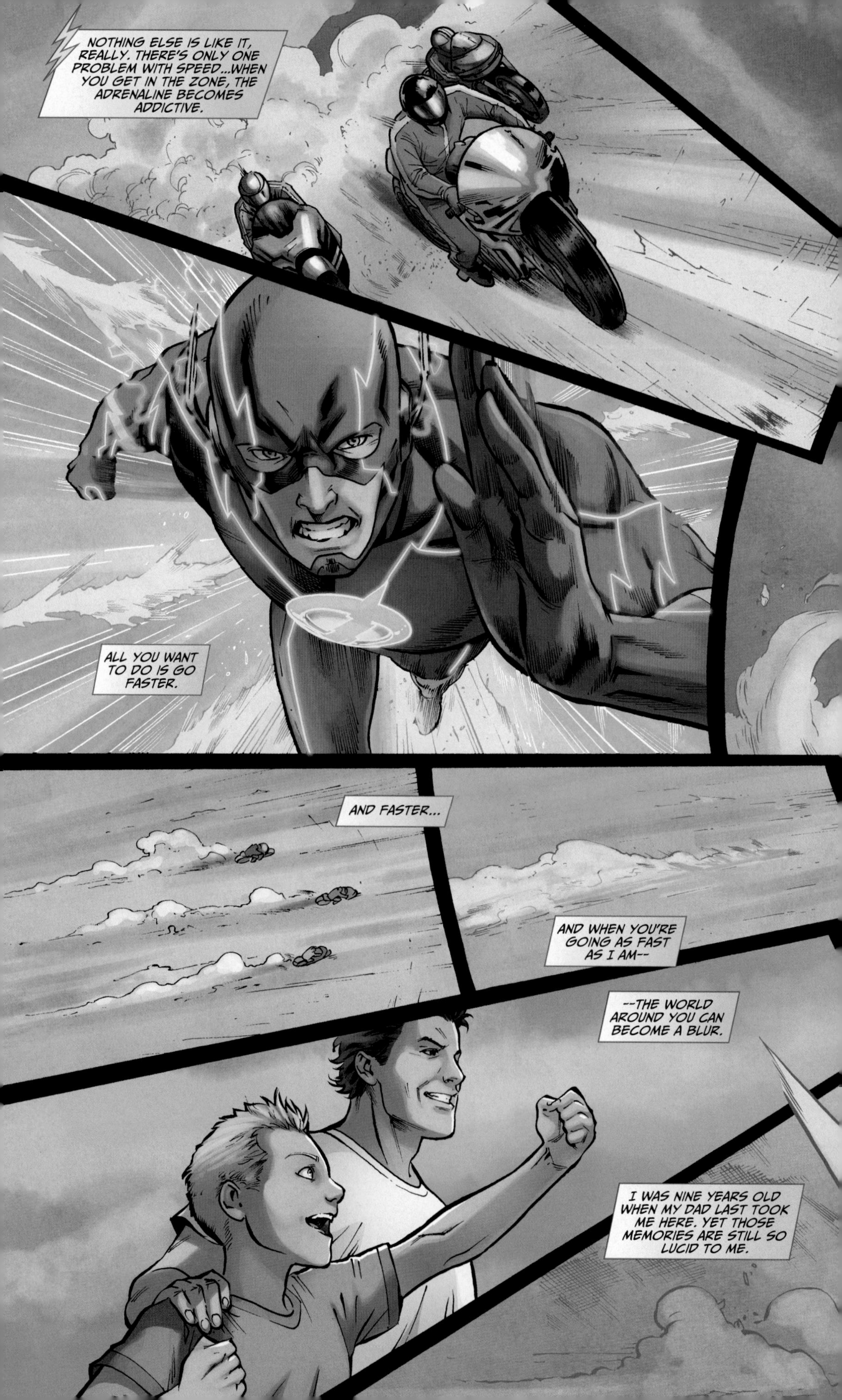
NOTHING ELSE IS LIKE IT, REALLY. THERE'S ONLY ONE PROBLEM WITH SPEED...WHEN YOU GET IN THE ZONE, THE ADRENALINE BECOMES ADDICTIVE.
ALL YOU WANT TO DO IS GO FASTER.
AND FASTER...
AND WHEN YOU'RE GOING AS FAST AS I AM--
--THE WORLD AROUND YOU CAN BECOME A BLUR.
I WAS NINE YEARS OLD WHEN MY DAD LAST TOOK ME HERE. YET THOSE MEMORIES ARE STILL SO LUCID TO ME.

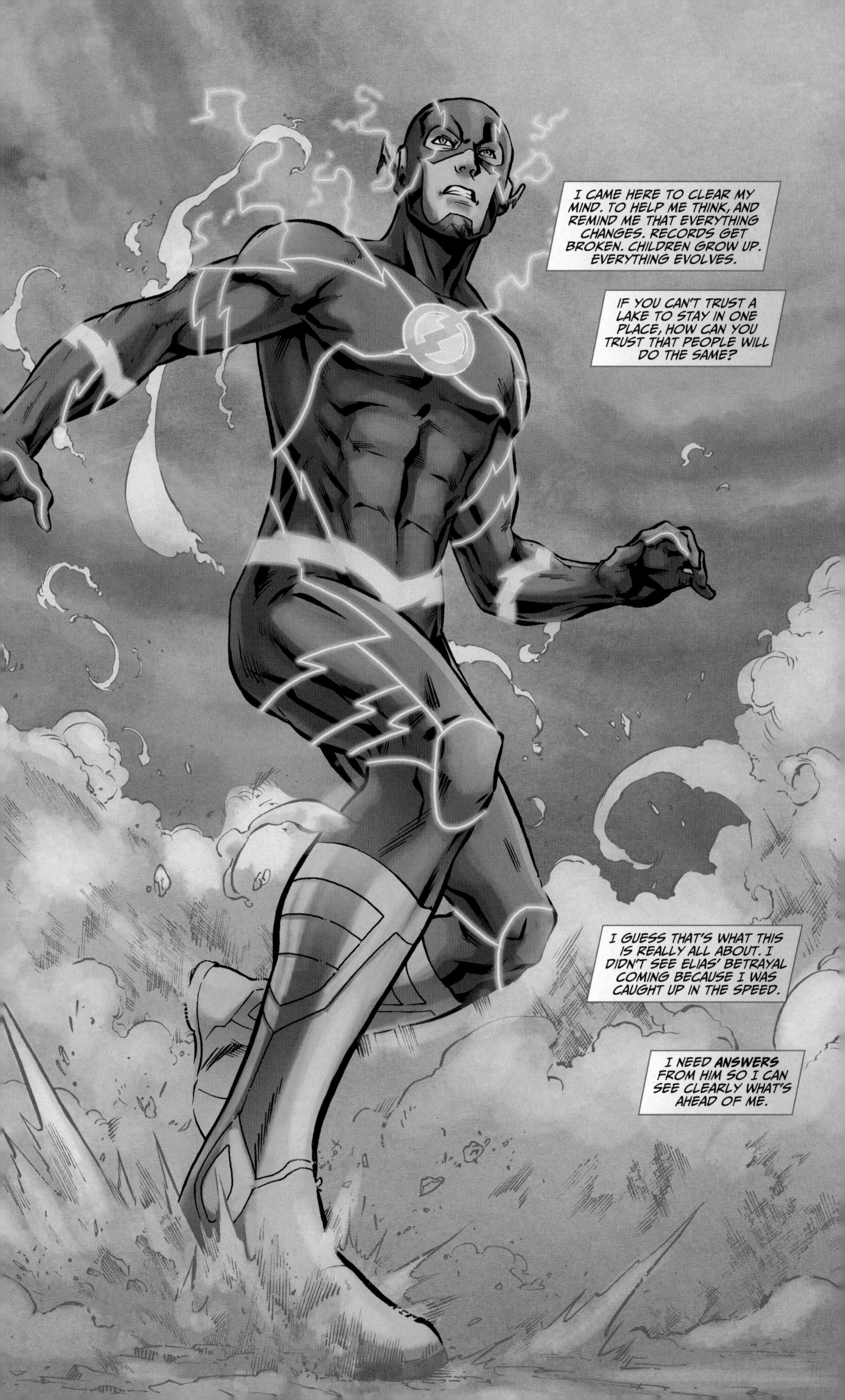
I CAME HERE TO CLEAR MY MIND. TO HELP ME THINK, AND REMIND ME THAT EVERYTHING CHANGES. RECORDS GET BROKEN. CHILDREN GROW UP. EVERYTHING EVOLVES.
IF YOU CAN'T TRUST A LAKE TO STAY IN ONE PLACE, HOW CAN YOU TRUST THAT PEOPLE WILL DO THE SAME?
I GUESS THAT'S WHAT THIS IS REALLY ALL ABOUT. I DIDN'T SEE ELIAS' BETRAYAL COMING BECAUSE I WAS CAUGHT UP IN THE SPEED.
I NEED **ANSWERS** FROM HIM SO I CAN SEE CLEARLY WHAT'S AHEAD OF ME.

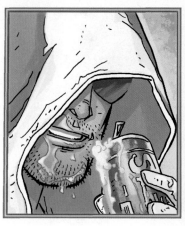

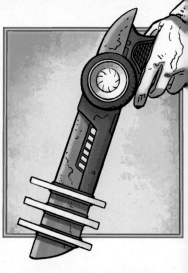

CHAPTER 2: THE OPPORTUNITY

A YEAR AND A HALF AGO...

IT'S EASY TO LOOK AT THIS PICTURE AND SAY THE ROGUES ARE A BUNCH OF "BAD GUYS." LET'S BE HONEST... WHAT WE'RE DOING IS TECHNICALLY ILLEGAL.

TRICKSTER

HEATWAVE

ALL OF YOU... FREEZE!!!!

CAPTAIN COLD

WEATHER WIZARD

BUT HERE'S THE THING... WE LIVE IN THE GREATEST COUNTRY IN THE WORLD-- THE LAND OF OPPORTUNITY, RIGHT? A PLACE WHERE EVERY MAN HAS THE RIGHT TO EARN A LIVING THE BEST WAY HE KNOWS HOW.

IS IT OUR FAULT THAT FOR US, THE BEST WAY MEANS ROBBING AND THIEVING?

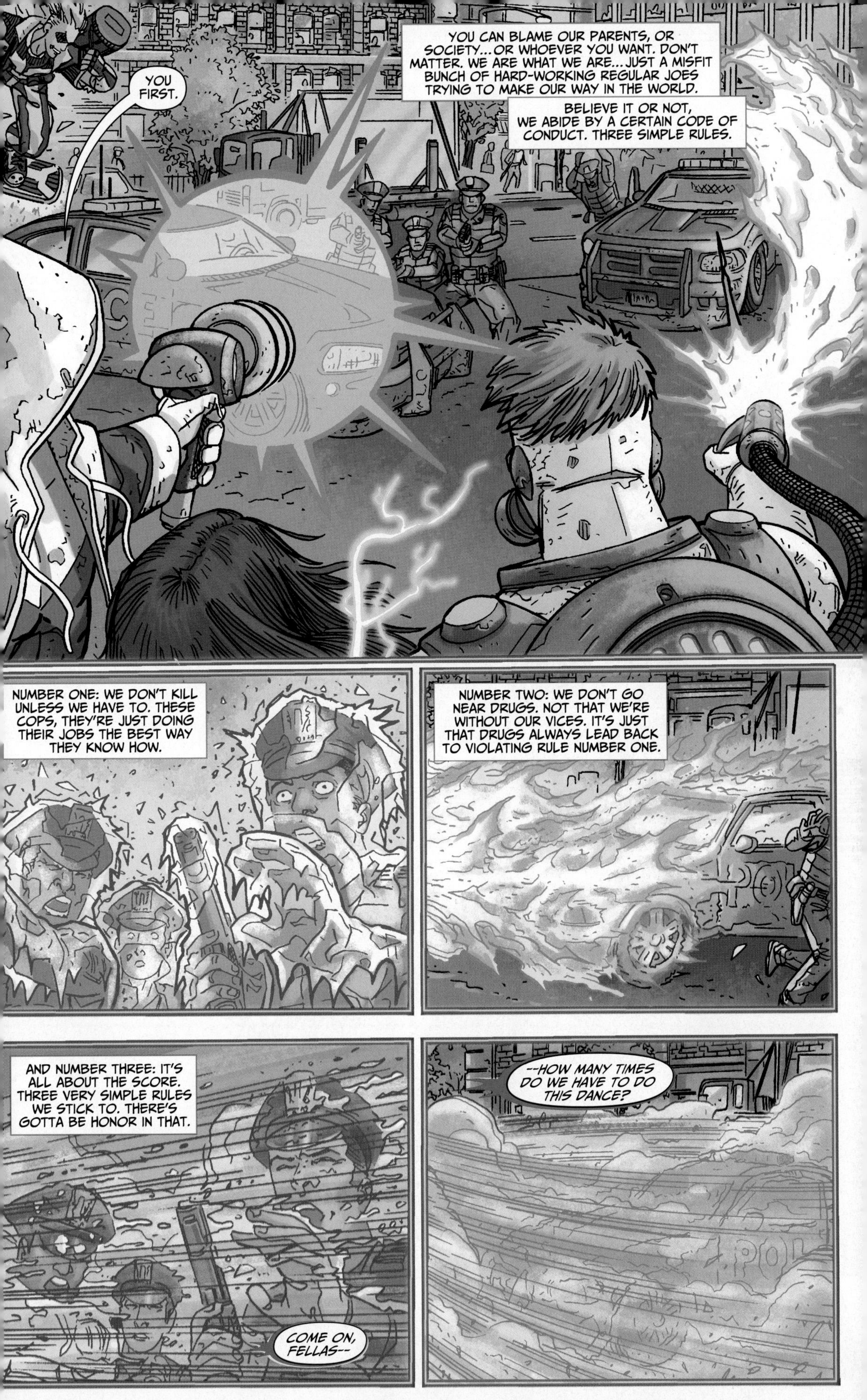
YOU CAN BLAME OUR PARENTS, OR SOCIETY...OR WHOEVER YOU WANT. DON'T MATTER. WE ARE WHAT WE ARE...JUST A MISFIT BUNCH OF HARD-WORKING REGULAR JOES TRYING TO MAKE OUR WAY IN THE WORLD.
YOU FIRST.
BELIEVE IT OR NOT, WE ABIDE BY A CERTAIN CODE OF CONDUCT. THREE SIMPLE RULES.
NUMBER ONE: WE DON'T KILL UNLESS WE HAVE TO. THESE COPS, THEY'RE JUST DOING THEIR JOBS THE BEST WAY THEY KNOW HOW.
NUMBER TWO: WE DON'T GO NEAR DRUGS. NOT THAT WE'RE WITHOUT OUR VICES. IT'S JUST THAT DRUGS ALWAYS LEAD BACK TO VIOLATING RULE NUMBER ONE.
AND NUMBER THREE: IT'S ALL ABOUT THE SCORE. THREE VERY SIMPLE RULES WE STICK TO. THERE'S GOTTA BE HONOR IN THAT.
COME ON, FELLAS--
--HOW MANY TIMES DO WE HAVE TO DO THIS DANCE?

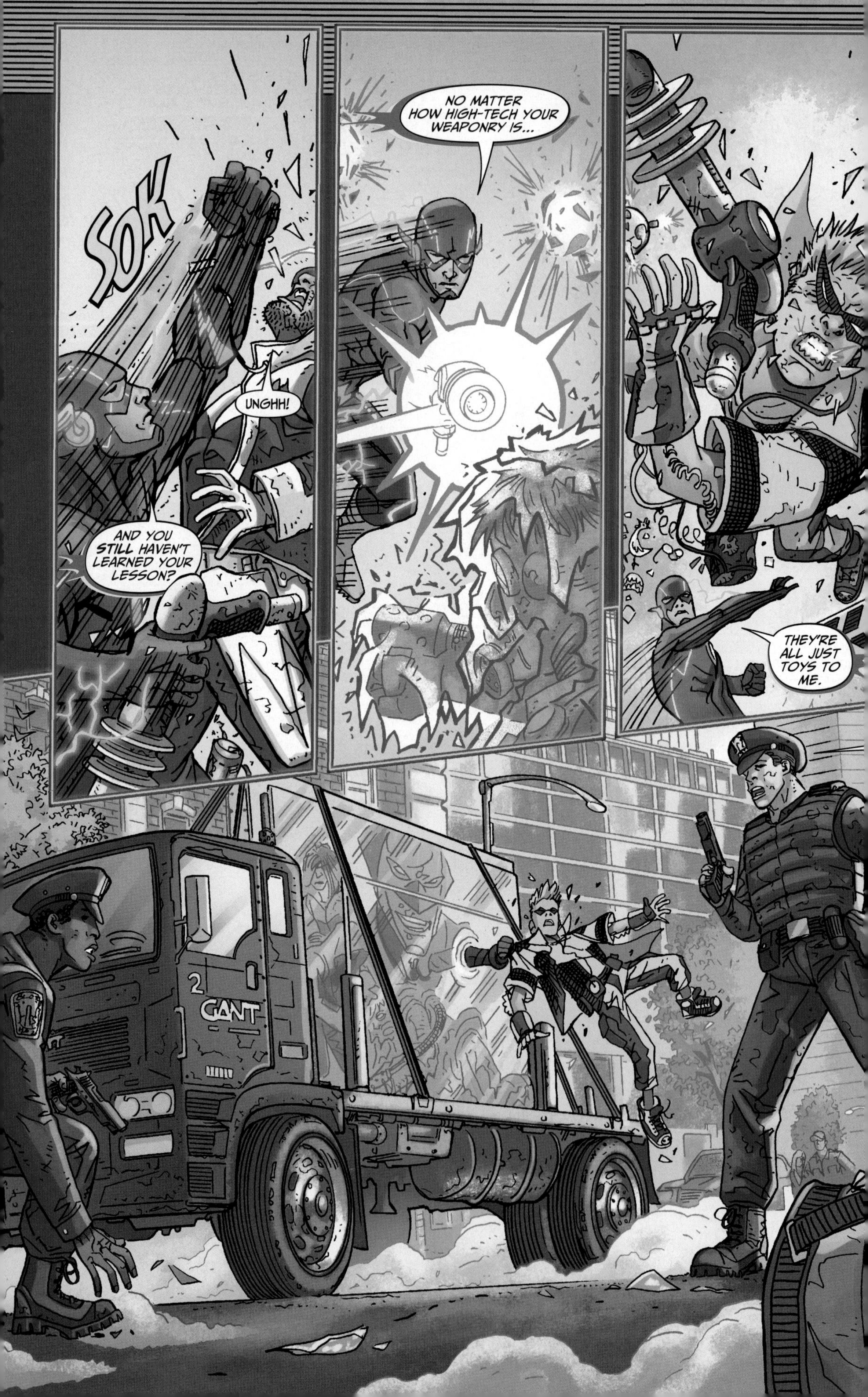
SOK
UNGHH!
AND YOU STILL HAVEN'T LEARNED YOUR LESSON?
NO MATTER HOW HIGH-TECH YOUR WEAPONRY IS...
THEY'RE ALL JUST TOYS TO ME.
2
GANT

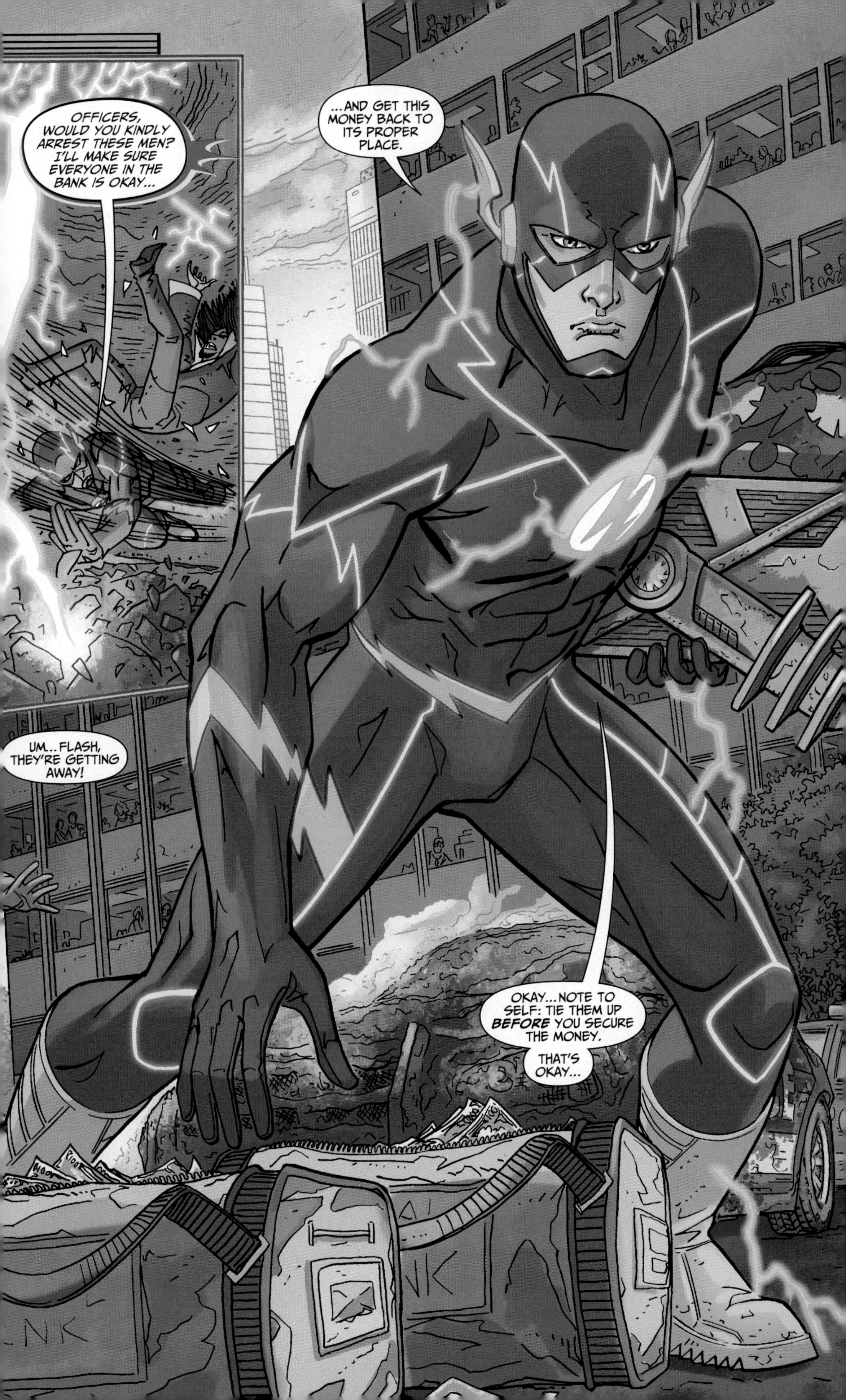
OFFICERS, WOULD YOU KINDLY ARREST THESE MEN? I'LL MAKE SURE EVERYONE IN THE BANK IS OKAY...
...AND GET THIS MONEY BACK TO ITS PROPER PLACE.
UM...FLASH, THEY'RE GETTING AWAY!
OKAY...NOTE TO SELF: TIE THEM UP **BEFORE** YOU SECURE THE MONEY.
THAT'S OKAY...

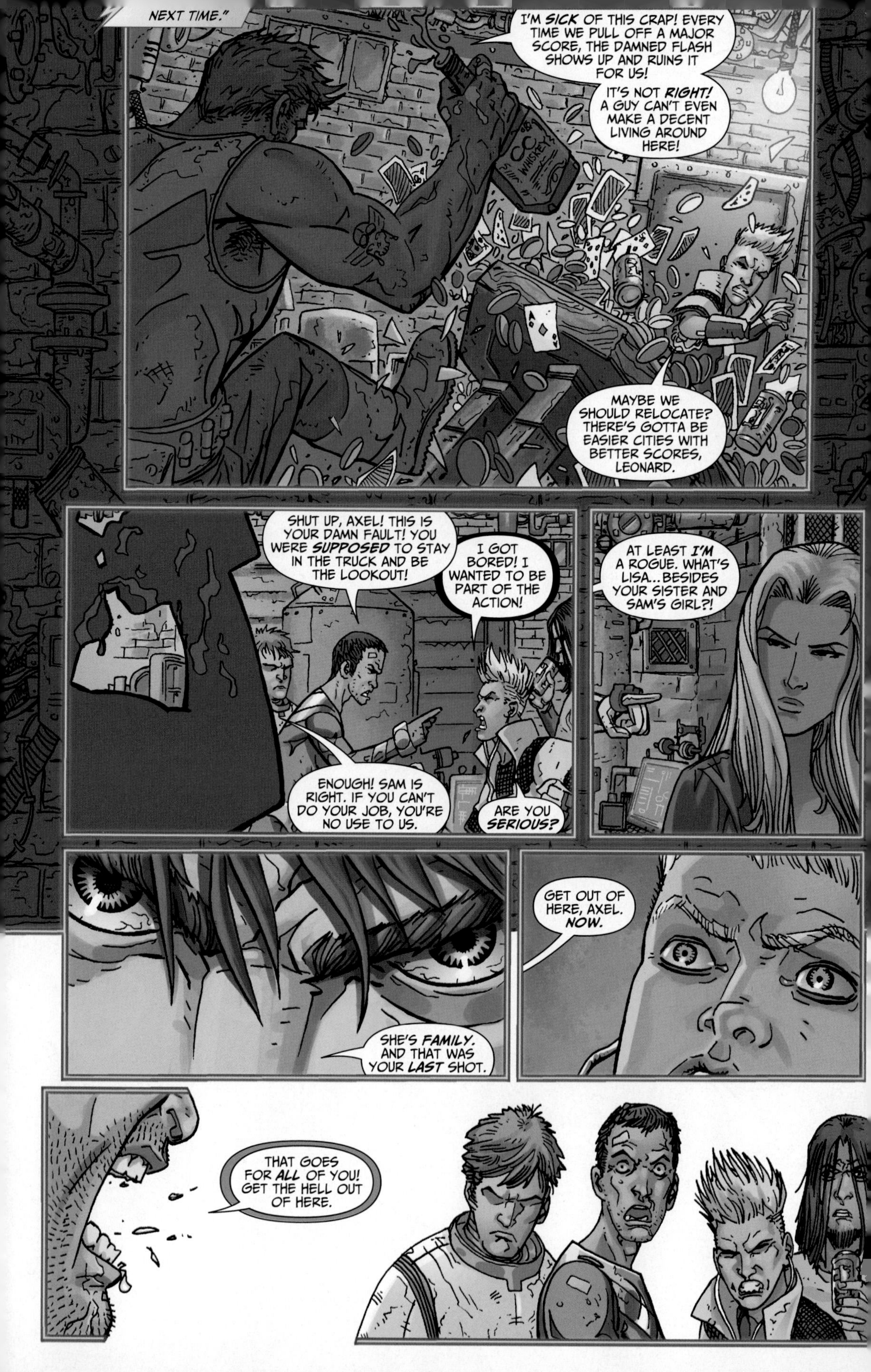

NEXT TIME."
I'M SICK OF THIS CRAP! EVERY TIME WE PULL OFF A MAJOR SCORE, THE DAMNED FLASH SHOWS UP AND RUINS IT FOR US!
IT'S NOT RIGHT! A GUY CAN'T EVEN MAKE A DECENT LIVING AROUND HERE!
MAYBE WE SHOULD RELOCATE? THERE'S GOTTA BE EASIER CITIES WITH BETTER SCORES, LEONARD.
SHUT UP, AXEL! THIS IS YOUR DAMN FAULT! YOU WERE SUPPOSED TO STAY IN THE TRUCK AND BE THE LOOKOUT!
I GOT BORED! I WANTED TO BE PART OF THE ACTION!
ENOUGH! SAM IS RIGHT. IF YOU CAN'T DO YOUR JOB, YOU'RE NO USE TO US.
ARE YOU SERIOUS?
AT LEAST I'M A ROGUE. WHAT'S LISA...BESIDES YOUR SISTER AND SAM'S GIRL?!
SHE'S FAMILY. AND THAT WAS YOUR LAST SHOT.
GET OUT OF HERE, AXEL. NOW.
THAT GOES FOR ALL OF YOU! GET THE HELL OUT OF HERE.

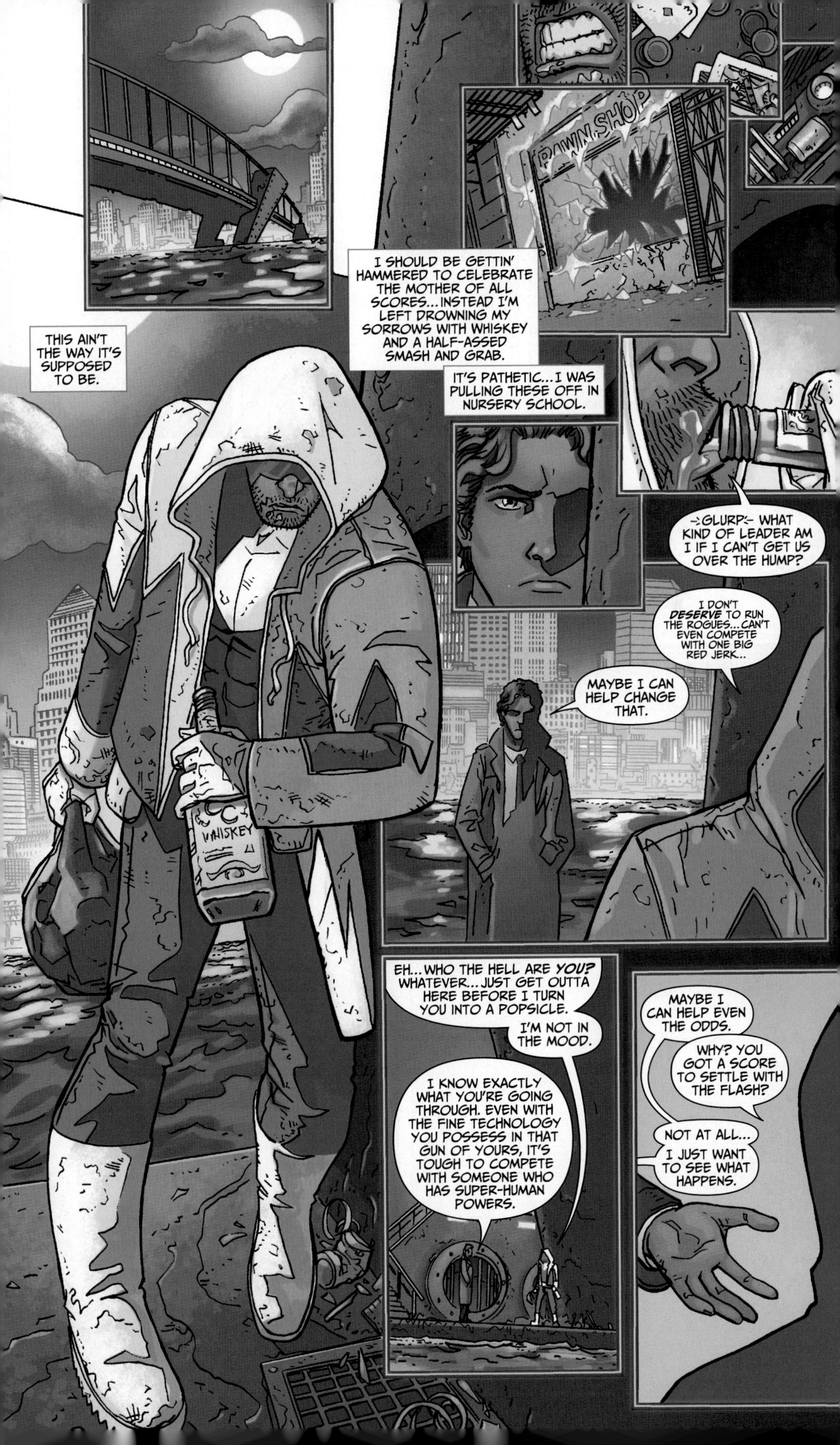
I SHOULD BE GETTIN' HAMMERED TO CELEBRATE THE MOTHER OF ALL SCORES... INSTEAD I'M LEFT DROWNING MY SORROWS WITH WHISKEY AND A HALF-ASSED SMASH AND GRAB.
PAWN SHOP
THIS AIN'T THE WAY IT'S SUPPOSED TO BE.
IT'S PATHETIC... I WAS PULLING THESE OFF IN NURSERY SCHOOL.
-GLURP- WHAT KIND OF LEADER AM I IF I CAN'T GET US OVER THE HUMP?
WHISKEY
I DON'T DESERVE TO RUN THE ROGUES... CAN'T EVEN COMPETE WITH ONE BIG RED JERK...
MAYBE I CAN HELP CHANGE THAT.
EH... WHO THE HELL ARE YOU? WHATEVER... JUST GET OUTTA HERE BEFORE I TURN YOU INTO A POPSICLE.
I'M NOT IN THE MOOD.
I KNOW EXACTLY WHAT YOU'RE GOING THROUGH. EVEN WITH THE FINE TECHNOLOGY YOU POSSESS IN THAT GUN OF YOURS, IT'S TOUGH TO COMPETE WITH SOMEONE WHO HAS SUPER-HUMAN POWERS.
MAYBE I CAN HELP EVEN THE ODDS.
WHY? YOU GOT A SCORE TO SETTLE WITH THE FLASH?
NOT AT ALL... I JUST WANT TO SEE WHAT HAPPENS.

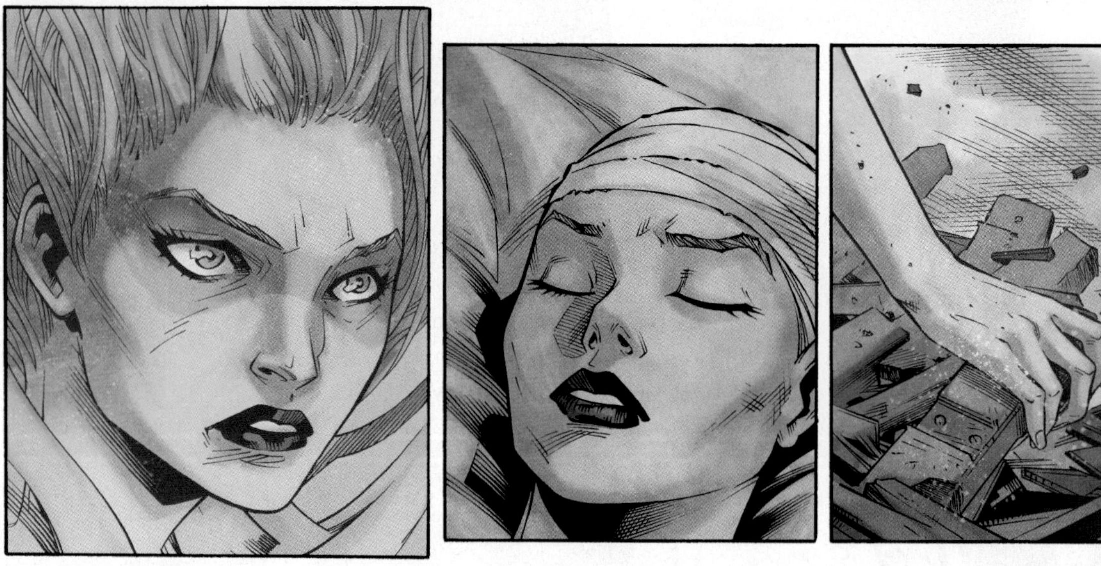

CHAPTER 3: THE PRICE

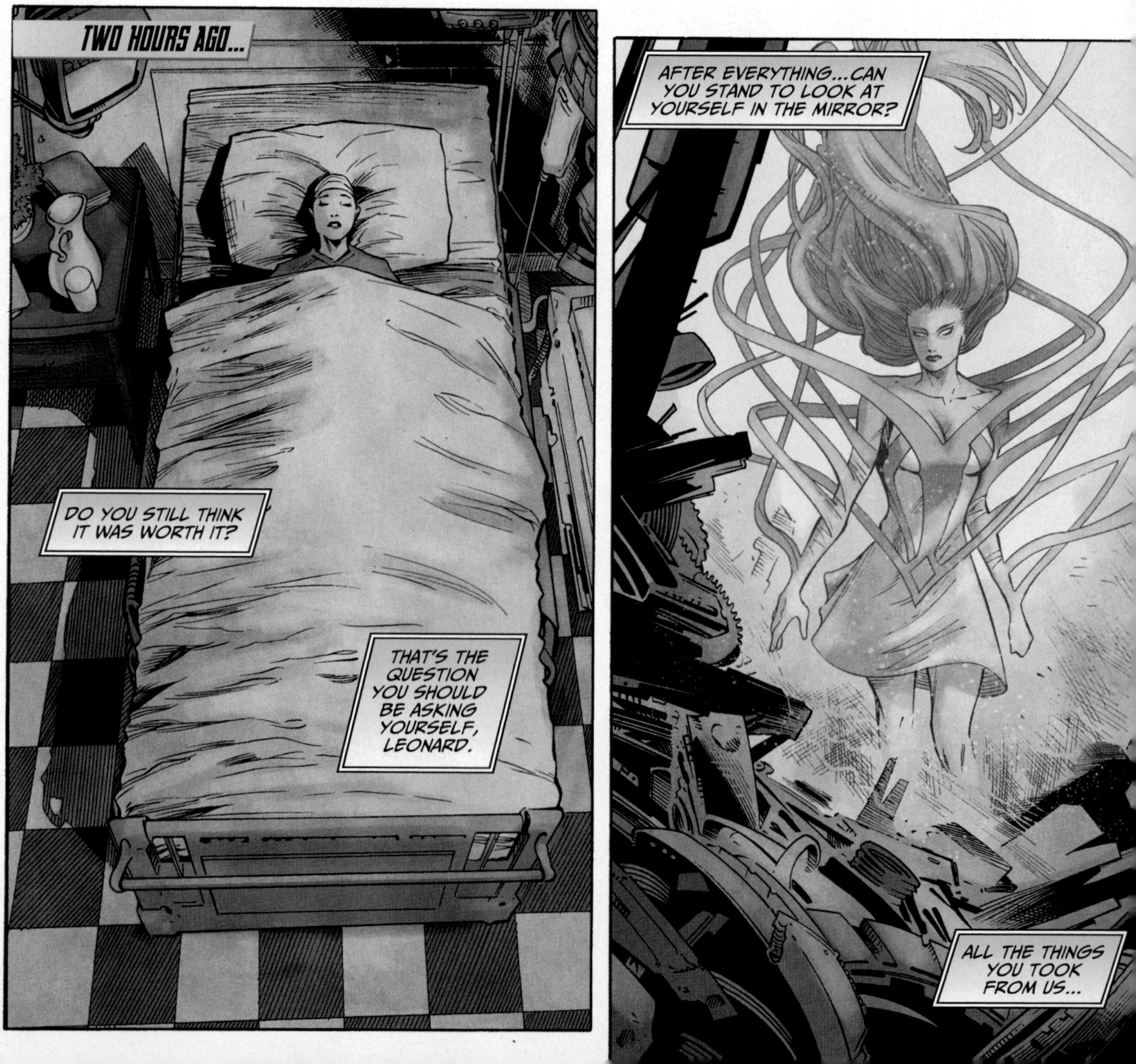
TWO HOURS AGO...
DO YOU STILL THINK IT WAS WORTH IT?
THAT'S THE QUESTION YOU SHOULD BE ASKING YOURSELF, LEONARD.
AFTER EVERYTHING...CAN YOU STAND TO LOOK AT YOURSELF IN THE MIRROR?
ALL THE THINGS YOU TOOK FROM US...

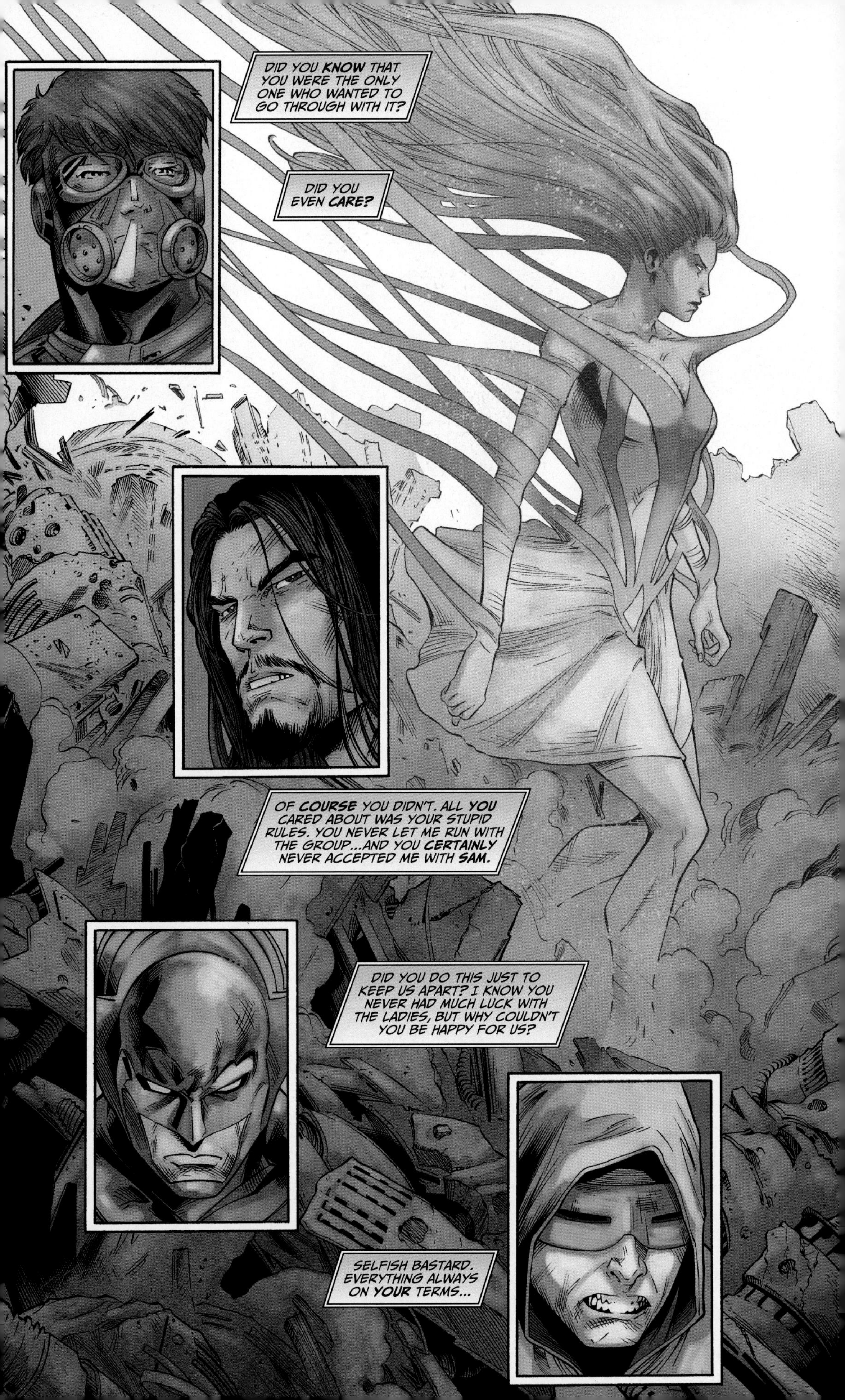

DID YOU KNOW THAT YOU WERE THE ONLY ONE WHO WANTED TO GO THROUGH WITH IT?
DID YOU EVEN CARE?
OF COURSE YOU DIDN'T. ALL YOU CARED ABOUT WAS YOUR STUPID RULES. YOU NEVER LET ME RUN WITH THE GROUP...AND YOU CERTAINLY NEVER ACCEPTED ME WITH SAM.
DID YOU DO THIS JUST TO KEEP US APART? I KNOW YOU NEVER HAD MUCH LUCK WITH THE LADIES, BUT WHY COULDN'T YOU BE HAPPY FOR US?
SELFISH BASTARD. EVERYTHING ALWAYS ON YOUR TERMS...

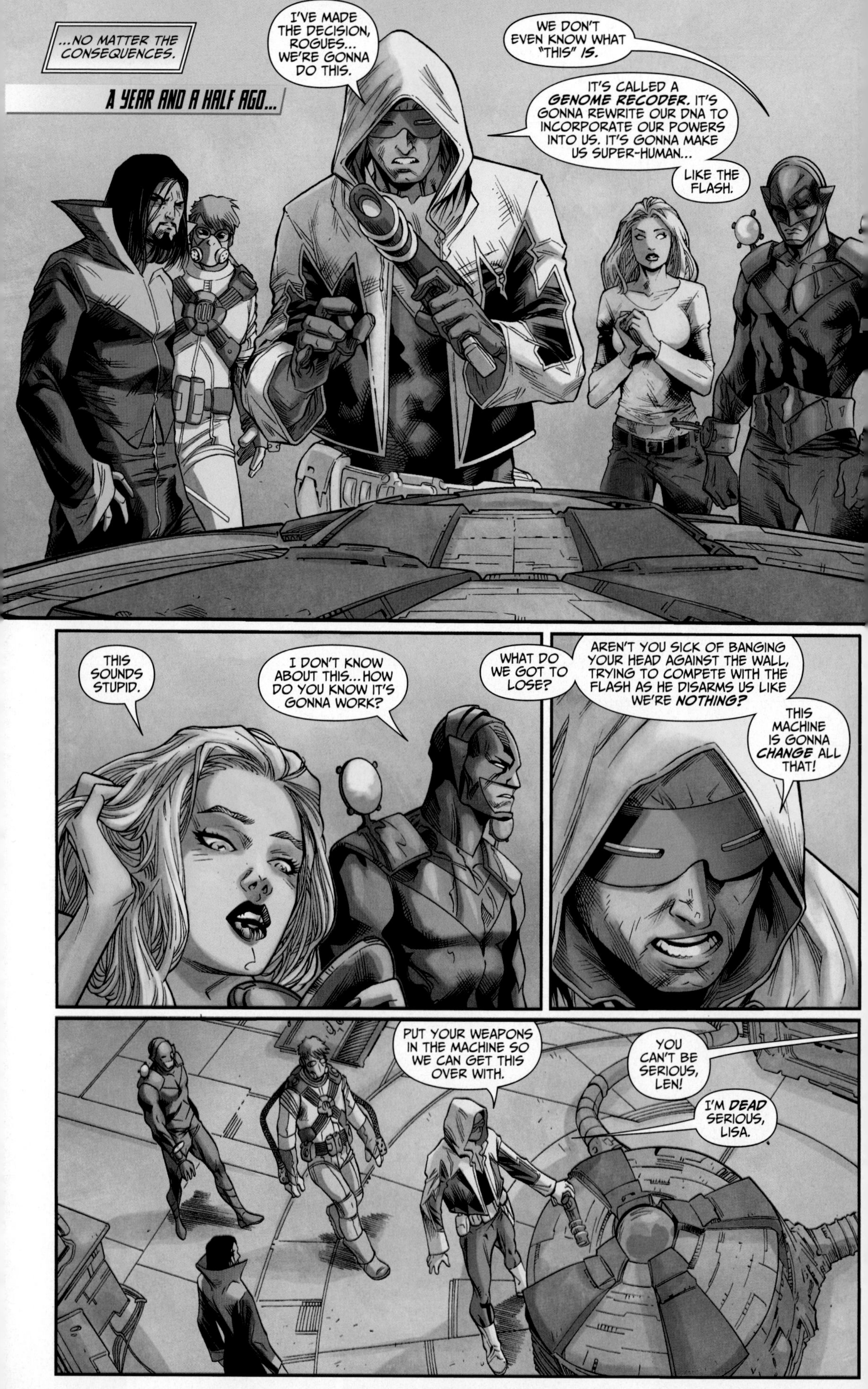
...NO MATTER THE CONSEQUENCES.
A YEAR AND A HALF AGO...
I'VE MADE THE DECISION, ROGUES... WE'RE GONNA DO THIS.
WE DON'T EVEN KNOW WHAT "THIS" IS.
IT'S CALLED A GENOME RECODER. IT'S GONNA REWRITE OUR DNA TO INCORPORATE OUR POWERS INTO US. IT'S GONNA MAKE US SUPER-HUMAN...
LIKE THE FLASH.
THIS SOUNDS STUPID.
I DON'T KNOW ABOUT THIS...HOW DO YOU KNOW IT'S GONNA WORK?
WHAT DO WE GOT TO LOSE?
AREN'T YOU SICK OF BANGING YOUR HEAD AGAINST THE WALL, TRYING TO COMPETE WITH THE FLASH AS HE DISARMS US LIKE WE'RE NOTHING?
THIS MACHINE IS GONNA CHANGE ALL THAT!
PUT YOUR WEAPONS IN THE MACHINE SO WE CAN GET THIS OVER WITH.
YOU CAN'T BE SERIOUS, LEN!
I'M DEAD SERIOUS, LISA.

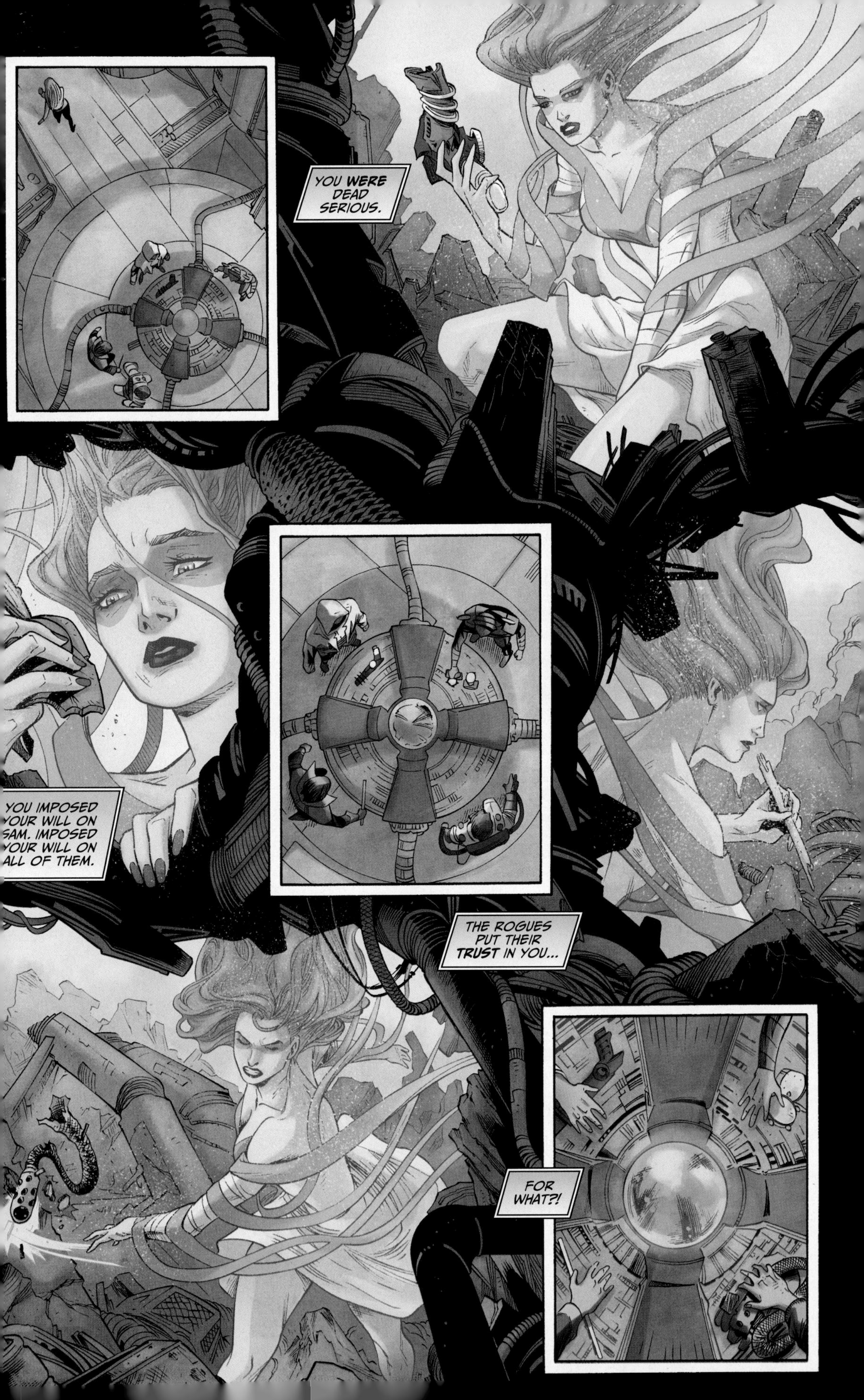
YOU WERE DEAD SERIOUS.
YOU IMPOSED YOUR WILL ON SAM. IMPOSED YOUR WILL ON ALL OF THEM.
THE ROGUES PUT THEIR TRUST IN YOU...
FOR WHAT?!

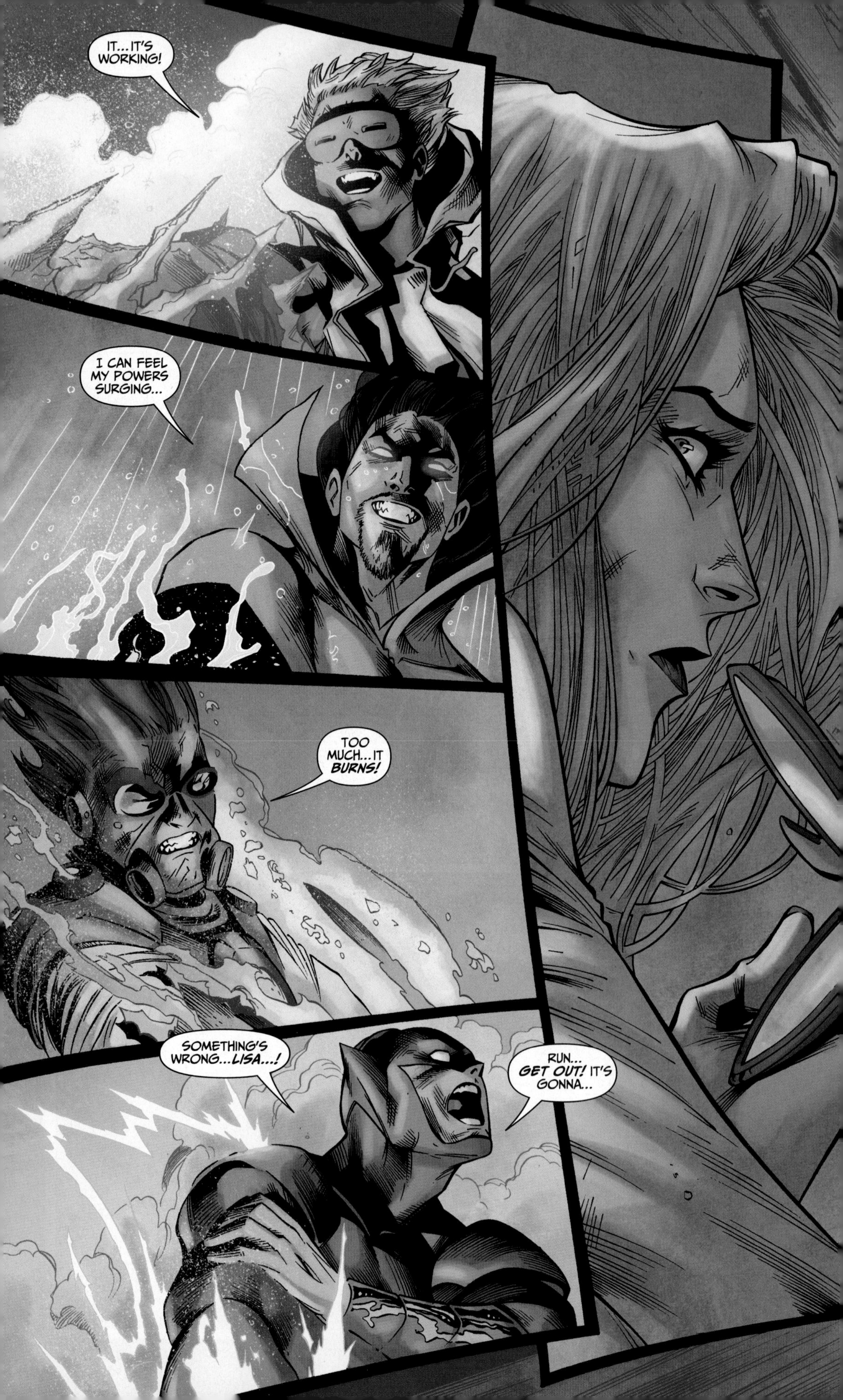

IT...IT'S WORKING!
I CAN FEEL MY POWERS SURGING...
TOO MUCH...IT **BURNS!**
SOMETHING'S WRONG...**LISA...!**
RUN... **GET OUT!** IT'S GONNA...

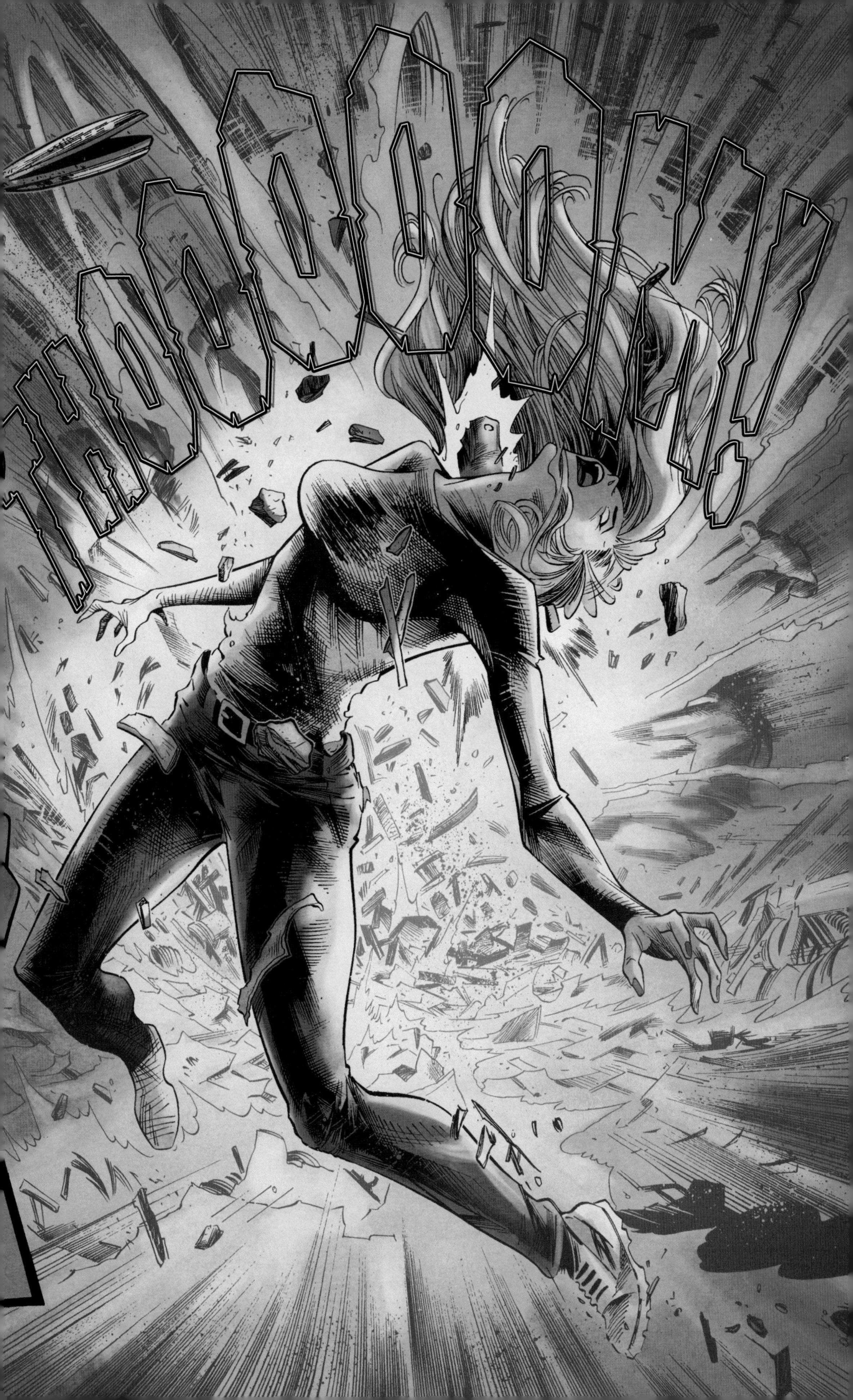
THOOOOOM!

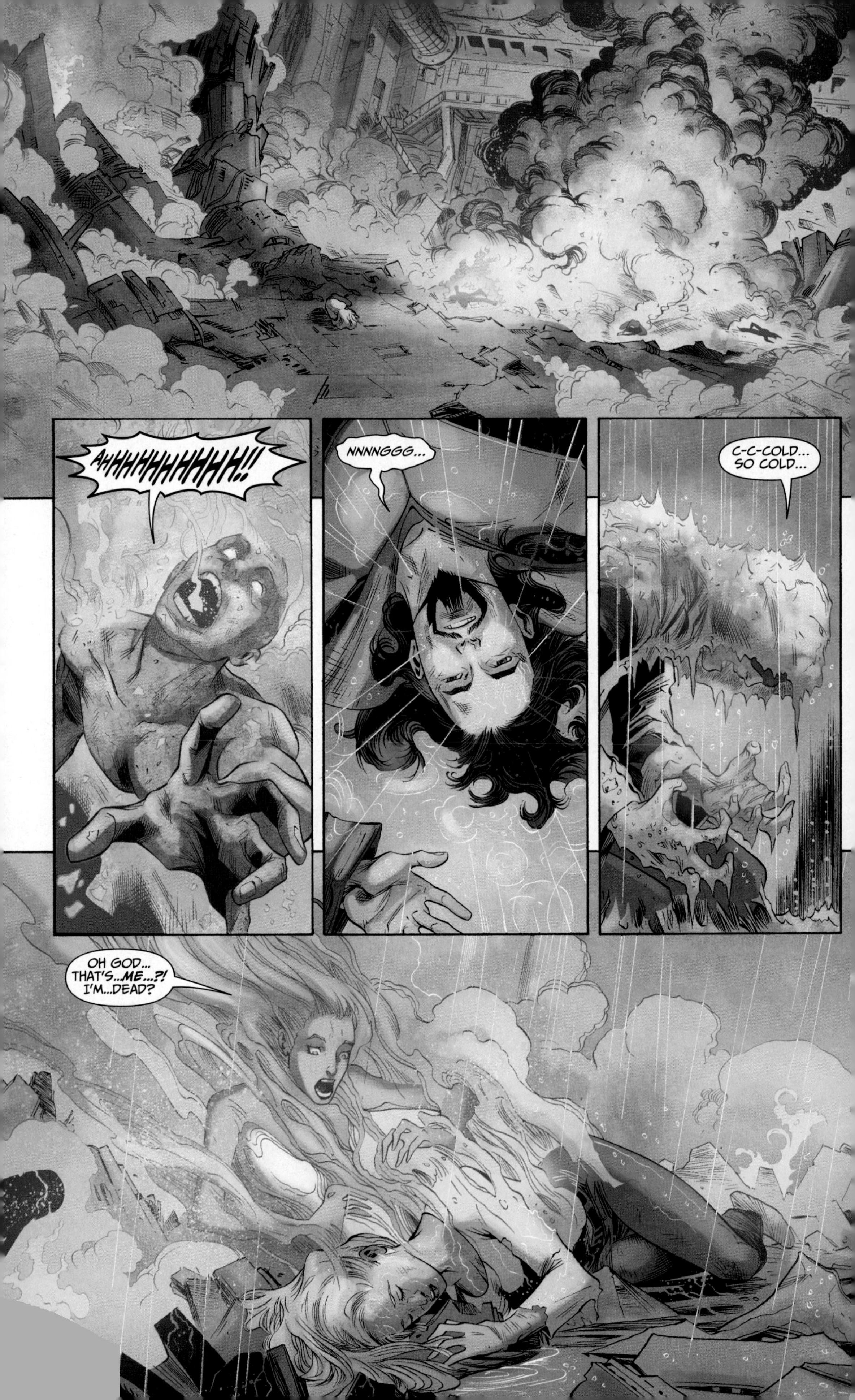
AHHHHHHHHHH!!
NNNNGGG...
C-C-COLD...
SO COLD...
OH GOD...
THAT'S...ME...?!
I'M...DEAD?

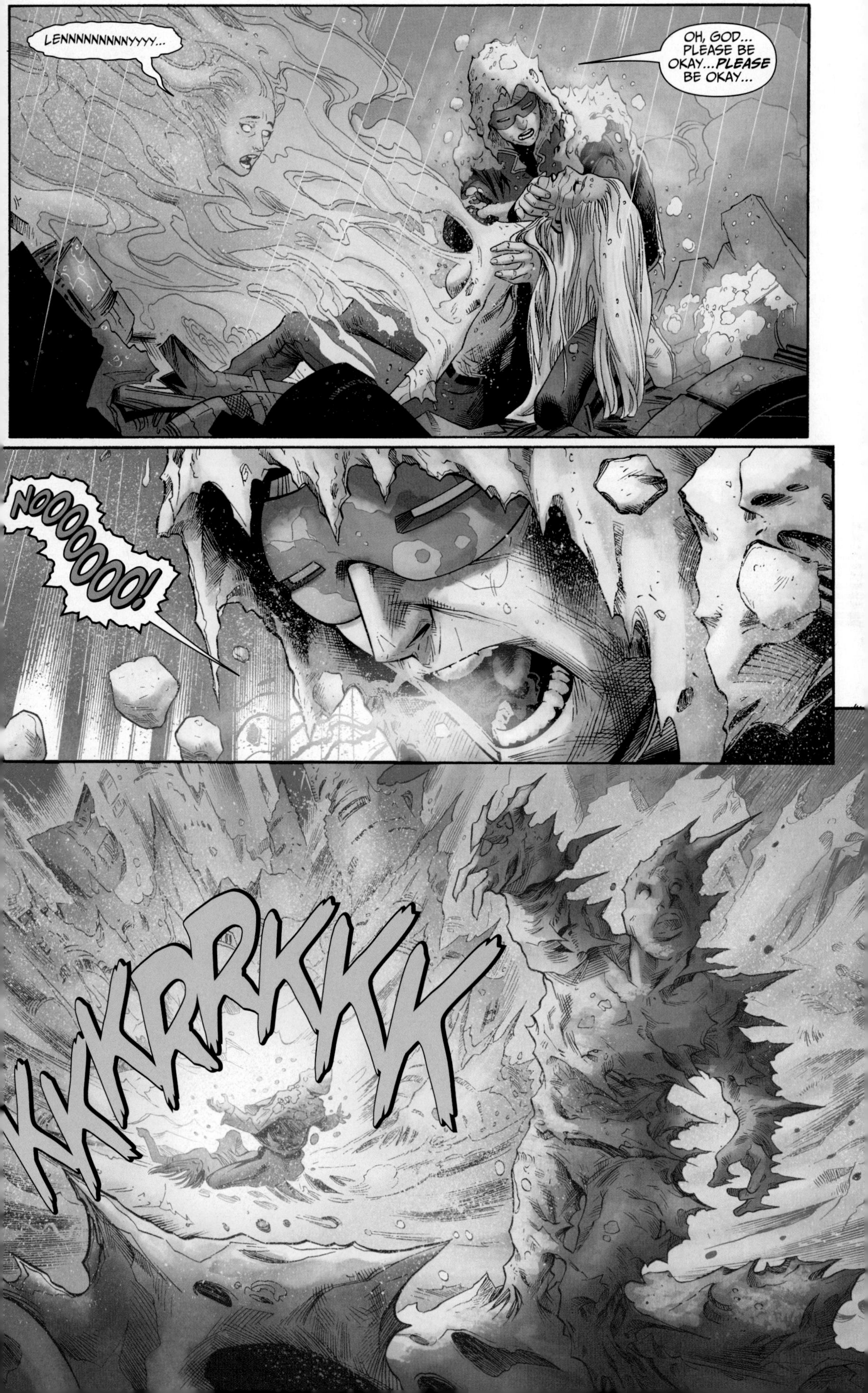
LENNNNNNNNNYYYY...
OH, GOD... PLEASE BE OKAY... **PLEASE** BE OKAY...
NOOOOOOOO!
KKKRRKKK

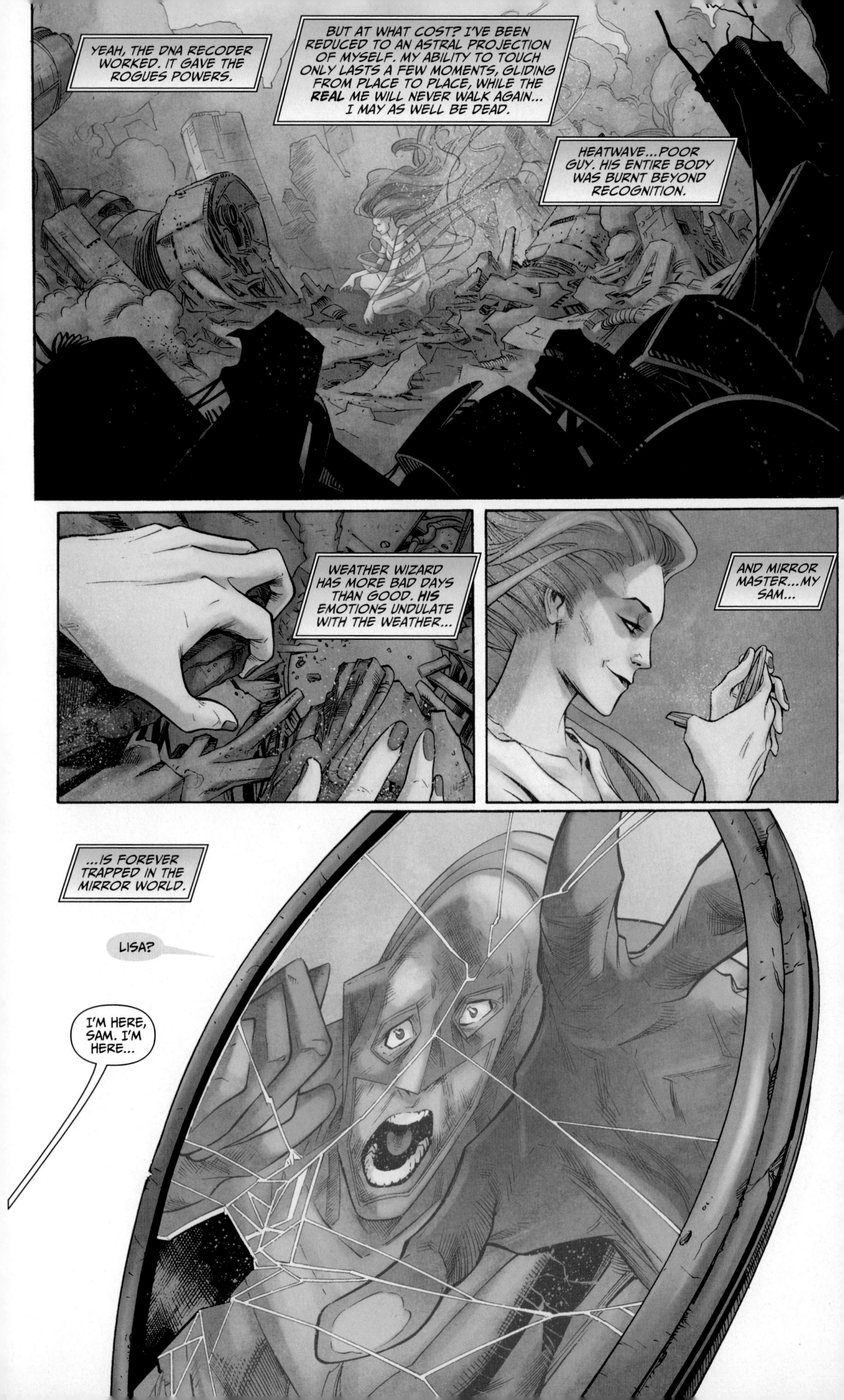
YEAH, THE DNA RECODER WORKED. IT GAVE THE ROGUES POWERS.
BUT AT WHAT COST? I'VE BEEN REDUCED TO AN ASTRAL PROJECTION OF MYSELF. MY ABILITY TO TOUCH ONLY LASTS A FEW MOMENTS, GLIDING FROM PLACE TO PLACE, WHILE THE REAL ME WILL NEVER WALK AGAIN... I MAY AS WELL BE DEAD.
HEATWAVE...POOR GUY. HIS ENTIRE BODY WAS BURNT BEYOND RECOGNITION.
WEATHER WIZARD HAS MORE BAD DAYS THAN GOOD. HIS EMOTIONS UNDULATE WITH THE WEATHER...
AND MIRROR MASTER...MY SAM...
...IS FOREVER TRAPPED IN THE MIRROR WORLD.
LISA?
I'M HERE, SAM. I'M HERE...

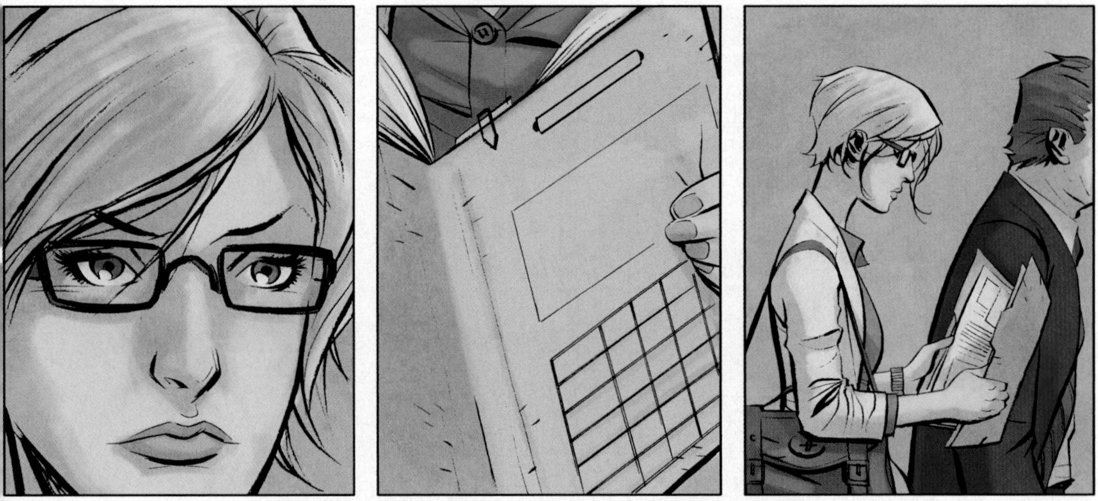

CHAPTER 4: THE SECRET

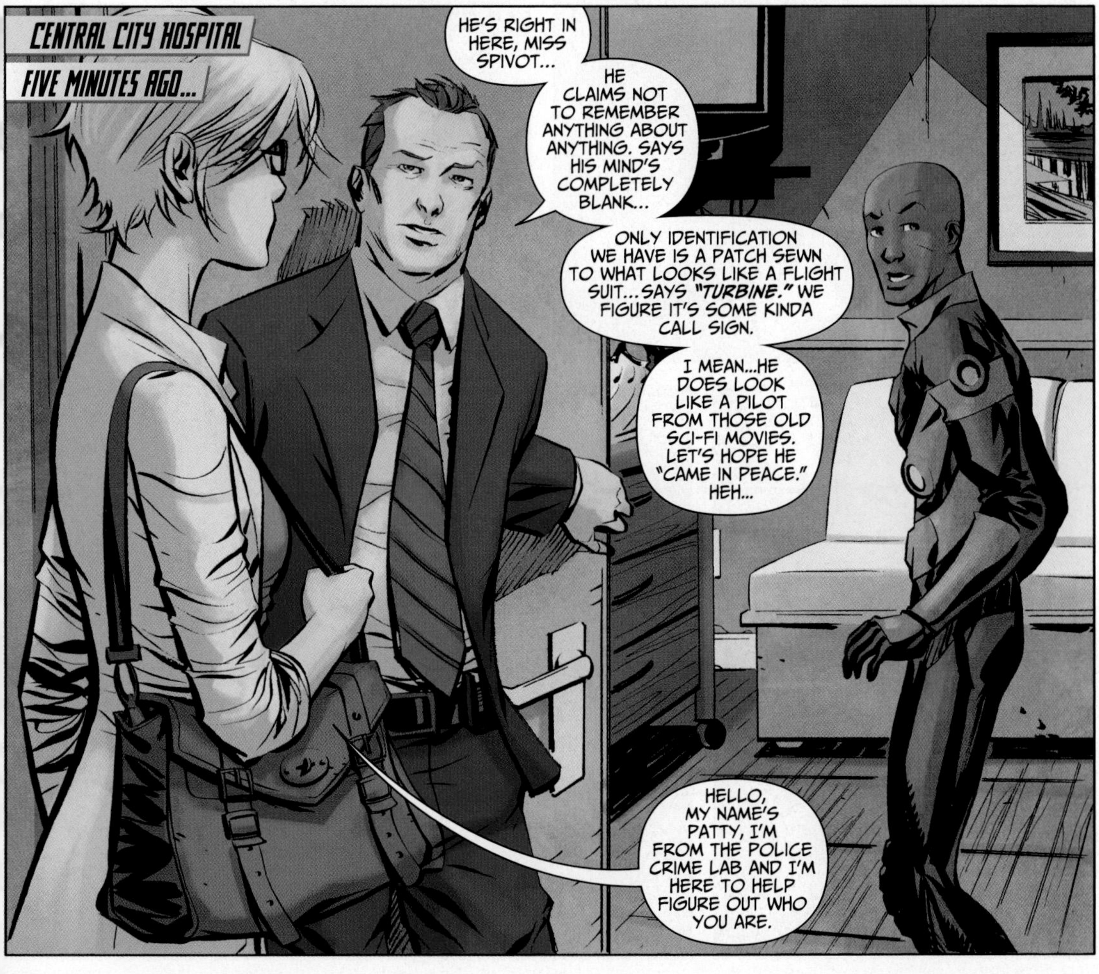
CENTRAL CITY HOSPITAL
FIVE MINUTES AGO...
HE'S RIGHT IN HERE, MISS SPIVOT...
HE CLAIMS NOT TO REMEMBER ANYTHING ABOUT ANYTHING. SAYS HIS MIND'S COMPLETELY BLANK...
ONLY IDENTIFICATION WE HAVE IS A PATCH SEWN TO WHAT LOOKS LIKE A FLIGHT SUIT...SAYS "TURBINE." WE FIGURE IT'S SOME KINDA CALL SIGN.
I MEAN...HE DOES LOOK LIKE A PILOT FROM THOSE OLD SCI-FI MOVIES. LET'S HOPE HE "CAME IN PEACE." HEH...
HELLO, MY NAME'S PATTY, I'M FROM THE POLICE CRIME LAB AND I'M HERE TO HELP FIGURE OUT WHO YOU ARE.

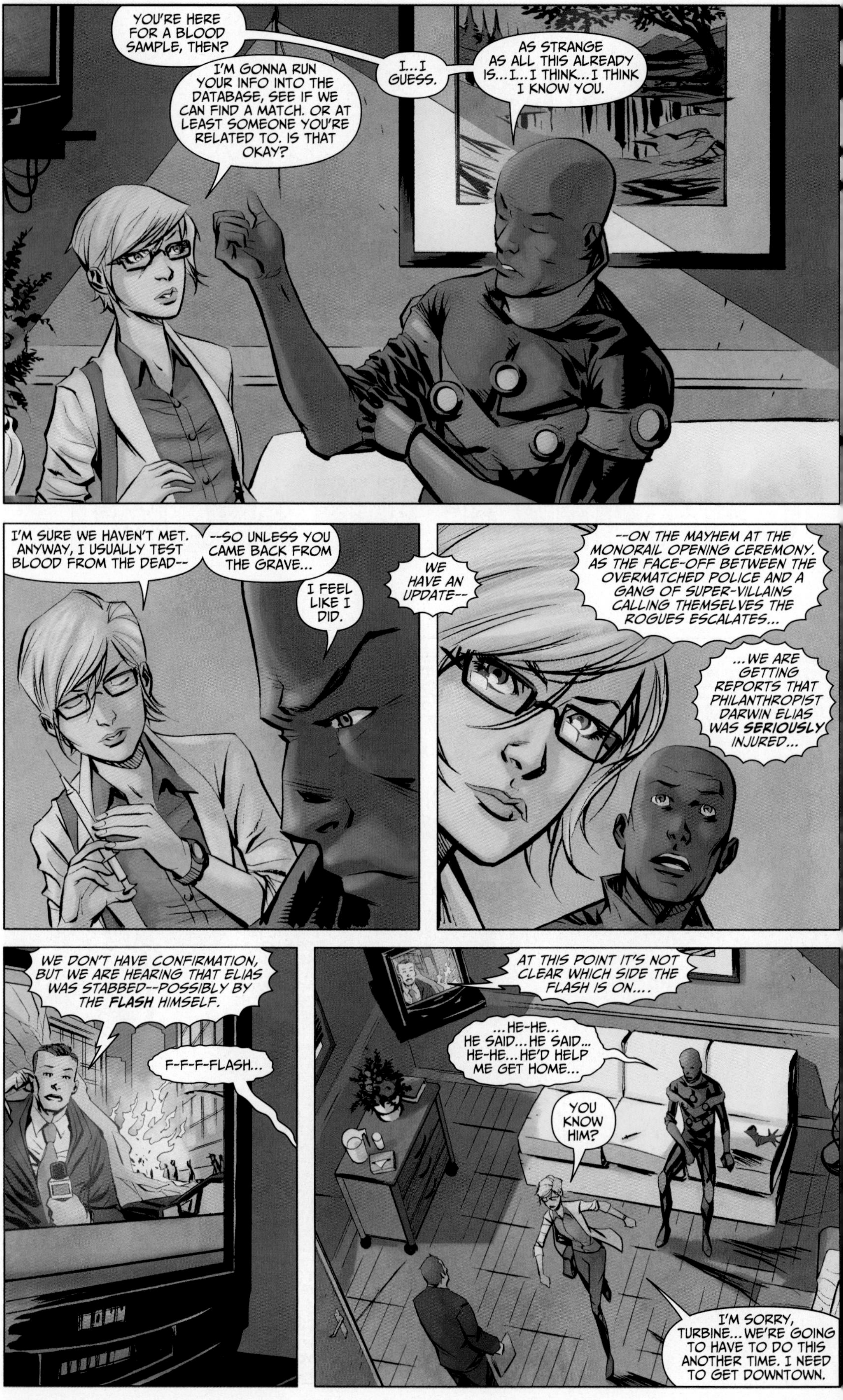
YOU'RE HERE FOR A BLOOD SAMPLE, THEN?
I'M GONNA RUN YOUR INFO INTO THE DATABASE, SEE IF WE CAN FIND A MATCH. OR AT LEAST SOMEONE YOU'RE RELATED TO. IS THAT OKAY?
I...I GUESS.
AS STRANGE AS ALL THIS ALREADY IS...I...I THINK...I THINK I KNOW YOU.
I'M SURE WE HAVEN'T MET. ANYWAY, I USUALLY TEST BLOOD FROM THE DEAD--
--SO UNLESS YOU CAME BACK FROM THE GRAVE...
I FEEL LIKE I DID.
WE HAVE AN UPDATE--
--ON THE MAYHEM AT THE MONORAIL OPENING CEREMONY. AS THE FACE-OFF BETWEEN THE OVERMATCHED POLICE AND A GANG OF SUPER-VILLAINS CALLING THEMSELVES THE ROGUES ESCALATES...
...WE ARE GETTING REPORTS THAT PHILANTHROPIST DARWIN ELIAS WAS SERIOUSLY INJURED...
WE DON'T HAVE CONFIRMATION, BUT WE ARE HEARING THAT ELIAS WAS STABBED--POSSIBLY BY THE FLASH HIMSELF.
F-F-F-FLASH...
AT THIS POINT IT'S NOT CLEAR WHICH SIDE THE FLASH IS ON....
...HE-HE... HE SAID...HE SAID... HE-HE...HE'D HELP ME GET HOME...
YOU KNOW HIM?
I'M SORRY, TURBINE...WE'RE GOING TO HAVE TO DO THIS ANOTHER TIME. I NEED TO GET DOWNTOWN.

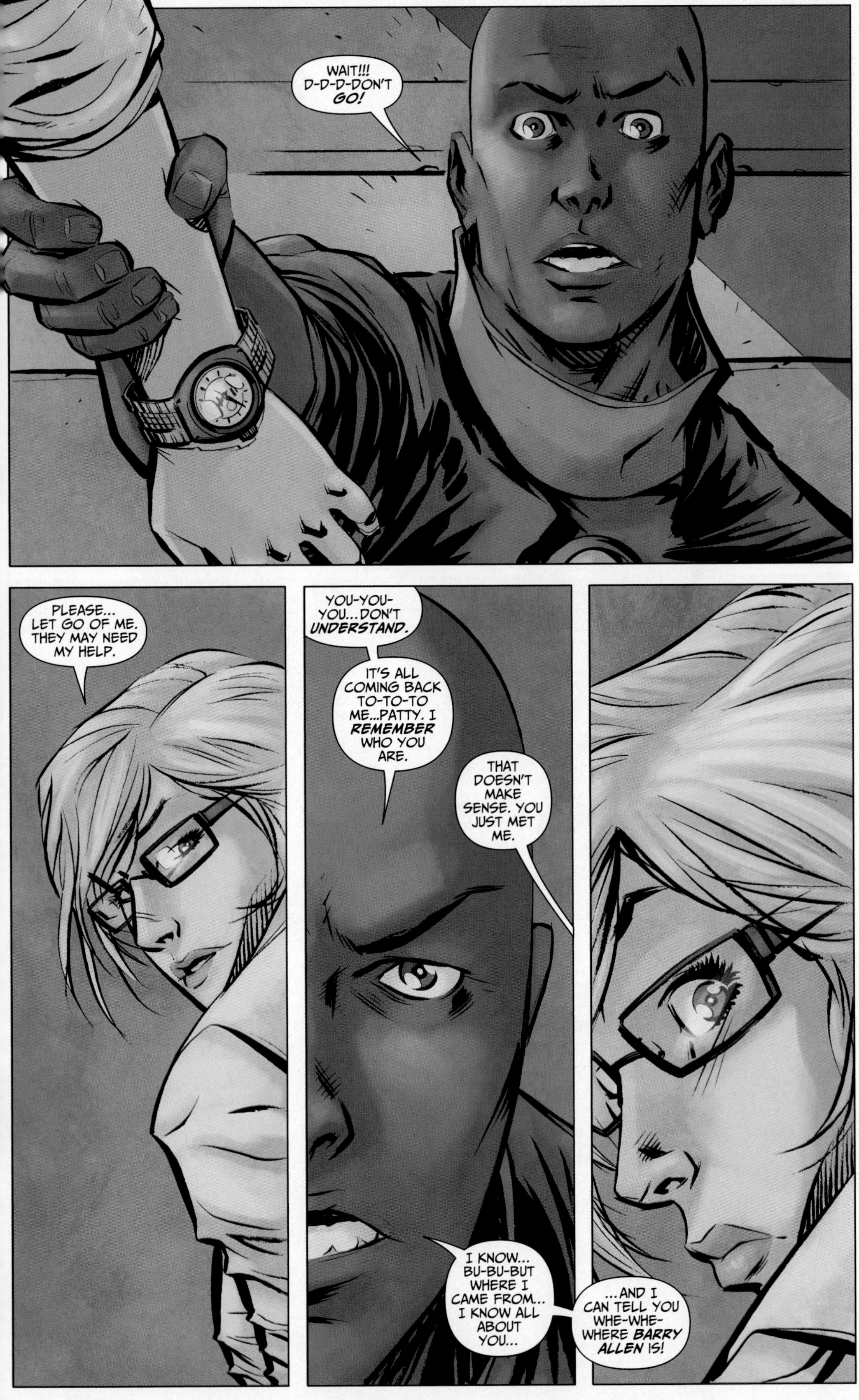
WAIT!!! D-D-D-DON'T GO!
PLEASE... LET GO OF ME. THEY MAY NEED MY HELP.
YOU-YOU-YOU...DON'T UNDERSTAND.
IT'S ALL COMING BACK TO-TO-TO ME...PATTY. I REMEMBER WHO YOU ARE.
THAT DOESN'T MAKE SENSE. YOU JUST MET ME.
I KNOW... BU-BU-BUT WHERE I CAME FROM... I KNOW ALL ABOUT YOU...
...AND I CAN TELL YOU WHE-WHE-WHERE BARRY ALLEN IS!

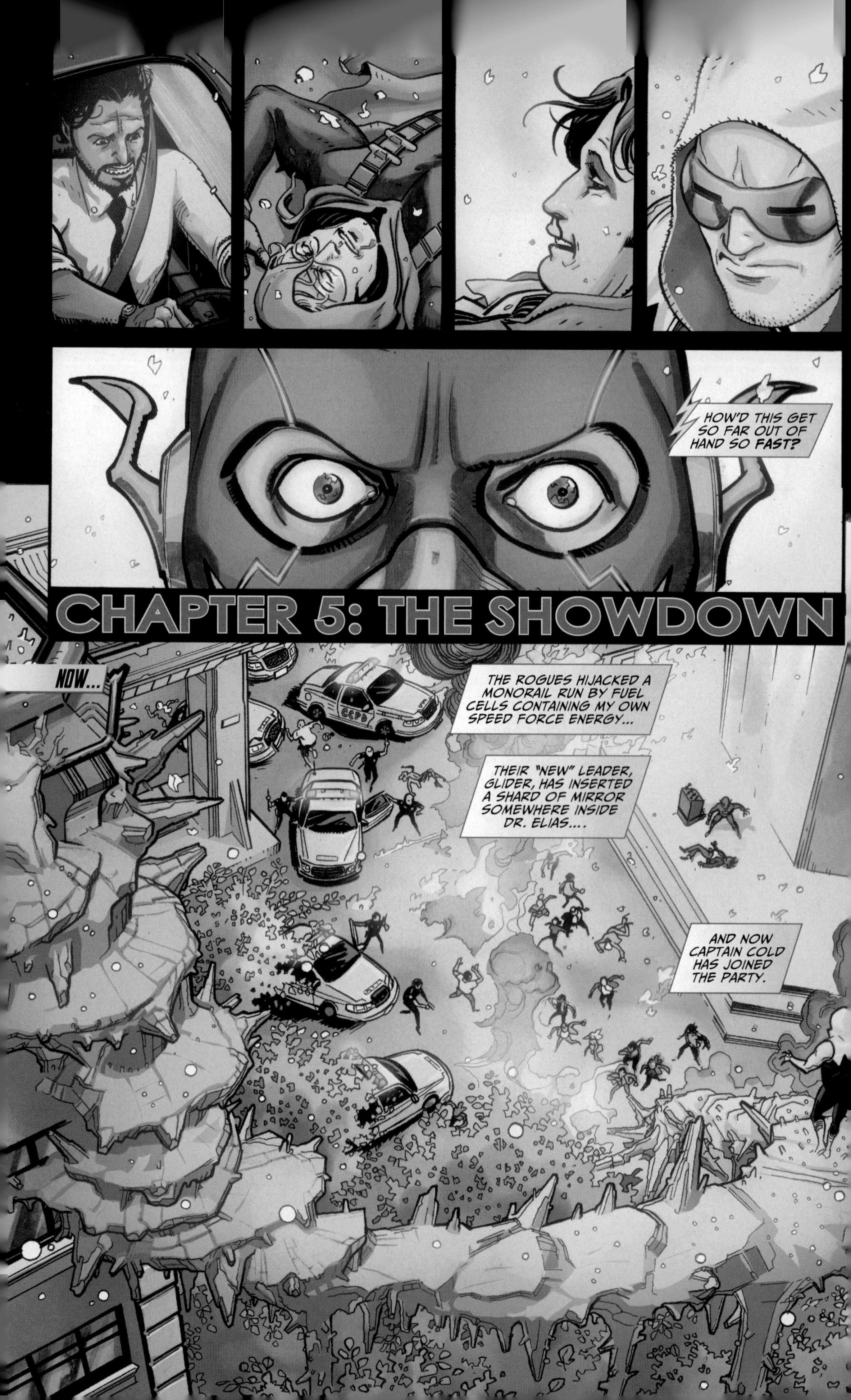
HOW'D THIS GET SO FAR OUT OF HAND SO FAST?
CHAPTER 5: THE SHOWDOWN
NOW...
THE ROGUES HIJACKED A MONORAIL RUN BY FUEL CELLS CONTAINING MY OWN SPEED FORCE ENERGY...
THEIR "NEW" LEADER, GLIDER, HAS INSERTED A SHARD OF MIRROR SOMEWHERE INSIDE DR. ELIAS....
AND NOW CAPTAIN COLD HAS JOINED THE PARTY.

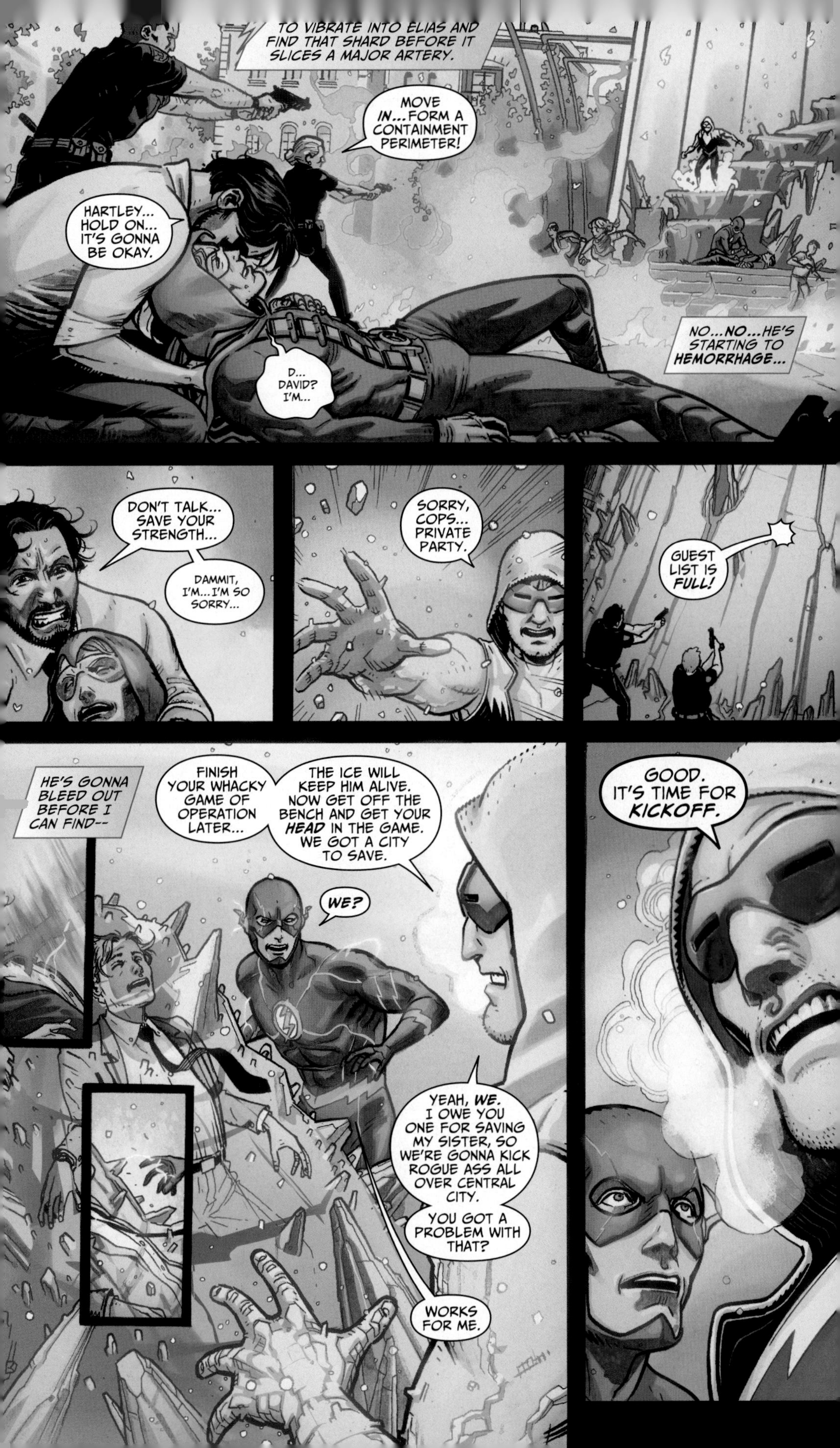
TO VIBRATE INTO ELIAS AND FIND THAT SHARD BEFORE IT SLICES A MAJOR ARTERY.
MOVE IN...FORM A CONTAINMENT PERIMETER!
HARTLEY... HOLD ON... IT'S GONNA BE OKAY.
D... DAVID? I'M...
NO...NO...HE'S STARTING TO HEMORRHAGE...
DON'T TALK... SAVE YOUR STRENGTH...
DAMMIT, I'M...I'M SO SORRY...
SORRY, COPS... PRIVATE PARTY.
GUEST LIST IS FULL!
HE'S GONNA BLEED OUT BEFORE I CAN FIND--
FINISH YOUR WHACKY GAME OF OPERATION LATER...
THE ICE WILL KEEP HIM ALIVE. NOW GET OFF THE BENCH AND GET YOUR HEAD IN THE GAME. WE GOT A CITY TO SAVE.
WE?
YEAH, WE. I OWE YOU ONE FOR SAVING MY SISTER, SO WE'RE GONNA KICK ROGUE ASS ALL OVER CENTRAL CITY.
YOU GOT A PROBLEM WITH THAT?
WORKS FOR ME.
GOOD. IT'S TIME FOR KICKOFF.

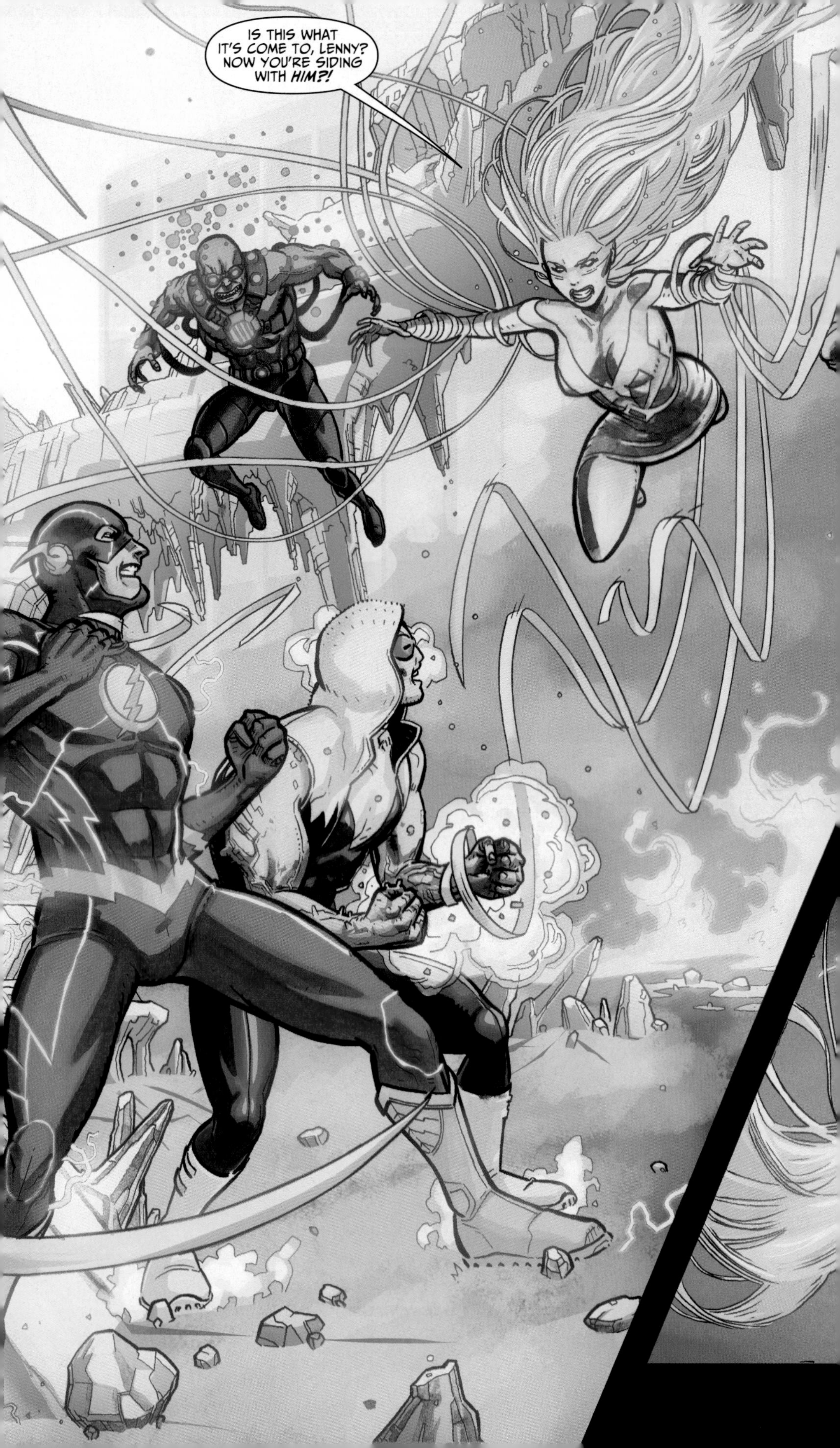
IS THIS WHAT IT'S COME TO, LENNY? NOW YOU'RE SIDING WITH *HIM?!*

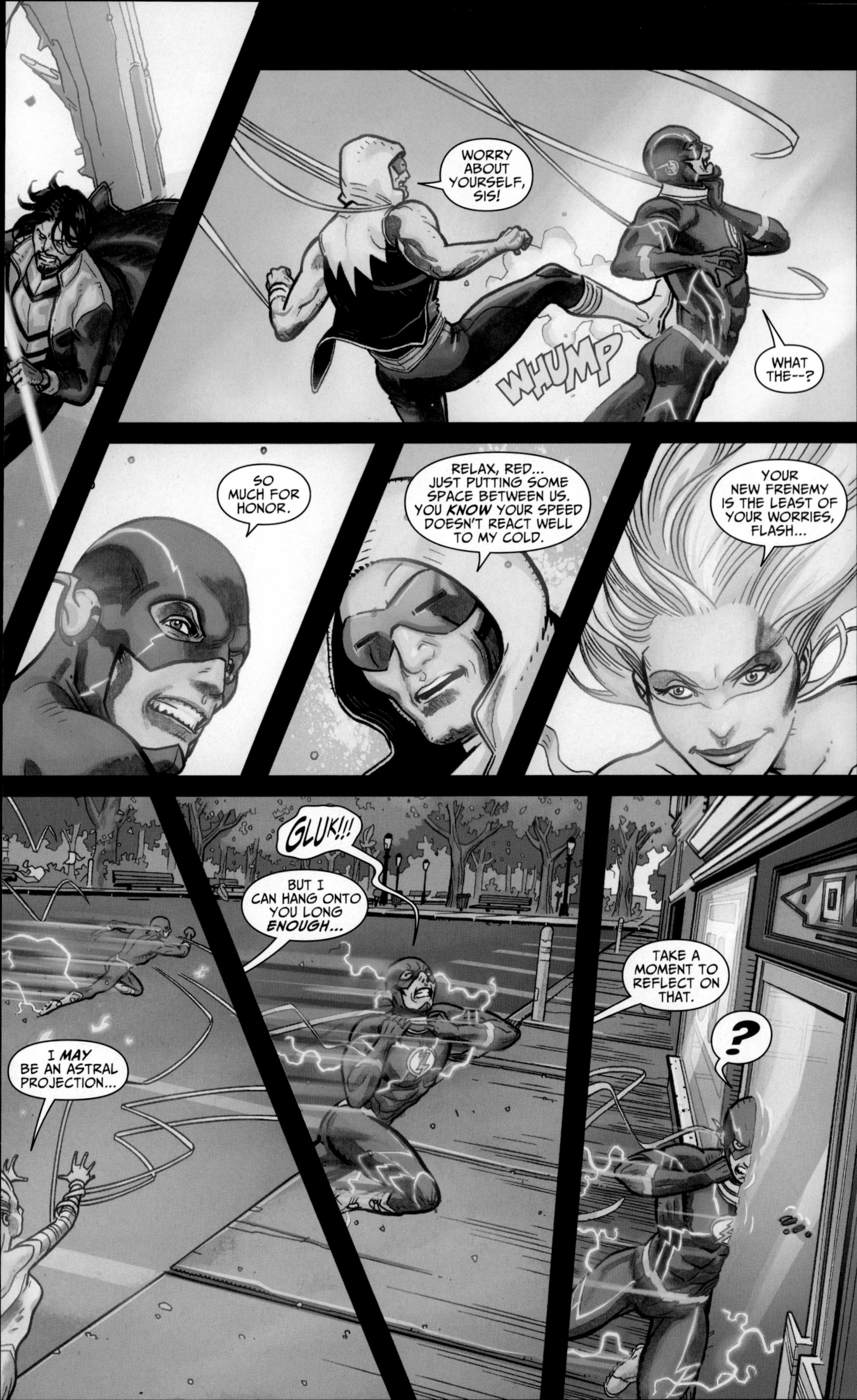
WORRY ABOUT YOURSELF, SIS!
WHUMP
WHAT THE--?
SO MUCH FOR HONOR.
RELAX, RED... JUST PUTTING SOME SPACE BETWEEN US. YOU KNOW YOUR SPEED DOESN'T REACT WELL TO MY COLD.
YOUR NEW FRENEMY IS THE LEAST OF YOUR WORRIES, FLASH...
I MAY BE AN ASTRAL PROJECTION...
GLUK!!!
BUT I CAN HANG ONTO YOU LONG ENOUGH...
TAKE A MOMENT TO REFLECT ON THAT.
?

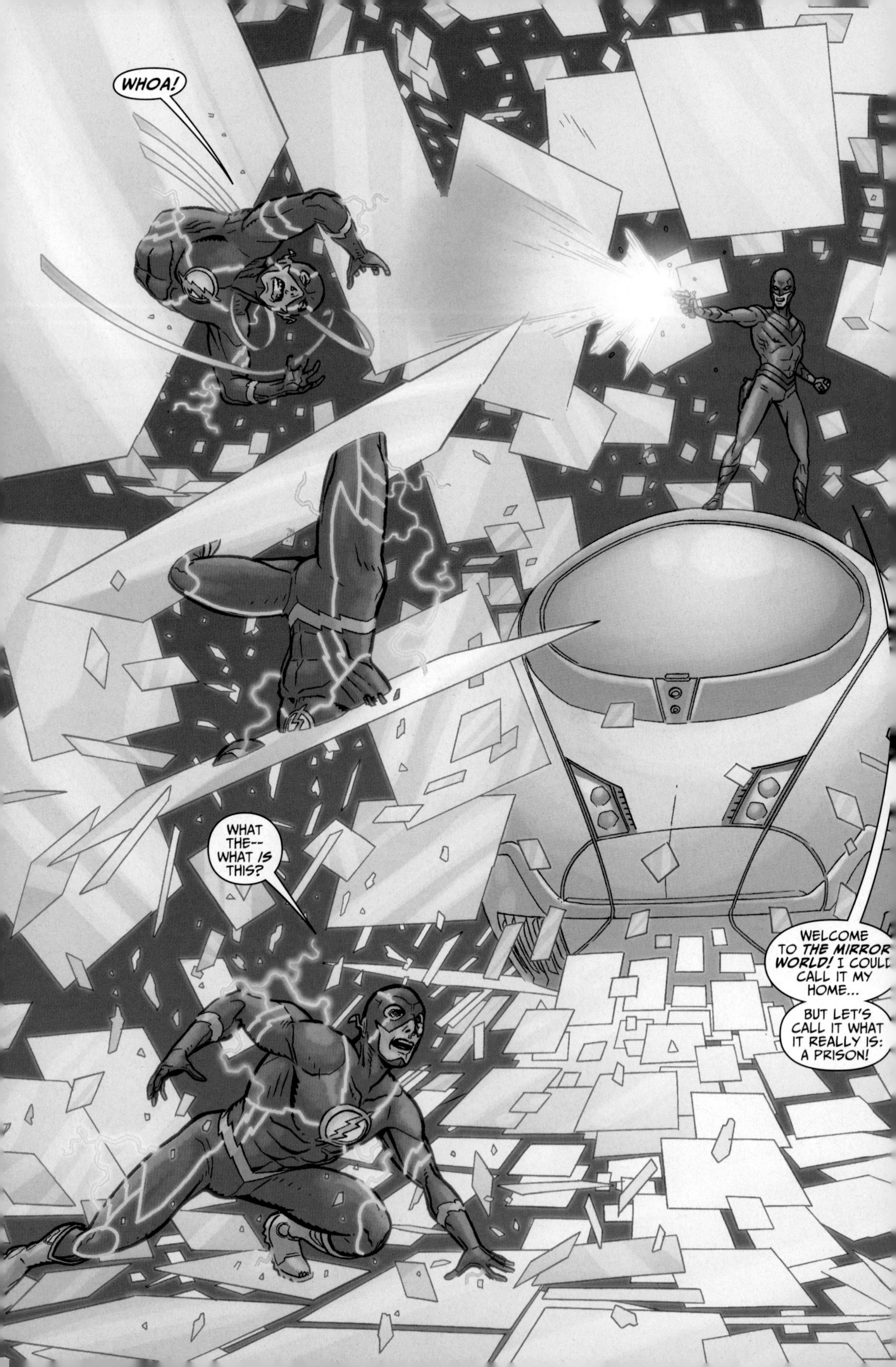
WHOA!
WHAT THE-- WHAT IS THIS?
WELCOME TO THE MIRROR WORLD! I COULD CALL IT MY HOME...
BUT LET'S CALL IT WHAT IT REALLY IS: A PRISON!

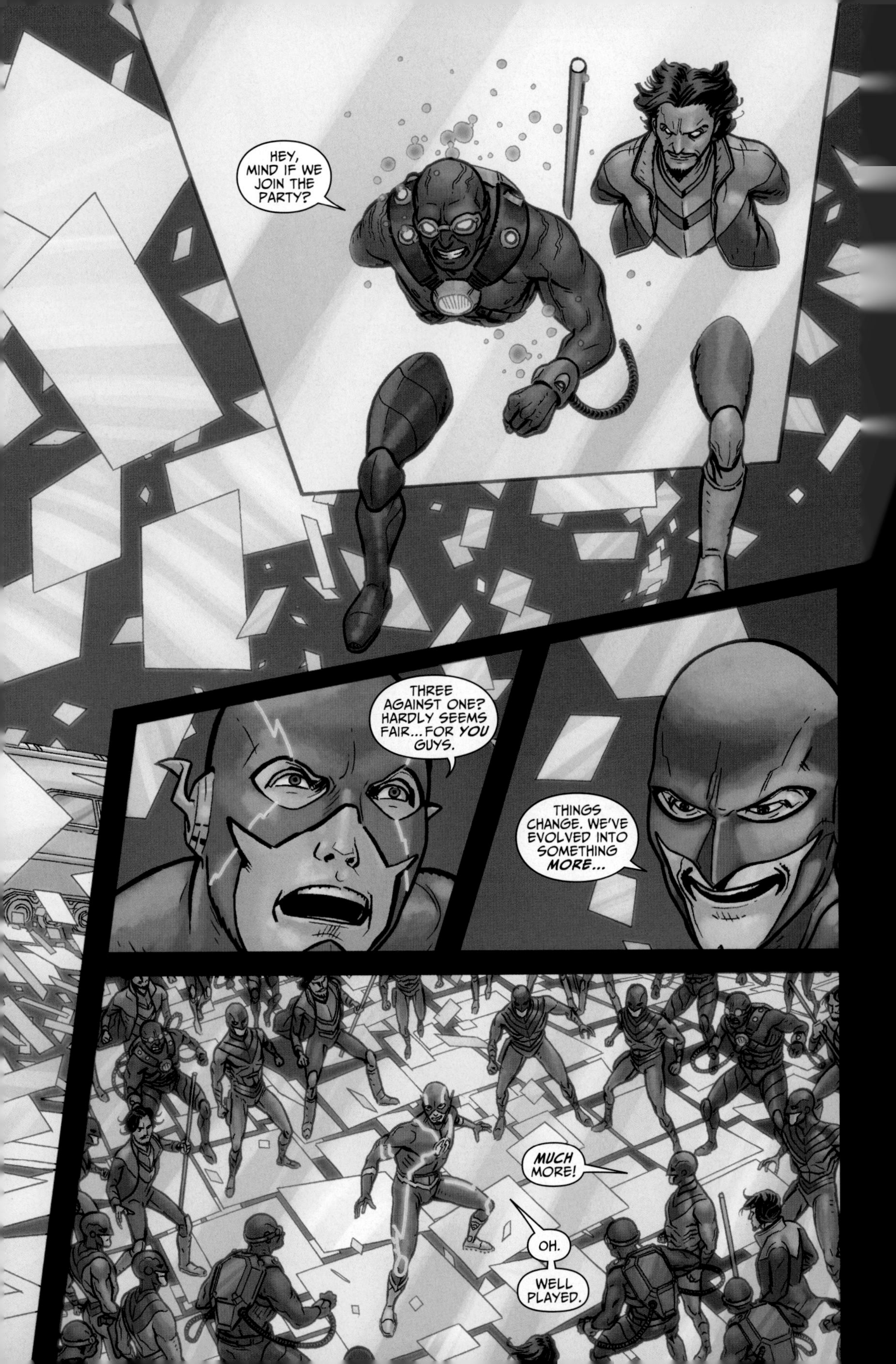
HEY, MIND IF WE JOIN THE PARTY?
THREE AGAINST ONE? HARDLY SEEMS FAIR... FOR *YOU* GUYS.
THINGS CHANGE. WE'VE EVOLVED INTO SOMETHING *MORE...*
MUCH MORE!
OH.
WELL PLAYED.

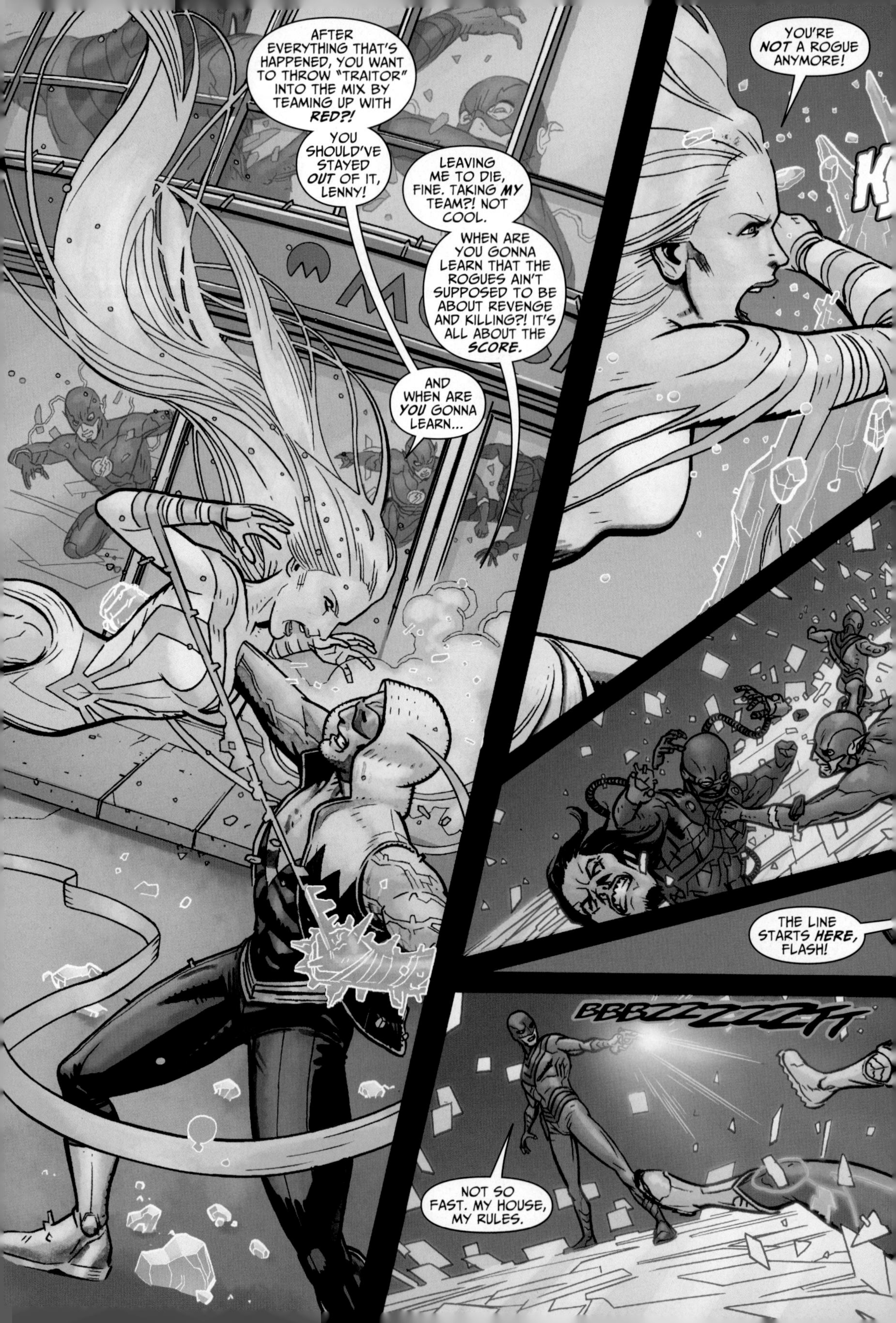

AFTER EVERYTHING THAT'S HAPPENED, YOU WANT TO THROW "TRAITOR" INTO THE MIX BY TEAMING UP WITH *RED?!*
YOU SHOULD'VE STAYED *OUT* OF IT, LENNY!
LEAVING ME TO DIE, FINE. TAKING *MY* TEAM?! NOT COOL.
WHEN ARE YOU GONNA LEARN THAT THE ROGUES AIN'T SUPPOSED TO BE ABOUT REVENGE AND KILLING?! IT'S ALL ABOUT THE *SCORE.*
AND WHEN ARE *YOU* GONNA LEARN...
YOU'RE *NOT* A ROGUE ANYMORE!
THE LINE STARTS *HERE,* FLASH!
BBBZZZZZZZT
NOT SO FAST. MY HOUSE, MY RULES.

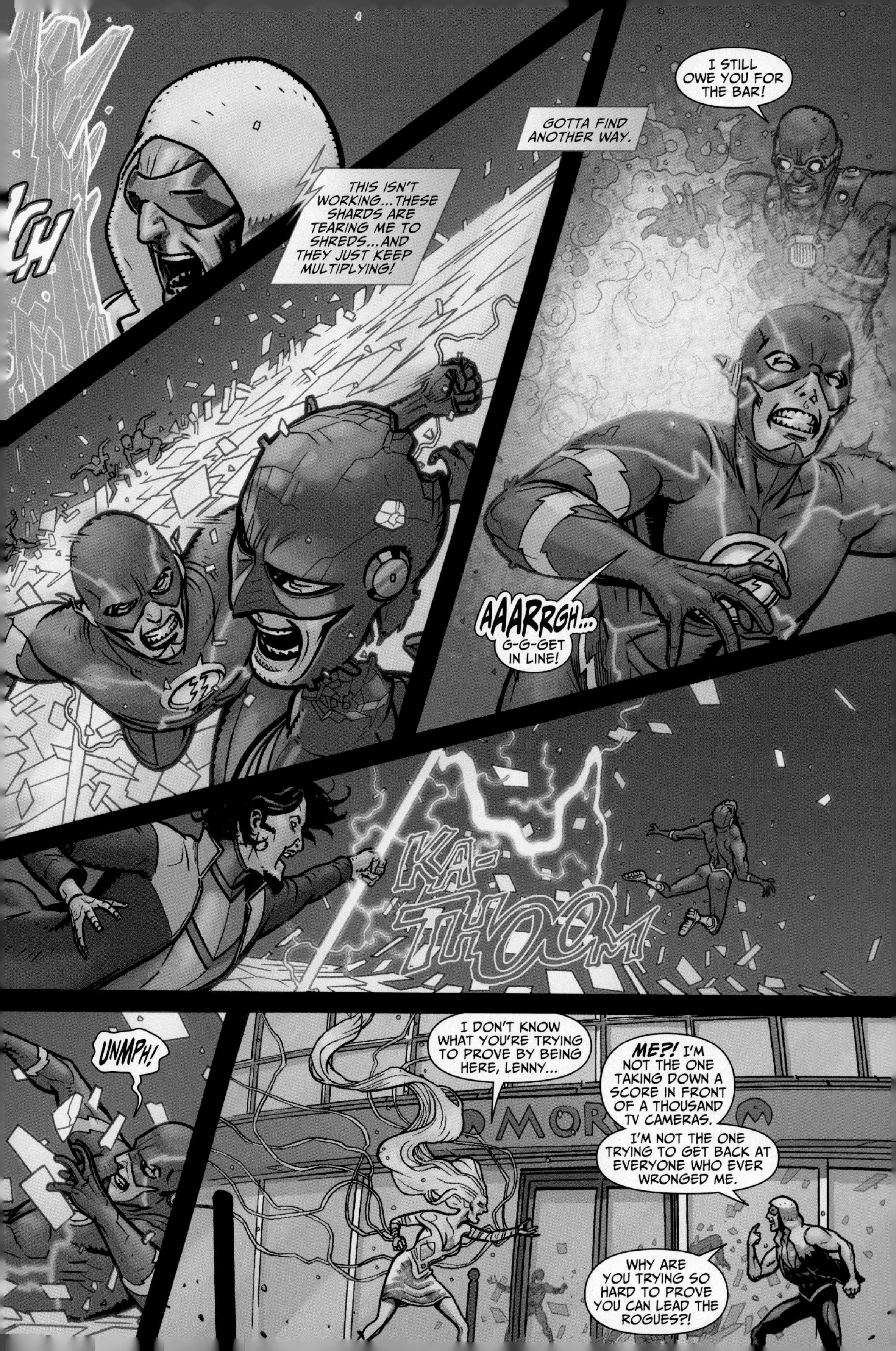
THIS ISN'T WORKING...THESE SHARDS ARE TEARING ME TO SHREDS...AND THEY JUST KEEP MULTIPLYING!
GOTTA FIND ANOTHER WAY.
I STILL OWE YOU FOR THE BAR!
AAARRGH... G-G-GET IN LINE!
KA-THOOM
UNMPH!
I DON'T KNOW WHAT YOU'RE TRYING TO PROVE BY BEING HERE, LENNY...
ME?! I'M NOT THE ONE TAKING DOWN A SCORE IN FRONT OF A THOUSAND TV CAMERAS.
I'M NOT THE ONE TRYING TO GET BACK AT EVERYONE WHO EVER WRONGED ME.
WHY ARE YOU TRYING SO HARD TO PROVE YOU CAN LEAD THE ROGUES?!

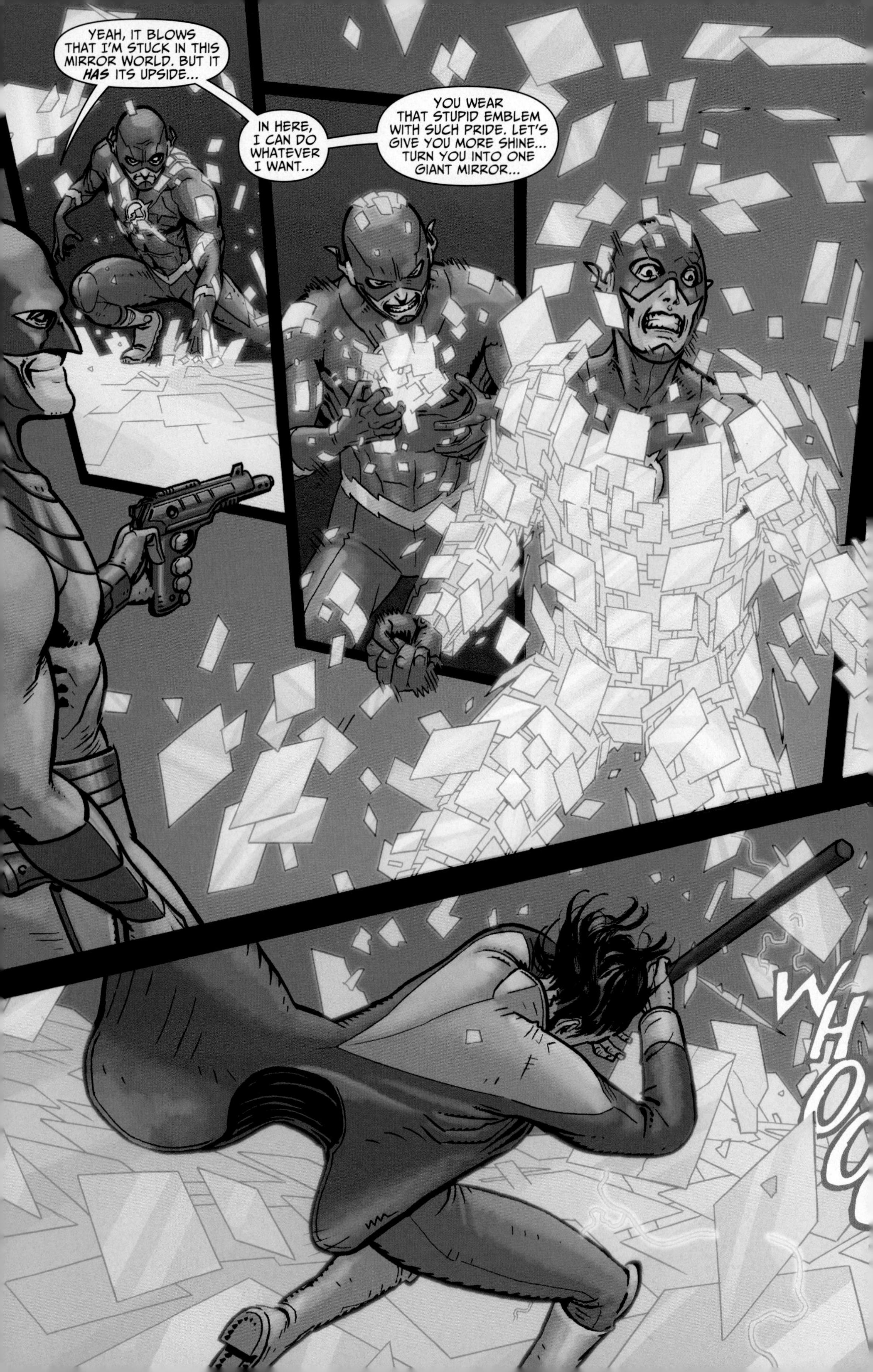
YEAH, IT BLOWS THAT I'M STUCK IN THIS MIRROR WORLD. BUT IT HAS ITS UPSIDE...
IN HERE, I CAN DO WHATEVER I WANT...
YOU WEAR THAT STUPID EMBLEM WITH SUCH PRIDE. LET'S GIVE YOU MORE SHINE... TURN YOU INTO ONE GIANT MIRROR...

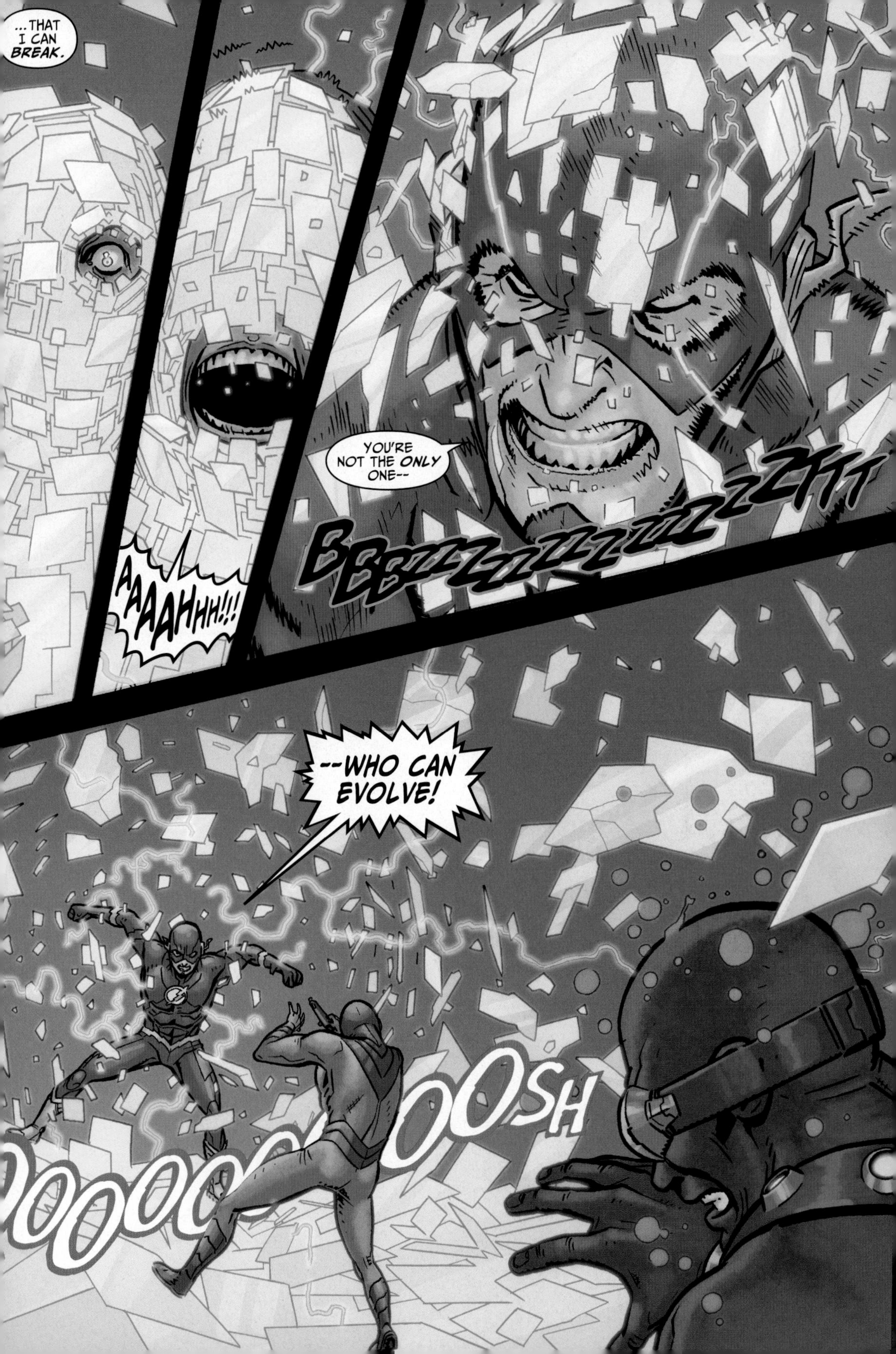
...THAT I CAN BREAK.
AAAAHHH!!!
YOU'RE NOT THE ONLY ONE--
BBBZZZZZZZZZZZZZTTT
--WHO CAN EVOLVE!
OOOOOOOOOSH

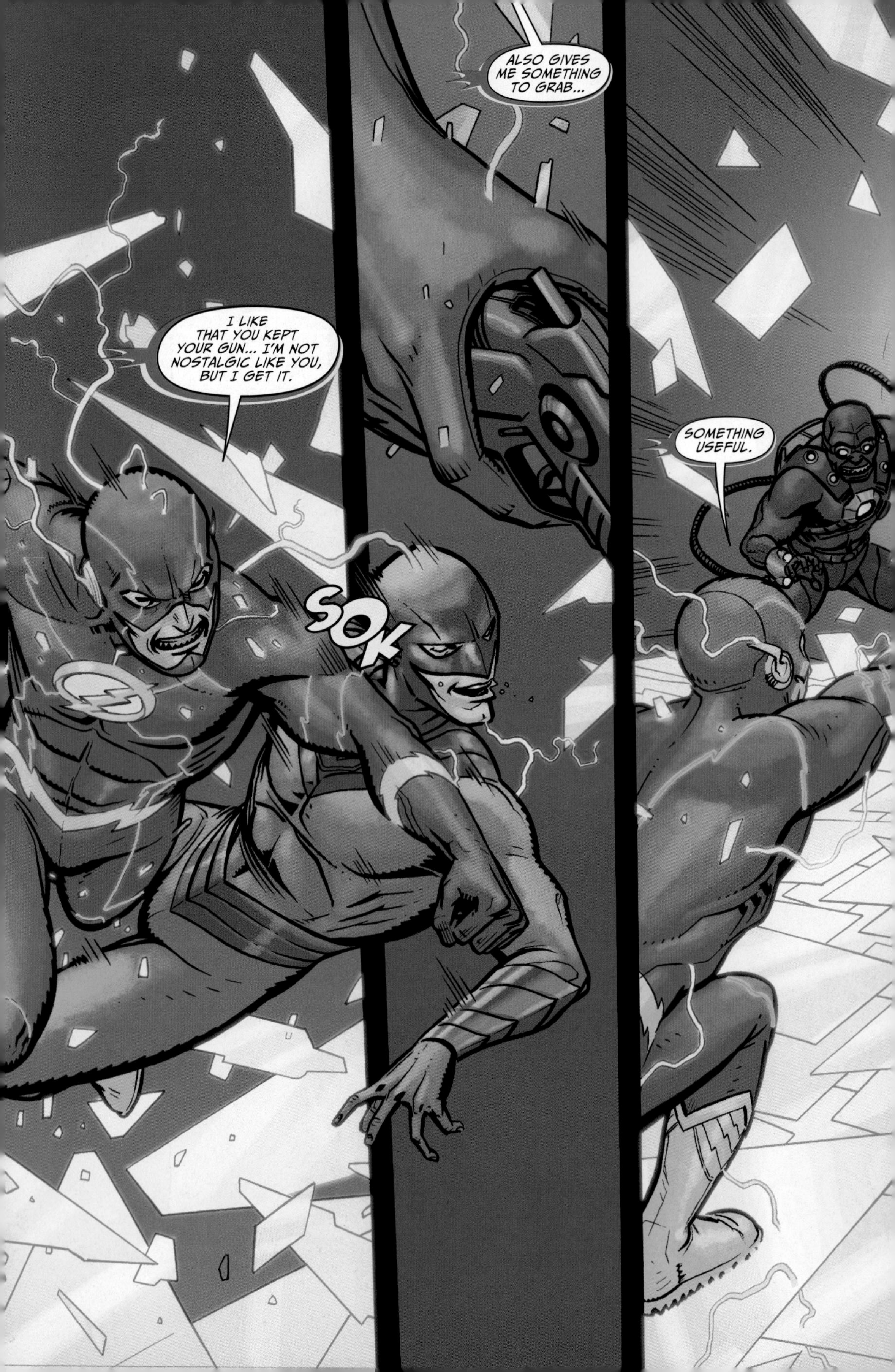
I LIKE THAT YOU KEPT YOUR GUN... I'M NOT NOSTALGIC LIKE YOU, BUT I GET IT.
SOK
ALSO GIVES ME SOMETHING TO GRAB...
SOMETHING USEFUL.

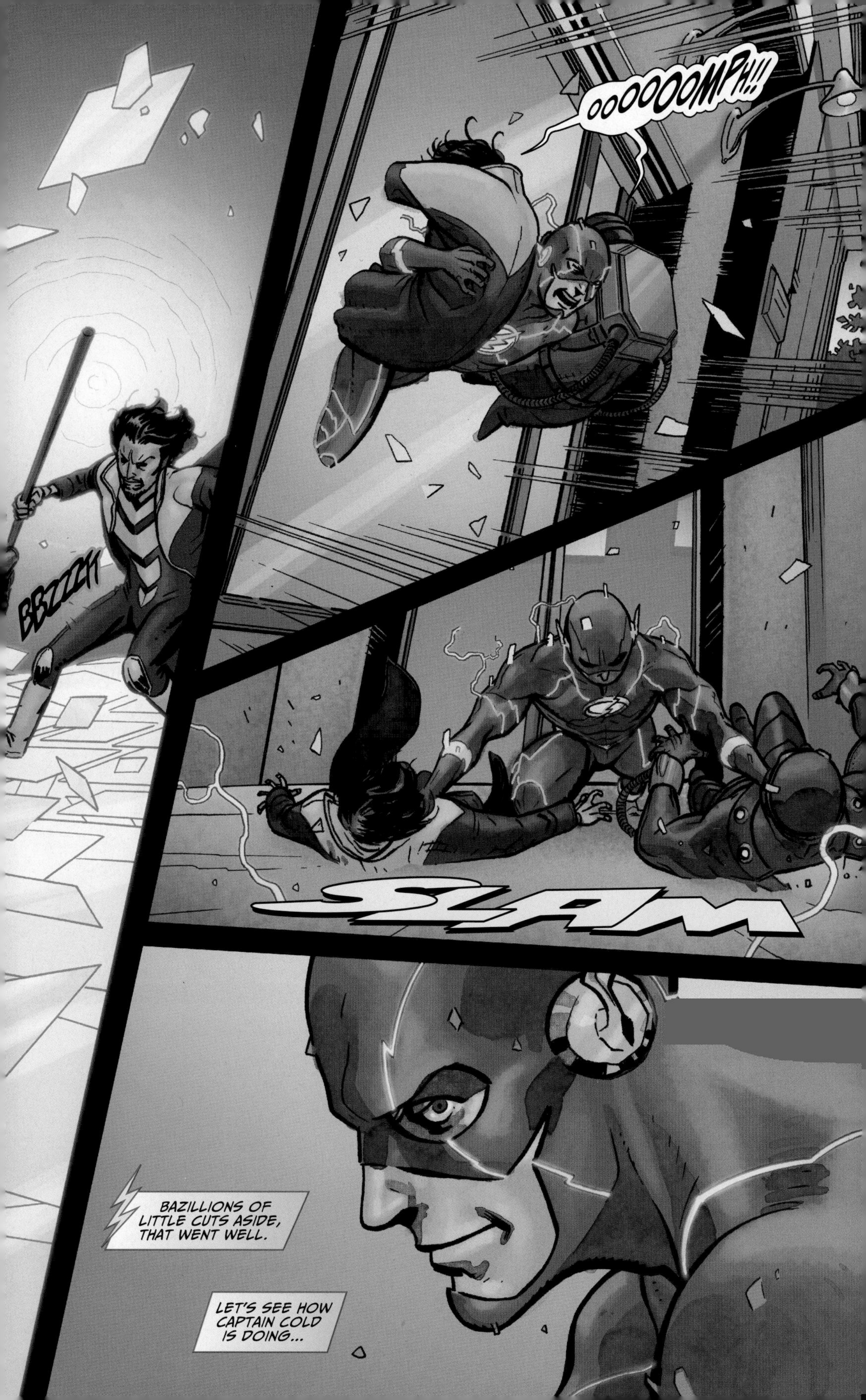

OOOOOOMPH!!
BBZZZZH
SLAM
BAZILLIONS OF LITTLE CUTS ASIDE, THAT WENT WELL.
LET'S SEE HOW CAPTAIN COLD IS DOING...

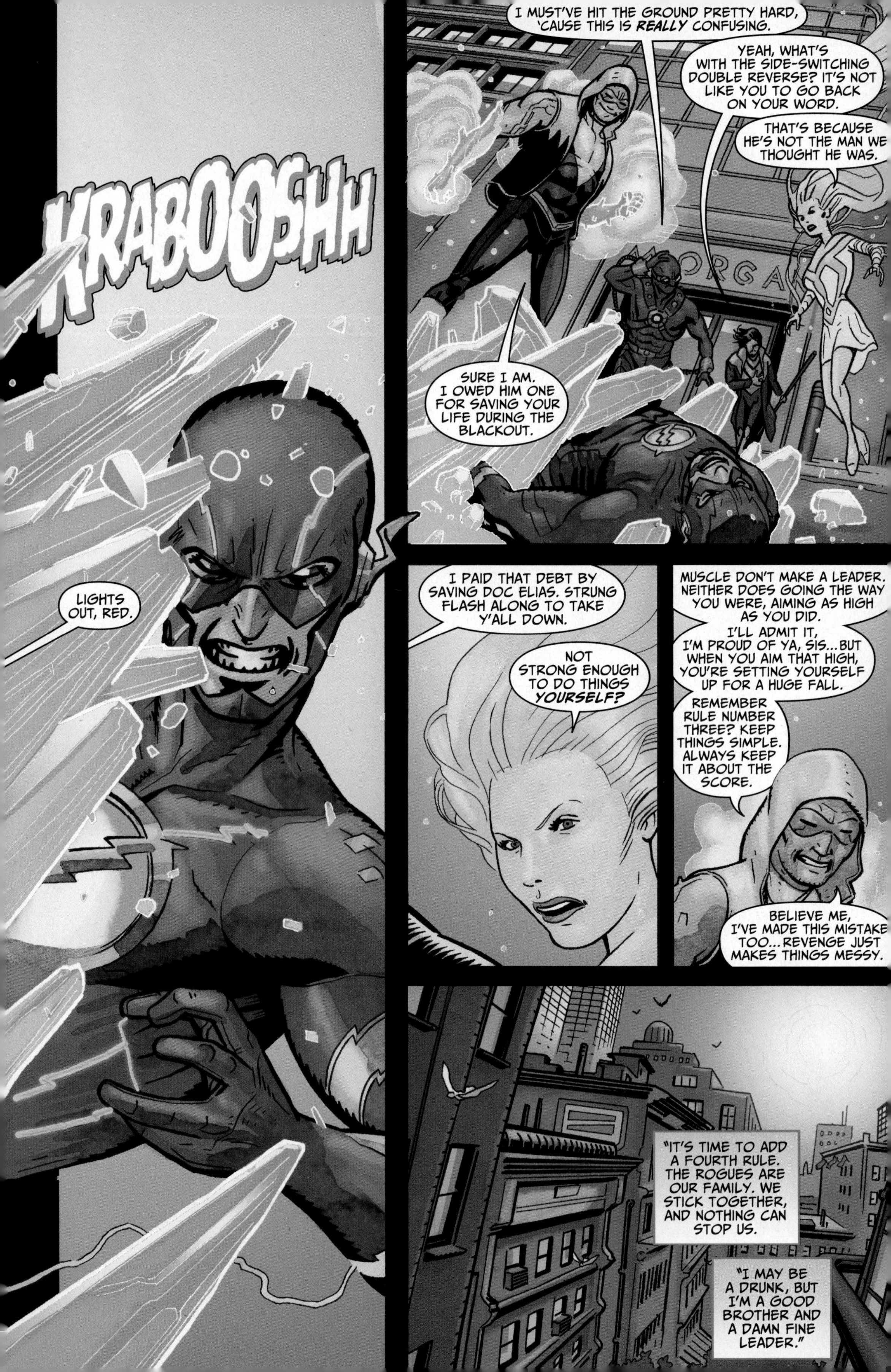
KRABOOSHH
LIGHTS OUT, RED.
I MUST'VE HIT THE GROUND PRETTY HARD, 'CAUSE THIS IS REALLY CONFUSING.
YEAH, WHAT'S WITH THE SIDE-SWITCHING DOUBLE REVERSE? IT'S NOT LIKE YOU TO GO BACK ON YOUR WORD.
THAT'S BECAUSE HE'S NOT THE MAN WE THOUGHT HE WAS.
SURE I AM. I OWED HIM ONE FOR SAVING YOUR LIFE DURING THE BLACKOUT.
I PAID THAT DEBT BY SAVING DOC ELIAS. STRUNG FLASH ALONG TO TAKE Y'ALL DOWN.
NOT STRONG ENOUGH TO DO THINGS YOURSELF?
MUSCLE DON'T MAKE A LEADER. NEITHER DOES GOING THE WAY YOU WERE, AIMING AS HIGH AS YOU DID.
I'LL ADMIT IT, I'M PROUD OF YA, SIS... BUT WHEN YOU AIM THAT HIGH, YOU'RE SETTING YOURSELF UP FOR A HUGE FALL.
REMEMBER RULE NUMBER THREE? KEEP THINGS SIMPLE. ALWAYS KEEP IT ABOUT THE SCORE.
BELIEVE ME, I'VE MADE THIS MISTAKE TOO... REVENGE JUST MAKES THINGS MESSY.
"IT'S TIME TO ADD A FOURTH RULE. THE ROGUES ARE OUR FAMILY. WE STICK TOGETHER, AND NOTHING CAN STOP US.
"I MAY BE A DRUNK, BUT I'M A GOOD BROTHER AND A DAMN FINE LEADER."

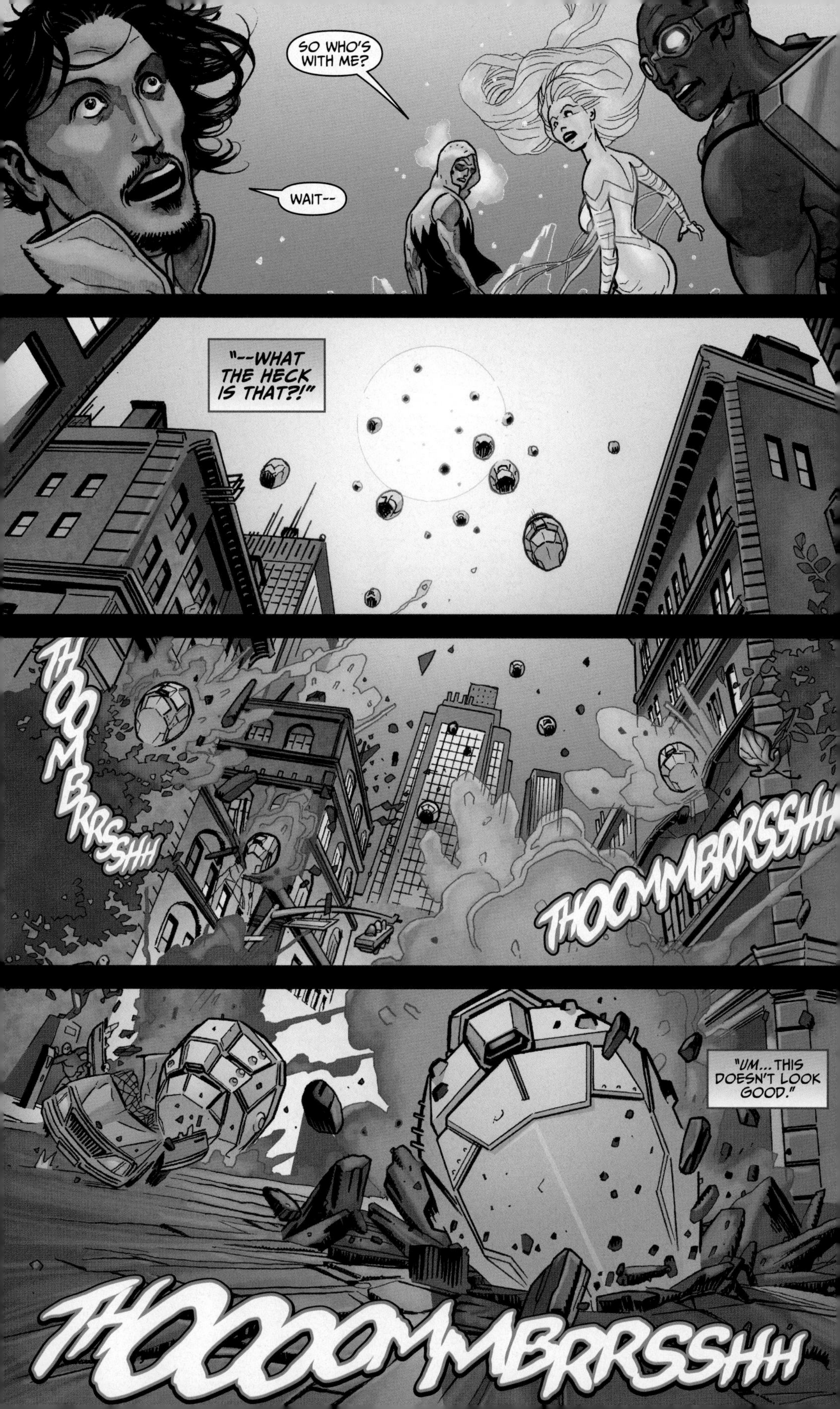
SO WHO'S WITH ME?
WAIT--
"--WHAT THE HECK IS THAT?!"
THOOMMBRRSSHH
THOOMMBRRSSHH
"UM... THIS DOESN'T LOOK GOOD."
THOOOOMMBRRSSHH

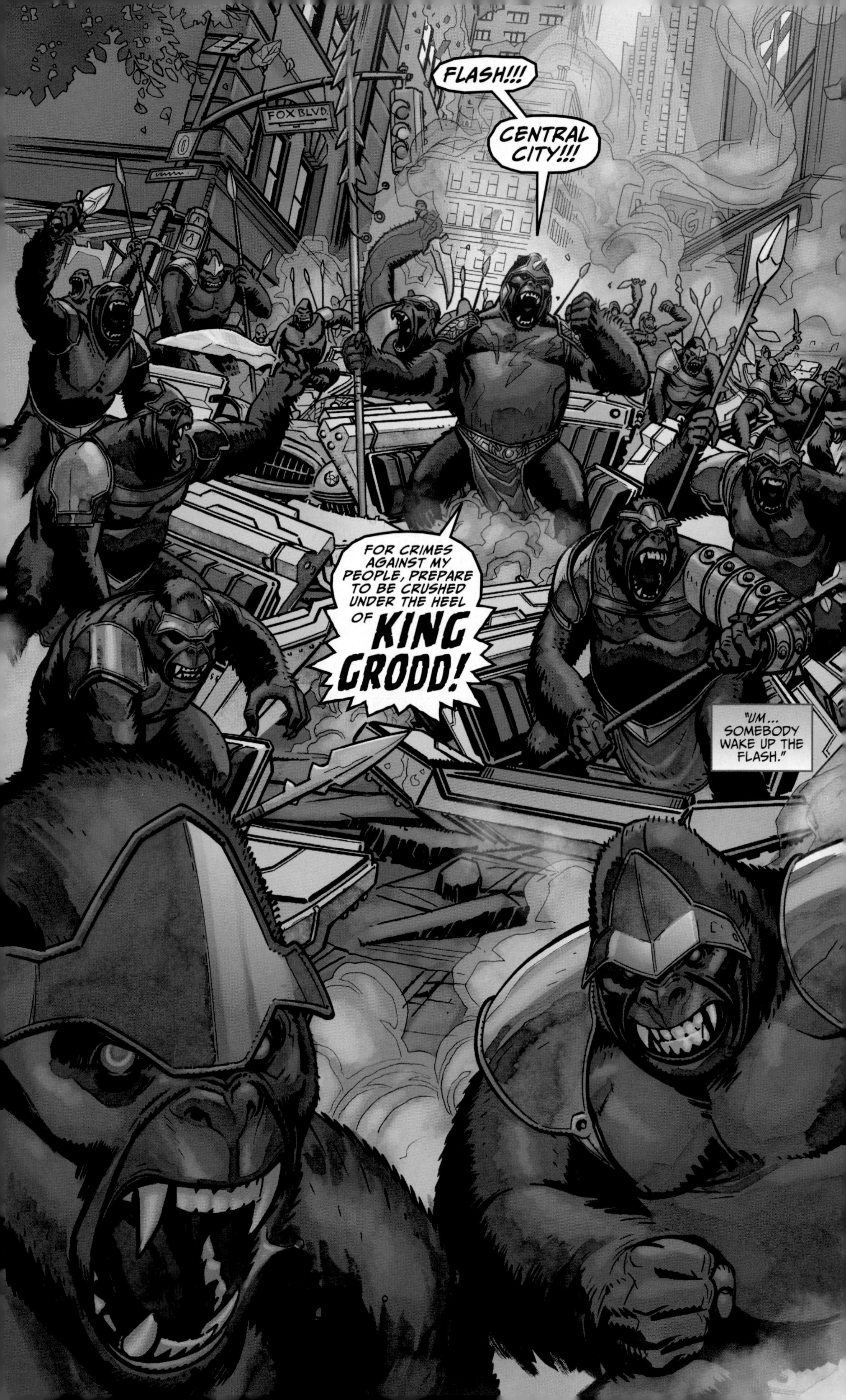

FOX BLVD.
FLASH!!!
CENTRAL CITY!!!
FOR CRIMES AGAINST MY PEOPLE, PREPARE TO BE CRUSHED UNDER THE HEEL OF KING GRODD!
"UM... SOMEBODY WAKE UP THE FLASH."

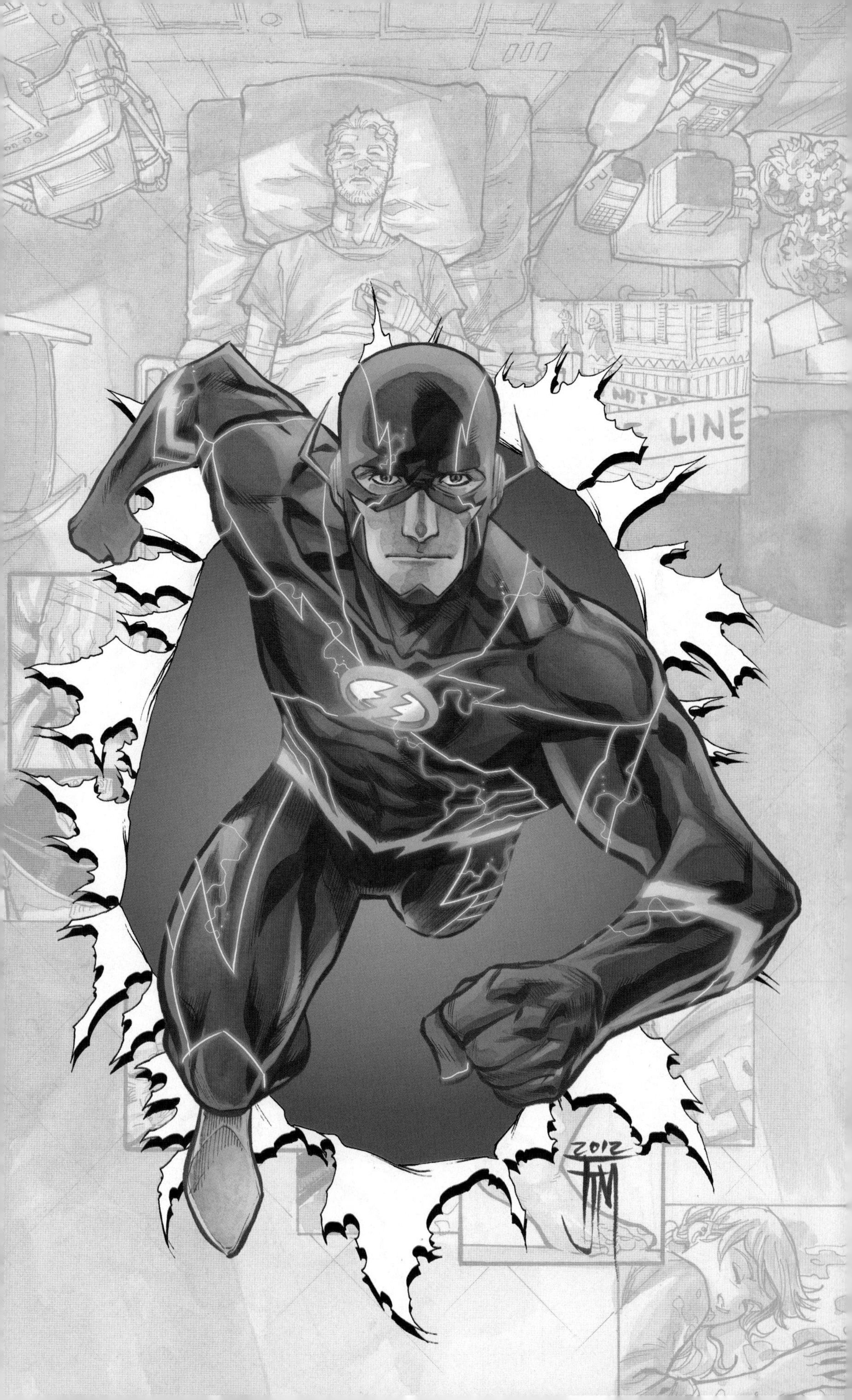
LINE
2012

FRANCIS MANAPUL & BRIAN BUCCELLATO writers FRANCIS MANAPUL artist

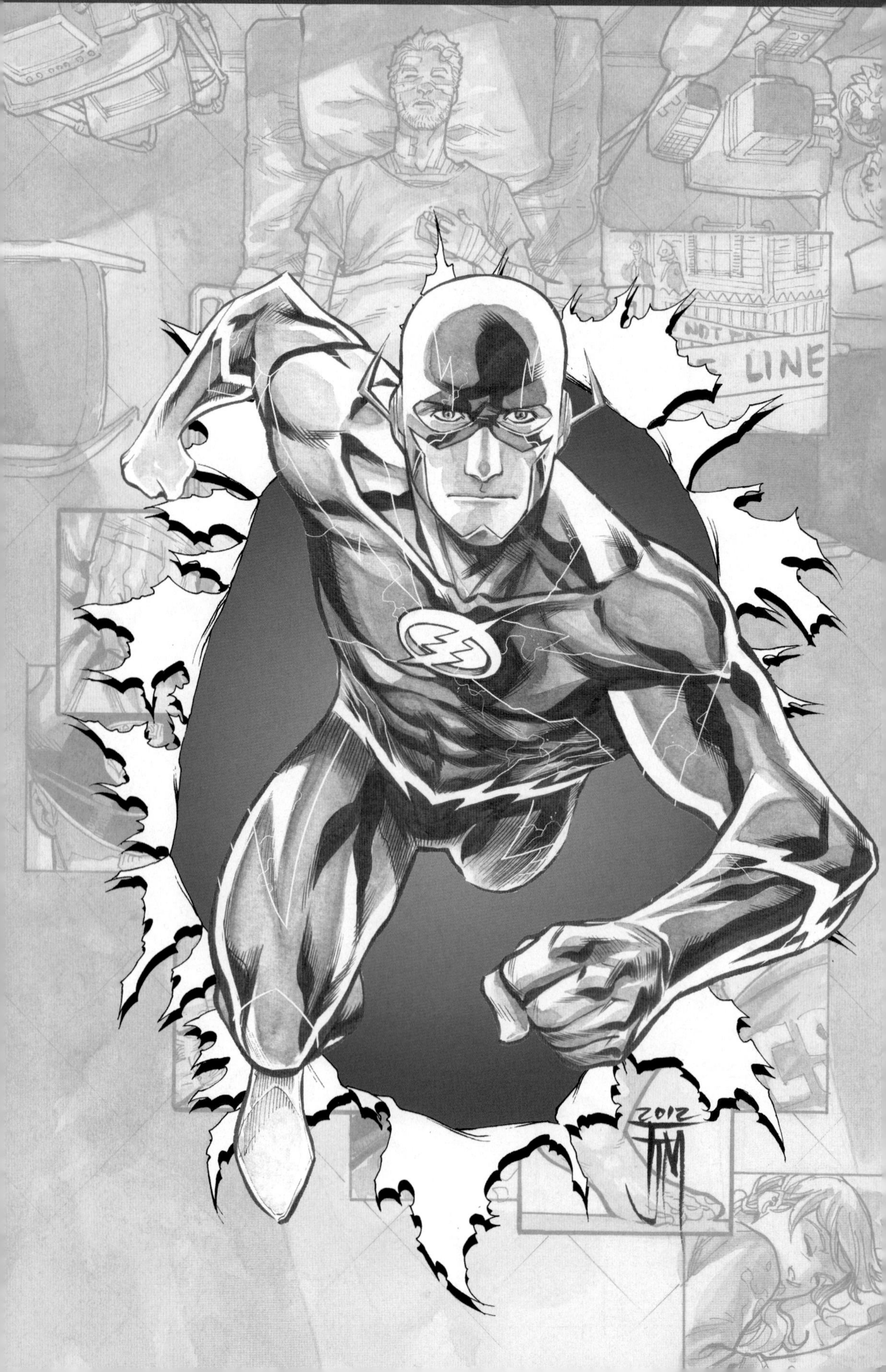

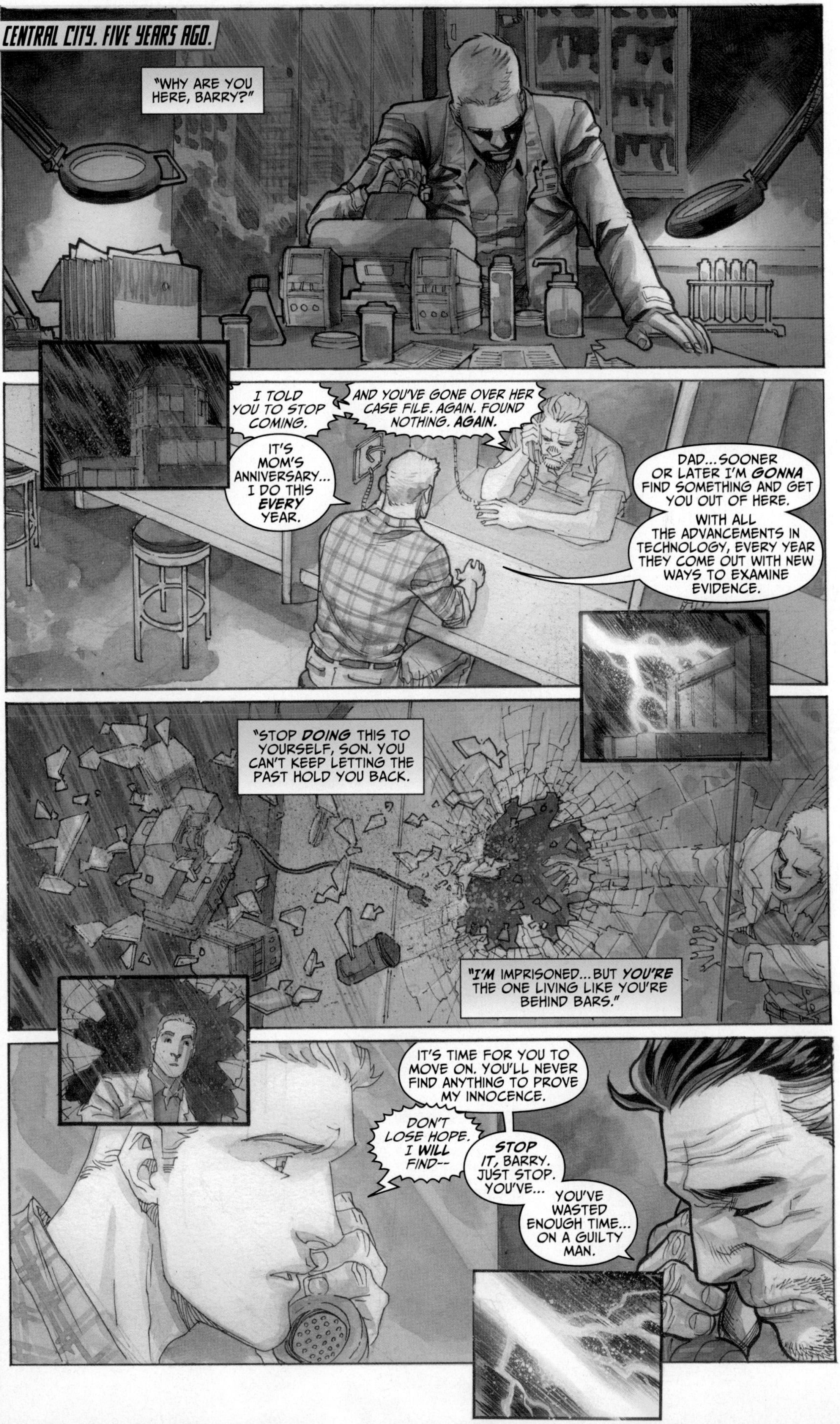
CENTRAL CITY. FIVE YEARS AGO.
"WHY ARE YOU HERE, BARRY?"
I TOLD YOU TO STOP COMING.
AND YOU'VE GONE OVER HER CASE FILE. AGAIN. FOUND NOTHING. AGAIN.
IT'S MOM'S ANNIVERSARY... I DO THIS EVERY YEAR.
DAD...SOONER OR LATER I'M GONNA FIND SOMETHING AND GET YOU OUT OF HERE.
WITH ALL THE ADVANCEMENTS IN TECHNOLOGY, EVERY YEAR THEY COME OUT WITH NEW WAYS TO EXAMINE EVIDENCE.
"STOP DOING THIS TO YOURSELF, SON. YOU CAN'T KEEP LETTING THE PAST HOLD YOU BACK.
"I'M IMPRISONED...BUT YOU'RE THE ONE LIVING LIKE YOU'RE BEHIND BARS."
IT'S TIME FOR YOU TO MOVE ON. YOU'LL NEVER FIND ANYTHING TO PROVE MY INNOCENCE.
DON'T LOSE HOPE. I WILL FIND--
STOP IT, BARRY. JUST STOP. YOU'VE...
YOU'VE WASTED ENOUGH TIME... ON A GUILTY MAN.

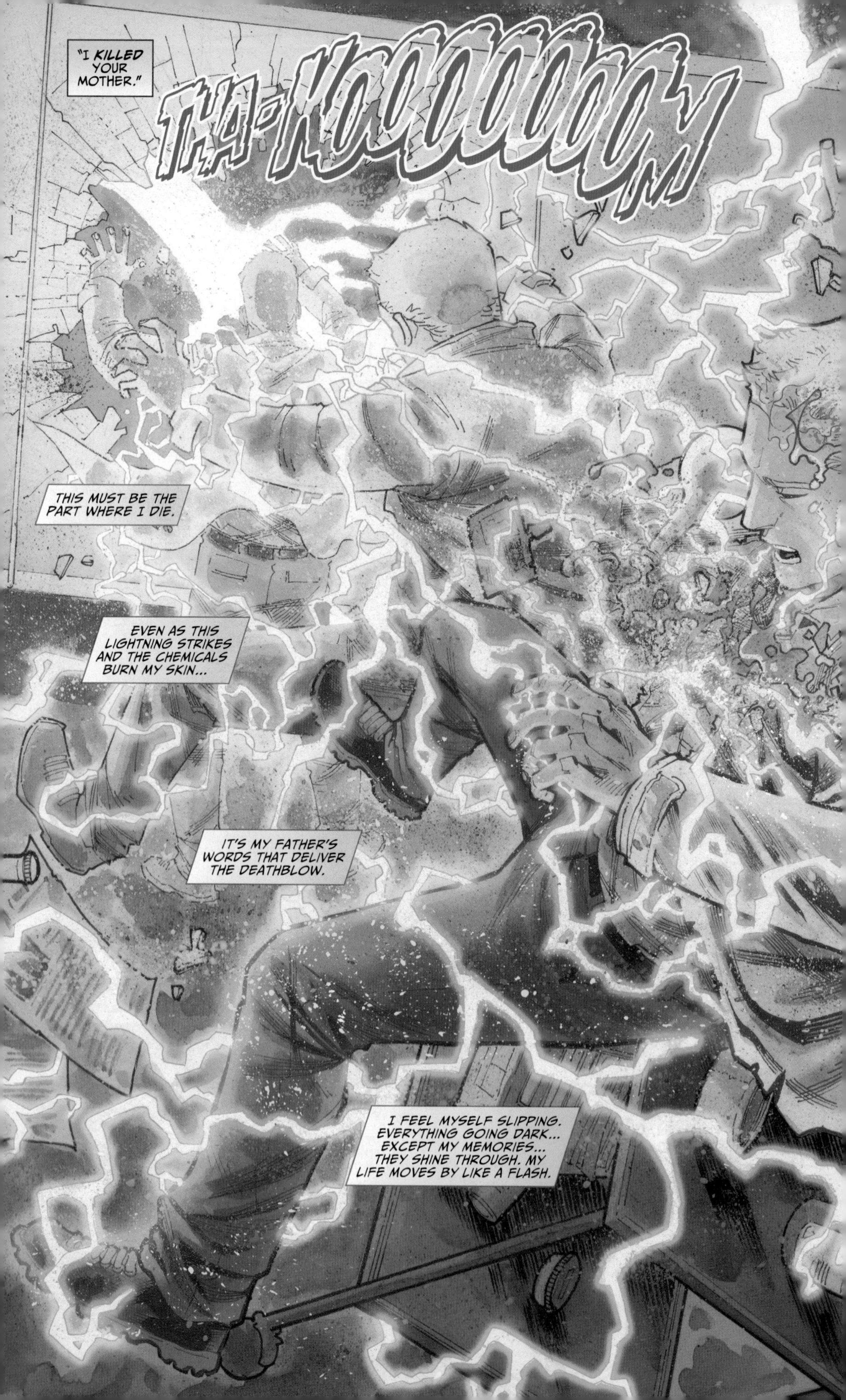
"I KILLED YOUR MOTHER."
THA-KOOOOOOOOM
THIS MUST BE THE PART WHERE I DIE.
EVEN AS THIS LIGHTNING STRIKES AND THE CHEMICALS BURN MY SKIN...
IT'S MY FATHER'S WORDS THAT DELIVER THE DEATHBLOW.
I FEEL MYSELF SLIPPING. EVERYTHING GOING DARK... EXCEPT MY MEMORIES... THEY SHINE THROUGH. MY LIFE MOVES BY LIKE A FLASH.

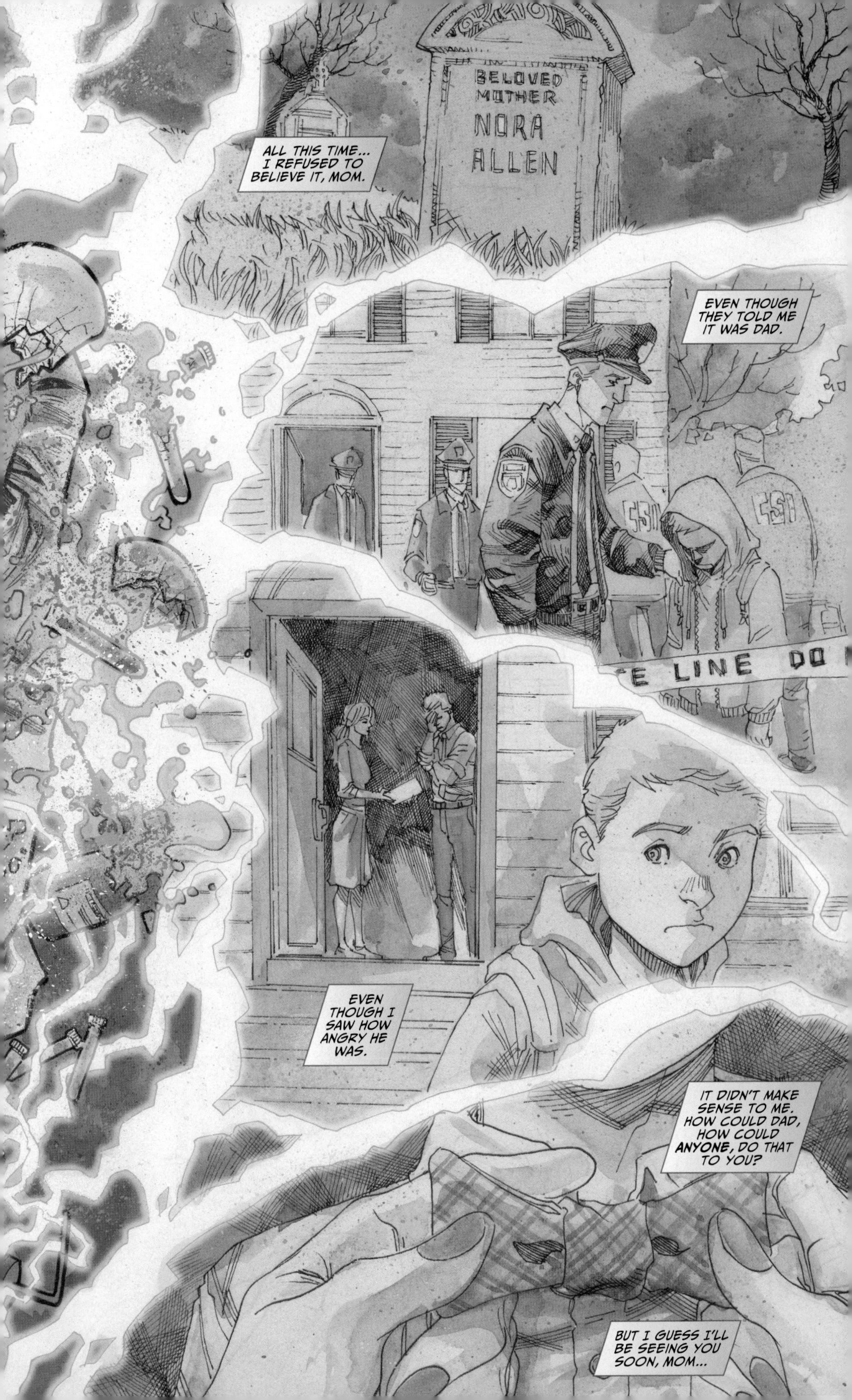
BELOVED MOTHER NORA ALLEN
ALL THIS TIME... I REFUSED TO BELIEVE IT, MOM.
EVEN THOUGH THEY TOLD ME IT WAS DAD.
CSI
CSI
E LINE DO
EVEN THOUGH I SAW HOW ANGRY HE WAS.
IT DIDN'T MAKE SENSE TO ME. HOW COULD DAD, HOW COULD ANYONE, DO THAT TO YOU?
BUT I GUESS I'LL BE SEEING YOU SOON, MOM...

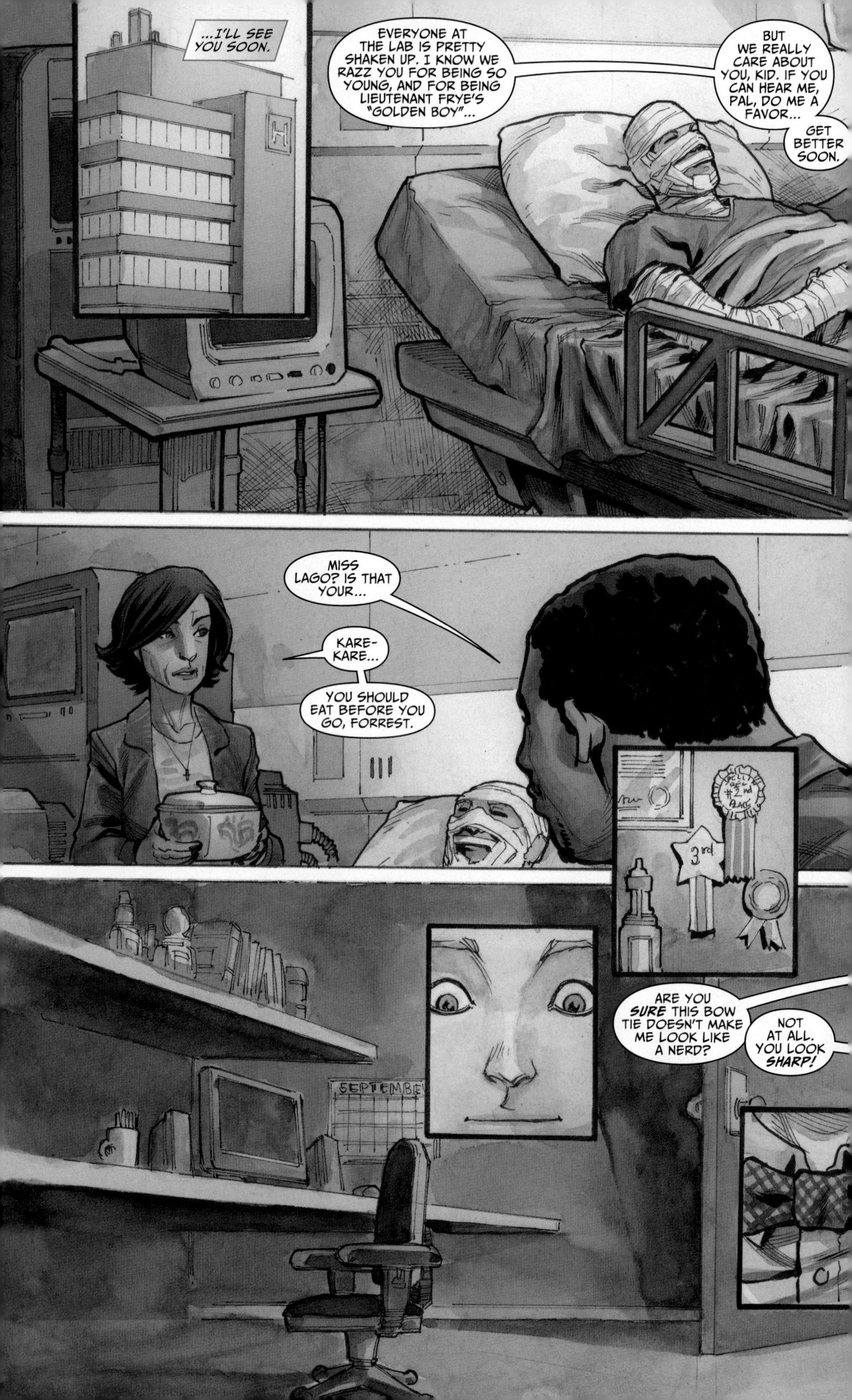
...I'LL SEE YOU SOON.
EVERYONE AT THE LAB IS PRETTY SHAKEN UP. I KNOW WE RAZZ YOU FOR BEING SO YOUNG, AND FOR BEING LIEUTENANT FRYE'S "GOLDEN BOY"...
BUT WE REALLY CARE ABOUT YOU, KID. IF YOU CAN HEAR ME, PAL, DO ME A FAVOR...
GET BETTER SOON.
MISS LAGO? IS THAT YOUR...
KARE-KARE...
YOU SHOULD EAT BEFORE YOU GO, FORREST.
3rd
SEPTEMBE
ARE YOU SURE THIS BOW TIE DOESN'T MAKE ME LOOK LIKE A NERD?
NOT AT ALL. YOU LOOK SHARP!

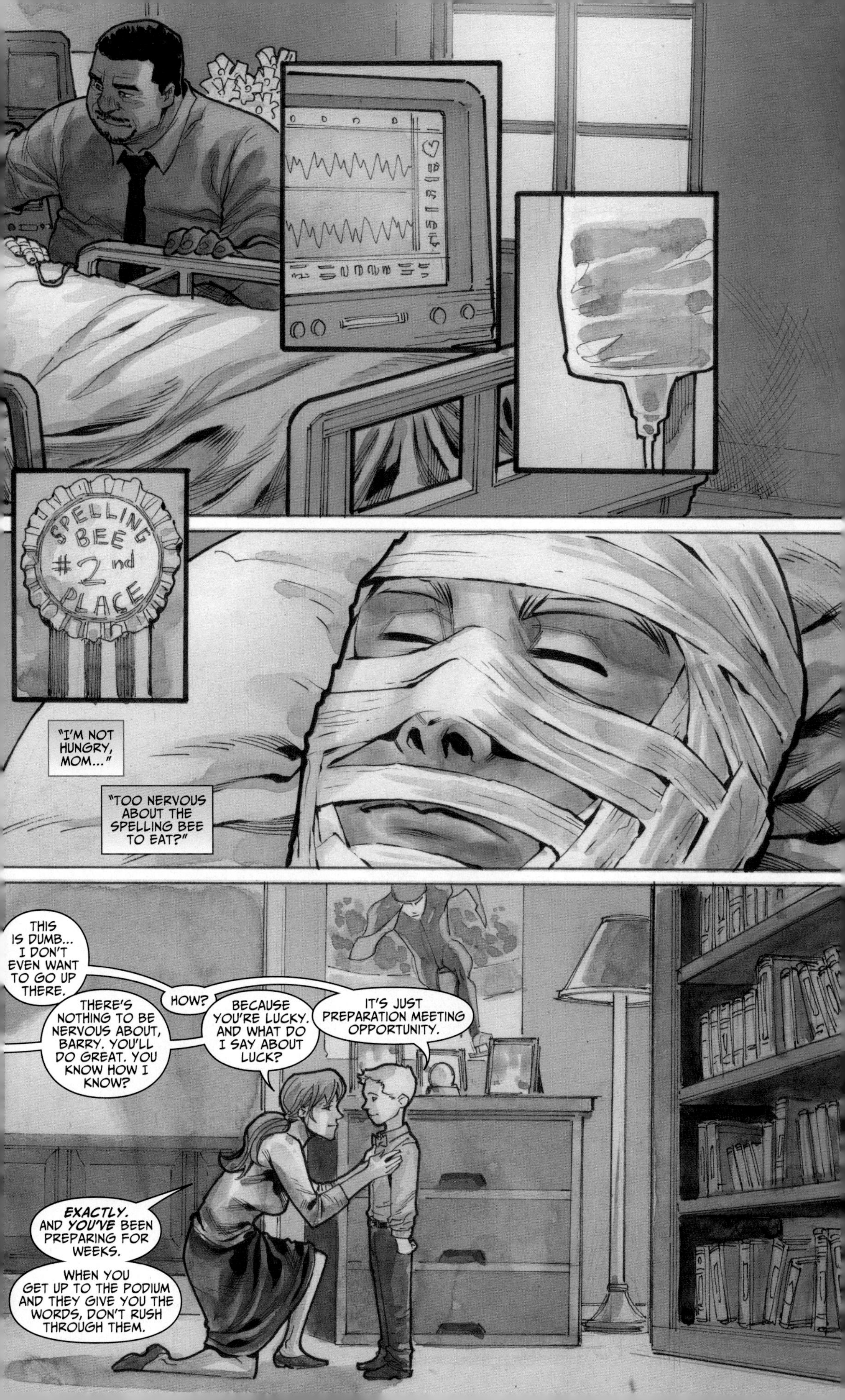
SPELLING BEE #2 nd PLACE
"I'M NOT HUNGRY, MOM..."
"TOO NERVOUS ABOUT THE SPELLING BEE TO EAT?"
THIS IS DUMB... I DON'T EVEN WANT TO GO UP THERE.
THERE'S NOTHING TO BE NERVOUS ABOUT, BARRY. YOU'LL DO GREAT. YOU KNOW HOW I KNOW?
HOW?
BECAUSE YOU'RE LUCKY. AND WHAT DO I SAY ABOUT LUCK?
IT'S JUST PREPARATION MEETING OPPORTUNITY.
EXACTLY. AND YOU'VE BEEN PREPARING FOR WEEKS.
WHEN YOU GET UP TO THE PODIUM AND THEY GIVE YOU THE WORDS, DON'T RUSH THROUGH THEM.

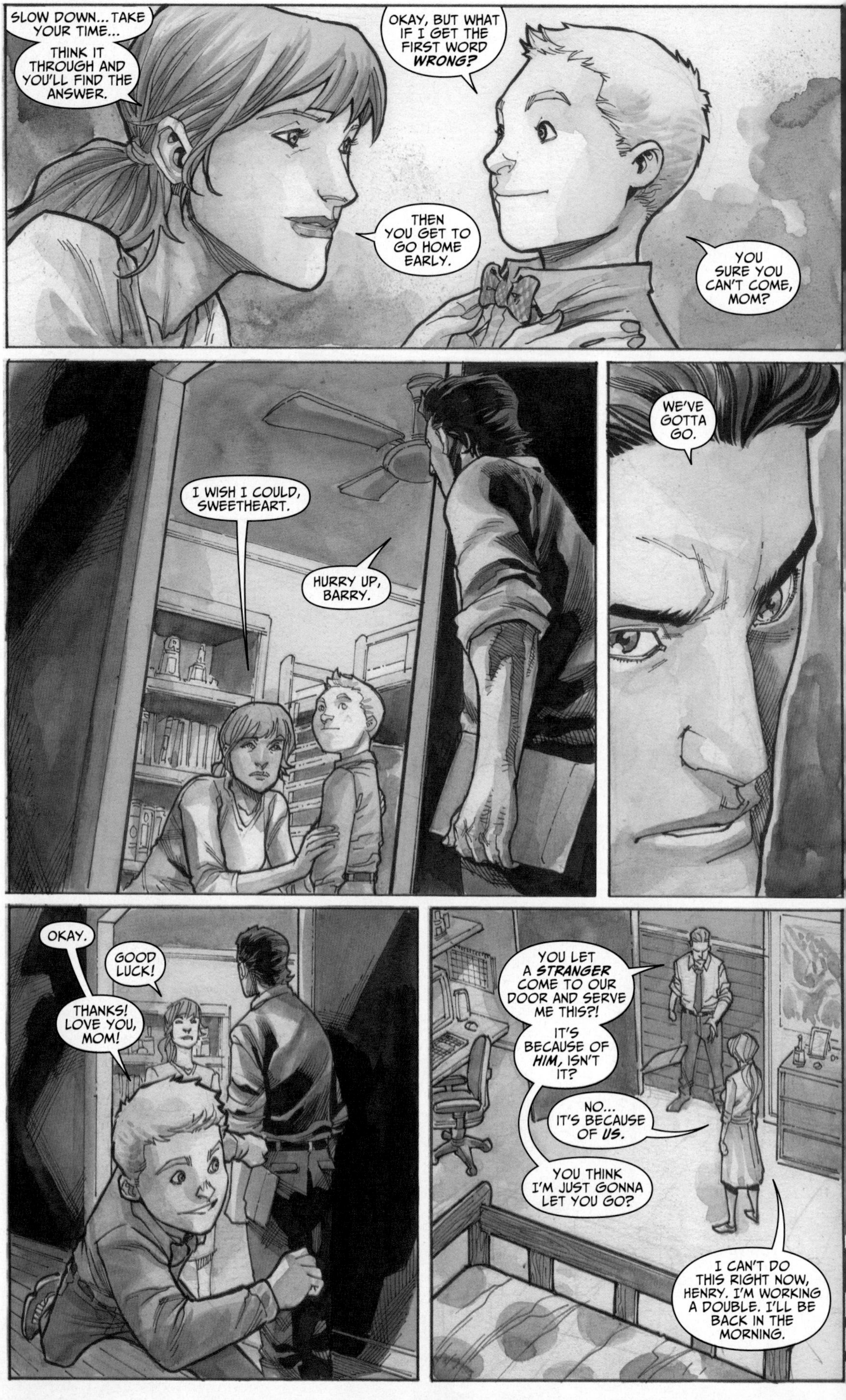
SLOW DOWN... TAKE YOUR TIME...
THINK IT THROUGH AND YOU'LL FIND THE ANSWER.
OKAY, BUT WHAT IF I GET THE FIRST WORD WRONG?
THEN YOU GET TO GO HOME EARLY.
YOU SURE YOU CAN'T COME, MOM?
I WISH I COULD, SWEETHEART.
HURRY UP, BARRY.
WE'VE GOTTA GO.
OKAY.
GOOD LUCK!
THANKS! LOVE YOU, MOM!
YOU LET A STRANGER COME TO OUR DOOR AND SERVE ME THIS?!
IT'S BECAUSE OF HIM, ISN'T IT?
NO... IT'S BECAUSE OF US.
YOU THINK I'M JUST GONNA LET YOU GO?
I CAN'T DO THIS RIGHT NOW, HENRY. I'M WORKING A DOUBLE. I'LL BE BACK IN THE MORNING.

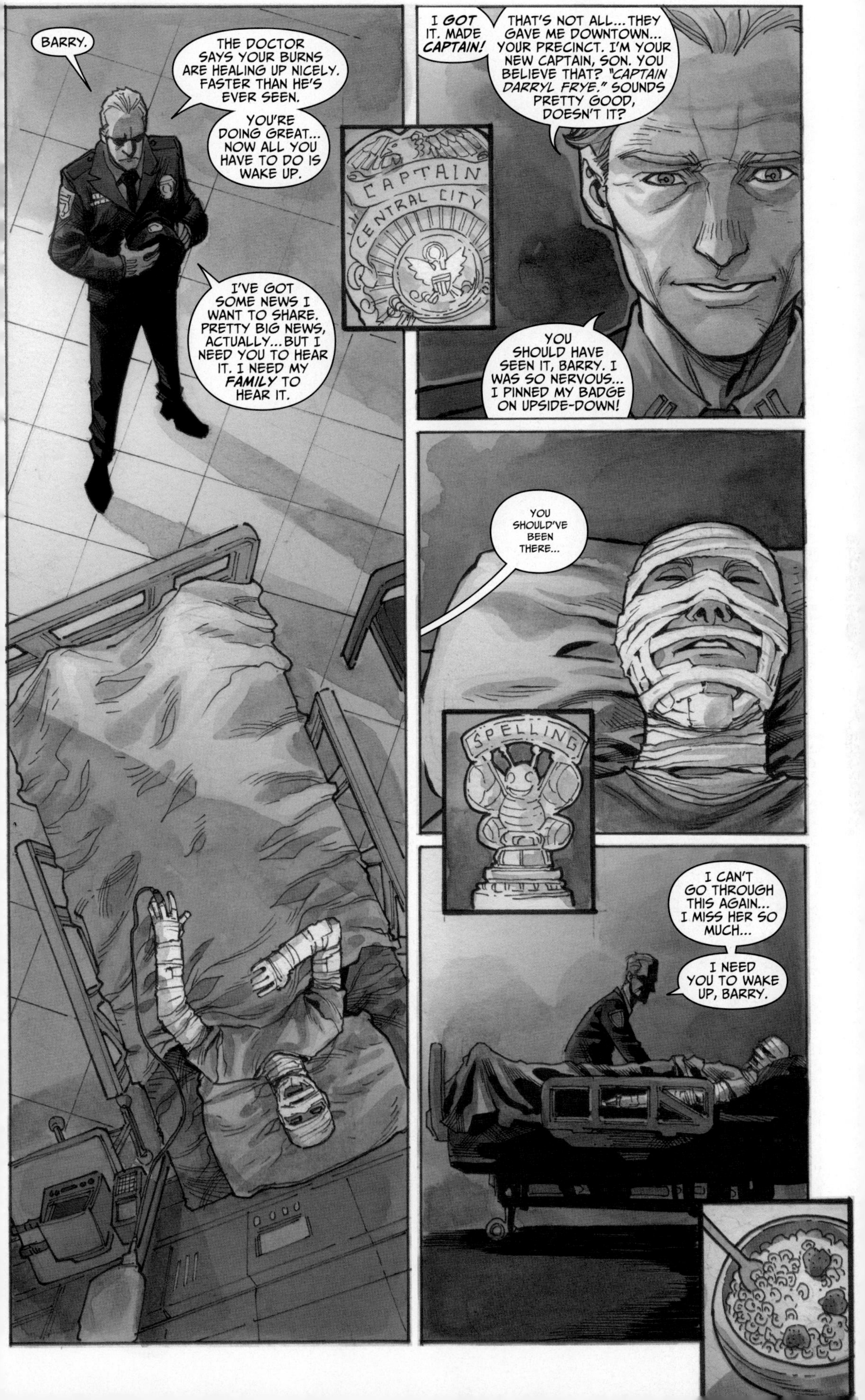
BARRY.
THE DOCTOR SAYS YOUR BURNS ARE HEALING UP NICELY. FASTER THAN HE'S EVER SEEN.
YOU'RE DOING GREAT... NOW ALL YOU HAVE TO DO IS WAKE UP.
I'VE GOT SOME NEWS I WANT TO SHARE. PRETTY BIG NEWS, ACTUALLY... BUT I NEED YOU TO HEAR IT. I NEED MY FAMILY TO HEAR IT.
CAPTAIN
CENTRAL CITY
I GOT IT. MADE CAPTAIN!
THAT'S NOT ALL... THEY GAVE ME DOWNTOWN... YOUR PRECINCT. I'M YOUR NEW CAPTAIN, SON. YOU BELIEVE THAT? "CAPTAIN DARRYL FRYE." SOUNDS PRETTY GOOD, DOESN'T IT?
YOU SHOULD HAVE SEEN IT, BARRY. I WAS SO NERVOUS... I PINNED MY BADGE ON UPSIDE-DOWN!
YOU SHOULD'VE BEEN THERE...
SPELLING
I CAN'T GO THROUGH THIS AGAIN... I MISS HER SO MUCH...
I NEED YOU TO WAKE UP, BARRY.

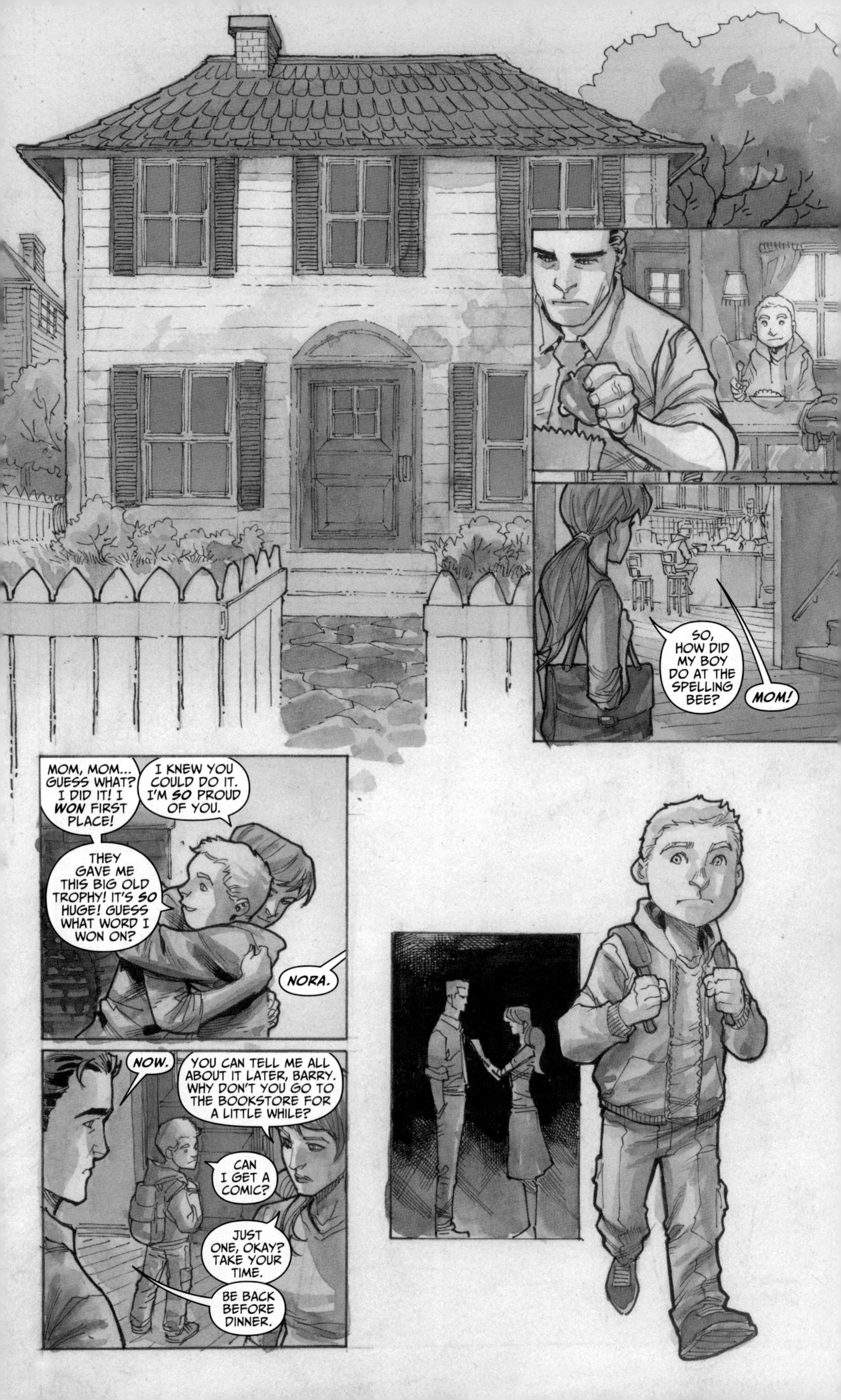

SO, HOW DID MY BOY DO AT THE SPELLING BEE?
MOM!
MOM, MOM... GUESS WHAT? I DID IT! I WON FIRST PLACE!
I KNEW YOU COULD DO IT. I'M SO PROUD OF YOU.
THEY GAVE ME THIS BIG OLD TROPHY! IT'S SO HUGE! GUESS WHAT WORD I WON ON?
NORA.
NOW.
YOU CAN TELL ME ALL ABOUT IT LATER, BARRY. WHY DON'T YOU GO TO THE BOOKSTORE FOR A LITTLE WHILE?
CAN I GET A COMIC?
JUST ONE, OKAY? TAKE YOUR TIME.
BE BACK BEFORE DINNER.

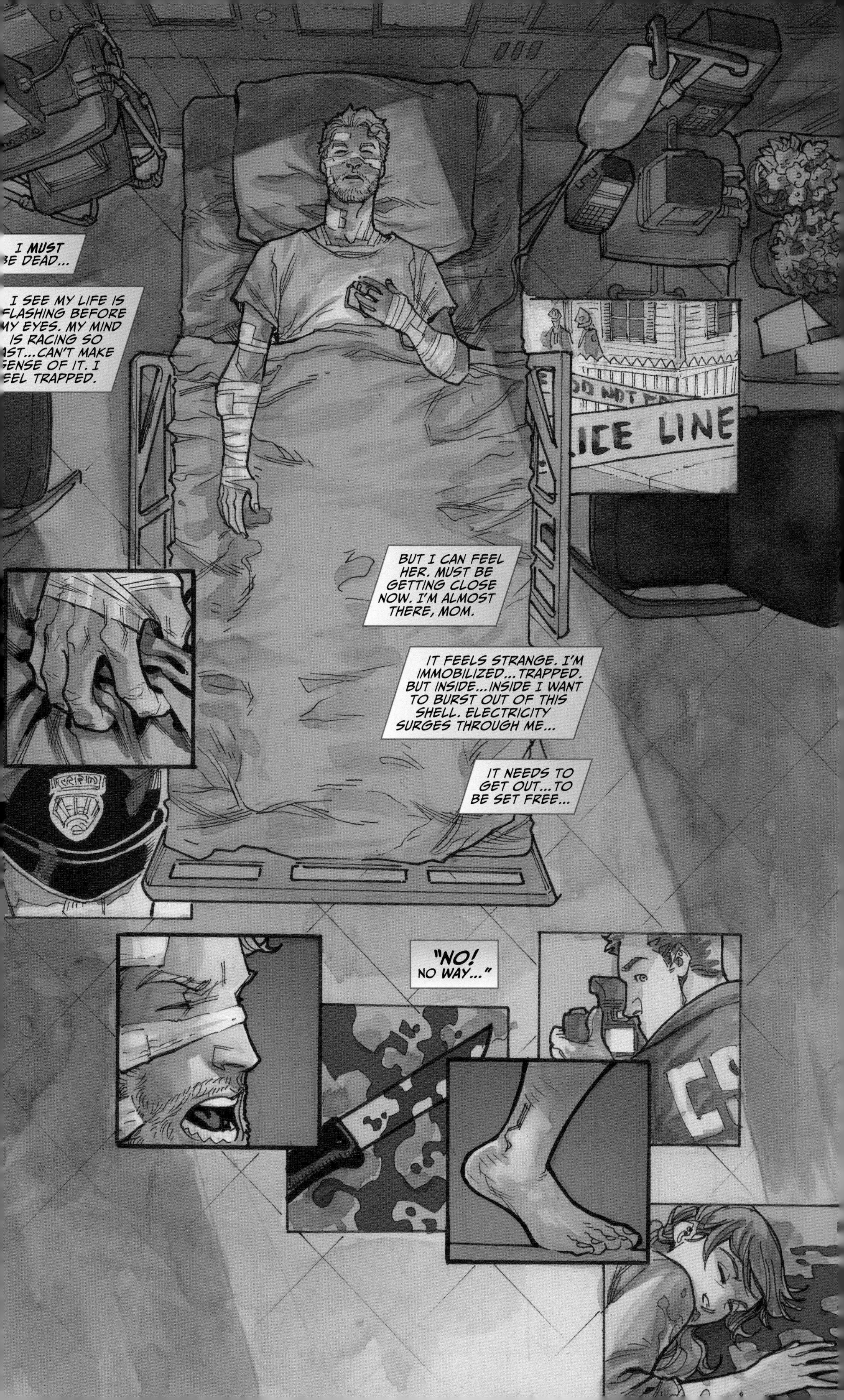
I MUST
BE DEAD...
I SEE MY LIFE IS FLASHING BEFORE MY EYES. MY MIND IS RACING SO FAST...CAN'T MAKE SENSE OF IT. I FEEL TRAPPED.
DO NOT
LICE LINE
BUT I CAN FEEL HER. MUST BE GETTING CLOSE NOW. I'M ALMOST THERE, MOM.
IT FEELS STRANGE. I'M IMMOBILIZED...TRAPPED. BUT INSIDE...INSIDE I WANT TO BURST OUT OF THIS SHELL. ELECTRICITY SURGES THROUGH ME...
IT NEEDS TO GET OUT...TO BE SET FREE...
"NO! NO WAY..."

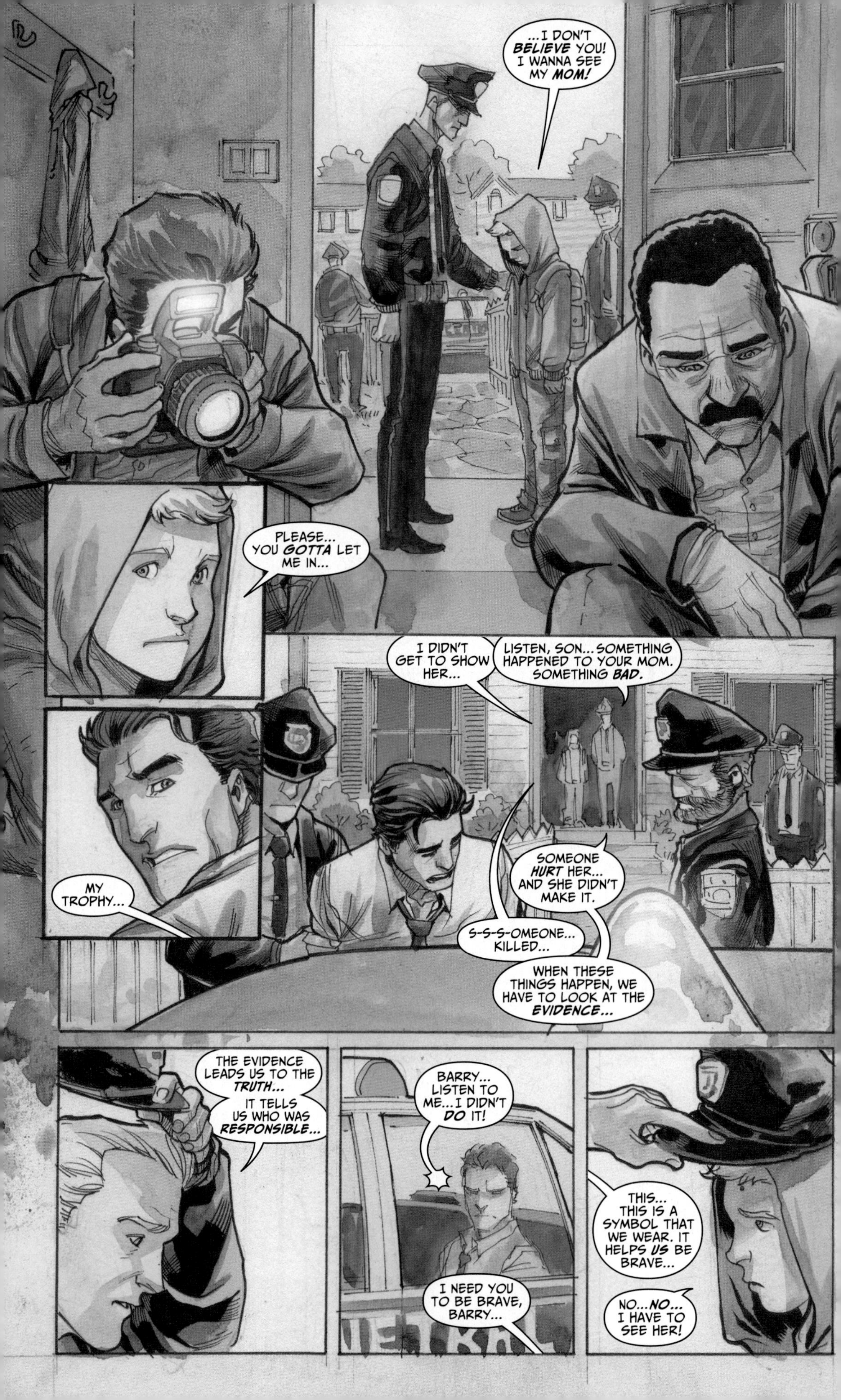
...I DON'T BELIEVE YOU! I WANNA SEE MY MOM!
PLEASE... YOU GOTTA LET ME IN...
I DIDN'T GET TO SHOW HER...
LISTEN, SON... SOMETHING HAPPENED TO YOUR MOM. SOMETHING BAD.
MY TROPHY...
SOMEONE HURT HER... AND SHE DIDN'T MAKE IT.
S-S-S-OMEONE... KILLED...
WHEN THESE THINGS HAPPEN, WE HAVE TO LOOK AT THE EVIDENCE...
THE EVIDENCE LEADS US TO THE TRUTH...
IT TELLS US WHO WAS RESPONSIBLE...
BARRY... LISTEN TO ME... I DIDN'T DO IT!
I NEED YOU TO BE BRAVE, BARRY...
THIS... THIS IS A SYMBOL THAT WE WEAR. IT HELPS US BE BRAVE...
NO...NO... I HAVE TO SEE HER!

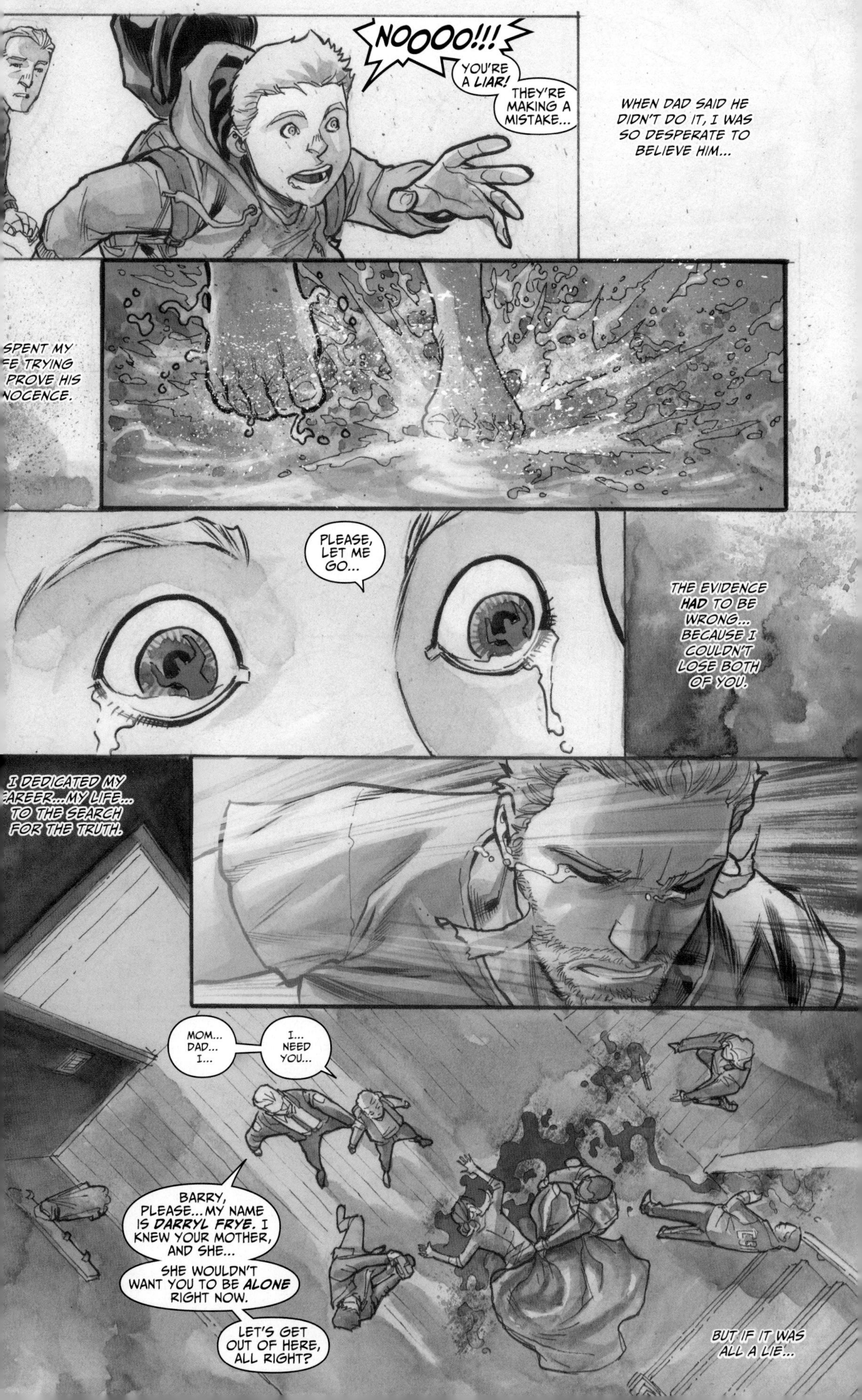
NOOOO!!!
YOU'RE A LIAR!
THEY'RE MAKING A MISTAKE...
WHEN DAD SAID HE DIDN'T DO IT, I WAS SO DESPERATE TO BELIEVE HIM...
SPENT MY FE TRYING PROVE HIS NOCENCE.
PLEASE, LET ME GO...
THE EVIDENCE HAD TO BE WRONG... BECAUSE I COULDN'T LOSE BOTH OF YOU.
I DEDICATED MY CAREER...MY LIFE... TO THE SEARCH FOR THE TRUTH.
MOM... DAD... I...
I... NEED YOU...
BARRY, PLEASE...MY NAME IS DARRYL FRYE. I KNEW YOUR MOTHER, AND SHE...
SHE WOULDN'T WANT YOU TO BE ALONE RIGHT NOW.
LET'S GET OUT OF HERE, ALL RIGHT?
BUT IF IT WAS ALL A LIE...

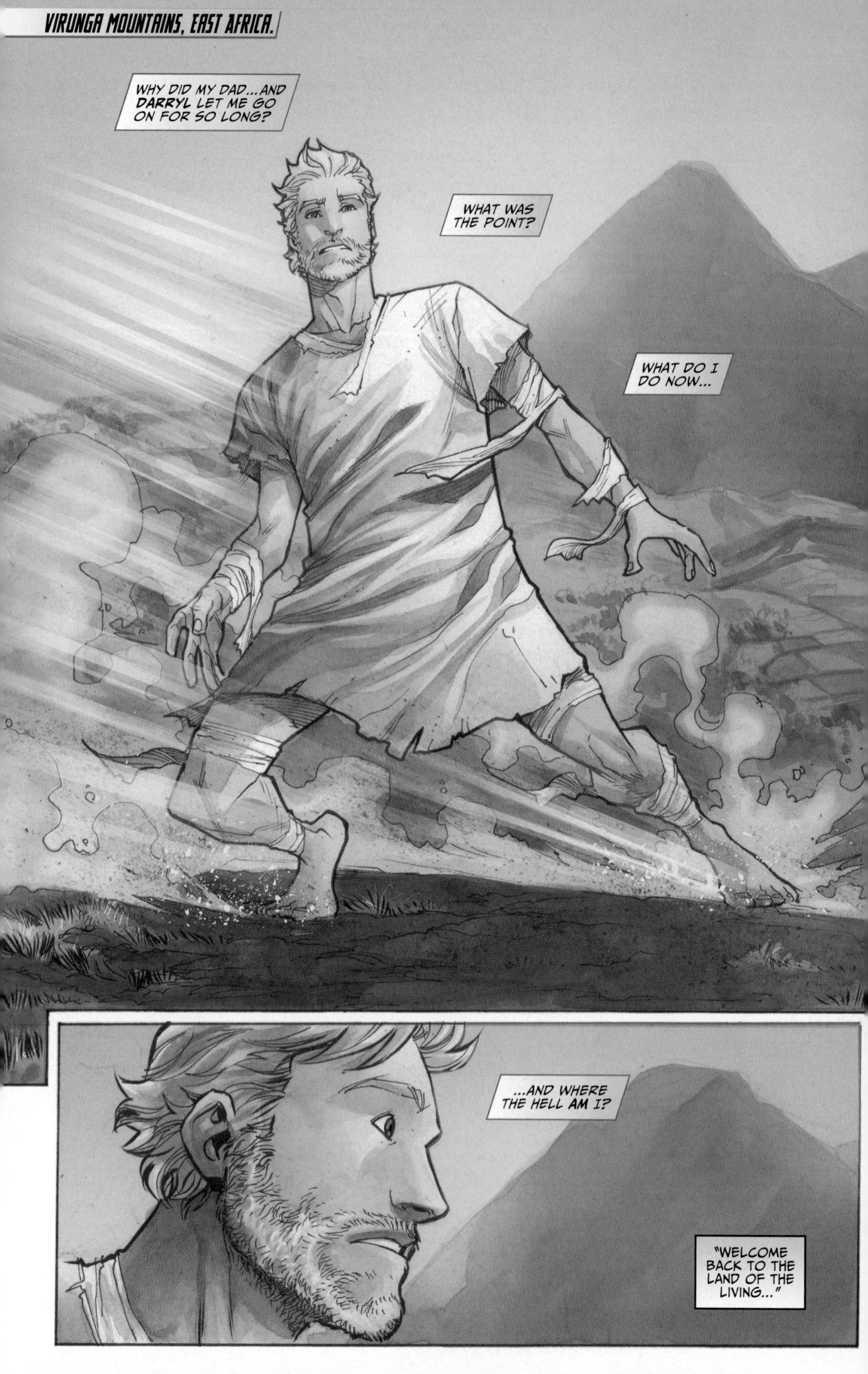
VIRUNGA MOUNTAINS, EAST AFRICA.
WHY DID MY DAD...AND DARRYL LET ME GO ON FOR SO LONG?
WHAT WAS THE POINT?
WHAT DO I DO NOW...
...AND WHERE THE HELL AM I?
"WELCOME BACK TO THE LAND OF THE LIVING..."

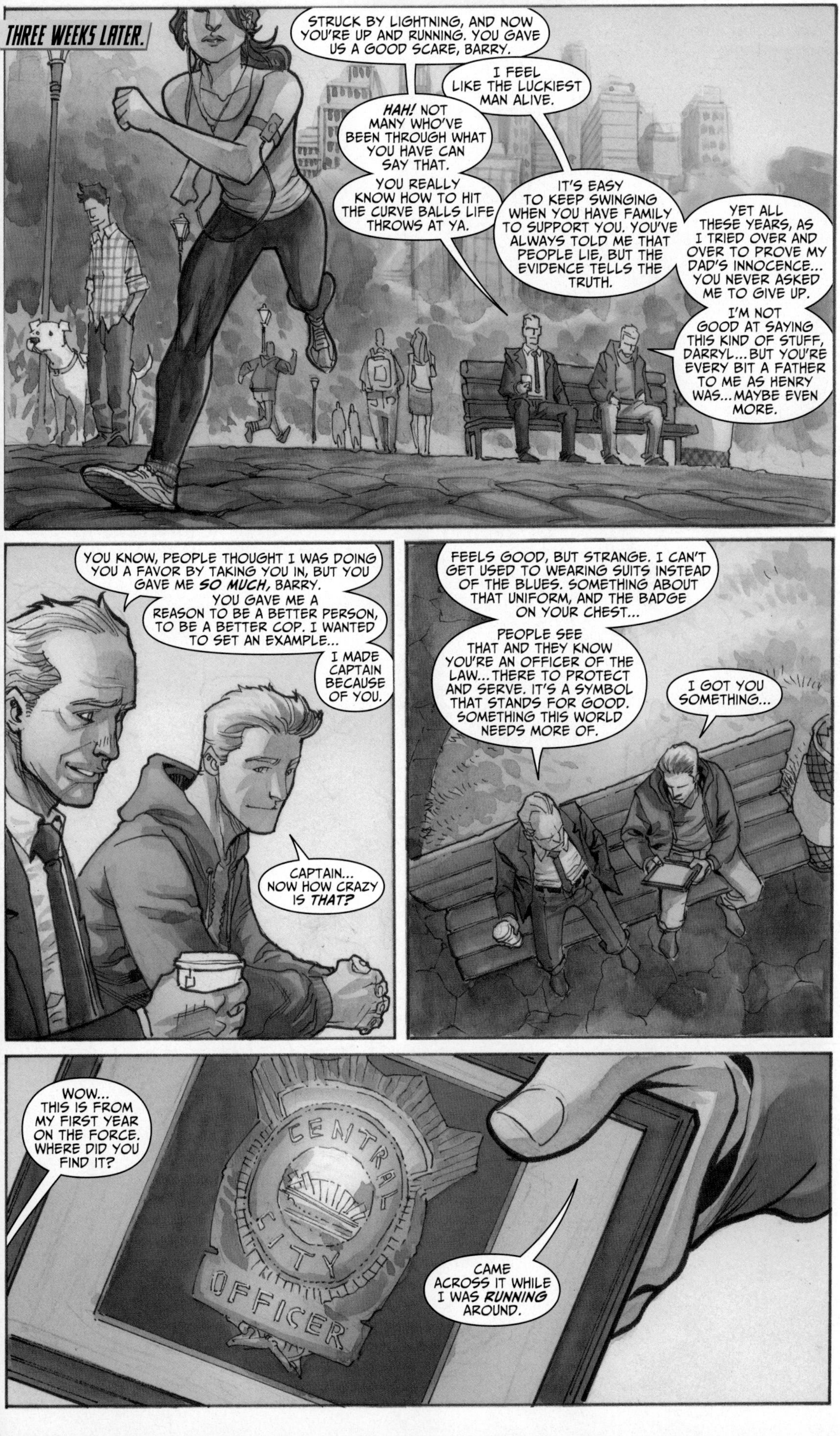
THREE WEEKS LATER.
STRUCK BY LIGHTNING, AND NOW YOU'RE UP AND RUNNING. YOU GAVE US A GOOD SCARE, BARRY.
I FEEL LIKE THE LUCKIEST MAN ALIVE.
HAH! NOT MANY WHO'VE BEEN THROUGH WHAT YOU HAVE CAN SAY THAT.
YOU REALLY KNOW HOW TO HIT THE CURVE BALLS LIFE THROWS AT YA.
IT'S EASY TO KEEP SWINGING WHEN YOU HAVE FAMILY TO SUPPORT YOU. YOU'VE ALWAYS TOLD ME THAT PEOPLE LIE, BUT THE EVIDENCE TELLS THE TRUTH.
YET ALL THESE YEARS, AS I TRIED OVER AND OVER TO PROVE MY DAD'S INNOCENCE... YOU NEVER ASKED ME TO GIVE UP.
I'M NOT GOOD AT SAYING THIS KIND OF STUFF, DARRYL... BUT YOU'RE EVERY BIT A FATHER TO ME AS HENRY WAS... MAYBE EVEN MORE.
YOU KNOW, PEOPLE THOUGHT I WAS DOING YOU A FAVOR BY TAKING YOU IN, BUT YOU GAVE ME SO MUCH, BARRY.
YOU GAVE ME A REASON TO BE A BETTER PERSON, TO BE A BETTER COP. I WANTED TO SET AN EXAMPLE...
I MADE CAPTAIN BECAUSE OF YOU.
CAPTAIN... NOW HOW CRAZY IS THAT?
FEELS GOOD, BUT STRANGE. I CAN'T GET USED TO WEARING SUITS INSTEAD OF THE BLUES. SOMETHING ABOUT THAT UNIFORM, AND THE BADGE ON YOUR CHEST...
PEOPLE SEE THAT AND THEY KNOW YOU'RE AN OFFICER OF THE LAW... THERE TO PROTECT AND SERVE. IT'S A SYMBOL THAT STANDS FOR GOOD. SOMETHING THIS WORLD NEEDS MORE OF.
I GOT YOU SOMETHING...
WOW... THIS IS FROM MY FIRST YEAR ON THE FORCE. WHERE DID YOU FIND IT?
CENTRAL CITY OFFICER
CAME ACROSS IT WHILE I WAS RUNNING AROUND.

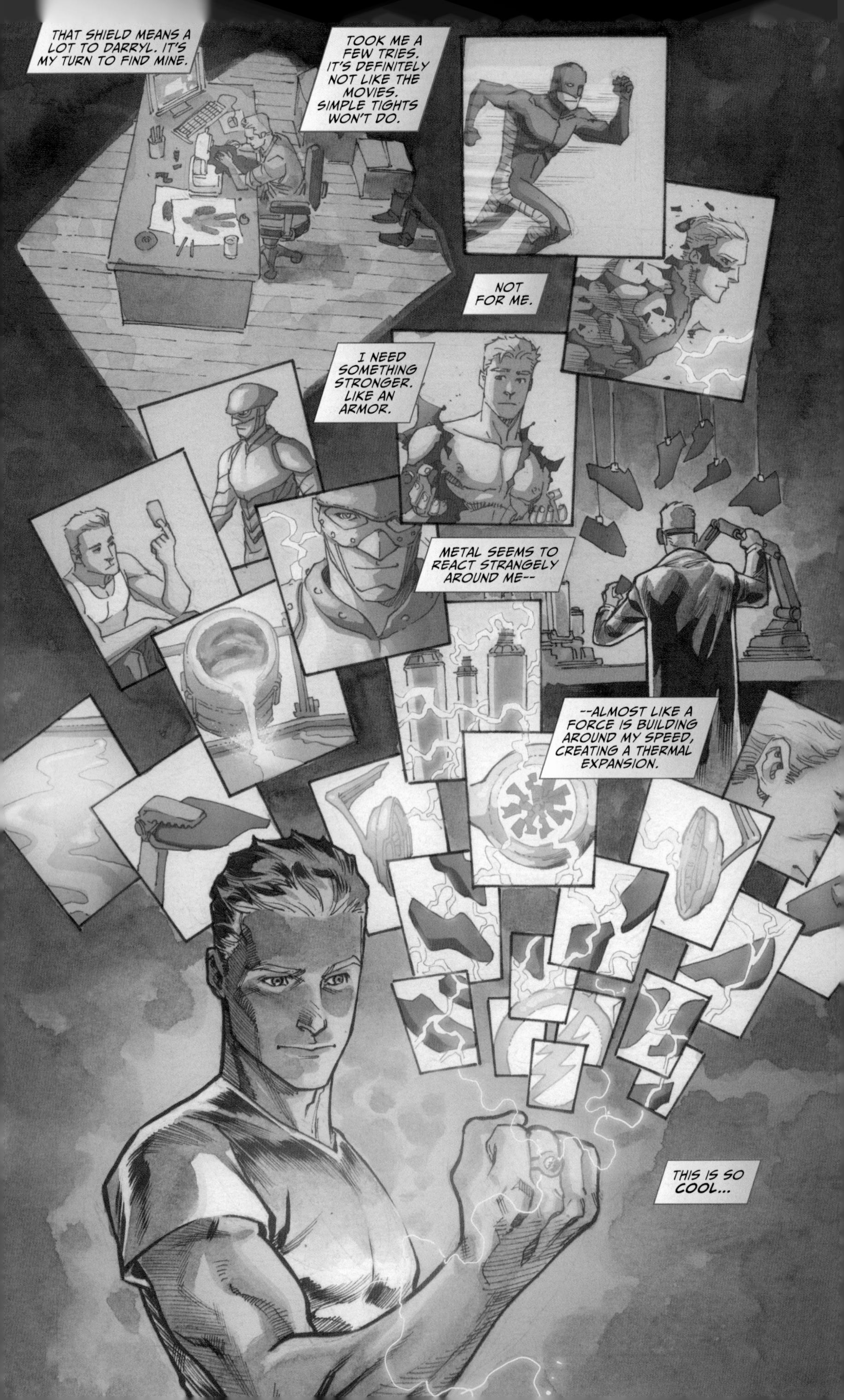

THAT SHIELD MEANS A LOT TO DARRYL. IT'S MY TURN TO FIND MINE.
TOOK ME A FEW TRIES. IT'S DEFINITELY NOT LIKE THE MOVIES. SIMPLE TIGHTS WON'T DO.
NOT FOR ME.
I NEED SOMETHING STRONGER. LIKE AN ARMOR.
METAL SEEMS TO REACT STRANGELY AROUND ME--
--ALMOST LIKE A FORCE IS BUILDING AROUND MY SPEED, CREATING A THERMAL EXPANSION.
THIS IS SO COOL...

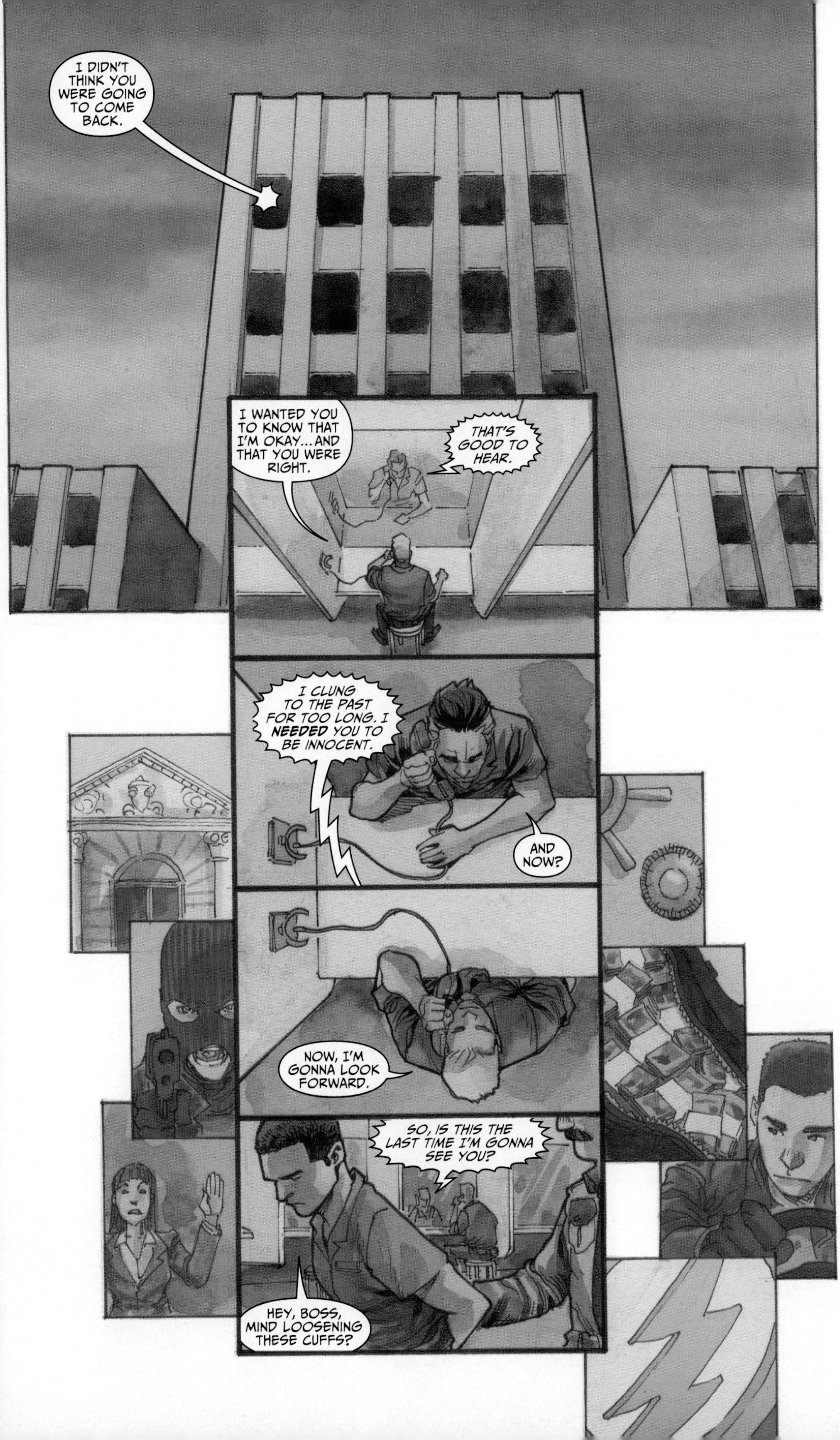
I DIDN'T THINK YOU WERE GOING TO COME BACK.
I WANTED YOU TO KNOW THAT I'M OKAY... AND THAT YOU WERE RIGHT.
THAT'S GOOD TO HEAR.
I CLUNG TO THE PAST FOR TOO LONG. I **NEEDED** YOU TO BE INNOCENT.
AND NOW?
NOW, I'M GONNA LOOK FORWARD.
SO, IS THIS THE LAST TIME I'M GONNA SEE YOU?
HEY, BOSS, MIND LOOSENING THESE CUFFS?

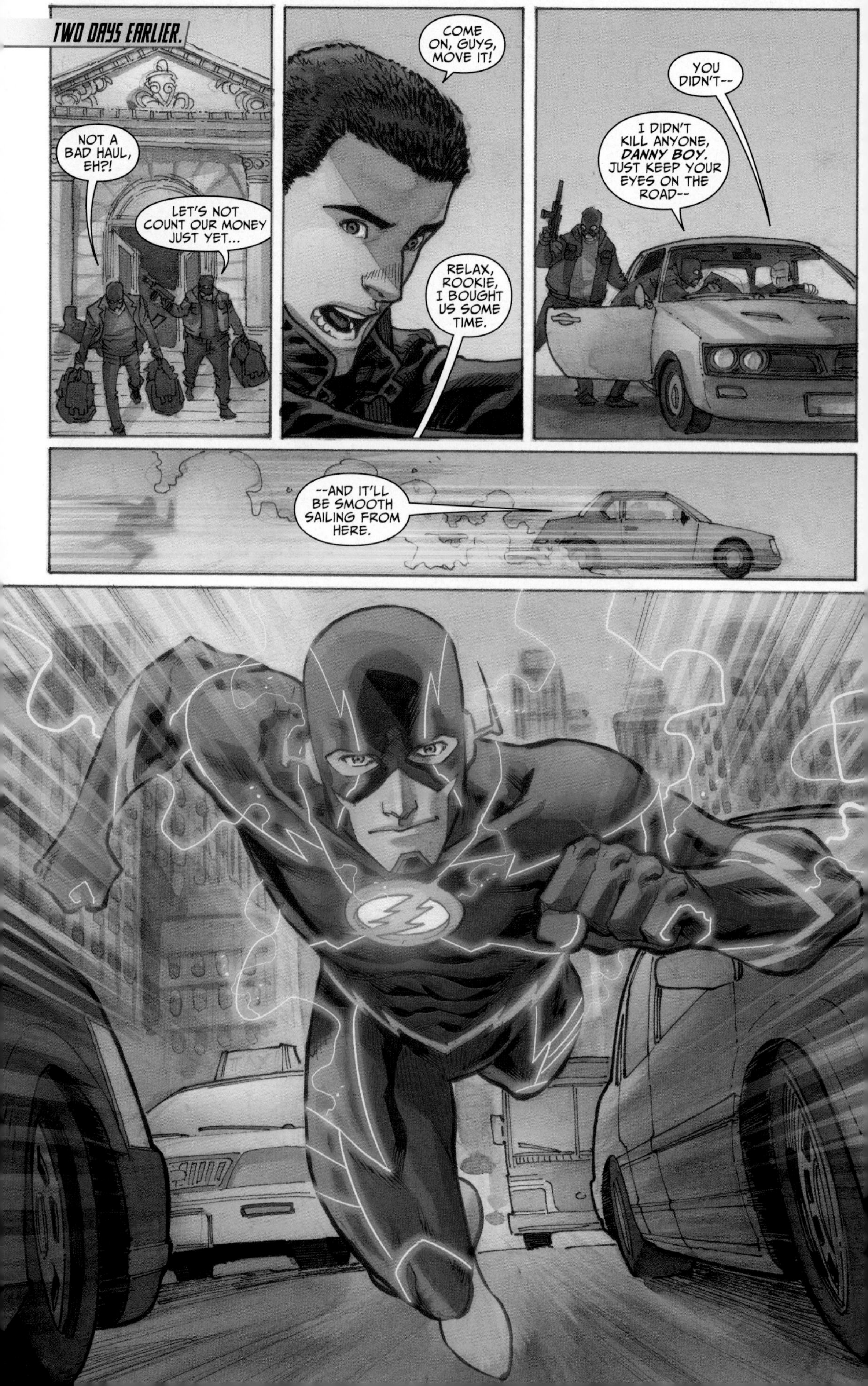
TWO DAYS EARLIER.
NOT A BAD HAUL, EH?!
LET'S NOT COUNT OUR MONEY JUST YET...
COME ON, GUYS, MOVE IT!
RELAX, ROOKIE, I BOUGHT US SOME TIME.
YOU DIDN'T--
I DIDN'T KILL ANYONE, DANNY BOY. JUST KEEP YOUR EYES ON THE ROAD--
--AND IT'LL BE SMOOTH SAILING FROM HERE.

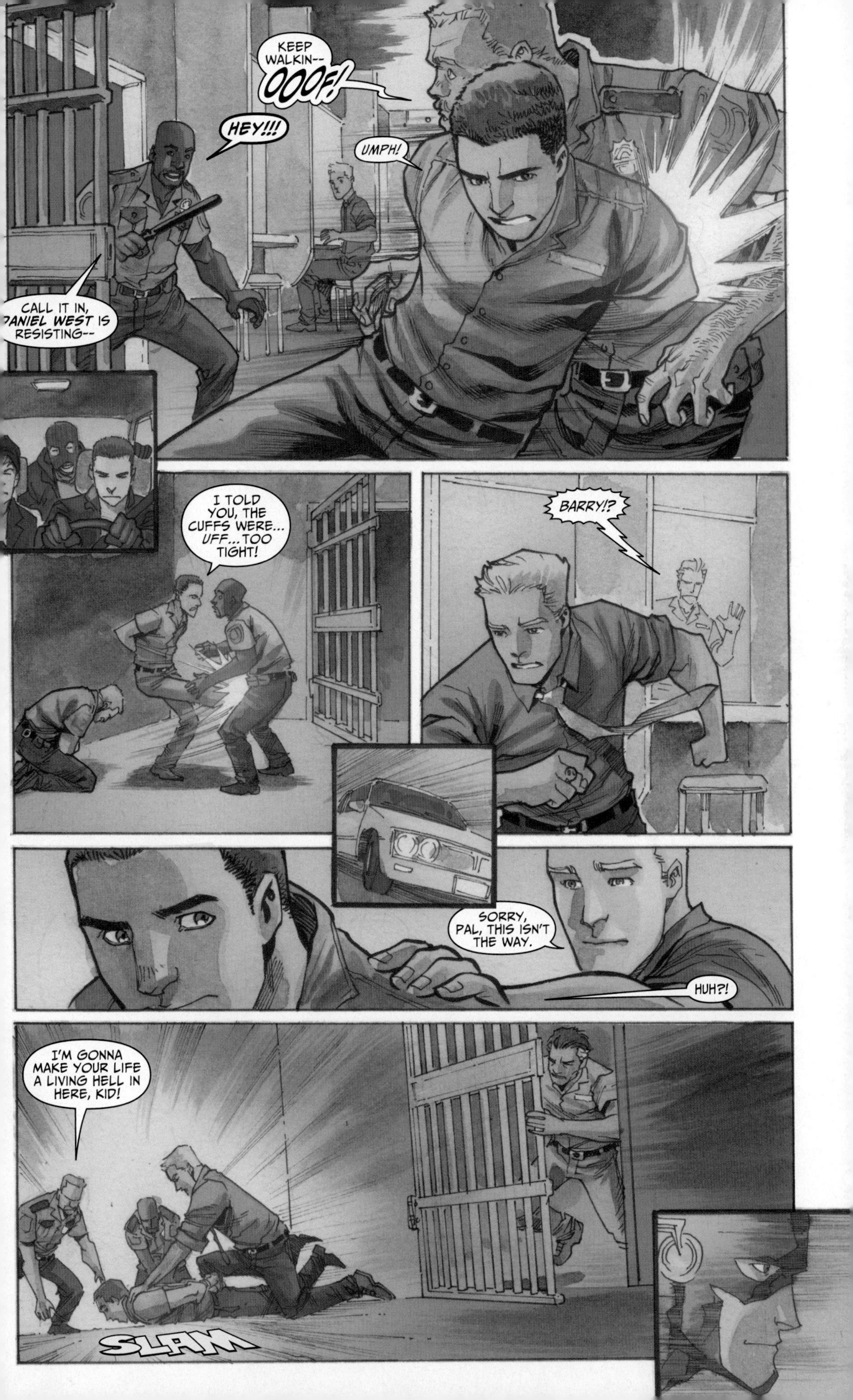
KEEP WALKIN--
OOOF!
HEY!!!
UMPH!
CALL IT IN, DANIEL WEST IS RESISTING--
I TOLD YOU, THE CUFFS WERE... UFF... TOO TIGHT!
BARRY!?
SORRY, PAL, THIS ISN'T THE WAY.
HUH?!
I'M GONNA MAKE YOUR LIFE A LIVING HELL IN HERE, KID!
SLAM

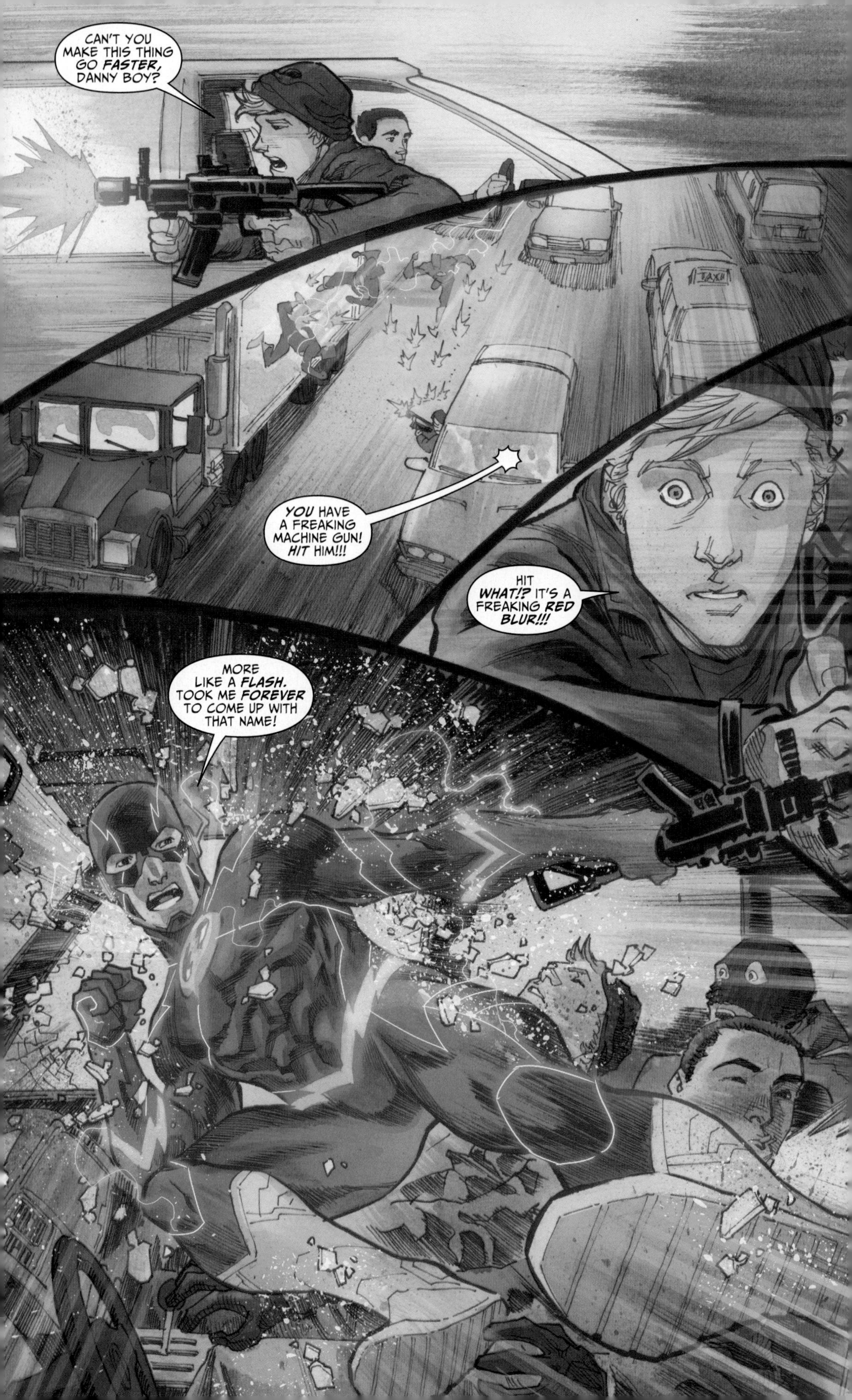
CAN'T YOU MAKE THIS THING GO *FASTER,* DANNY BOY?
YOU HAVE A FREAKING MACHINE GUN! *HIT* HIM!!!
HIT *WHAT!?* IT'S A FREAKING *RED BLUR!!!*
MORE LIKE A *FLASH.* TOOK ME *FOREVER* TO COME UP WITH THAT NAME!

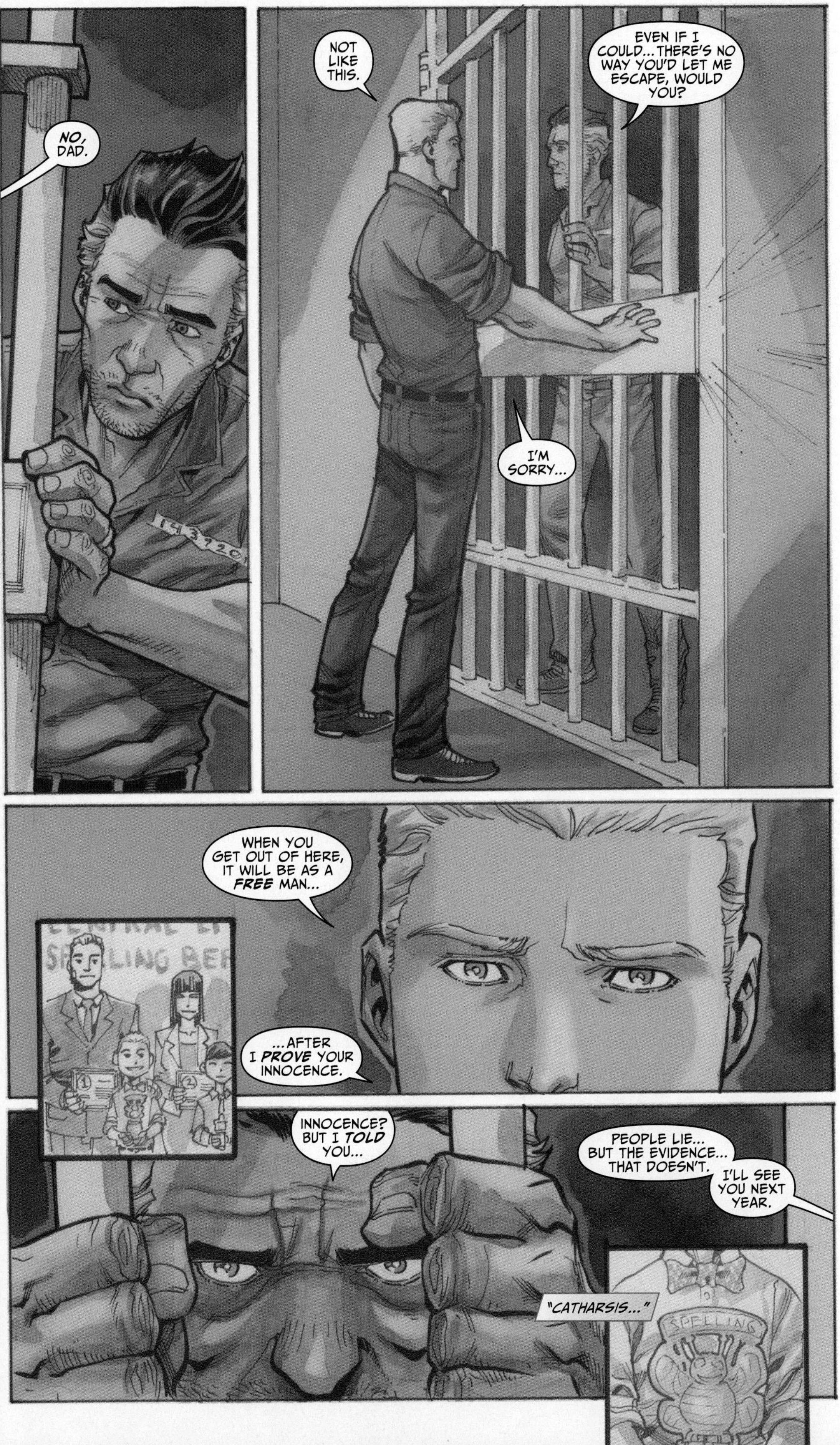
NO, DAD.
NOT LIKE THIS.
EVEN IF I COULD...THERE'S NO WAY YOU'D LET ME ESCAPE, WOULD YOU?
I'M SORRY...
WHEN YOU GET OUT OF HERE, IT WILL BE AS A *FREE* MAN...
...AFTER I *PROVE* YOUR INNOCENCE.
INNOCENCE? BUT I *TOLD* YOU...
PEOPLE LIE... BUT THE EVIDENCE... THAT DOESN'T.
I'LL SEE YOU NEXT YEAR.
"CATHARSIS..."

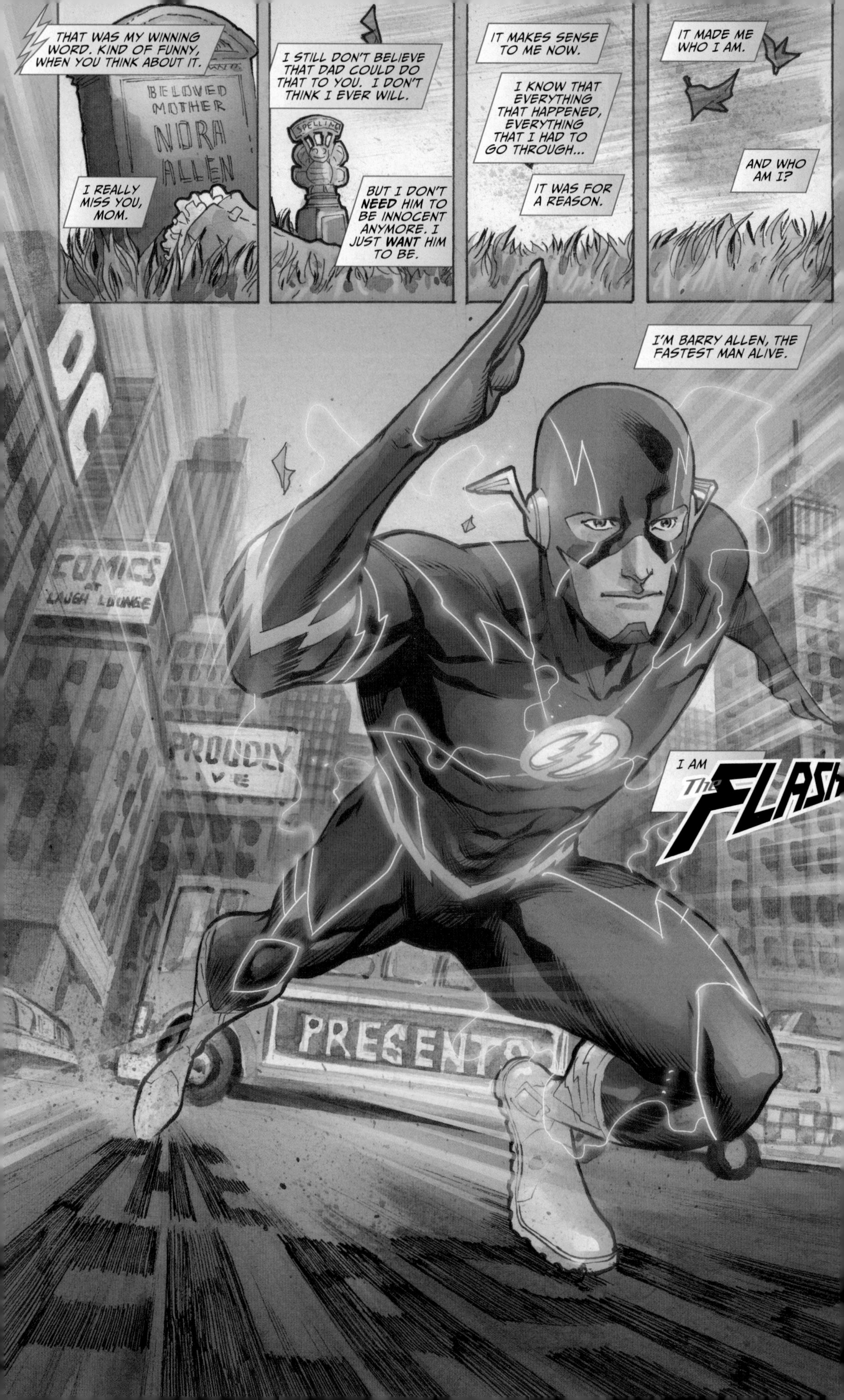
THAT WAS MY WINNING WORD. KIND OF FUNNY, WHEN YOU THINK ABOUT IT.
BELOVED MOTHER NORA ALLEN
I REALLY MISS YOU, MOM.
I STILL DON'T BELIEVE THAT DAD COULD DO THAT TO YOU. I DON'T THINK I EVER WILL.
SPELLING
BUT I DON'T **NEED** HIM TO BE INNOCENT ANYMORE. I JUST **WANT** HIM TO BE.
IT MAKES SENSE TO ME NOW.
I KNOW THAT EVERYTHING THAT HAPPENED, EVERYTHING THAT I HAD TO GO THROUGH...
IT WAS FOR A REASON.
IT MADE ME WHO I AM.
AND WHO AM I?
I'M BARRY ALLEN, THE FASTEST MAN ALIVE.
COMICS AT LAUGH LOUNGE
PROUDLY LIVE
PRESENTS
I AM The FLASH

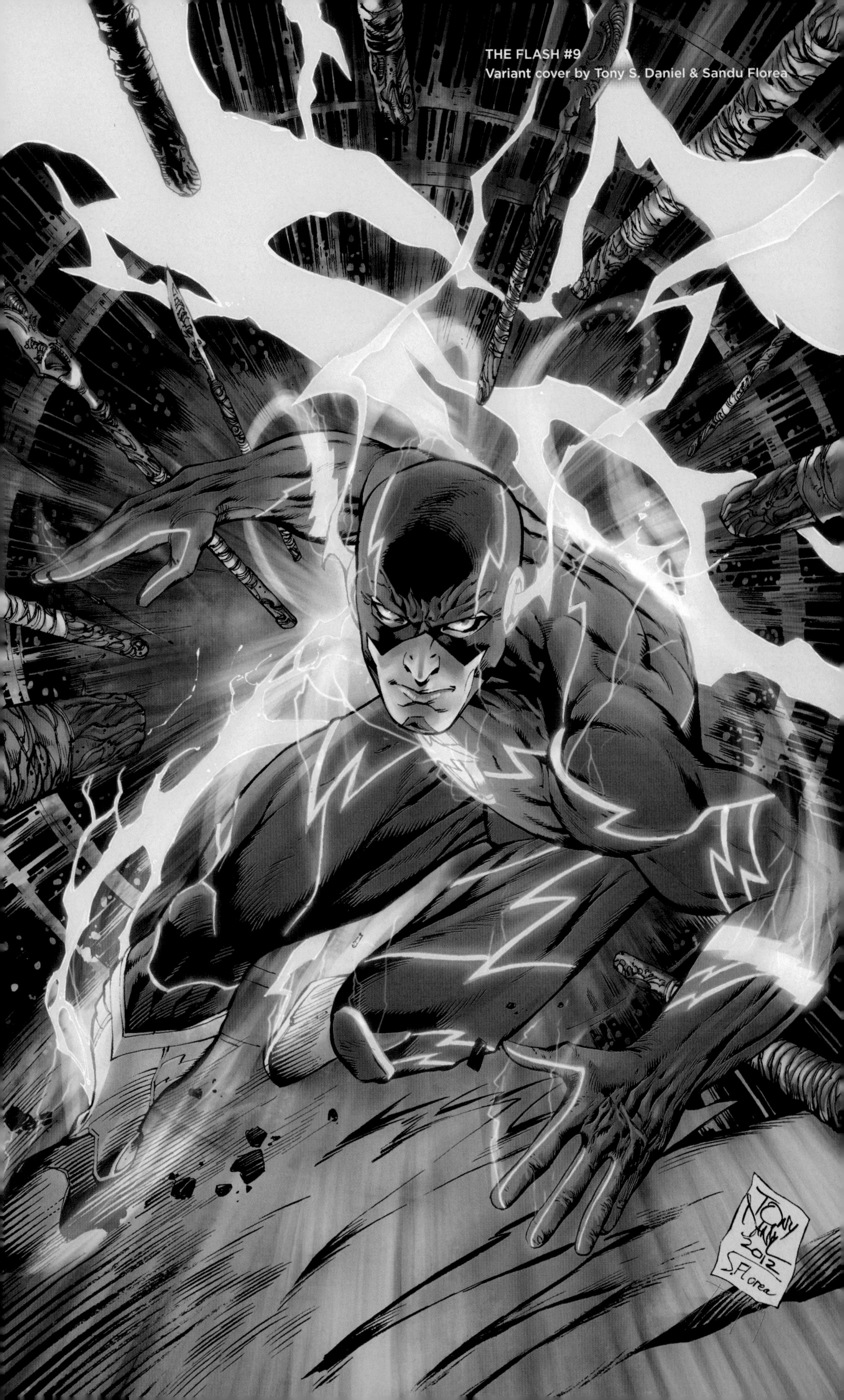

THE FLASH #9
Variant cover by Tony S. Daniel & Sandu Florea

THE FLASH #9 cover pencils

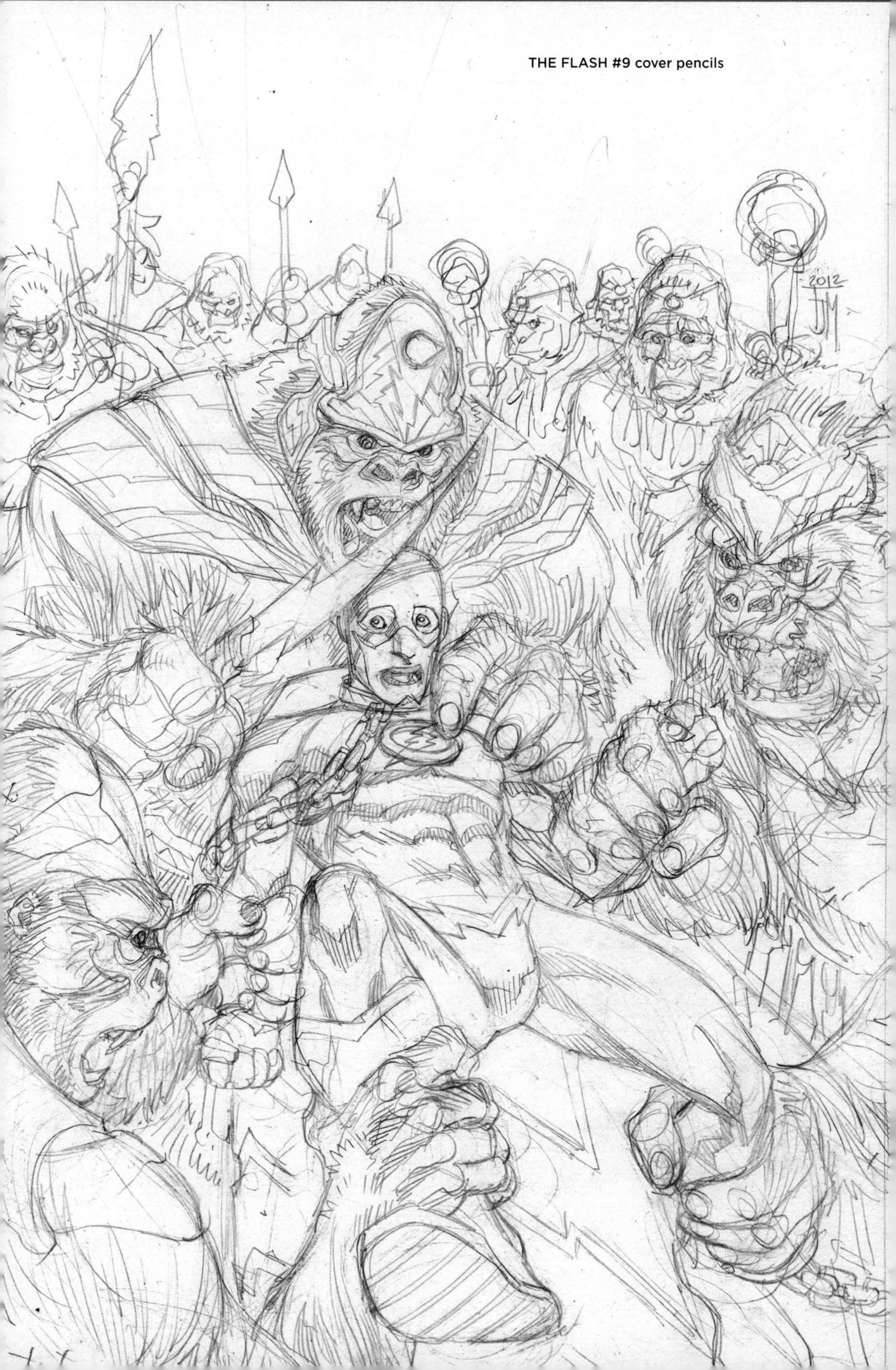
2012
FM

THE FLASH #9 cover sketches and final inked cover

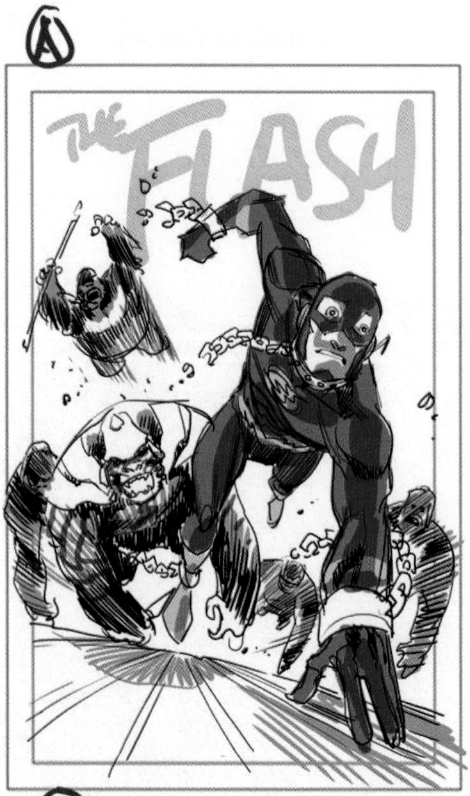
A
THE FLASH

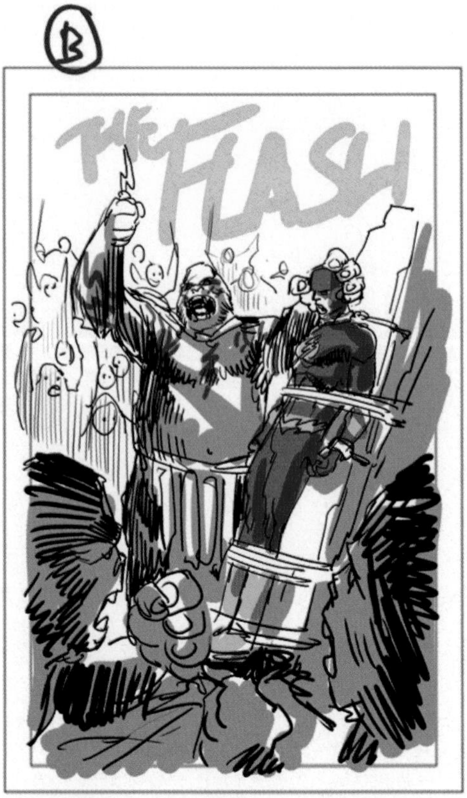
B
THE FLASH

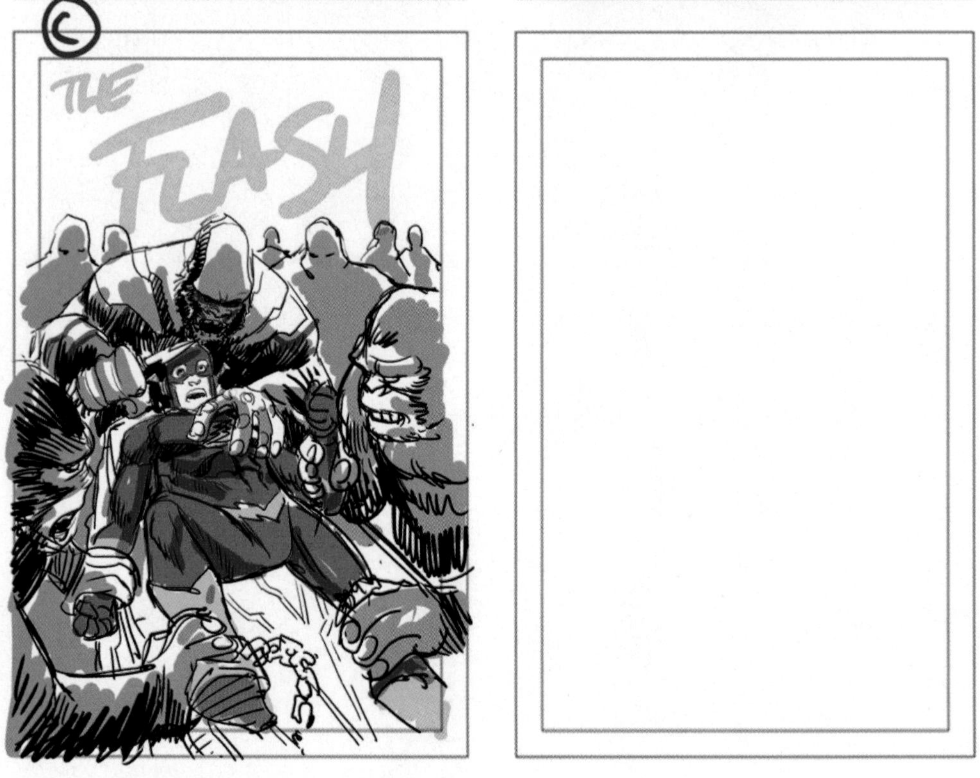
C
THE FLASH

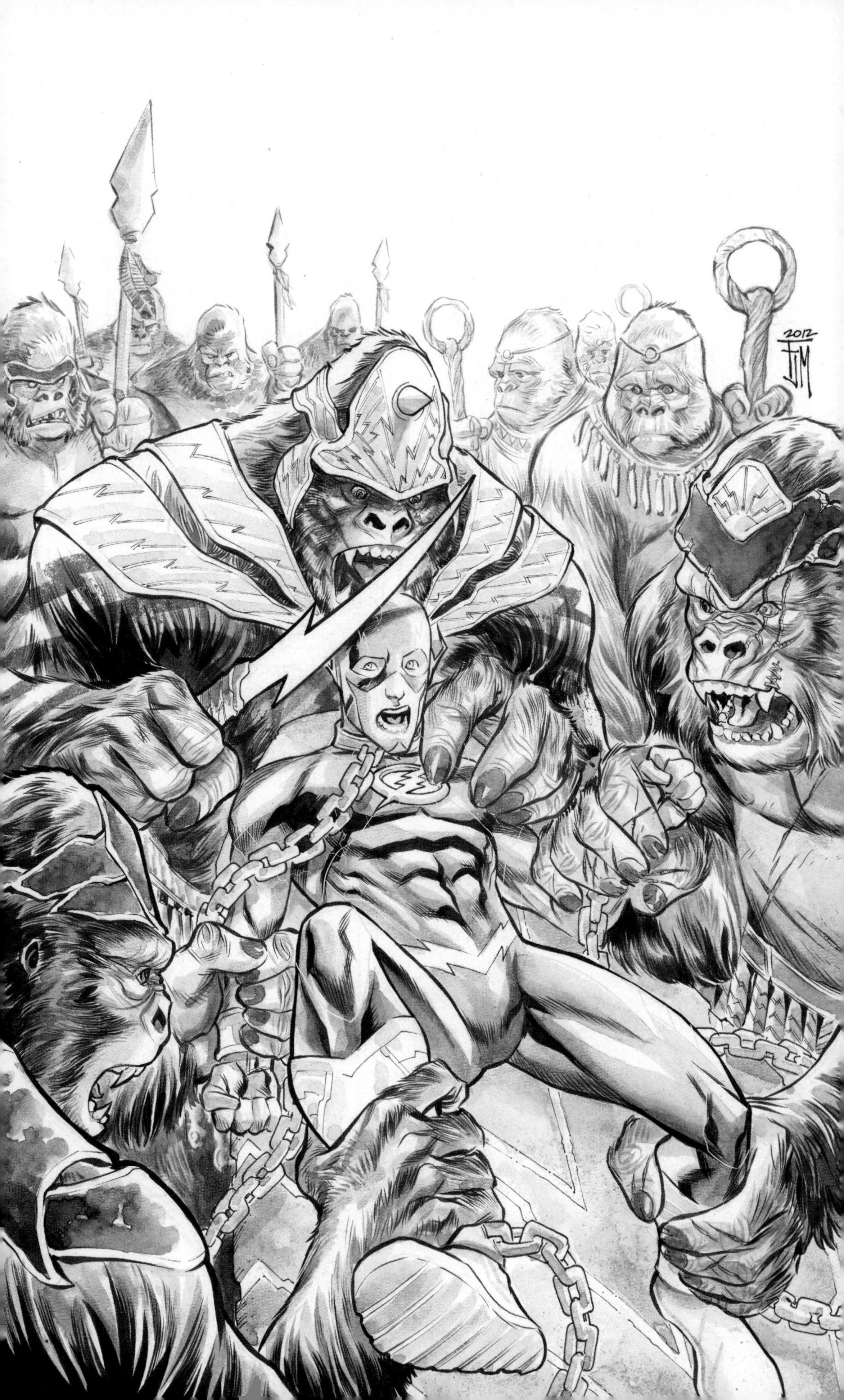

THE FLASH #10 cover sketches and final inked cover

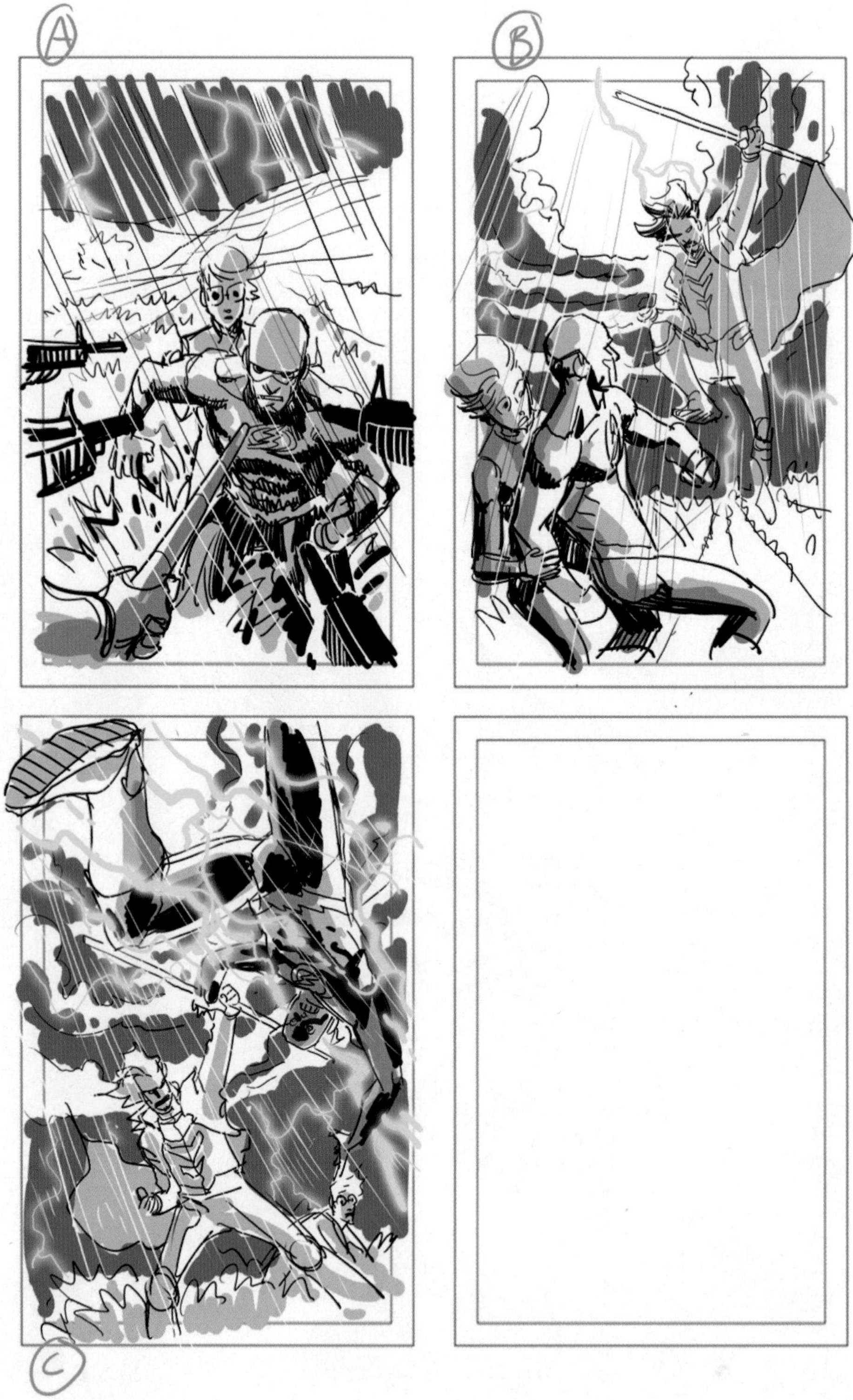
A
B
C

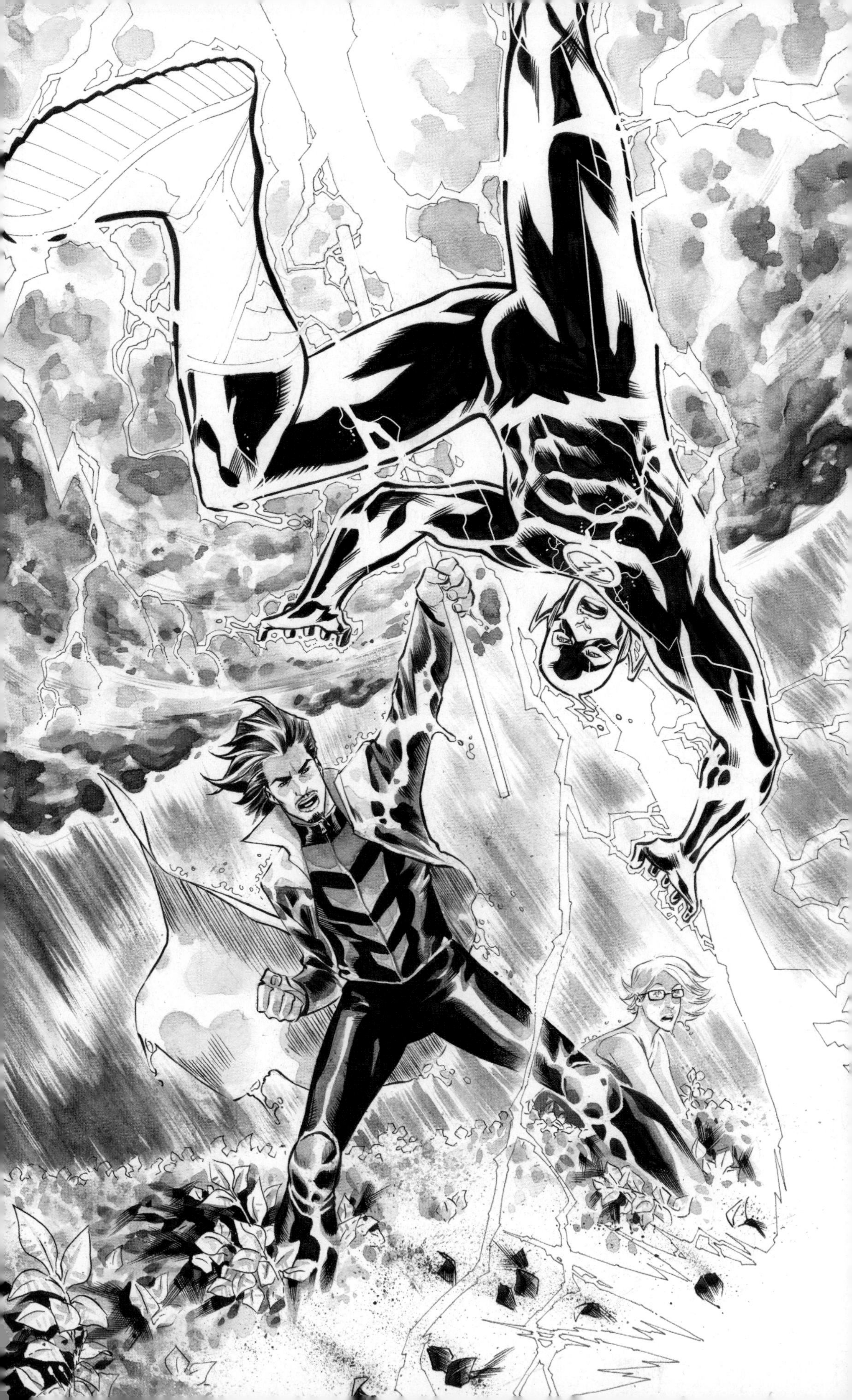

THE FLASH #11 cover sketches and final inked cover

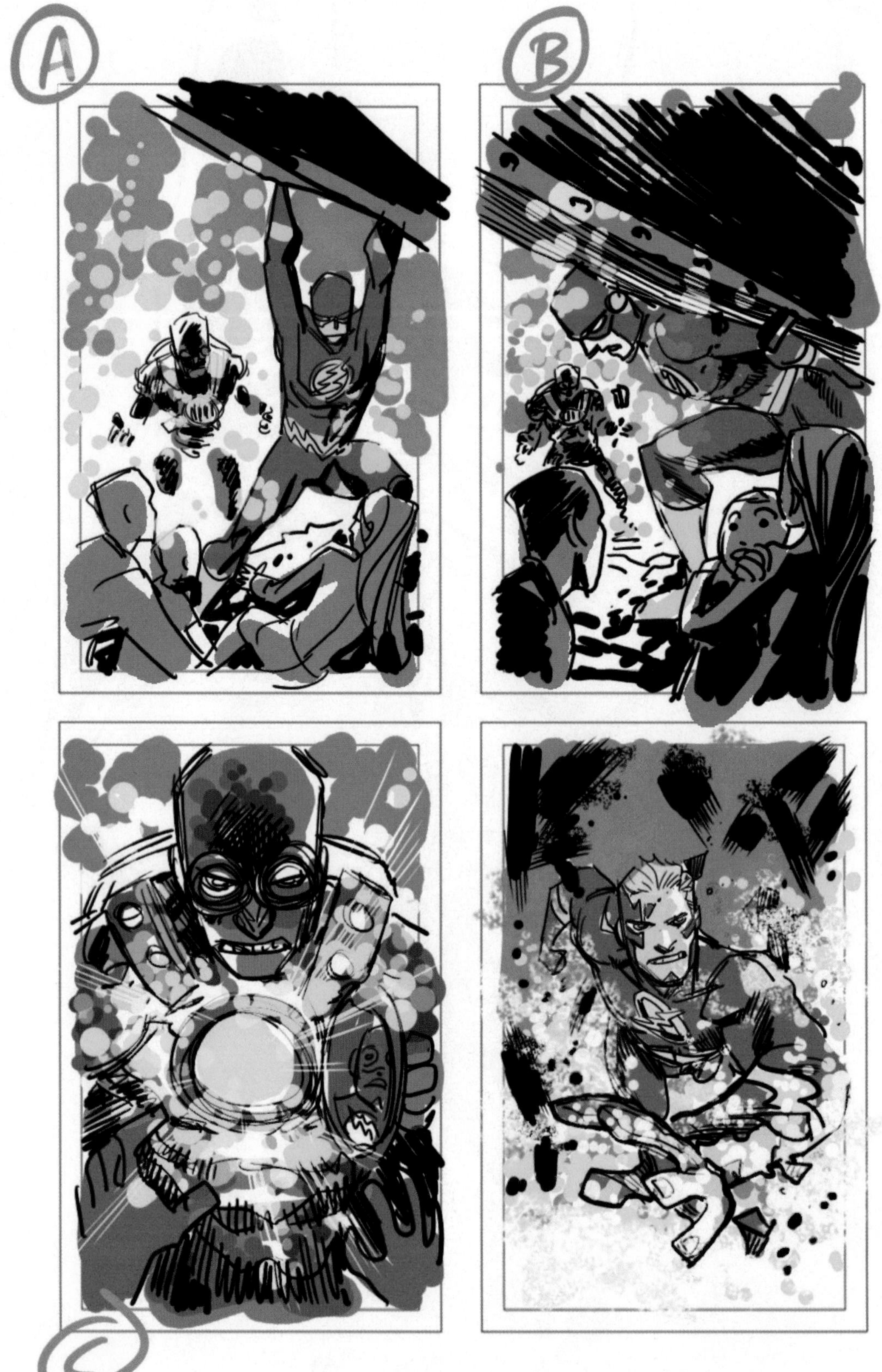
A
B
C

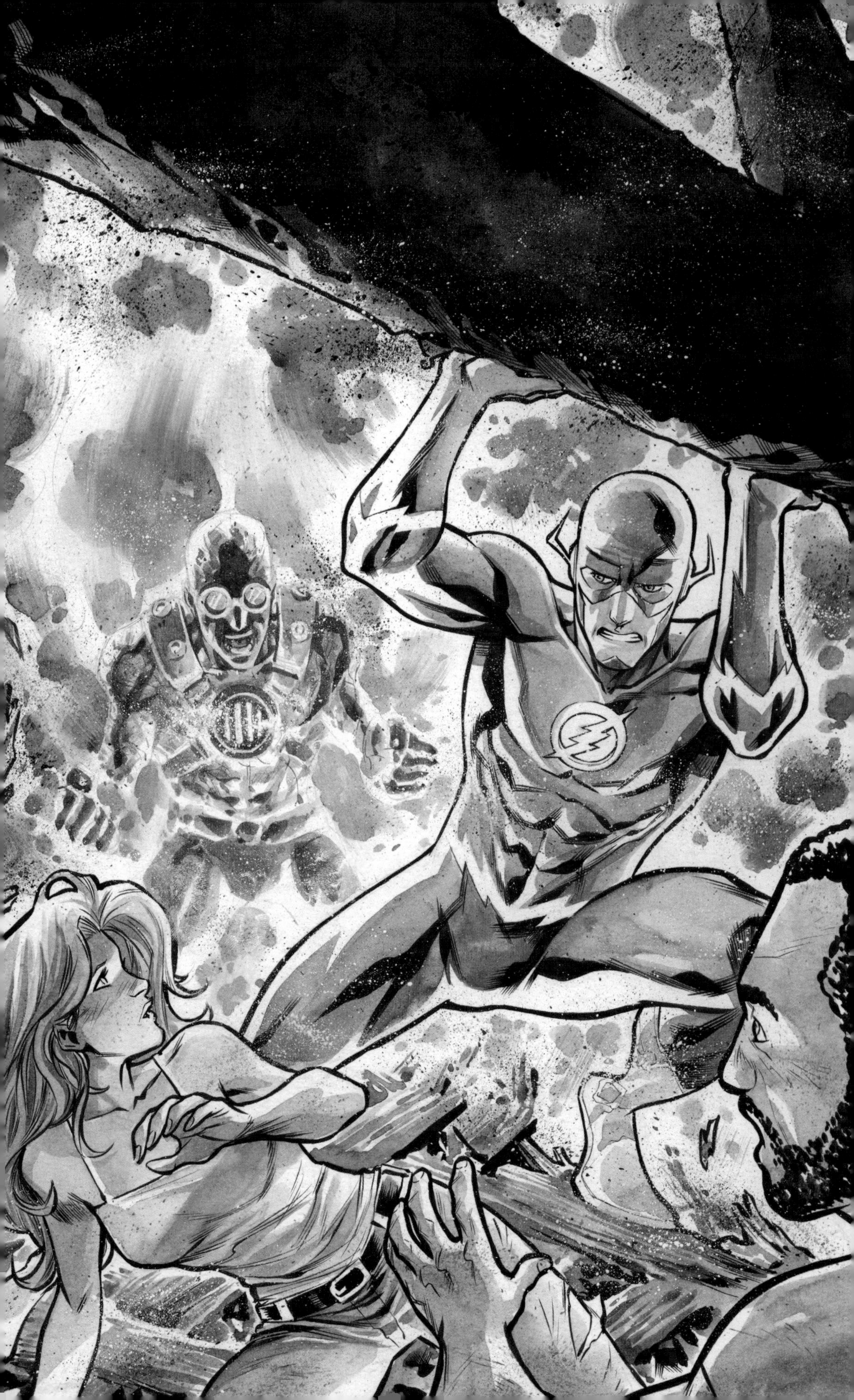

THE FLASH #12 cover inks

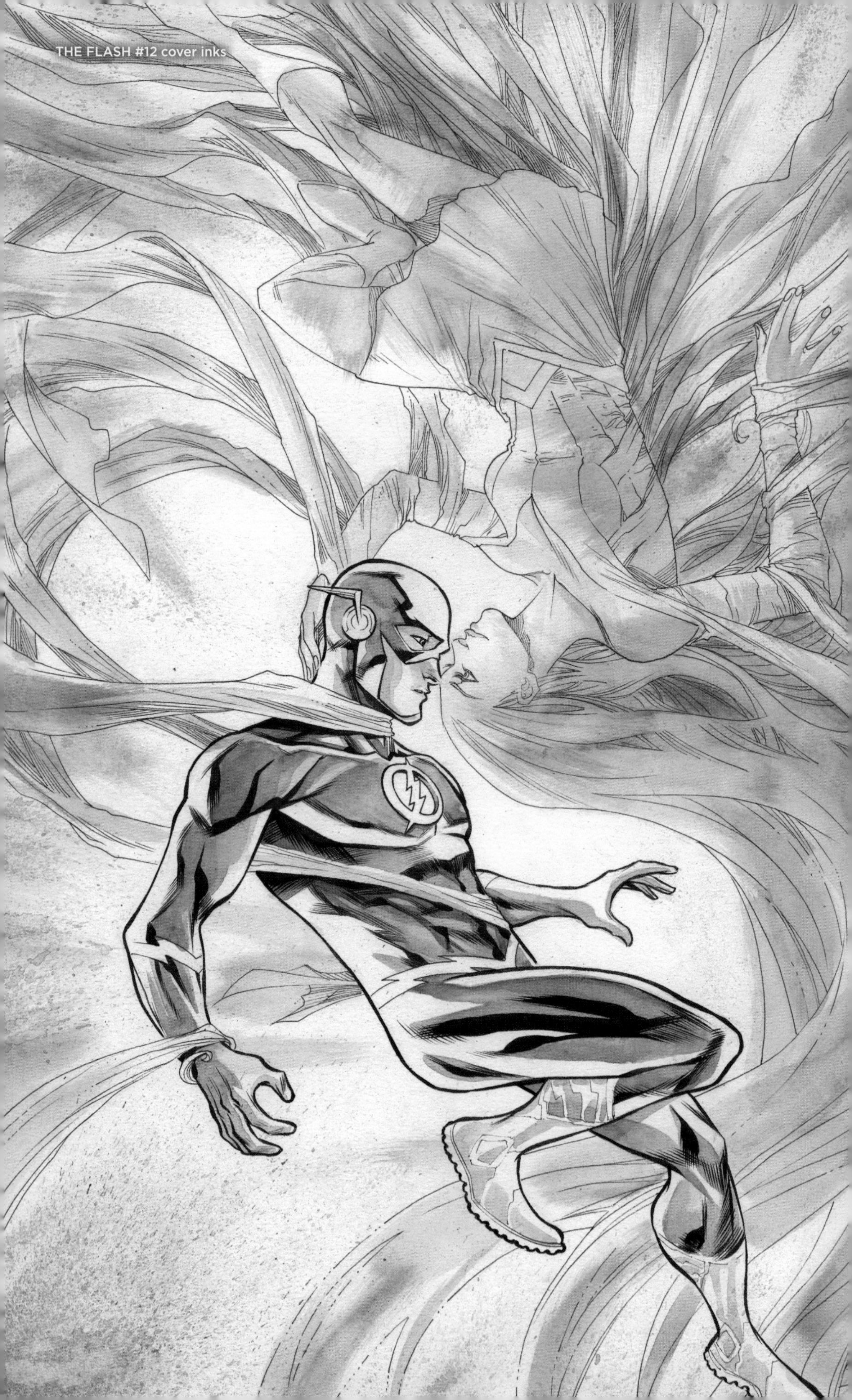

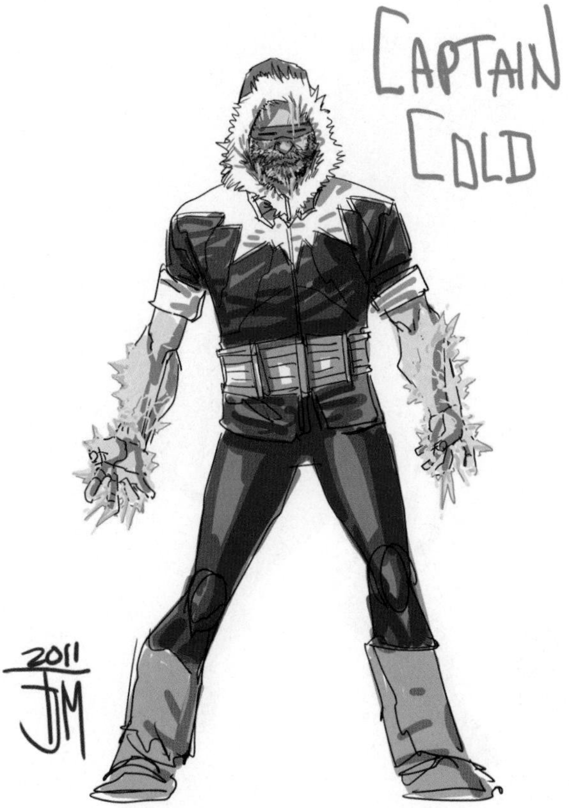
CAPTAIN
COLD
2011
FJM

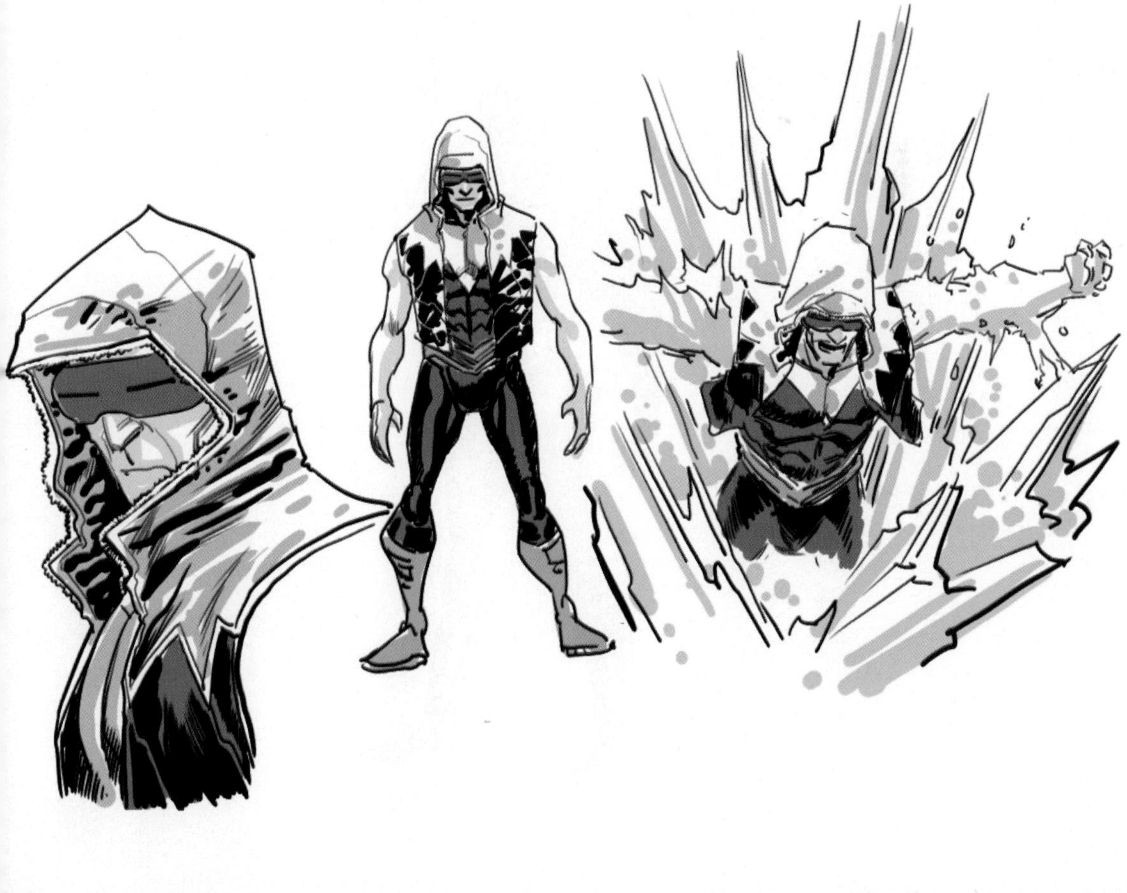

HEATWAVE

MIRROR MASTER

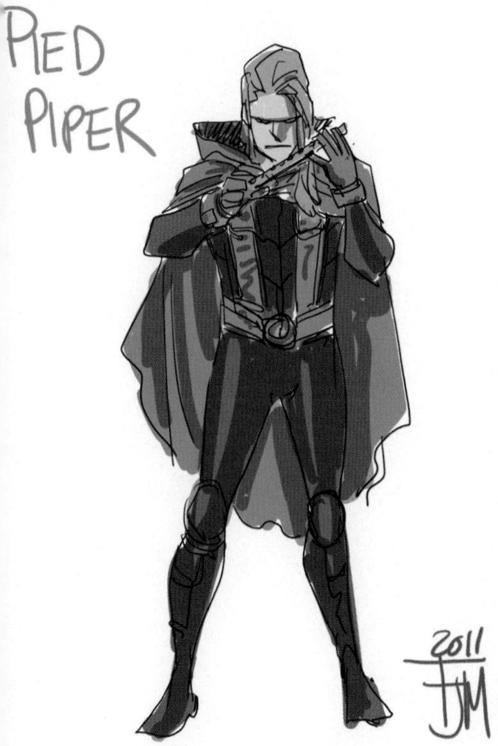
PIED
PIPER
2011

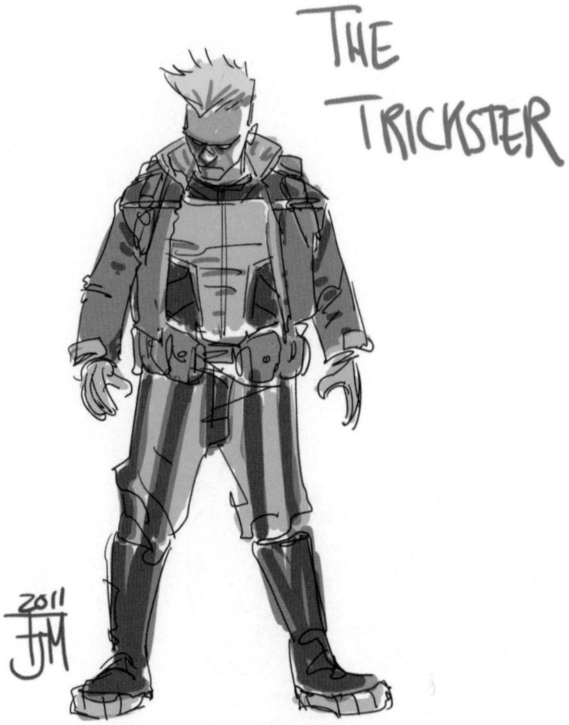
THE
TRICKSTER
2011

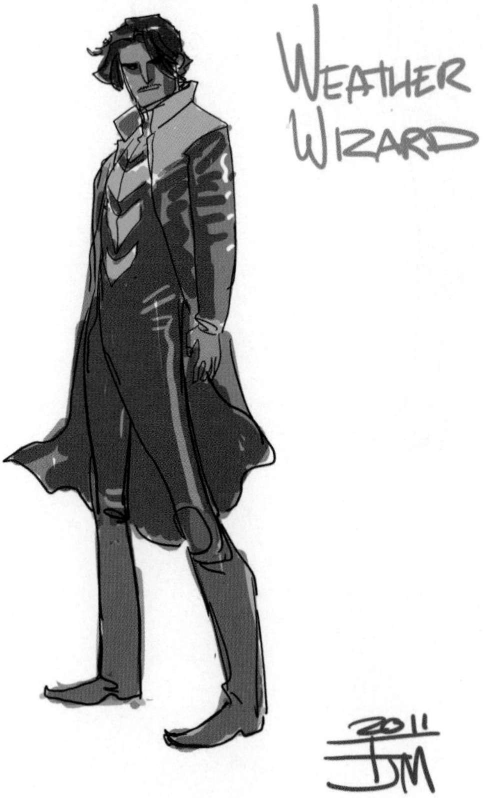
WEATHER
WIZARD
2011

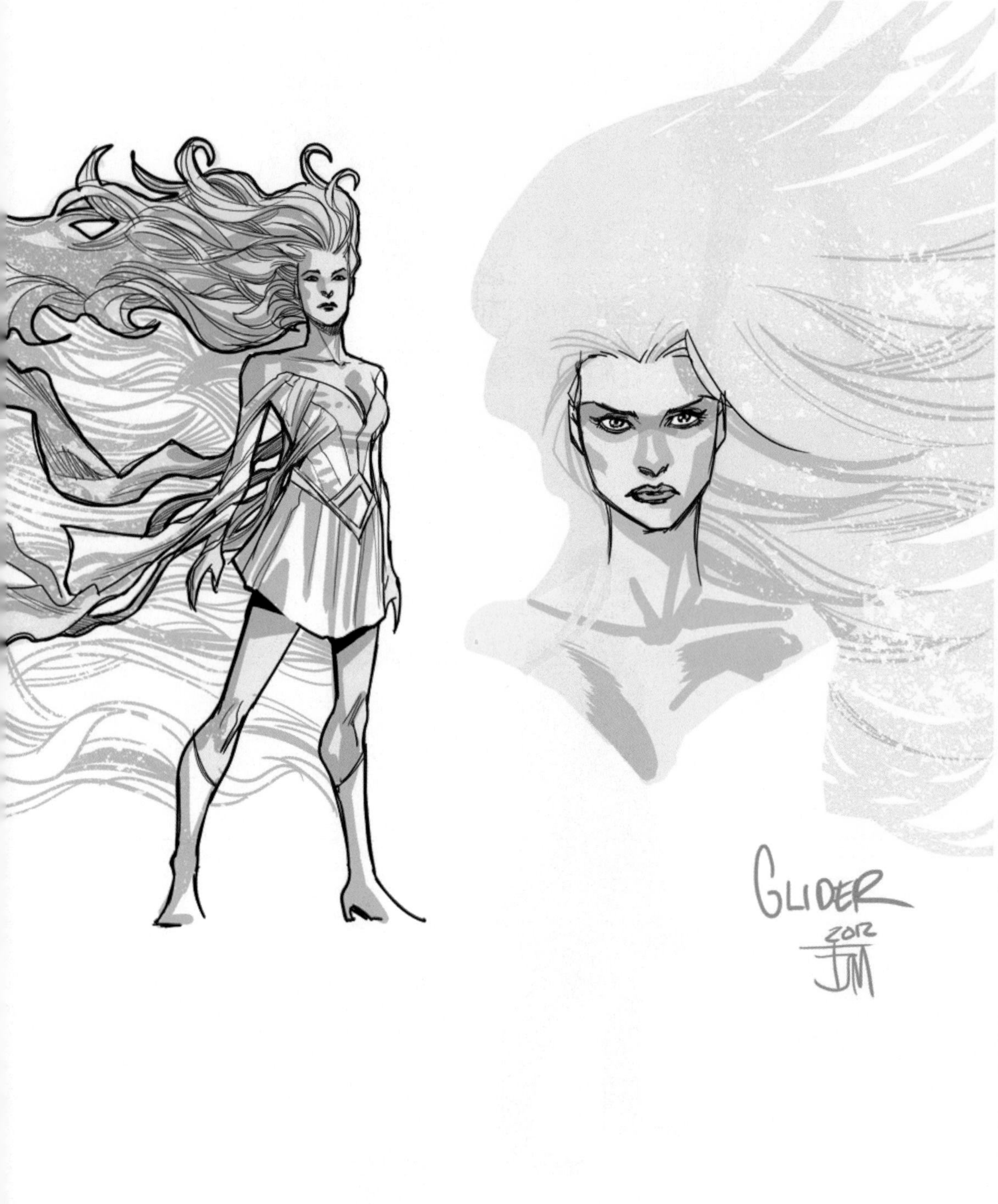
GLIDER
2012

THE FLASH #9 & 10 rough layouts

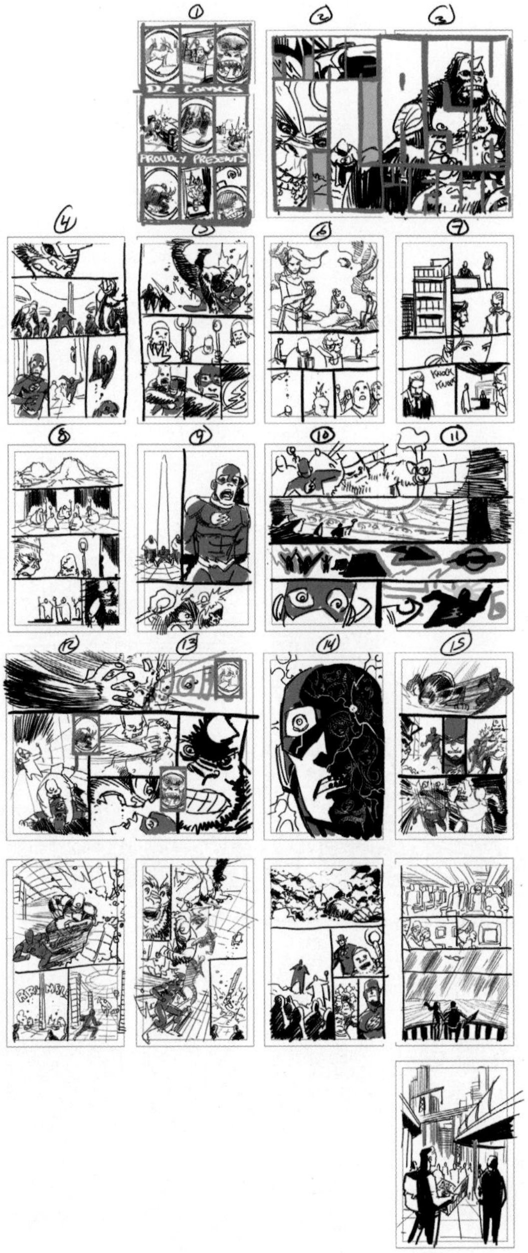
DC COMICS
PROUDLY PRESENTS

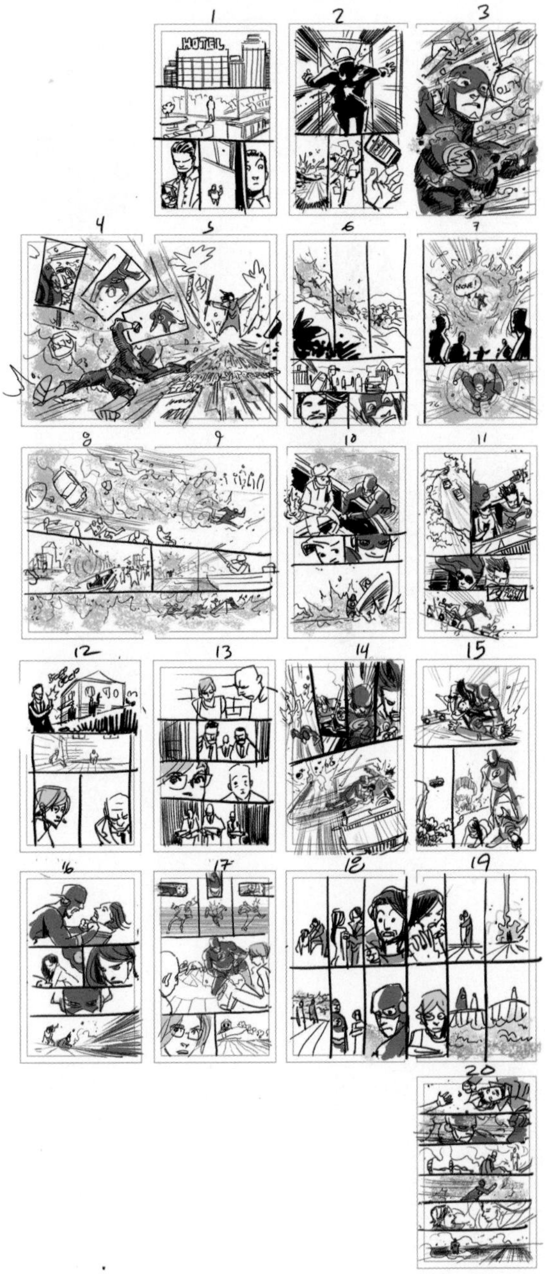
HOTEL

THE FLASH #11 & 12 rough layouts

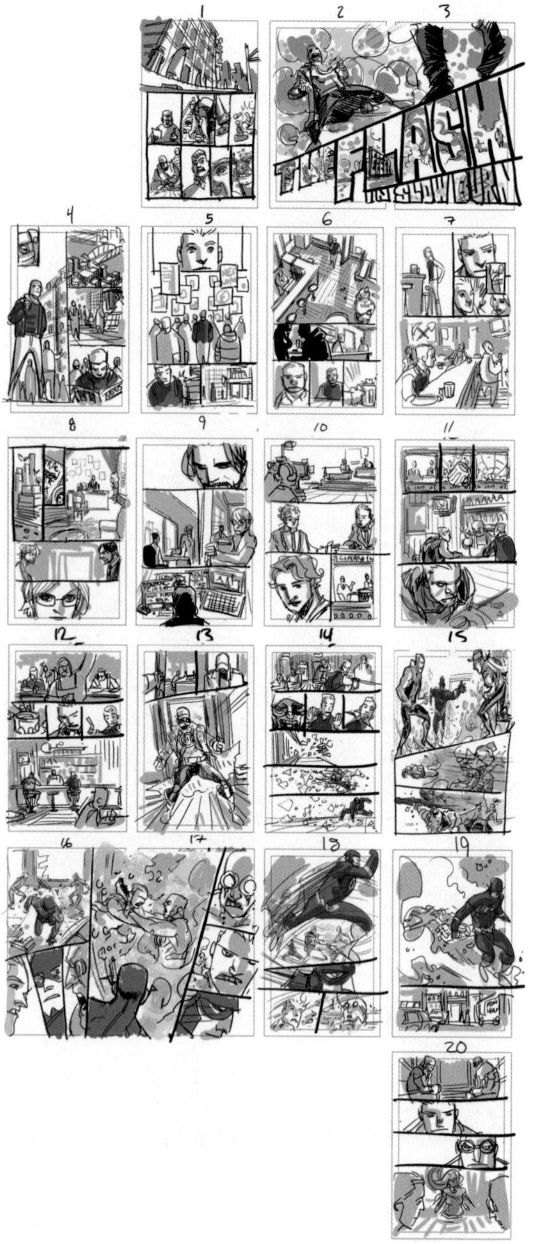

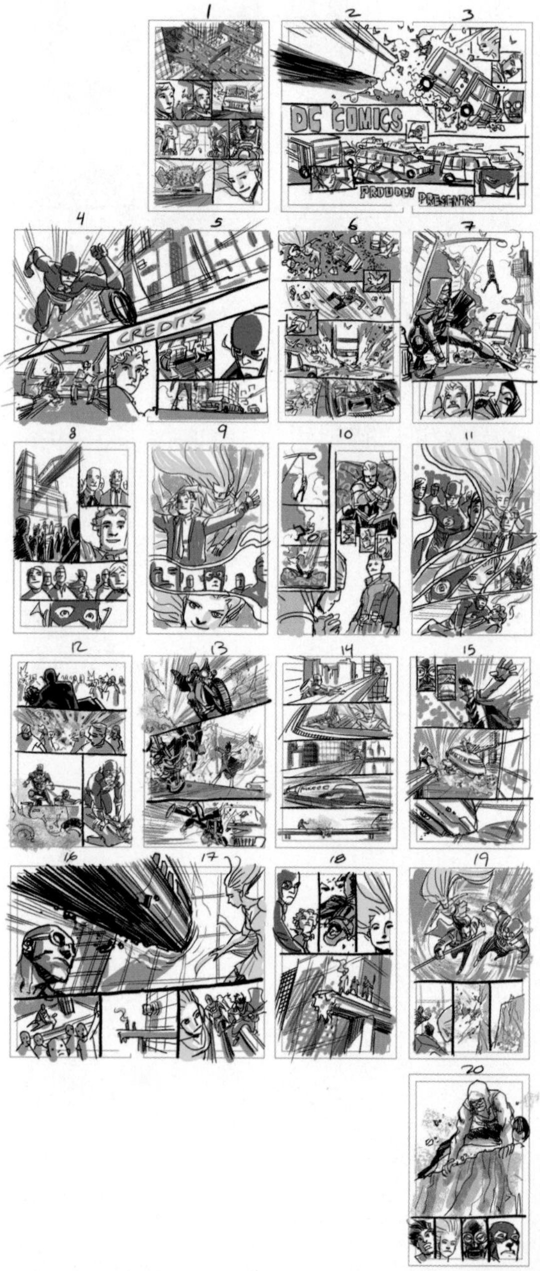
DC COMICS
PROUDLY PRESENTS
CREDITS

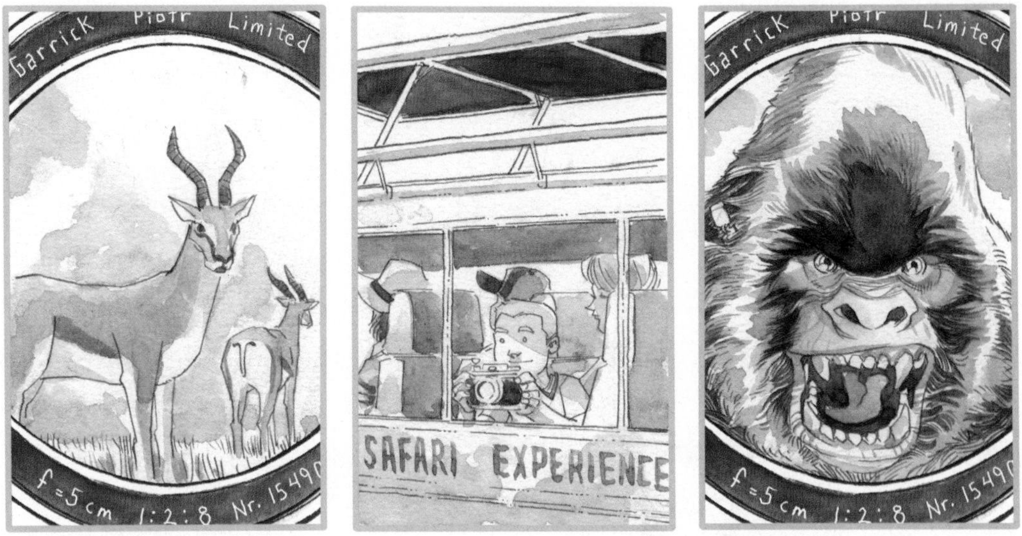
Garrick Piotr Limited
f=5cm 1:2:8 Nr. 1549
SAFARI EXPERIENCE
Garrick Piotr Limited
f=5cm 1:2:8 Nr. 1549

THE FLASH #9 page 1 inks

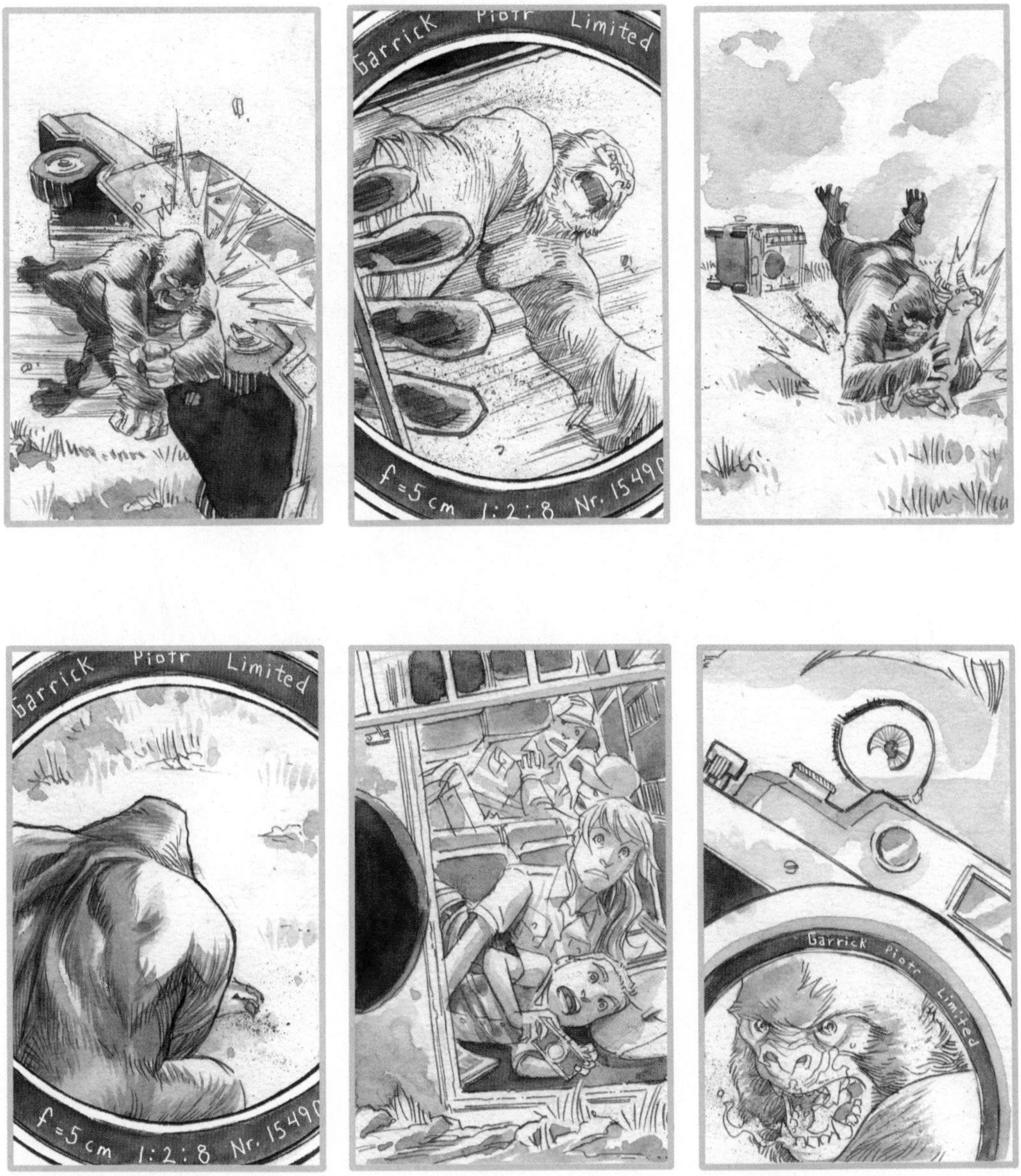
Garrick Piotr Limited
f=5cm 1:2:8 Nr. 1549
Garrick Piotr Limited
f=5cm 1:2:8 Nr. 1549
Garrick Piotr Limited

THE FLASH #9 pages 2-3 inks

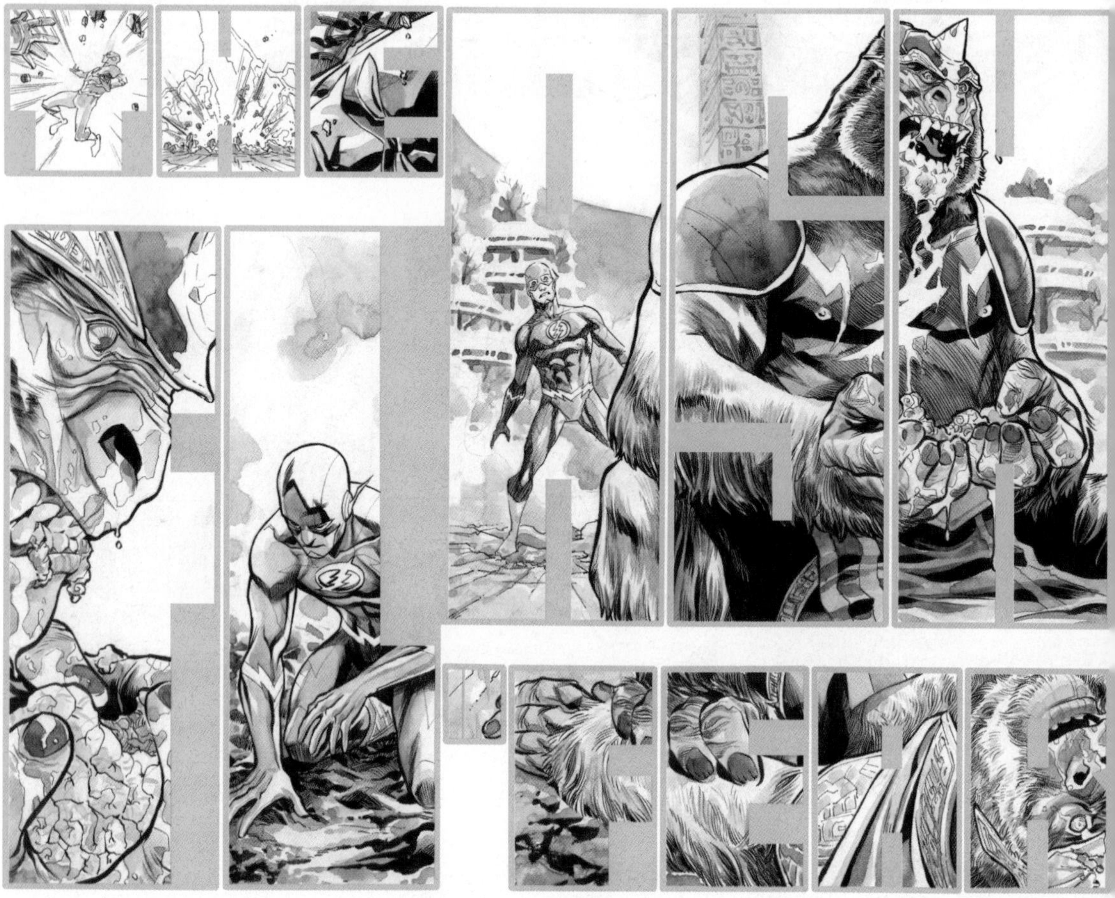

THE FLASH #12 pages 4-5 inks

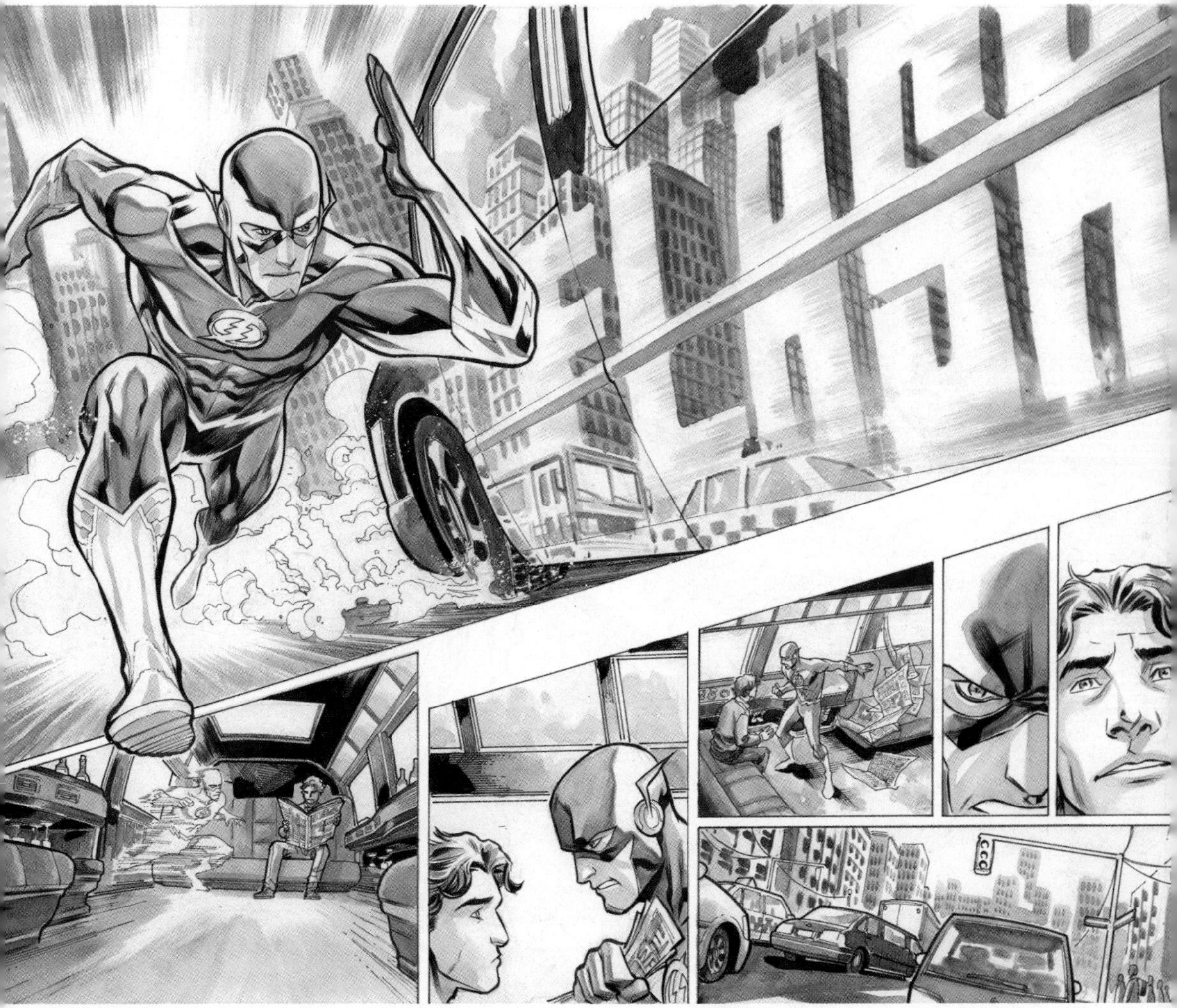

THE FLASH #12 page 9 inks

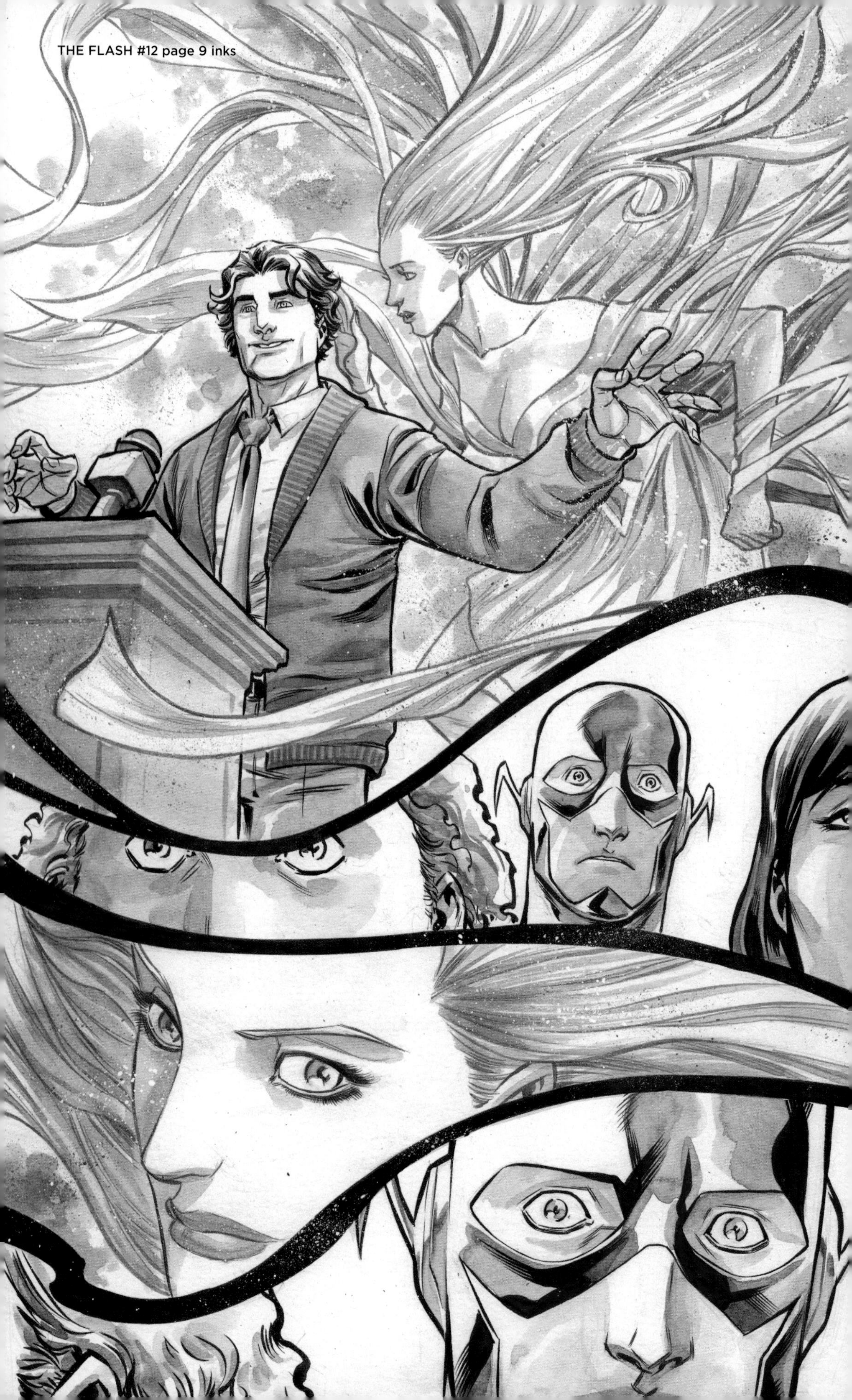

"Flash fans should breathe a sigh of relief that the character is 100% in the right hands."—MTV GEEK

START AT THE BEGINNING!

THE FLASH
VOLUME 1: MOVE FORWARD

THE FLASH VOL. 2: ROGUES REVOLUTION

THE FLASH VOL. 3: GORILLA WARFARE

JUSTICE LEAGUE VOL. 1: ORIGIN

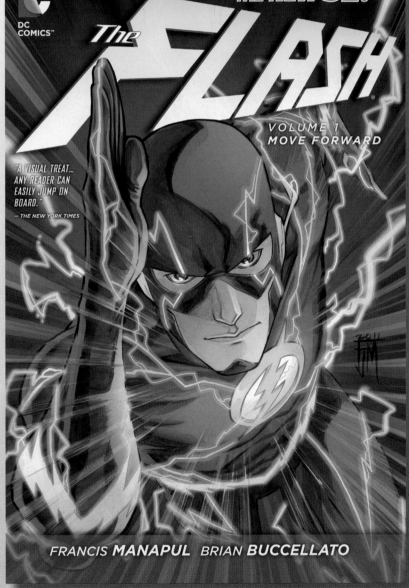

FROM THE WRITER OF *JUSTICE LEAGUE* AND *GREEN LANTERN*

GEOFF JOHNS
with ETHAN VAN SCIVER

THE FLASH:
THE DASTARDLY
DEATH
OF THE ROGUES!

with FRANCIS MANAPUL

THE FLASH: THE ROAD
TO FLASHPOINT

with FRANCIS MANAPUL
and SCOTT KOLINS

FLASHPOINT

with ANDY KUBERT